Praise for *July 1914*

'A work of meticulous scholarship … McMeekin's description of the details of life in the European capitals – small events that influenced great decisions – makes *July 1914* irresistible.'

Roy Hattersley, *The Times*

'A genuinely exciting, almost hour-by-hour account of the terrible month when Europe's diplomats danced their continent over the edge and into the abyss.'

Nigel Jones, *BBC History Magazine*

'Sean McMeekin's splendid *July 1914* unravels all the shenanigans, bluffs and bunglings by which Europe's leaders and diplomats turned a minor murder in a Balkans backwater into total war … There are scenes in *July 1914* that linger long after the cover is closed.'

John Lewis-Stempel, *Sunday Express*

'McMeekin shows us precisely why the conflict happened … [he] tells these stories with clarity and skill, drawing expert portraits of all the characters involved.'

Mail on Sunday

'Lucid, convincing and full of rich detail, the book is a triumph for the narrative method and a vivid demonstration that chronology is the logic of history.'

The Independent

'[S]timulating and enjoyable … Sean McMeekin's [*July 1914*] is controversial, arguing that Russia and France were more bent than Germany on war in July 1914 … [A] well-written book.'

Financial Times

'Sean McMeekin is establishing himself as a – or even *the* – leading young historian of modern Europe. Here he turns his gifts to the outbreak of war in July 1914 and has written another masterpiece.'

Norman Stone, author of *World War Two: A Short History*

SEAN McMEEKIN

JULY 1914

COUNTDOWN TO WAR

ICON

First published in the UK in 2013 by Icon Books Ltd

This edition published in the UK in 2014 by
Icon Books Ltd, Omnibus Business Centre,
39–41 North Road, London N7 9DP
email: info@iconbooks.net
www.iconbooks.net

First published in the United States in 2013 by Basic Books,
a member of the Perseus Books Group

Sold in the UK, Europe and Asia
by Faber & Faber Ltd, Bloomsbury House,
74–77 Great Russell Street,
London WC1B 3DA or their agents

Distributed in the UK, Europe and Asia
by TBS Ltd, TBS Distribution Centre, Colchester Road,
Frating Green, Colchester CO7 7DW

Distributed in South Africa
by Book Promotions, Office B4, The District
41 Sir Lowry Road, Woodstock 7925

Distributed in Australia and New Zealand
by Allen & Unwin Pty Ltd,
PO Box 8500, 83 Alexander Street,
Crows Nest, NSW 2065

ISBN: 978-184831-657-7

Designed by Pauline Brown
Typeset in Palatino

Printed by CPI Group (UK) Ltd, Croydon CR0 4YY

For the fallen

ABOUT THE AUTHOR

Sean McMeekin's books include *The Berlin-Baghdad Express: The Ottoman Empire and Germany's Bid for World Power* (Penguin/Allen Lane) and *The Russian Origins of the First World War* (Harvard University Press). He lives in Istanbul with his wife, Nesrin, and their daughter, Ayla.

ALSO BY SEAN McMEEKIN:

History's Greatest Heist

The Red Millionaire

CONTENTS

CONTENTS

AUTHOR'S NOTE

I WOULD LIKE TO THANK MY AGENT, Andrew Lownie, for taking on this project and sharpening it with his suggestions. Likewise, I am indebted to Lara Heimert of Basic Books for believing in the book and to Roger Labrie and Beth Wright for sharpening my prose. It is always a pleasure to find editors who share one's enthusiasm for a subject. I am also indebted to the archivists without whom I could not have told my story. I have spent many happy months in the Foreign Office archives of Germany, Austria, Russia, France, and England. While it is impossible to thank everyone, I would like to single out Joachim Tepperberg of the Haus-, Hof- und Staatsarchiv in Vienna and Mareike Fossenberg of the Politisches Archiv des Auswärtigen Amtes in Berlin, both of whom performed wonders on my behalf.

I have drawn inspiration from secondary works. Like many other historians (particularly Americans, for whom the First World War is not quite as central to our own national story as it is for Europeans), I first fell in love with the subject when I devoured Barbara Tuchman's *The Guns of August* (1962). I still have my tattered old paperback edition, with its cover price (75 cents) reminding me that it comes from another era. While not all of her conclusions have stood up over time, Tuchman's perfectly wrought character sketches and incomparable scene settings ensure that her book will always find an audience among history lovers. The best thing about *The Guns of August*, for my purposes, is that she left the July crisis alone, picking up her narrative only on 1 August.

The historical literature on the July crisis of 1914 is vast, although not quite so vast as that on the First World War, which resulted from it. Anyone who tackles the July crisis realises that, on almost any issue of scholarly dispute, Sidney Fay, Bernadotte Schmitt, or Luigi Albertini got there first. It is impossible to write about July 1914 without developing an intimate relationship with Albertini's three-volume history. This is also true of the great documentary collections compiled by the major powers after the war. While the odd document slipped through the cracks, and revelations continue to emerge from former Soviet or Eastern Bloc archives opened in 1991 (of which I can claim credit for some), for the most part the basic documentation on the July crisis has remained unchanged since the 1930s. Like Albertini's, like that of nearly all historians, my narrative draws primarily on these great documentary collections. I am grateful to their editors, particularly those behind the famous Kautsky-Montgelas-Schückert series of German documents, which reproduces not only the full text of most key telegrams but also marginalia scribbled on them, with precise time-dating, down to the minute, for dispatch, decoding, and even when they were read by the chancellor or kaiser.

It has always been my preference to go back to the sources directly, rather than to filter my interpretation through those of others. For this reason, while acknowledging my debts to the historians in the bibliography, I have kept my narrative as clean as possible, eschewing scholarly disputation in the main text. Those wishing to read further may consult the bibliography; those interested in sources and the fine points of debate will find them in the endnotes.

For readers, I can offer a note on 1914-era diplomatic terminology.

'Chorister's Bridge' is shorthand for the Imperial Russian Foreign Ministry. 'Whitehall' stands for the British Foreign Office (and/or government), the 'Wilhelmstrasse' for the German Foreign Office (and/or the Chancellery), the 'Ballhausplatz' (or 'Ballplatz') for the Austro-Hungarian government, and 'Quai d'Orsay' for the French Foreign Ministry.

DRAMATIS PERSONAE

Austria-Hungary

Berchtold, Leopold von, Count. Foreign minister of
Austria-Hungary, 1912–1915.

Bienerth, Karl von, Count, Lieutenant-Colonel. Austrian military
attaché in Berlin, 1910–1914.

Biliński, Leon von. Austrian minister for Bosnia-Herzegovina
and common imperial finance minister.

Conrad von Hötzendorf, Franz. Austria-Hungary's army chief of
staff, 1912–1916.

Czernin, Otto. Austrian legation secretary in St Petersburg,
and interim ambassador there in absence of Count
Friedrich Szapáry.

Franz Ferdinand, Archduke. Heir to the Habsburg throne of
Austria-Hungary.

Franz Josef I. Emperor of Austria and king of Hungary,
1848–1916.

Friedrich, Archduke, Duke of Teschen. Appointed supreme
commander of the Common Imperial Army in July 1914.

Giesl von Gieslingen, Baron. Austrian minister in Serbia,
1913–1914.

Hoyos, Alexander, Count. Berchtold's secretary and special
envoy to Berlin, July 1914.

Krobatin, Alexander, General. Common imperial war minister.

Mensdorff, Albert, Count. Austria-Hungary's ambassador to
England, 1904–1914.

Potiorek, Oskar. Austrian military governor of
Bosnia-Herzegovina.

Ritter von Storck, Wilhelm. Austrian chargé d'affaires in
Belgrade.

Stürgkh, Karl, Count. Austrian minister-president.

Szapáry, Friedrich, Count. Austria-Hungary's ambassador to
Russia, 1913–1914.

Szögyény, Ladislaus, Count. Austria-Hungary's ambassador to Germany, 1892–1914.

Tisza, Stefan, Count. Minister-president of Hungary, 1903–1905, 1913–1917.

Belgium

Albert I. King of Belgium, 1909–1934.

France

Barrère, Camille. France's ambassador to Italy, 1897–1924.

Bienvenu-Martin, Jean-Baptiste. French Minister of Justice and acting director of foreign affairs at the Quai d'Orsay in July 1914.

Boppe, Jules August. French minister to Belgrade, 1914.

Caillaux, Joseph. French prime minister (1911–1912) and finance minister, 1899–1902, 1906–1909, 1913–1914.

Cambon, Jules. France's ambassador to Germany, 1907–1914.

Cambon, Paul. France's ambassador to Britain, 1898–1920.

Dumaine, Alfred. France's ambassador to Austria-Hungary, 1912–1914.

Joffre, Joseph. Chief of staff of the French army, 1911–1916.

Laguiche, Pierre de, General. French military attaché in St Petersburg.

Messimy, Adolphe. France's minister of war, 1911–1912 and June–August 1914.

Paléologue, Maurice. France's ambassador to Russia, 1914–1917.

Poincaré, Raymond. President of France, 1913–1920.

Robien, Louis de. French embassy attaché in St Petersburg.

Viviani, René. France's premier and foreign minister at various points in 1914 and 1915, including both offices in June–July 1914.

Germany

Below-Selaske, Klaus von. German minister at Brussels, 1913–1914.

Bethmann Hollweg, Theobald von. Chancellor of Imperial Germany, 1909–1917.

Bülow, Bernhard von, Prince. Chancellor of Imperial Germany, 1900–1909.

Chelius, Oskar von, General. German military attaché in St Petersburg and aide-de-camp to Tsar Nicholas II, 1914.

Falkenhayn, Erich von. Prussian minister of war, 1913–1915.

Griesinger, Julius Adolph, Baron. Germany minister to Belgrade, 1911–1914.

Jagow, Gottlieb von. State secretary of Imperial Germany, 1913–1916.

Lichnowsky, Prince Karl Max von. Germany's ambassador to Britain, 1912–1914.

Moltke 'the Younger,' Helmuth von. Chief of staff of the German army, 1906–1914.

Müller, Georg Alexander von, Admiral. Chief of German naval cabinet, 1906–1918.

Plessen, Hans G. H. von, General, adjutant to Kaiser Wilhelm II.

Pourtalès, Friedrich. Germany's ambassador to Russia, 1907–1914.

Riezler, Kurt. Private secretary to Chancellor Bethmann Hollweg, 1909–1914.

Schlieffen, Alfred von, Count, Field Marshal. Chief of German General Staff, 1891–1906.

Schoen, Wilhelm von, Baron. Germany's ambassador to France, 1910–1914.

Stumm, Wilhelm von. Political director of the German Foreign Office, 1911–1916.

Tirpitz, Alfred von. Secretary of state of the German Imperial Naval Office, 1897–1916.

Tschirschky, Heinrich von, Count. German ambassador to Austria-Hungary, 1907–1914.

Wilhelm II. Emperor ('Kaiser') of Imperial Germany, 1888–1918.

Zimmermann, Arthur. Undersecretary of state of Imperial Germany, 1911–1916.

Great Britain

Asquith, Herbert Henry. Liberal British prime minister, 1908–1916.

Bertie, Sir Francis. Britain's ambassador to France, 1905–1918.

Buchanan, Sir George. Britain's ambassador to Russia, 1910–1918.

Churchill, Winston. Britain's first lord of the Admiralty, 1911–1915.

Crackanthorpe, Dayrell. British chargé d'affaires in Belgrade, 1912–1915.

Crowe, Sir Eyre. Senior clerk in the British Foreign Office.

De Bunsen, Sir Maurice. Britain's ambassador to Austria, 1913–1914.

George V. King of England, 1910–1936.

Goschen, Sir W. Edward. Britain's ambassador to Germany, 1908–1914.

Grey, Sir Edward. His Majesty's foreign secretary, 1905–1916.

Morley, Lord John. Lord President of the Council, 1910–1914.

Nicolson, Sir Arthur. Permanent undersecretary in the British Foreign Office, 1910–1916.

Wilson, Sir Henry, General. Director of military operations in British War Office, 1910–1914.

Russia

Artamonov, Viktor A., General. Russian military attaché in Belgrade, 1912–1914.

Bark, Peter. Russian minister of finance, 1914–1917.

Benckendorff, Alexander K., Count. Russian ambassador to England, 1903–1917.

Dobrorolskii, Sergei, General. Chief of Russian army's mobilisation section, 1914.

Goremykin, Ivan L. Chairman of Russian Council of Ministers, 1914–1916.

Grigorevich, Ivan K., Admiral. Russian naval minister, 1911–1916.

Hartwig, Nikolai. Russia's minister in Serbia, 1909–1914.

Izvolsky, Alexander. Russia's ambassador to France, 1910–1917.

Krivoshein, A. V. Russian minister of agriculture, 1906–1915.

Nicholas II (Romanov). Tsar of Russia, 1894–1917.

Nicholas Nikolaevich (Romanov). Grand Duke and commander in chief of the Russian Imperial Army, 1914–1915.

Sazonov, Sergei. Foreign minister of Russia, 1910–1916.

Schilling, Moritz F., Baron. Head of Chancery (i.e., chief of staff) of the Russian Foreign Ministry, 1912–1914.

Shebeko, Nikolai. Russia's ambassador to Austria-Hungary, 1913–1914.

Stolypin, Peter. Chairman of Russian Council of Ministers, 1906–1911.

Sukhomlinov, V. A. Chief of Russian Army General Staff, 1908–1909, and Russian war minister, 1909–1915.

Yanushkevitch, N. N. General, chief of Russian Army General Staff.

Serbia

Chabrinovitch, Nedjelko. Bosnian Serb terrorist and co-conspirator of Gavrilo Princip, trained in Belgrade.

Ciganovitch, Milan. Bosnian-born Serb; liaison between Black Hand leaders and Gavrilo Princip in Belgrade. Furnished arms to the terrorists plotting to assassinate Franz Ferdinand.

Dimitrijevitch, Dragutin ('Apis'), Colonel. Head of Serbian Military Intelligence and the Black Hand.

Grabezh, Trifko. Bosnian Serb terrorist and co-conspirator of Gavrilo Princip, trained in Belgrade.

Ilitch, Danilo. Recruiter of local terrorists in Sarajevo, in order to camouflage Serbian involvement in the assassination plot in Belgrade.

Paĉu, Laza, Dr Serbian Minister of Finance, 1912–1915.

Pašić, Nikola. Prime minister of Serbia, 1912–1918.

Princip, Gavrilo. Bosnian Serb terrorist, trained in Belgrade.

Spalaiković, M. Serbia's ambassador to Russia, 1914.

Tankositch, Voja, Major. Co-founder of Black Hand.

CHRONOLOGY

28 June 1914	assassination of Archduke Franz Ferdinand in Sarajevo
5–6 July 1914	Count Hoyos mission to Berlin leads to the 'blank check'
10 July 1914	Berlin first learns of Austrian plans for a Serbian ultimatum
14 July 1914	Tisza converts to the Austrian 'war party'
18 July 1914	Sazonov returns from vacation and learns of Austrian ultimatum plans
19 July 1914	the Ministerial Council in Vienna approves text of Serbian ultimatum
20–23 July 1914	the French presidential summit in St Petersburg
21 July 1914	Sazonov threatens Berchtold: 'There must be no talk of an ultimatum'
23 July 1914	France and Russia try to warn Vienna not to issue a Serbian ultimatum; Vienna issues its ultimatum to Serbia anyway
24–25 July 1914	Russia's Council of Ministers decrees 'partial mobilisation'; Tsar Nicholas II ratifies this; France's ambassador gives imprimatur
26 July 1914	Russia begins its 'Period Preparatory to War'
28 July 1914	Austria-Hungary declares war on Serbia
29 July 1914	Tsar Nicholas II orders general mobilisation, then changes his mind
30 July 1914	Russian general mobilisation is ordered
31 July 1914	Germany issues ultimatum to Russia to halt its mobilisation

1 August 1914	first France and then Germany orders general mobilisation; Germany declares war on Russia
3 August 1914	Grey gives speech to the Commons, making case for war if Germany violates Belgian neutrality; Germany declares war on France
4 August 1914	German troops enter Belgium; Britain issues ultimatum to Germany; it expires at eleven PM London time; Britain and Germany at war

PROLOGUE: SARAJEVO, SUNDAY, 28 JUNE 1914

O<small>N</small> S<small>UNDAY</small> <small>MORNING</small>, 28 June 1914, Archduke Franz Ferdinand awoke in the Hotel Bosnia with a sense of relief that he would soon depart. His suite, located in the spa town of Ilidža ten kilometres (about six miles) west of Sarajevo, had a certain garish charm, adorned with Persian carpets, Arabesque lamp figurines, and Turkish scimitars. But three days of Oriental-Muslim kitsch had been plenty for this proper Catholic archduke. After arriving Thursday afternoon, the heir to the Habsburg throne had attended two full days of Austrian military manoeuvres. On Friday evening, Ferdinand had accompanied his wife, Sophie, on what was intended to be an informal shopping expedition in the bazaars of Sarajevo. The Muslim mayor, Fehim Efendi, had instructed his multifaith constituents to show these illustrious guests their best 'Slavic hospitality,' and they did not disappoint, mobbing Ferdinand and Sophie everywhere they went. The archduke had then repaid this cumbersome hospitality by hosting the mayor, along with Bosnian officials and religious leaders (Catholic, Orthodox, and Muslim), at his Ilidža hotel for a 'sumptuous banquet' on Saturday night. The menu was mostly French, but, in a nod to the locals, the aperitifs included *žilavka*, a white wine from the Mostar region in Herzegovina.

'Thank God,' Ferdinand was heard to remark as his guests at last began returning to Sarajevo, 'this Bosnian trip is over.' Franz Conrad von Hötzendorf, who, as chief of the General Staff, had presided over the military exercises, slipped off quietly at nine PM, following the last toasts. Ferdinand would have liked to leave with Conrad, and nearly did – only to be warned by

Archduke Franz Ferdinand, heir to the throne of Austria-Hungary, with his wife, Sophie, and their three children. *Source: Bain News Service, Library of Congress.*

advisers that breaking off the Sunday programme would damage Austrian prestige in Bosnia. Still, it would all be over in several hours. All that remained on the Sunday programme was a town hall photo op, a brief museum visit, and lunch at Konak, the governor's mansion. After dressing and attending an early Mass 'in a room specially converted to a chapel' in the hotel, Ferdinand dashed off a telegram to his children, telling them that 'Papi' and 'Mami' could not wait to see them on Tuesday.[1]

That final day of the visit, 28 June, was an anniversary of painful significance for the archducal couple. On this date in 1900, the heir to the Austrian throne had been forced by his uncle, Emperor Franz Josef I, to sign an Oath of Renunciation, stipulating that any children issuing from his morganatic marriage to Sophie be excluded from the imperial succession. Although hardly a commoner, Sophie Chotek came from a Czech noble family far too obscure and impoverished for the grand Habsburgs. Adding to the scandalous impropriety of the match, Sophie had been lady-in-waiting to the Habsburg archduchess, Marie Christine, whom Ferdinand had been expected to marry. One day, the story went, Franz Ferdinand changed clothes to play tennis, leaving his locket behind in the dressing room. The mother of the presumed heiress opened the locket, expecting to find a picture of her daughter – only to see instead the likeness of her lady-in-waiting.

Rather than renounce his passion in the name of family dignity, Ferdinand had married his secret love. Most of the Habsburgs had never forgiven him this humiliation. Nor was Sophie allowed to forget it. Although she was created Duchess of Hohenberg, Ferdinand's wife was subjected to endless humiliations at imperial banquets, where she was forced to enter each room last, after much younger, unmarried archduchesses, 'alone and without escort,' being then seated at the foot of the table, nowhere near her husband. Even at the Saturday dinner banquet in Ilidža, far from the court in Vienna, Sophie had been forced to sit between two archbishops and to endure her husband's painfully 'wifeless toast' (Franz Ferdinand was not allowed to mention her in public on official occasions).[2]

A legend claims that Ferdinand's entire Bosnian trip was conceived as a sop to Sophie, who did not often get to enjoy the elaborate ceremonies most Habsburg duchesses expected as a matter of course. In fact the visit was eminently political, which is why he was so keen to get it over with. Ferdinand had fervently opposed the annexation of Bosnia-Herzegovina by the dual monarchy in 1908 as a needless provocation of the South Slavs, especially the Orthodox Serbs, who comprised more than 40 per cent of the 1.9 million residents of Bosnia-Herzegovina in 1914 (as against Muslims at 30 per cent, Roman Catholic Croats at 20 per cent, and a smattering of Jews, Protestants, and gypsies). It was not that the archduke cared for Serbs, whom he regarded as a 'pack of thieves and murderers and scoundrels.'[3] He did, however, care to maintain Austria's precarious relations with Serbophile Russia, and he therefore viewed the whole Bosnian business with distaste.

The annexation, as Ferdinand knew, had wounded Russian pride deeply, not least because Austria's then foreign minister, Baron Alois Lexa von Aehrenthal, had famously tricked his Russian counterpart, Alexander Izvolsky, into supporting it in a cynical quid pro quo, in exchange for Austrian endorsement of Russian naval access to the Ottoman Straits, before reneging on his phony promise. Izvolsky had then reneged in turn, only for his hand to be forced by an implied German threat to go to war with Russia in March 1909. Aehrenthal's humiliation of Izvolsky in this First Bosnian Crisis was severe enough that the latter was forced to resign (only to re-emerge in Paris as Russian ambassador to France, from which post he plotted his revenge). Austria's annexation of Bosnia-Herzegovina in the teeth of Serbian hatred and Russian resentment was a ticking diplomatic time bomb that could go off at any time. The archduke could only hope that it would not detonate during his visit.

In 1910, Franz Josef I had made a royal progress in Bosnia-Herzegovina to win over the loyalty of his reluctant new subjects – although, in a not-so-subtle nod to Serbian opposition, his advance team had made sure to blanket Sarajevo with a thick police presence. Having experienced a similarly stiff setup on a state visit to Romania, Franz Ferdinand had demanded a less suffocating cordon for his own progress in 1914. He had also demanded that he be allowed to bring to Bosnia his beloved wife, who kept his spirits up during tedious official occasions (when, that is, she was allowed to speak to him). Still, security was taken seriously, with planning handled by the archduke's own military staff, with assistance from Conrad; Leon von Biliński, the minister for Bosnia-Herzegovina; and Oskar Potiorek, the province's military governor. Contrary to claims by Serbian critics, the manoeuvres by the XV and XVI Army Corps that were the point of Ferdinand's trip were held not along the Bosnian-Serbian border but in the area of southwestern Herzegovina facing the Adriatic, as far from Serbia as possible.

Aside from sensibly avoiding a provocation near the Serbian border, these men had not, alas, distinguished themselves in planning the trip, which had begun with a series of ill omens. The luxurious rail car Ferdinand usually travelled in, built to order for him by the Ringhoffer firm in Prague, had sprung an axle loose en route from the Czech-Austrian resort town Chlumetz bei Wittengau (where Ferdinand and Sophie had left their children, until their expected return on Tuesday). The archduke had then been deposited in an ordinary first-class wagon as far as Vienna, where he was to be transferred to a backup royal rail car for the long journey to Trieste – only for its electric lights to fail while he was still in the station. As there was not enough time to repair the wiring without disturbing the trip's itinerary, the archduke and his staff continued all the way to the Adriatic coast in a wagon lit by candlelight. It was, Ferdinand remarked, like travelling 'in a tomb.'[4]

The worst omen of all, however, was the choice of date for the final royal progress in Sarajevo. For Ferdinand and Sophie, 28 June brought a painful reminder of the exclusion of their children from the Habsburg succession. For Serbs, this date brought the even more painful reminder of their terrible defeat at Kosovo Polje in 1389, when the Turks had wiped out independent Serbia. For Serbs, however, 28 June was not only a day of mourning. Because a Serbian knight, Miloš Obilić, had slain Ottoman sultan Murad I on the battlefield, the anniversary had been turned into a celebration of national resistance, a feast day in honour of the Slavic deity of war and fertility: St Vitus's Day, or Vidov Dan. Even as Archduke Ferdinand, heir to the throne, would be (reluctantly) consecrating Habsburg rule over Serbs with an official visit to Sarajevo, Serbs at Kosovo would be feasting to honour the patriot who had slain their Turkish conqueror on this day 525 years before. Considering the recent history of

Serbian regicidal terrorism – in 1903 a clique of hypernationalist military officers led by the future head of Serbian army intelligence, Dragutin Dimitrijevitch ('Apis'), had murdered Serbia's own king and queen* to protest their insufficient devotion to the Serbian cause – staging a royal progress in Sarajevo on Vidov Dan was provocative, if not downright foolhardy.

Making the Sunday tour still more risky, news of the visit had been made public months in advance, such that any Serb with a grudge against the dual monarchy had plenty of time to plan for it. A Zaghreb newspaper, *Srbobran*, had divulged the principal details of the archduke's upcoming trip to Bosnia-Herzegovina in March 1914. Although the exact date of the Sarajevo tour was not then known, *Srbobran* announced as definite that Archduke Ferdinand would come to Bosnia in early summer to observe military manoeuvres.

Intrigued by the news report, which had reached him in Sarajevo, a Bosnian Serb activist of the irredentist group Young Bosnia clipped the announcement and mailed it to his friend Nedjelko Chabrinovitch in Belgrade, addressed – in the bohemian style of the Serbian underground – via the coffeehouse Eichelkranz. Chabrinovitch, in turn, showed the clipping to his friend Gavrilo Princip, a radical Serb nationalist from Bosnia, over lunch. After spending the afternoon brooding over the news, Princip sought out Chabrinovitch that night in another Belgrade café, the Grüner Kranz, to propose that the two travel to Sarajevo to assassinate the heir to the Habsburg throne. The nineteen-year-old Chabrinovitch, more of an anarchist by temperament than Princip, would rather have gone after Governor Potiorek, who symbolised what he called the 'Mameluke' or Muslim slave-caste class of government officials sent down by

---

* Also murdered were the queen's brothers and several government ministers.

Vienna to make Bosnian Serbs suffer. But Princip won over Chabrinovitch by force of conviction.[5]

Princip's suggestion was not an idle one. Although neither he nor Chabrinovitch possessed weapons of his own, they both were in touch with Serbia's network of semi-official terrorist groups. Princip was a former recruit of the Narodna Odbrana (National Defence), an organisation launched in 1908 to oppose Austria's annexation of Bosnia-Herzegovina by training underground *comitaji* warriors in 'bomb-throwing, the blowing up of railways and bridges,' and other sundry arts of guerrilla warfare. Princip had been trained by Narodna Odbrana in 1912 under Major Voja Tankositch (who had personally murdered the Serbian queen's brothers in 1903), the intention being to smuggle him across the Turkish border prior to the First Balkan War, launched by the Balkan League of Serbia, Bulgaria, Greece, and Montenegro against Ottoman Turkey that October. Then just eighteen, thin, and in poor health, Princip had washed out of training, but he maintained contacts in both the Narodna Odbrana and its more radical spin-off organization, Ujedinjenje ili Smrt (Union or Death), known as the Black Hand.

The Black Hand, run by many of the same people who had founded Narodna Odbrana – including Apis and Major Tankositch – was enveloped in layers of secrecy. New members would be led into 'a darkened room, lighted only by wax candles,' where they would swear an oath 'by the blood of my ancestors . . . that I will from this moment till my death . . . be ready to make any sacrifice for [Serbia].' The organisation's seal suggested what sacrifice was meant: it displayed an unfurled flag, the skull and bones sign, a dagger, a bomb, and, last, a bottle of poison meant for the member himself, after he had committed his murderous deed.[6]

Princip and Chabrinovitch were not active members of the Black Hand, but they knew men who were. Milan Ciganovitch, for one, was a fellow Bosnian Serb who had trained with Princip under Major Tankositch in 1912, only more successfully. Ciganovitch had pilfered a personal arsenal of six handheld bombs during the Balkan Wars. Learning of Princip's idea, Ciganovitch offered the use of his stash of explosives but also suggested that the two would-be assassins try to obtain pistols, in case the bombs failed. Major Tankositch, almost certainly on orders from Apis, duly provided them with four Browning revolvers plus ammunition, 150 dinars in cash, and, not least, cyanide of potassium, with which the assassin was to commit suicide after killing the archduke. Finally, Tankositch instructed Ciganovitch, a veteran, to give Princip and Chabrinovitch shooting practice so that they would not miss their target.[7]

The Black Hand provided more to the would-be assassins than weapons and training. Over the years, the organisation had built a sort of underground railroad, or tunnel, of terrorism. It was not hard to smuggle individuals with fake papers onto Austrian territory, but smuggling weapons required a deft touch. On 26 May 1914, when Princip, Chabrinovitch, and a third conspirator, Trifko Grabezh, arrived at Šabac, near the border, a Serbian army officer, Major Popovitch, was waiting with instructions he had received from Major Tankositch. Chabrinovitch, with papers provided by Popovitch, was to cross the border en route for Zvornik, on the Bosnian side; from there another confidence man would drive him to Tuzla, a town connected by railway to Sarajevo. Princip and Grabezh, carrying the weapons, crossed the Drina River into Bosnia near Lješnica, being carefully ferried by a Serbian customs official from one island to another and then passed on by friendly Serbian peasant guides as far as Priboj. There they met their next handler, Veljko Chubrilovitch, the town's schoolmaster, a secret member of Narodna Odbrana.

To make their rendezvous with Chabrinovitch at Tuzla, they would have to pass a checkpoint of Austrian gendarmes at Lopare. In a clever bit of derring-do, Princip and Grabezh left

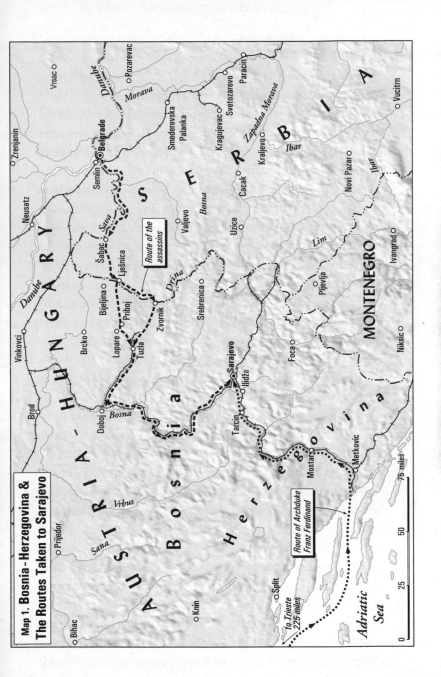

Map 1. Bosnia - Herzegovina &
The Routes Taken to Sarajevo

Route of the
assassins

Route of Archduke
Franz Ferdinand

to Trieste
225 miles

Adriatic
Sea

MONTENEGRO

S   E   R   B   I   A

A U S T R I A - H U N G A R Y

B o s n i a

H e r z e g o v i n a

Belgrade
Semlin
Šabac
Ljesnica
Bijeljina
Priboj
Lopare
Tuzla
Zvornik
Srebrenica
Doboj
Bosna
Tarcin
Ilidža
Sarajevo
Mostar
Metkovic
Foca
Niksic
Ivangrad
Pljevlja
Novi Pazar
Vucitrn
Kraljevo
Cacak
Užice
Valjevo
Kragujevac
Svetozarevo
Paracin
Smederevska
Palanka
Pozarevac
Vrsac
Zrenjanin
Neusatz
Vinkovci
Brcko
Brod
Prijedor
Knin
Split
Bihac
Sana
Vrbus
Drina
Sava
Morava
Danube
Ibar
Lim
Zapadna Morava
Bosna

0   25   50   75 miles

9

their stash of bombs, pistols, and poison in the cart of a peasant they were travelling with for cover, circled the village on foot and then rejoined him on the other side. Finally, in Tuzla, the three terrorists, having been reunited, turned over their deadly cargo to another confidence man, Mishko Jovanovitch, who, like Chubrilovitch, was both an upstanding local citizen (he owned a bank and a movie theatre) and a member of Narodna Odbrana. Jovanovitch hid the weapons in his attic, while the terrorists proceeded on to Sarajevo. Showing a mastery of underground tradecraft, the four men agreed that a fifth man would return from Sarajevo to retrieve the weapons, identifying himself 'by offering a package of Stephanie cigarettes.'[8]

While Princip, Chabrinovitch, and Grabezh bided their time in the Bosnian capital, their handlers swung into action. Danilo Ilitch, a former schoolmaster and bank clerk turned full-time activist ne'er do well, who now lived with his mother in Sarajevo, took in Princip and Chabrinovitch (Grabezh's own family lived nearby). Ilitch knew the terrorists well from previous visits to Belgrade. Princip had written him back in April, speaking vaguely of his plans to assassinate Franz Ferdinand and suggesting that Ilitch recruit local assassins in Sarajevo as well. Ilitch was thus already knee-deep in the conspiracy even before the terrorist trio arrived; he would now go deeper still. After presenting the package of Stephanie cigarettes in Tuzla, Ilitch asked Jovanovitch to carry the weapons on to Doboj, fearing that he would be arrested in Tuzla, where he was not known.

Jovanovitch duly took the weapons and, with panache, hid them in a box of sugar, which he wrapped in white paper and bound with twine. While looking for Ilitch in Doboj, Jovanovitch at one point left the box hidden underneath his raincoat in the rail station waiting room; he later left it unattended, for a time, in a friend's workshop. Ilitch, after finally taking the dangerous cargo to Sarajevo, placed it 'in a small chest, which I locked, under a couch' in his mother's bedroom. Fittingly, on the morning of 28 June 1914, Ilitch at last returned the 'sugar' to Princip, Chabrinovitch, and Grabezh in the Vlajinitch pastry shop (minus several revolvers turned over to his own local recruits). Princip took a pistol, Chabrinovitch a bomb, and Grabezh one of each. The assassins were ready.[9]

There was no great mystery about the route the archduke's motorcade would follow that morning. Sarajevo was a small enough city, with obvious enough features, that one could have guessed at it without inside knowledge of the itinerary. Sarajevo is a low-lying valley town, split in the middle by the Miljăcke River (although 'river' is a misnomer during the summer months, when it dries to a trickle) and surrounded by high hills that frame the town's dramatic skyline. Any royal progress would likely proceed down the Appelquai, the main avenue running parallel to the Miljăcke.

As if to confirm what everyone suspected already, in the same decree in which he had exhorted Sarajevo's subjects to show the Habsburg heir their best Slavic hospitality, Mayor Fehim Efendi had also informed them of the itinerary of the archduke's Sunday visit, including the Appelquai (to be travelled both to and from town hall), the idea being that residents and shop owners along the route should bedeck the streets with imperial flags and flowers. Many Sarajevans had gone the mayor one better, displaying large portraits of the archduke on their walls and windows. Judging from the ubiquitous displays of hospitality blanketing the city all weekend, and the overwhelming warmth with which the locals had greeted him during his impromptu Friday night tour of the bazaar, Franz Ferdinand had no reason to expect anything different on Sunday.

But Sunday *was* different, because the travel itinerary – including both the route and the timing of the visit – had been published beforehand. The archduke's private secretary,

Paul Nikitsch-Boulles, later wrote that during the spontaneous Friday tour 'any would-be murderer would have had a thousand chances to assault Franz Ferdinand, undefended.' And yet, although accessing the victim would have been easy, none of the assassins had made a move on Friday because they did not have their weapons. On Sunday, they did.[10]

The sun shone brilliantly across Bosnia on the morning of Vidov Dan, as the Habsburg heir prepared to run out the clock on his visit. Franz Ferdinand wore the uniform of an Austrian cavalry general, with a blue tunic over black trousers with red stripes, topped off by a gold collar with three silver stars. Sophie was elegantly outfitted in a 'gossamer white veil' and white hat, with a bouquet of roses tucked into her red sash. Together they arrived in Sarajevo by train from Ilidža at 9:20 AM, accompanied by Governor Potiorek, who acted as tour guide. A brief review of local troops followed, at which Sophie, significantly, was allowed to walk side by side with her husband. The archducal couple then took the position of honour in an open car in the imperial motorcade, behind the lead car holding the mayor and police chief, with three other staff cars trailing behind. The cannons boomed a '24-fold salute' to announce the start of the royal progress, followed by shouts of 'Zivio!' ('long live the heir') from the crowds. As everyone in town knew, the motorcade would now, between 10 and 10:30 AM, proceed down the length of the Appelquai towards the town hall, along the right side of the road bordering the river; on the return route, the motorcade would proceed on the opposite, landward side of the quai.[11]

There, along the Appelquai, the assassins waited. Counting Ilitch himself, there were seven in all. Chabrinovitch, Grabezh, and Princip, fresh from Belgrade, formed the core muscle of the conspiracy. Ilitch had recruited three more locals: Vaso Chubrilovitch and Cvjetko Popovitch, both Bosnian Serbs,

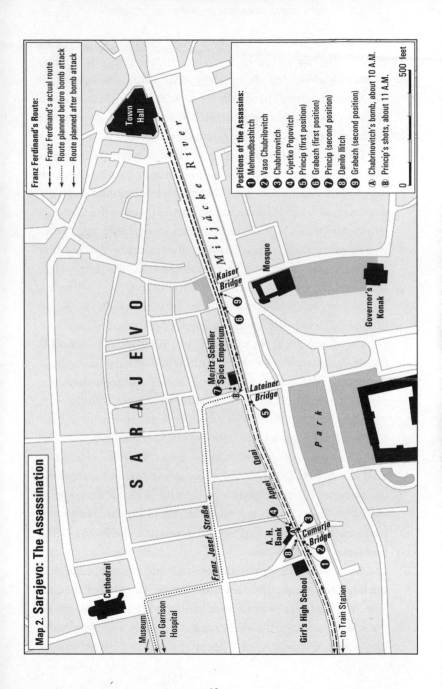

Map 2. Sarajevo: The Assassination

Franz Ferdinand's Route:
- – – – Franz Ferdinand's actual route
- ·········· Route planned before bomb attack
- ——— Route planned after bomb attack

Positions of the Assassins:
1. Mehmedbashitch
2. Vaso Chubrilovitch
3. Chabrinovitch
4. Cvjetko Popovitch
5. Princip (first position)
6. Grabezh (first position)
7. Princip (second position)
8. Danilo Ilitch
9. Grabezh (second position)

Ⓐ Chabrinovitch's bomb, about 10 A.M.
Ⓑ Princip's shots, about 11 A.M.

0   500 feet

Cathedral

Museum
to Garrison Hospital

Franz Josef Straße

S   A   R   A   J   E   V   O

A. H. Bank

Appel Quai

Moritz Schiller Spice Emporium

Lateiner Bridge

Kaiser Bridge

Town Hall

Miljäcke River

Mosque

Park

Governor's Konak

Cumurja Bridge

Girl's High School

to Train Station

13

and, perhaps to throw investigators off the scent of the crime, a token Bosnian Muslim with the wonderfully evocative name of Mehmedbashitch ('Mehmed' being a Turkic variant of Mohammad and 'bashitch' the Slavicisation of the Turkish word for kickback, *baksheesh*). Ilitch, the organiser, chose a post for himself on the landward side of the Appelquai across from the Cumurja Bridge, flanked by Popovitch. Directly opposite, Mehmedbashitch, Chubrilovitch, and Chabrinovitch took up key positions along the river. The motorcade would pass by the first two, who carried pistols, just before passing the Cumurja Bridge and then Chabrinovitch, with his handheld fuse bomb. In case these three missed their chance, Princip was waiting with his revolver right before the cars reached the next bridge, the Lateiner. Finally, if the first four failed, the motorcade would have to get by Grabezh – the only assassin who carried both bomb and pistol – short of the Kaiser Bridge.

For all the brilliant redundancy of Ilitch's plan, there was a glaring weakness. Perhaps overestimating the dedication of his own recruits, the organiser of the assassination plot had given the two most important positions to Vaso Chubrilovitch, a young Bosnian with little training and less courage, and Mehmedbashitch, a Muslim of questionable loyalty to the Serbian cause. Neither man raised a finger when the motorcade passed him by. Only the third assassin and first of the Belgrade conspirators, Chabrinovitch, acted. As the motorcade was passing by the Cumurja Bridge, Chabrinovitch knocked the cap off his bomb and hurled it at the archduke's car. Luckily, the driver had seen the assassin readying to strike; he accelerated rapidly, and the fuse bomb, after grazing Ferdinand's face, bounced off the back hood and detonated underneath the staff car that followed behind. The explosion did serious damage to the latter vehicle, wounding Potiorek's adjutant and several bystanders on the quai. Chabrinovitch jumped into the dry riverbed, only to be seized by policemen before he could pop his poison pill (if he intended to).

Never was the quiet dignity of the Habsburgs more in evidence than in the minutes following the attempt on the archduke's life. Dismissing his own minor scratch, Franz Ferdinand calmly surveyed the damage to the car, asked if anyone had been injured, and made sure all wounded men were sent forthwith to the garrison hospital for treatment. 'Come on,' he remarked, 'the fellow is insane. Gentlemen, let us proceed with the programme.' When the motorcade resumed its course along the Appelquai at a higher speed than before, so as to discourage further attempts on the archduke's life, Ferdinand scoffed and asked his driver to slow down so that his subjects might see him better. His instinct was sound: having seen Chabrinovitch's bomb fail to hit its target, Princip and Grabezh had abandoned their positions.[12]

Despite his show of pluck in the face of this act of terrorism, the archduke was in a foul mood when the party reached the town hall. Sophie, uninjured but for a small scratch and not too badly shaken, went off to meet with a deputation of Muslim women, while Ferdinand prepared to endure one last round of public speeches. The scene was novel, at least. Underneath a canopy of 'red-gold Moorish loggias' – a nod to Sarajevo's Ottoman past – the archduke was greeted by 'turbaned mullahs, bishops in miters and gilt vestments, rabbis in kaftans.' But there was an unmistakable air of awkwardness. When Mayor Fehim Efendi, unsure of how to behave in the wake of the incident on the quay, simply read off his prepared text of platitudes and compliments for the Habsburg heir – read in German, which he spoke decently well for a Bosnian – Ferdinand finally snapped, interrupting Fehim Efendi to say, 'That's rich! We come here to visit this city and we are greeted with bombs. Very well, then, go on.'[13]

It was approaching eleven AM. The programme called for a visit to the museum before lunch, which would require navigating the most crowded part of the city by way of Franz Josef Strasse. To avoid further trouble, the archduke's military advisers suggested he skip the museum and proceed to Potiorek's gubernatorial Konak, turning left at the first bridge along the quai – the Kaiser – to avoid the trouble spot at the Cumurja farther down; from the Kaiser it was a straight shot to the Konak (this route also passed through the Muslim quarter, presumably safer than the Serbian neighbourhoods). With his characteristic sense of honour, Ferdinand chose a third option: visiting the garrison hospital to check on Potiorek's adjutant and the other wounded before proceeding to the Konak for the luncheon that would, at last, terminate his duties in Bosnia. While the hospital, like the museum, was most directly reached via the narrow Franz-Josef Strasse, Potiorek insisted that the motorcade proceed straight along the broad Appelquai at high speed so as to foil bomb throwers, reaching the garrison hospital by the long – but presumably safe – way.[14]

It was a sensible plan. Meanwhile, Princip and Grabezh were still milling about the quai, despondent after watching Chabrinovitch's arrest following his near miss. Ilitch and his Bosnian recruits, despite being perfectly located to make mischief after the motorcade had been halted after the bombing, had all slunk away to hide. Grabezh had not distinguished himself either, having failed to strike – even after the motorcade resumed its progress along the quay – because, he claimed later, the crowds at the Lateiner Bridge were too thick. The Serbs' one remaining hand bomb, held by Grabezh, would have almost no chance to hit a car travelling at full speed. Grabezh and Princip were both carrying pistols, but the idea that either one of them could, after a few weeks' target practice, hit the archduke with a kill shot in a rapidly moving car was fanciful. Grabezh, knowing this, had taken up a new position at the

Kaiser Bridge, hoping that, if the returning motorcade turned there towards the gubernatorial Konak, it would slow down enough for him get off a shot at close range. Had the archduke not insisted on visiting the wounded men at the garrison hospital, his car would have had to slow down, briefly, turning onto the bridge where Grabezh was waiting – although the Serb would have had only a second, at most, to get off his shot.[15]

Gavrilo Princip had not given up, either. He, along with Chabrinovitch, had set the conspiracy in motion. Both men were committed terrorists. Both had taken oaths to carry out this terrible deed over the Sarajevo gravestone of Bogdan Zherajitch, a Herzogovinian Serb revered for his assassination attempt on General Vareshanin, Potiorek's predecessor as military governor of Bosnia, in 1910. Zherajitch, like Princip and Chabrinovitch, had been trained by the Black Hand. Although he had failed to kill the governor, Zherajitch had got off five shots before committing suicide. Princip, in the days before the archduke's arrival, spent hours next to Zherajitch's grave, gathering strength for his task. On the night before Vidov Dan, Princip had made one last pilgrimage, covering the terrorist's tombstone with flowers to consecrate his own expected martyrdom on the morrow.[16]

So far, Princip had failed his hero. Chabrinovitch had at least made his attempt on the archduke (even if failing to kill himself, as Zherajitch had done). Thus far Princip had not even done that much. True, it was not his fault that Ilitch had placed him fourth in line on the riverside that morning. In the tense aftermath of the bombing, with officers and onlookers blanketing the scene, it would have been nearly impossible for him to get close enough to the archduke to get off a good shot. And yet, for a Serbian terrorist committed to die for his cause, this was no excuse.

Fortified by his graveside pilgrimages, Princip did not lose faith after Chabrinovitch was arrested. As Grabezh had

Princip's murder weapon, an FN Model 1910 Browning semi-automatic pistol. *Source: Heeresgeschichtliches Museum, Vienna, Austria.*

the Konak route covered, Princip took up a new position on the museum route, opposite the Lateiner Bridge, in front of the Moritz Schiller spice emporium at the corner of Franz Josef Strasse, where the archduke's car would turn right from the Appelquai if it followed the original programme. So dangerous was the publication of the archduke's itinerary that now, whether he proceeded to either of his two remaining destinations, his motorcade would have to slow down at a sharp corner where a Serb terrorist was waiting, loaded pistol in hand. Still, Ferdinand's stubbornness in choosing a third destination, and Potiorek's decision to abandon the Franz Josef Strasse and run all cars at high speed, had dramatically lowered the odds of a successful second attack. If everything proceeded according to the new plan, both Grabezh and Princip would watch the motorcade pass by in a blur, just out of reach. Princip would be a bit closer, but – at nine metres or 30 feet from his new position – a fast-moving car would present an almost impossible target.

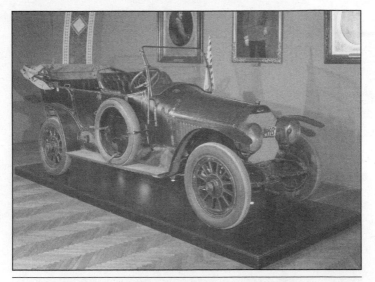

The 1911 Gräf & Stift convertible in which Franz Ferdinand and his wife, Sophie, were travelling when shot by Gavrilo Princip on 28 June 1914. *Source: Heeresgeschichtliches Museum, Vienna, Austria.*

It was just past eleven AM when the archduke, his wife, Potiorek, the mayor, and their beefed-up police escort left town hall, proceeding at full throttle along the river side of the Appelquai. As a further precaution, the driving order had been reconfigured, with a police car leading, the mayor's car second, followed by the Ferdinand-Sophie-Potiorek car, and three more staff cars behind. A close friend of the archduke, Count Harrach, had volunteered for good measure to ride on the car's left running board so he could fend off any assault from the river, from which side the earlier bomb had been thrown. With the principals now in the middle of a long, tightened, fast-moving motorcade, they would be harder to single out by any bomb thrower and almost invulnerable to a shooter.

Grabezh, on the Kaiser Bridge, could only watch the cars as they zoomed by him without turning. As they neared the Lateiner Bridge, about a quarter-mile distant from town hall, the motorcade should have reached full speed – should have, but did not. Whether because they had forgotten about Potiorek's rerouting or because Potiorek had been negligent in informing everyone, the first two cars turned right onto Franz Josef Strasse. The third car, too, carrying Potiorek and the archduke, turned. Realising the error, Potiorek ordered the driver to turn back just as they rounded the sharp corner in front of the spice emporium. After hitting the brakes, the archduke's chauffeur struggled for a fatal moment before he could shift the car into reverse gear. Gavrilo Princip thus found his target sitting motionless for a period of two or three seconds, just 2.5 metres (about 8 feet) away, with Count Harrach – acting as bodyguard – marooned helplessly on the wrong side of the car. Stepping in to point-blank range, Princip fired two shots with his Browning pistol. The first pierced Franz Ferdinand's neck and the second Sophie's abdomen.

As the archduke's car, having turned around at last, sped in the other direction towards the Konak, it was not yet clear to the others in the car that the shots had hit their target. Sophie, sensing something was amiss, thought only of her husband, asking him, 'In God's name, what has happened to you?' Franz Ferdinand, likewise, although knowing he had been hit, could think only of Sophie. 'Sopherl, Sopherl,' he managed to say even as blood dripped from his mouth, 'don't die on me. Live for our children.' Asked by Count Harrach whether he was badly injured, the archduke replied, with all the reserve expected of a Habsburg, 'It is nothing.' As both he and his wife slowly expired, Ferdinand repeated again and again, each time more softly than the last: 'It is nothing.'[17]

By eleven thirty AM on 28 June 1914, Ferdinand and Sophie were dead.

I

REACTIONS

1

Vienna: Anger, Not Sympathy

I T WAS A GORGEOUS DAY ACROSS EUROPE, typical of the glorious summer of 1914. 'Throughout the days and nights,' the novelist Stefan Zweig recalled, 'the heavens were a silky blue, the air soft yet not sultry, the meadows fragrant and warm.' On Sunday afternoon, 28 June, Zweig, like nearly everyone in Austria, was outdoors enjoying the weather, sitting on a park bench in the spa town of Baden, reading a Tolstoy novel. Shortly after two PM, a notice announcing the death of the heir to the throne was posted near the bandstand. Seeing the announcement, the musicians abruptly stopped playing, which alerted everyone that something was amiss. Before long, everyone in town knew the story.[1]

News of the murders in Sarajevo spread quickly across the country. Among government officials, Chief of Staff Conrad, who had taken leave of Franz Ferdinand just hours before the archduke was murdered, was the first to know. Conrad had taken the ten thirty PM train from Sarajevo to Croatia, where he was to supervise manoeuvres. Shortly after noon on Sunday, as Conrad passed through Zaghreb, Baron Rhemen, a general of cavalry, entered his coupé and passed on the terrible story. At his final stop, in Karlstadt, Conrad received an official telegram

23

informing him of the deaths of the Habsburg heir and his wife, and that the assassin was a 'Bosnian of Serbian nationality.' Conrad concluded right then that the assassinations could not have been 'the deed of a single fanatic,' but rather must be 'the work of a well-organised conspiracy.' In effect, the murder of Archduke Franz Ferdinand was 'the declaration of war by Serbia on Austria-Hungary.' This act of war, he resolved, 'could only be answered by war.' Without delay, Conrad wired to Emperor Franz Josef I at his alpine villa at Bad Ischl, asking whether he should break off the planned manoeuvres in Croatia and return to the capital. The answer was yes. For the second evening in a row, Conrad boarded the night train, this time en route to Vienna.[2]

Conrad's coolly belligerent reaction to the news was wholly in character. Army fit and ramrod-thin, the chief of staff was every bit as stubborn as Franz Ferdinand, to whom he owed his elevation to the position. The slain archduke had secured Conrad's appointment in 1906 and his reappointment in 1912 following a short-lived sack the previous November, both times over the objection of Emperor Franz Josef, who found Conrad's ambitious military reforms irksome. (It had not helped that the ever-belligerent Conrad had advocated invading Italy, Austria's nominal ally, in November 1911, when Italy was at war with the Ottoman Empire.) That Conrad was keen to crush Serbia was one of the worst-kept secrets in Europe. As Cato the Elder had signed off his speeches in the Roman Senate with the reminder that 'Carthage must be destroyed,' so Conrad had been consistently urging his colleagues to 'solve the Serbian question once and for all' since the First Bosnian Crisis of 1908–1909.*

---

* It has been estimated that in 1913 alone, Conrad proposed going to war with Serbia 25 times. There is a popular theory that his belligerent attitude owed much to a desire to impress his young mistress, Gina von Reininghaus, into leaving her husband, Hermann, a wealthy beer merchant. While one never knows what secret motivations lie in our heart of hearts, this seems to be taking psychoanalysis a bit far.

Although, thanks to Germany's firm backing against Russia in this crisis, Vienna was able to win European recognition of Austria's annexation of Bosnia-Herzegovina, Serbian nationalists had never accepted its legitimacy: both Narodna Odbrana and the Black Hand had been formed in order to overturn the annexation. Although unsuccessful so far in overthrowing Austrian rule in Bosnia, Serbs were scoring victory after victory elsewhere. Serbia had nearly doubled in size and population during the Balkan Wars of 1912–1913, gaining at the expense of Turkey and Bulgaria. Serbia's prestige was skyrocketing, while Austria's, owing to her failure to intervene in the Balkan Wars, was plummeting. Small wonder the Bosnian Serbs had embraced irredentism – and political terrorism.[3]

Rounding out the atmosphere of menace facing Vienna, Russia, Serbia's Great Power patron, was flexing her muscles again. In a period of internal weakness following her humiliation in the Russo-Japanese War and her subsequent Revolution of 1905, Russia had backed down during the First Bosnian Crisis. Four years later, her pan-Slavist minister to Belgrade, Nikolai Hartwig, had all but single-handedly organised the Balkan League (Serbia, Bulgaria, Greece, and Montenegro), which declared war on the Ottoman Empire in October 1912, launching the First Balkan War. True, Russia had not mobilised herself in this conflict, which saw Turkey defeated on all fronts, nor did she in the Second Balkan War, launched by Bulgaria against her former allies in June 1913 in a quarrel over the spoils from the First (a quarrel Bulgaria lost soundly, after Romania and Turkey piled on her, too). But then, with Austria sitting on the sidelines during both wars even as her Serbian archenemy won victory after victory, Russia had not had to get involved. With the Serbs humiliating Turkey and scaring off Austria from intervening even without Russian backing, Conrad feared that the dual monarchy was running out of time to resolve its smoldering problems with Slavic minorities. That Franz Ferdinand

Map 3. The Balkans, circa 1914

RUSSIAN EMPIRE

AUSTRIA-HUNGARY

Vienna ⊙   ○ Pressburg

○ Budapest

○ Klausenburg

○ Arad

Agram (Zagreb) ○

Trieste

Kronstadt (Brașov) ○

Transylvanian Alps

○ Sinaia

ROMANIA

⊙ Bucharest

○ Constanta

Bosnia Herzegovina

Tuzla ○   Belgrade ⊙

Sarajevo ○

Split ○

Mostar ○

Ragusa ○

MONTE NEGRO

Scutari ○

SERBIA

Danube

Silistra ○

Balchik ○

○ Varna

Balkan Mountains

Sofia ⊙   BULGARIA

○ Burgas

Black Sea

Adriatic Sea

Durazzo ○   Tirana ⊙

ALBANIA

Skopje (Üsküp) ○

Bitola (Monastir) ○

Rhodope Mts.

○ Edirne (Adrianople)

Constantinople ⊙

Taranto ○

Salonica ○

Ioannina ○

GREECE

Dedeagatch ○

Lemnos

Imbros

Aegean Sea

Lesbos

Chios ○

Samos

○ Smyrna

OTTOMAN EMPIRE

Ionian Sea

Corinth ○   Athens ⊙

Dodecanese (Under Italian Occupation)

────── Boundaries 1914

┄┄┄┄┄ Areas lost by the Ottoman Empire

0 ————— 300 Miles

Crete

Mediterranean Sea

26

Count Leopold von Berchtold, foreign minister of Austria-Hungary, found himself at
the centre of the diplomatic storm of July
1914. *Source: Bundesarchiv, Bild 183-2004-
1110-500.*

had himself disapproved of Conrad's belligerent line during
the Balkan Wars did nothing to dampen Conrad's fire – nor did
the archduke's death now prompt a reconsideration. Conrad
spared no time for sentiment as he plotted Austria's vengeance.
It was now or never.

Count Leopold von Berchtold, Austria-Hungary's foreign
minister, was attending a country fair at Buchlowitz, near his
ancestral estate at Buchlau, when he learned the news. He and
his wife, Nandine, had been close with Ferdinand and Sophie.
Not long ago, they had all spent a happy weekend together
at the archduke's estate at Konopischt, where the brilliantly
redesigned gardens were in full springtime bloom. Berchtold,

a handsome, fashionable, stupendously wealthy aristocrat not taken terribly seriously at court – he had been the emperor's third choice when appointed to the post in 1912 – had neither the Habsburg stoicism of his friend Franz Ferdinand nor the ruthless focus of Conrad. Intelligent, well-mannered, and thoughtful, Berchtold was believed to dread making decisions. It was Berchtold who had stood in Conrad's way during the Balkan Wars, teaming up with Franz Ferdinand and the emperor against the war party and consigning Austrian policy to a listless, reactive passivity that had done nothing to keep Serbia in check. True to form, the foreign minister was stunned with grief upon learning of his friend's death, which left him speechless. After taking a long moment to compose himself, Berchtold walked to the station and boarded the next train to Vienna, arriving late Sunday afternoon.

Berchtold found the city 'seized by a kind of monstrous agitation.' In part because the government was cagey at first in revealing details about the assassinations, wild rumours were spreading through the city. Some thought the attacks were some kind of inside job, cooked up by German or Austrian intelligence; others fingered the Freemasons, while yet others heirs of the deceased Crown Prince Rudolf, who might have wished to avenge their father's 1889 suicide based on the idea that Franz Ferdinand, Rudolf's successor as heir to the throne, had murdered him. Some even suspected Stefan Tisza, the Hungarian minister-president, who may have seen Franz Ferdinand as a threat to Hungary's privileged position in the dual monarchy (the archduke had disliked Tisza intensely, and the feeling was mutual). Others were certain of Serbian involvement in the crime, naming (correctly, as it turned out) the intelligence chief Apis, already a notorious bogeyman of Serbian villainy. Franz Ferdinand had been unloved at court and not better liked in Viennese society; his murder was not so much mourned in the city as appreciated for its titillating shock value. Guessing at the motivation for the crime became something of a parlor game, which added to the general air of festivity during a long holiday weekend – Monday, 29 June, was the Catholic feast day of Peter and Paul. In the Prater, after a brief interruption to digest the news from Sarajevo, the music played on through the night as if in defiance of the Sarajevo assassins, whosoever they might be.[4]

There was a curious parallel to the holiday gaiety in Vienna out on the 'blackbird field' of Kosovo Polje in Serbia that Sunday, where the nationalist ecstasies of Vidov Dan were ramping up to fever pitch when a report of the Sarajevo assassinations reached the crowd around five PM. In a remarkable instance of life imitating art, the traditional re-enactment of the Serbian martyr's assassination of Sultan Murad I had, in recent years, featured Austrians rather than Turks as the villains, and now here was news that a real Austrian 'sultan' had been slain, presumably by a Serb. The crowds, an eyewitness told Ritter von Storck, the Austrian chargé d'affaires in Belgrade, 'collapsed in each other's arms out of joy' when they heard that Franz Ferdinand had been murdered. 'We have waited so long for such news,' said one. Another Serb, more political, declared that the assassination was 'small vengeance for the annexation' of Bosnia-Herzegovina. (After citing this remark, Ritter asked, 'and what, I wonder, would be large vengeance?') Although the Vidov Dan ceremony officially came to a close at ten PM, Ritter informed Berchtold that the euphoric celebration had continued long into the night.[5]

At Bad Ischl, the alpine spa town southwest of Vienna where the Habsburg sovereign preferred to spend the summer months, the atmosphere was more somber. Late Sunday evening, a telegram reporting the murder of the Habsburg heir was presented in the formal manner, on royal plate, to Franz Josef I by his adjutant-general, Count Paar. Like Berchtold, the emperor fell momentarily speechless, although his own thoughts were less sympathetic. At last, he is said to have told the count: 'Horrible! Horrible! It is God's will.'* Having not yet learned about the Serbian connection, Franz Josef saw in the murders, at this stage, something like divine punishment for Franz Ferdinand's morganatic marriage to Sophie Chotek, a punishment that had, at least, cleansed the Habsburg line of dynastic impurity. The emperor coldly forbade the burial of the slain archducal couple in the Habsburg vault in Vienna's Church of the Capuchins.[6]

At the Ballplatz, the seat of the Austro-Hungarian government, the mood was just as serious as at Bad Ischl, although considerably less somber. As Berchtold noted in his diary, during the first cabinet meeting following the Sarajevo outrage, 'one noted, yes, consternation and indignation but also a certain easing of mood.' The picture beginning to emerge in reports from Sarajevo was disturbing but also clarifying: there had been multiple assassins on the Appelquai, all of them, it seemed, Bosnian Serbs with murky ties to secret societies inside Serbia. While it was not clear yet whether there was any *official* Serbian involvement in plotting the assassination of the Habsburg heir, strong evidence suggested that 'threads of the conspiracy . . . come together in Belgrade,' as Berchtold told Germany's ambassador, Heinrich von Tschirschky, in a phrase he would repeat over and over in the coming weeks. Tschirschky sympathised with Berchtold's concerns but, lacking clear instructions from Berlin, strongly urged caution.[7]

Few Austrians did so. 'The word "war,"' Berchtold recalled of the Monday following the assassination, 'was on everyone's

---

* Different versions have the emperor remarking that 'the Almighty is not mocked,' the idea being that Franz Ferdinand's morganatic marriage had offended God. This is perhaps too lyrical, according to those most familiar with Franz Josef's manner of speaking. 'It is God's will' is the most likely phrasing.

lips.' As if to pre-empt any possible wavering on the part of the foreign minister, Berchtold was besieged all day by officials hoping to put steel into him for a clash with Serbia. Opinion was nearly unanimous. Austria's minister-president, Count Karl Stürgkh, was all in for war, as were General Alexander Krobatin, the war minister, and Leon von Biliński, the common imperial finance minister. Because Biliński was also minister for Bosnia-Herzegovina, sharing blame with Potoriek for the lax security arrangements in Sarajevo (Biliński was later exonerated by the emperor for any wrongdoing), he had extra motivation to avenge the crime. The burgeoning war party need not have worried. Berchtold's blood was now up.[8]

This was made clear in a fateful encounter that took place sometime late Monday afternoon. Tisza, the Hungarian minister-president, had shrewdly called on Franz Josef I that morning, offering condolences for the loss of his nephew – having no inkling, if we are to believe his protestations, that the murder of the Habsburg heir would have any impact on imperial foreign policy. Tisza first learned something important was brewing when he stopped by the Ballplatz, where he was astonished to find the normally harmless Berchtold breathing fire. There is no record of what was said, but the conversation made a dramatic impression on the Hungarian, who went so far as to compose a letter of protest to Franz Josef I that the Habsburg foreign minister intended 'to make the Sarajevo outrage the occasion for a settlement of accounts with Serbia.'

Tisza was a formidable figure in the dual monarchy, whose opinion Berchtold could not ignore. Stern and colourless where Berchtold was dapper and charming, Tisza was a man of few words, but he meant what he said. Like many ambitious Magyars of his generation, he preferred Germany to Austria, seeing in the former all the go-ahead dynamism the worm-eaten Habsburg empire now lacked. Tisza had studied at Berlin and Heidelberg in the early 1880s, at the height of Otto von Bismarck's glory and prestige, and admired the founder of the German Reich so fervently that he devoted a book to him. A strict and somewhat dour Calvinist, Tisza was closer in faith and temperament to the sober Prussian Protestant-dominated Reich than to Catholic Austria, with her elaborate ceremonial and pretensions of grandeur. Despite viewing Hungary as the strongest nation in the realm, Tisza was loyal to the crown, and he believed too much in German efficiency to countenance weakening Austria's army by giving in to nationalists who wanted Hungarian added to German as a second language of command.

Tisza had no love for Serbs or Serbia, but for that very reason he wanted the dual monarchy to avoid deeper involvement in Serbian affairs, or in the southern Balkans more generally: any enlargement of the empire could only undermine Hungary's privileged position within it, by bringing in yet more Slavic minorities (as it was, Magyars barely made up a majority even in Hungary). Above all, Tisza believed it his duty, as a Calvinist, to oppose war in all but the most exceptional of circumstances. Going to war with Serbia, Tisza told Berchtold on Monday (or at least, this is what he claimed to have said in his protest note to the emperor, delivered two days later), 'would be a fatal mistake.' 'We have no sufficient grounds,' Tisza objected, 'for holding Serbia responsible [for the crime] and for provoking a war with her.' If Austria-Hungary invaded Serbia in retaliation for the assassination of the archduke, Tisza warned Franz Josef I, 'we should appear before the world as the disturber of the peace and would kindle the fires of a great war in the most unfavourable conditions.'[9]

Monday evening, Conrad arrived at the Ballplatz to sound out Berchtold, without knowing that the foreign minister had just taken a hawkish stand in conversation with Tisza. The chief of staff had endured enough of Berchtold's prevarications over the years; this time he wanted a decisive course of action. Skipping the usual pleasantries, Conrad proposed straightaway that Austria-Hungary mobilise against Serbia, beginning on Wednesday, 1 July. Berchtold, taking a markedly different tack than he had with Tisza, replied that 'the outward occasion [for mobilisation] was lacking' and that 'public opinion must first be prepared.' To create the necessary impression, he suggested that the Ballplatz send a sharp note to Belgrade, asking the Serbian government to dissolve 'certain societies' such as Narodna Odbrana, the more respectable public face of the secret Black Hand – the latter's existence was apparently unknown to the Austrians – and sack its minister of police. Doing this, Conrad objected, would achieve nothing: Serbia would simply appoint another minister and carry on as before. 'Nothing will have the slightest effect,' the chief of staff argued, 'but the use of force.' Berchtold agreed that the time had come for some kind of reckoning with Serbia, but he cautioned Conrad that he would have to speak with the emperor before authorising any military measures. Conrad then left the Ballplatz with three parting words for Berchtold, intoned with monotonous gravity, of which Cato would have approved: 'War. War. War.'[10]

Despite what these blunt remarks suggest, the chief of staff was a reflective man who had given serious thought to the roiling national tensions that threatened to tear asunder the dual monarchy. The imperial army (or Common Army, as it had been officially designated since the Ausgleich, or Compromise, granting Hungary autonomy in 1867) was an almost perfect microcosm of the multiethnic empire. Germans, to be sure, dominated the officer corps, of which they comprised 76 per cent (as against 24 per cent of the population), and German was the language of command. Nevertheless, the remaining quarter of officers was drawn from a broad mixture of national groups, led by the Hungarians (at 11 per cent), Czechs (5 per cent), and Croats (a bit less than 5 per cent, although this was far larger than their share of the population). Recruits were expected to learn at least a dozen or so words of 'command German' (*Kommandosprache*) and the German terms for their rifle parts and other essential equipment, but officers in turn were expected, and strongly encouraged, to learn the language of their men (Conrad himself spoke seven languages). For the most part, it worked – better, certainly, than did the empire's parliamentary assemblies, which had all run aground on 'tower of Babel' language difficulties (the main Reichsrat, in Vienna, had shut down indefinitely by 1914; the Hungarian Diet in Budapest functioned, barely, only because the Hungarians had kept most non-Hungarian speakers, such as Serbs, Slovaks, and especially Romanians, out of it).[11]

Giving Hungary equal status in the empire had been, to Conrad's thinking – a view shared prominently by the slain Franz Ferdinand – a gross political error, inviting Hungary's persecution of its minorities, such that all the empire's other national groups were jealous for autonomy they could use to persecute their enemies, too. Austria's failure to intervene during the Balkan Wars had left an 'impression of impotence,' Conrad believed, encouraging irredentists of all national stripes and calling forth the Sarajevo outrage, as clearly as night followed day. The assassination of the Habsburg heir presented the empire with a final test of strength. Would Austria fight to preserve the unity of the Habsburg empire, or would it allow the Serbs to pry Bosnia-Herzegovina loose, thus signalling the empire's final dissolution into a seething morass of jealous nation-states?[12]

The answer to this question would depend largely on Berchtold, the man in the middle. Conrad, who spoke for the Common Army, was bent on war, backed by Austria's minister-president and the common imperial finance and war ministers. Tisza, speaking for Hungary, was dead-set against. To Conrad, Berchtold had come off sounding like his usual wavering self, but to Tisza, the hitherto doddering foreign minister now seemed just as dangerous a warmonger as Conrad.

In truth, Berchtold was still unsure of what to do, as he confessed to the emperor at Schönbrunn Palace outside Vienna on Tuesday, 30 June. Any course of action would bring peril, but the worst thing of all would be to show weakness. If Austria let this act of terrorist aggression go unpunished, Berchtold told the emperor, 'our southern and eastern neighbours would be so certain of our powerlessness that they would consequently bring their work of destruction [of the empire] to its conclusion.' Nevertheless, the foreign minister reassured his sovereign that he would not act hastily – not until he had reliable information confirming Serbian involvement in the crime. Once a guilty verdict was in, Berchtold wanted to prepare 'a clear plan of action against Serbia.' The emperor was agreed that Berchtold should wait, but his own primary concern was not the investigation into the crime per se, but rather the need for imperial unity. Any policy Berchtold wished to pursue, the emperor insisted, must have Tisza's, and thus Hungary's, full backing.[13]

Franz Josef I, now 83, had ruled Austria, and then Austria-Hungary, since 1848. In those days, the Holy Roman Empire was still in living memory, such that the Habsburg emperor could, and did, see himself as heir to a 'Mandate of Heaven reaching back a thousand years to his ancestor, Charlemagne.' The emperor demanded of everyone at court rigid adherence to the 'stiff, Burgundian rituals' of the Habsburg dynasty. He spoke all fifteen official languages of his realm (or at least, Vienna wags retorted, he could utter platitudes in them), and he claimed, in a swipe at the chauvinistic trend of the age, not to favour any single national group. In the later years of his reign, Franz Josef I had come to truly embody the ancient empire as a living symbol of its grace, manners, style, and stubborn refusal to modernise (except for the Hungarian Ausgleich, which he had accepted reluctantly), and

Emperor Franz Josef I, emperor of Austria-Hungary, proud custodian of a Habsburg mandate to rule 'reaching back a thousand years.' *Source: Harris and Ewing Collection, Library of Congress.*

not least in that both were visibly showing their age and fragility. The octogenarian emperor had just recovered from a bout of bronchitis severe enough that, in April, Franz Ferdinand had 'kept an engine under steam' for several days to whisk him to Vienna if the emperor died.* Many had feared, even before the murder of the heir, that once the old man went, the empire, too, would die, as reverence for his august figure was the last bond holding its many nations together.[14]

---

* Doubtless the emperor got wind of this. The rumour in Vienna was that Franz Josef's surprisingly rapid recovery was owed to 'his keen desire to spite his nephew.'

Despite the appearance of fragility, however, the emperor remained fully in possession of his faculties. He was no figurehead. While he was necessarily noncommittal during his audiences with Berchtold and Tisza, urging both men to forge a common imperial policy, Franz Josef's own views on the Sarajevo outrage were probably closer to those of his foreign minister, if not quite as belligerent as those of Conrad. On Thursday, 2 July, the day after he had received Tisza's written statement opposing war with Serbia, the emperor told Tschirschky, the German ambassador, that he was 'not sure how much longer things could remain calm in the Balkans,' and that he hoped Germany's sovereign, Kaiser Wilhelm II, was able 'to appreciate the danger posed to the [dual] monarchy by the presence of Serbia as a neighbour.' Behind Serbia stood Russia. Serbia's prime minister, Franz Josef believed, 'did nothing without consulting [Nikolai] Hartwig,' Russia's minister to Serbia. Hartwig, the emperor told Tschirschky, was 'the real boss in Belgrade.' Franz Josef said he was 'particularly disquieted by the Russian trial mobilisation planned for fall, just at the time we are shifting our recruit contingents.'[15]

It is significant that the Habsburg emperor revealed his deepest forebodings about Russia not to Berchtold or Tisza, but to the ambassador of Germany, Austria's only real ally. The belle of the ball in Metternich's day, when Vienna had been the fulcrum of a 'holy alliance' of the three eastern empires (Austria, Prussia, and Russia) that had pledged to suppress any revolutionary or irredentist-nationalist challenges to the status quo in the wake of the French Revolution and Napoleonic Wars, Austria had declined so precipitously that she was now rated barely worth an alliance by the Western powers. Since breaking with St Petersburg in the Crimean War of 1853–1856, when then–foreign minister Count Buol had demanded that Russian troops evacuate Danube lands at a time when Russia was locked in war

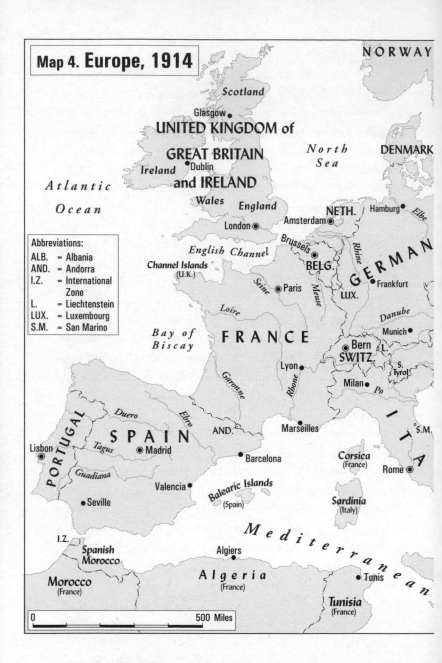

Map 4. **Europe, 1914**

NORWAY

Scotland

Glasgow •

UNITED KINGDOM of

GREAT BRITAIN

North Sea

DENMARK

Ireland • Dublin

and IRELAND

Wales   *England*

Atlantic

Ocean

NETH.   Hamburg • Elbe

London ◉   Amsterdam ◉

Abbreviations:
ALB. = Albania
AND. = Andorra
I.Z. = International Zone
L. = Liechtenstein
LUX. = Luxembourg
S.M. = San Marino

Brussels

English Channel

G E R M A N

Channel Islands
(U.K.)

BELG.

Rhine

Seine ◉ Paris

LUX.   • Frankfurt

Meuse

Loire

Danube

Bay of Biscay

F R A N C E

Munich •

◉ Bern   L.

SWITZ.

S. Tyrol

Lyon •

Garonne

Milan •   *Po*

Rhone

Duero

Ebro

AND.

Marseilles •

I T A

S.M.

PORTUGAL

S P A I N

Tagus

◉ Madrid

Corsica
(France)

Rome ◉

Lisbon •

Guadiana

Valencia •

Balearic Islands
(Spain)

Sardinia
(Italy)

• Seville

M e d i t e r r a n e a n

I.Z.

Spanish
Morocco

Algiers •

Morocco
(France)

A l g e r i a
(France)

• Tunis

Tunisia
(France)

0   500 Miles

with Britain, France, Sardinia, and the Ottoman Empire, Vienna had been adrift in European diplomacy. Otto von Bismarck, architect of Germany's unification under Prussian auspices in 1871, had tried to rope mutually suspicious Austria and Russia together in his Machiavellian Three Emperors League (1873–1879, 1881–1887), the spirit of which was maintained in his still more Machiavellian (and secret) Reinsurance Treaty of 1887, but this improbable grouping worked only so long as the Russians did not intuit Bismarck's real purpose, which was to keep Paris and St Petersburg from teaming up against Germany. This they duly did shortly after Bismarck's fall from power in 1890, concluding a bilateral Franco-Russian military alliance against Germany in 1894.

With Austria having lost its strategic role as a smokescreen for Bismarckian diplomacy, Germany maintained her alliance with Austria largely out of diplomatic inertia – and the fact that the two empires now, since the collapse of Bismarck's system, shared a Russian enemy. True, Vienna could theoretically count on Italy, third wheel of a Triple Alliance with Austria and Germany dating to 1882, but the tie with Rome was far weaker than the one with Berlin. Italy shared a common potential wartime enemy with Germany (France), but not with Austria, which did not border France. Moreover, Italy's well-known designs on Austrian Trieste and the South Tyrol made nonsense of the notion that Rome was Vienna's ally. Conrad had gone too far in proposing a pre-emptive war with Italy in 1911, but no one at the Ballplatz entertained any illusions that Italy would take Austria's side in a Balkan or European war. In the face of the Serbian threat, the Austrians knew that Germany alone stood between them and utter isolation. Without the Germans, they could do nothing. On this, if little else, everyone in Vienna – and Budapest – was agreed.

On 1 July, the same day Tisza presented his anti-war memorandum to the Emperor, Conrad visited the Ballplatz again to sound out the foreign minister. Berchtold informed the chief of staff of Tisza's stout opposition to waging war on Serbia: Tisza believed that Russia would intervene and that 'Germany would leave us in the lurch.' Conrad himself was forced to concede that, if Austria's main ally did not offer support, 'our hands would be tied.' Berchtold himself shared this concern, adding to it the fear that Romania, which Vienna was actively courting as a possible ally in the Balkans, would not likely support an Austrian war against Serbia unless it was clear that the war had German backing. Berchtold told the chief of staff that he had recently prepared a memorandum exhorting Berlin to help cajole Bulgaria and Romania into the Triple Alliance. Conrad was intrigued. The chief of staff concluded his audience with Berchtold by saying, 'before anything else we must ask Germany whether she intends to back us up against Russia or not.'[16]

It is significant that Berchtold told Conrad that he himself had prepared the Balkan policy memorandum that both men agreed must now be dispatched to Berlin. In fact the original memorandum, outlining a new Austro-German 'peace initiative' centred on bringing Bulgaria, Romania, and Ottoman Turkey into the Triple Alliance in order to deter Russian aggression in the Balkans, had been prepared on Tisza's instructions back in March. The most recent draft had been completed on 24 June, four days before the Sarajevo incident. Had the foreign minister told Conrad that the Berlin initiative represented Tisza's pseudo-pacifist thinking, the chief of staff may not have assented with such alacrity. Berchtold had clearly thought this through, because Tisza's Berlin peace initiative offered him a possible way out of the current impasse. Ostensibly to do with the bric-a-brac of Balkan politics, Tisza's memorandum was, at root, about strengthening the German alliance. Austria's goal, Tisza argued, must be to force Berlin to plunge ever deeper into Austria's Balkan affairs, so as to take joint ownership of them. 'There can be no talk of success,' Tisza had concluded his

March missive, 'unless we have complete assurance of being understood, respected, and supported by Germany. Germany must see that the Balkans are of decisive importance not only for us but for the German Empire.' Continuing the same line of thought in his 1 July note to the emperor, Tisza had urged Franz Josef I to approach Wilhelm II at the upcoming memorial service for the archduke, making use of the 'recent monstrous events' to win him over to a 'wholehearted support of [Austrian] policy in the Balkans.' Conrad wanted to use the Sarajevo outrage as a pretext for settling scores with Serbia. Tisza wished to use it as a pretext for bringing Germany into harmony with Austria on Balkan issues, to prevent another destructive war, as he assumed the Germans wanted to do. Berchtold's idea was to approach the Germans with Tisza's peace initiative but use it to win their support for Conrad's war policy.[17]

Franz Ferdinand's funeral, scheduled to take place in Vienna on Friday, 3 July, would, as Tisza suggested, offer the perfect setting for an approach to the Germans. Unlike his Austrian counterpart, Germany's Emperor Wilhelm II had been fond of Franz Ferdinand and Sophie. He had visited them for a long weekend at Konopischt in June, just days before the archduke was assassinated. The kaiser was notoriously impetuous and emotional. The murder of his close friend, a fellow royal, was bound to send him into a rage. So long as the Austrians could direct this rage in the right direction – against Serbia – Germany would be as good as won over.

It was not to be. On the morning of Thursday, 2 July, while the embalmed remains of Ferdinand and Sophie were still en route to Vienna from the port of Trieste, it was announced that Kaiser Wilhelm II would not be attending the funeral; an attack of lumbago had left him unable to travel. Tisza would not have his chance to sell the German sovereign on his Balkan peace initiative, but then neither could Berchtold or Conrad exploit

Wilhelm's anger to win German backing for a Serbian war. In fact, not a single foreign royal or statesman came to Vienna for the funeral. Supposedly, Berchtold claimed, invitations were withheld to spare the aging Franz Josef from the fatigue sure to result from a lengthy ceremony. Separate memorial services would be arranged by Austrian ambassadors abroad instead. The emperor's own feelings towards the deceased, as everyone knew, were not warm; despite strong protests from inside the family, he had not yielded on his decision not to bury the archducal couple in the Habsburg vault. A more intriguing explanation has been suggested by Ballplatz insiders: Berchtold did not want foreign sovereigns' access to the emperor's ear, for fear they would exercise a moderating influence on the war party.[18]

The flat memorial service for the heir to the Habsburg throne forms an instructive comparison with the grandiose state funeral of King Edward VII of England in May 1910, so memorably chronicled by Barbara Tuchman in *The Guns of August*. Then, London had seen no fewer than nine kings, on splendid mounts, ride 'through the palace gates, with plumed helmets, gold braid, crimson sashes, and jeweled orders flashing in the sun,' followed by 'five heirs apparent, 40 more imperial or royal highnesses, seven queens,' and 'a scattering of ambassadors from uncrowned countries.'[19] Franz Ferdinand's death, by contrast, went nearly unmourned in Vienna. The emperor refused even to meet the funeral train from Trieste, nor did he attend the memorial service. Those few members of the Habsburg dynasty willing to brave the emperor's wrath were free to attend, but they were given less than fifteen minutes to view the body. Franz Ferdinand's own children were not allowed even this dignity (although they were allowed to send flowers). Ferdinand's coffin, at least, bore the full insignia of the second-highest ranking prince of the dual monarchy: his body was properly adorned by the archducal crown, a plumed general's helmet, his ceremonial sword, and his principal decorations, including the Order of the Golden Fleece. Sophie's coffin, by contrast, was not only smaller than her husband's but stood twenty inches lower. It was bare except for a pair of white gloves and a black fan, symbolising her former station as a mere lady-in-waiting. The bodies were buried in a modest chapel in Artstetten – a 'provincial hole' well removed from imperial Vienna – which Franz Ferdinand had had specially built in case the couple were denied entry to the imperial vault. It was the Habsburg equivalent of an unmarked grave.[20]

The stiff and socially awkward archduke had, it is true, never been as popular as the gregarious and charming Edward VII, nor was Austria remotely as powerful a country as England, which ruled an empire that literally bestrode the globe. Still, the sharp contrast between the two occasions suggests that something important had been lost in the intervening four years. The year 1910 had seen a kind of Indian summer of Old Europe, a year blissfully free of international tension in between the First Bosnian Crisis of 1908–1909 and the Moroccan crisis of 1911 and the Italian-Turkish and Balkan Wars that followed on its heels. Then, Austria had not yet been humiliated, nor Serbia enlarged; nor had the Ottoman Empire been dealt a series of near-death blows by Italy and the Balkan League. The monarchical principle was still operative in 1910: no matter how loudly the nationalist press of each country bayed for blood against its enemies, sovereigns still shared ties of marriage and blood, some level of mutual comity and trust, which helped to defuse tensions before things went too far.

Had this still been true in 1914, there should have been a powerful international upwelling of sympathy for the slain archduke, whose brutal murder was an obvious affront to rulers everywhere (notwithstanding the frigid feelings of Austria's own sovereign). Instead, not even Wilhelm II, Franz Ferdinand's best and only true friend among Europe's royal houses, came to Vienna to pay his respects. There was a good – and revealing – reason why Wilhelm stayed home, and it was not, contrary to the public report, owing to lower-back pain. 'As a result of warnings I have received from Sarajevo,' German Chancellor Theobald von Bethmann Hollweg informed Franz Josef I in a secret telegram sent via the Ballplatz, 'of which the first dates all the way back to April of this year, I have been obliged to request His Majesty the Kaiser to abandon his trip to Vienna.' Assassinations such as those of the archduke and his wife, Bethmann explained, 'are well known to have a suggestive effect on criminal elements.'[21]

Here was a damning judgment on Vienna. So poorly did the Germans rate their ally's level of administrative competence after Sarajevo that they did not think the Austrians could secure an imperial funeral in their own capital. On the bright side, the chancellor's fingering of Bosnian-based terrorism as grounds for cancelling a state visit suggested that Berlin might be sympathetic to the cause of the Austrian war party. On the other hand, Bethmann had been careful not to mention Serbs, or Serbia, as complicit in the Sarajevo outrage. After all, the Austrians had not yet linked Belgrade to the crime. Germany's chancellor, like Tisza, Franz Josef I, and Berchtold, would need proof.

It is a reflection of the strategic impotence of Austria-Hungary in 1914 that her statesmen were unable to formulate a response to Sarajevo without running it by the Germans first. True, the impasse was also the result of internal political dynamics: namely, the presence of a towering Hungarian in the upper ranks of the government who had the unique ability to veto a policy based on his ability to represent literally half of the dual monarchy. But then it was impossible to separate foreign and domestic policy in an empire of fifteen nationalities. Tisza's 'pacifist' views on Balkan policy were intimately tied to his goal of maintaining Magyar supremacy over Hungary's subject nationalities, just as Conrad, and now Berchtold, wished to crush Serbia in order to weaken national irredentism in the empire, beginning with the insufferable pretensions of Magyars like Tisza. The interests of Hungary, the Austrian-dominated Imperial Foreign Office, and the Common Army appeared irreconcilable – without someone from outside knocking heads together. In this curious way Germany had, by 1914, become the arbiter of not only Austria's foreign policy but also her constitutional dilemmas. If and when Berchtold's and Conrad's suspicions about Serbian involvement in the Sarajevo outrage were confirmed by investigators, the Ballplatz could then pose the question on everyone's mind: What will the Germans say? For now, all Berchtold could do was wait.

2

St Petersburg: No Quarter Given

T HE REASON AUSTRIAN STATESMEN needed German support in case of a war with Serbia was plain as day: Russia might intervene. St Petersburg had gone to war against Ottoman Turkey on behalf of Balkan Slavs (mostly the Bulgarians) in 1877 and had nearly done so again against Austria on Serbia's behalf during the First Bosnian Crisis in 1909, only to back down in the face of an unsubtle threat from Berlin. True, Russia had not gone to war in either of the Balkan Wars of 1912–1913, but this was because both times her Serbian clients were winning and Vienna was doing nothing to stop them: there had been no need for Petersburg to bail out Belgrade, as there would be in case Austria-Hungary invaded Serbia.

While the popular cliché of the 'Russian steamroller' greatly exaggerated the real striking power of the tsarist armies, no one in either Vienna or Petersburg doubted that Russia could best Austria-Hungary easily alone. Only with German backing against Russia could the Austrians even entertain the idea of going to war in the Balkans; only with German backing could they win. This had been the argument of Tisza, the Hungarian minister-president, against going to war with Serbia: Russia would fight, and Germany would not back Austria. The line taken by the Habsburg foreign minister, Berchtold, and the belligerent chief of staff, Conrad, was the reverse of Tisza's: Germany would back Vienna, and Russia would not fight – so they hoped, at least. With the Germans, once the evidence from Belgrade was in, the Austrians could take a direct approach. With St Petersburg, it was like taking a leap in the dark. What would the Russians do?

The early signs were not encouraging for Austria. Although few foreigners other than Kaiser Wilhelm II truly grieved the loss of Franz Ferdinand, British, French, Italian, and German consuls across Europe all responded to the news from Sarajevo with the sympathy and decorum one expected of trained diplomats. Grave official condolences were offered; flags were lowered to half-mast; heads were nodded in deep if somewhat strained sympathy for Austria's loss. In stark contrast, Austrian diplomats throughout the Balkans complained that no condolences were offered by their Russian counterparts. In Rome, the Russian embassy was alone in refusing to lower its flag in honour of Archduke Ferdinand. Likewise, the tsarist legation in Belgrade declined to fly its flag at half-mast, even during the official funeral requiem for Franz Ferdinand, as if intentionally to insult the memory of the slain Habsburg heir.[1]

This calculated insult was almost certainly the work of Nikolai Hartwig, the pan-Slavist Russian minister whom Emperor Franz Josef had told Germany's ambassador was the real 'boss of Belgrade.' According to an Italian diplomat, upon hearing the news from Sarajevo on 28 June, Hartwig had exclaimed, 'In the name of Heaven! So long as it is not a Serb' (*pourvu que ça ne soit pas un Serbe*). As the Austrian chargé d'affaires in Belgrade, Ritter von Storck, interpreted this ambiguous remark for Berchtold, 'Hartwig, as someone in the know . . . evidently took it a priori that the murderer could only be a Serb.' Unperturbed in any case by the news, Hartwig held a bridge party that evening, at which he shared his real views confidentially with the Italian diplomat (who later betrayed him to the Austrians). The murder of Franz Ferdinand, Hartwig said, 'should be regarded as a boon for the [dual] monarchy,' as 'the archduke was sick through and through,' illustrating how 'the Austrian dynasty is an exhausted race.' The new heir to the throne, Franz Ferdinand's nephew Karl, was, Hartwig informed the Italian by way of further explanation, 'syphilitic,' which made nonsense of his earlier protestation that Franz Ferdinand's death was good news – unless, of course, he meant good news for Russia.[2]

It was hard for Austrians not to think the worst of Hartwig, the man widely viewed as the mastermind of the predatory Slavic-Orthodox coalition of Serbia-Bulgaria-Greece-Macedonia, which had launched the First Balkan War against Turkey in 1912, giving a powerful spur to Serbian irredentism. Franz Josef's contention that Hartwig secretly ruled Serbia was tinged with a certain exaggeration, but it contained a grain of truth. Serbia's People's Radical Party prime minister, Nikola Pašić, was an impressive political survivor. A former mayor of Belgrade, Pašić had served as prime minister of Serbia nearly continuously since 1904, overseeing Serbia's heroic irredentist aggrandisement during the Balkan Wars while fending off plots against him hatched by Serbian and 'South Slav' activists more radical still, such as Colonel Dimitrijevitch (Apis) and his Black Hand conspirators. With his colossal white beard and stern visage, Pašić looked like an Orthodox monk from the pages of Dostoevsky, still virile at 68 in 1914. Still, for all his appearance of vigour, Pašić – and Serbia – would not have amounted to much without Russia's backing. It was with Russian subsidies, and Russian and French arms, that Serbia had fought the Balkan Wars, and it was Russia's threats to intervene that had kept the Austrians off Belgrade's back while Serbian armies were carving up Turkey and Bulgaria. Hartwig had stood behind Pašić's every action during the Balkan Wars, and he remained Pašić's closest adviser still.[3]

Nikola Pašić, Serbia's great political survivor. *Source: Getty Images.*

Moreover, Hartwig was not the only influential Russian patron in town. Just as Russia's minister to Belgrade provided public pan-Slavist support for Pašić's populist regime, so did Russia's military attaché, General Viktor Artamonov, help advise and arm Serbia's more radical shadow government. Apis, after all, was not merely the secret organiser of the Black Hand and (as we know today) of the plot to murder Franz Ferdinand; he was also chief of Serbian army intelligence. Asked by an Italian journalist after the war how closely he had worked with Apis in Belgrade, Artamonov admitted readily that 'of course I was in practically daily contact with Dimitri[jevitch].' Predictably, the Russian attaché denied having prior knowledge of the Sarajevo plot, producing a perfect alibi – he was on leave from 19 June to 28 July 1914 – but a strange one, considering that the whole point of Archduke Ferdinand's ill-fated visit to Bosnia was to observe Austrian manoeuvres, which would have been of great interest to Russia's official military observer in Serbia. Still, in a revealing aside, Artamonov conceded that 'in the little Belgrade of the time, where public life was confined to a very few cafés, the plot could not have been kept secret.' Russia's military attaché was out of town on 28 June, but he was in Belgrade in late May and early June, when the plot had been set in motion.[4]

Hartwig, meanwhile, *was* in town that fateful day, hosting his soon-to-be-notorious bridge party. From post-war confessions, we know that Prime Minister Pašić knew of the assassination plot; in fact he had tried discreetly, via an emissary, to warn Vienna in early June, not wanting to provide Austria with a pretext for war, while Serbia was still recovering its strength from the Balkan Wars. (Pašić's warning was either ignored or later erased from memory by Habsburg officials, such as the minister for Bosnia-Herzegovina, Biliński, who were embarrassed not to have heeded it.) Serbia's prime minister and his Russian advisers were thus not complicit in the Black Hand plot to assassinate the archduke, but they almost certainly knew that some kind of plot had been hatched prior to his visit, and Pašić had done nothing decisive to foil it.[5]

Franz Josef was therefore not wrong to point the finger at Hartwig as an abettor of Serbian aggression and a menace to peace in the Balkans. It was still not clear, however, whether the views of the minister in Belgrade were representative of Russian policymakers in St Petersburg. During the Balkan Wars, Hartwig had behaved as something of a free agent, frequently overstepping the bounds of the brief laid down by Russia's more cautious foreign minister, Sergei Sazonov. Shortly before the outbreak of the First Balkan War in October 1912, Hartwig had all but questioned Sazonov's manhood: after the foreign minister issued a pre-emptory declaration guaranteeing the territorial

Sergei Sazonov, Russia's beleaguered and much-pilloried foreign minister, trying to live down a reputation for cowardice. *Source: Nikolai Aleksandrovich Bazili Papers, Envelope A, Hoover Institution Archives.*

status quo in the Balkans, Hartwig told the Serbs to go ahead and attack Turkey and not worry about 'foolish Sazonov.'[6]

Sazonov had never been anyone's idea of a strongman. To begin with, he did not look the part. Slim and small in stature, with a bland face and receding hairline, Sazonov had a classic Russian bureaucrat's mien: he could have been the inspiration for Gogol's empty overcoat. The foreign minister had been pilloried by pan-Slavists in Petersburg for his mild-mannered timidity during the Balkan Wars, even as Hartwig emerged as their conquering hero. For a time there were serious rumours in Petersburg that Hartwig would replace Sazonov, but in the end Tsar Nicholas II had stuck by his man out of simple loyalty.

Like Berchtold in Vienna, Russia's foreign minister was in a precarious position at the time of the Sarajevo incident, having just barely survived in office through the tumult of the Balkan Wars. There was a Francophile (that is, anti-German) 'war party' in Petersburg akin to Conrad's belligerent faction in Vienna, led by the agriculture minister, A.V. Krivoshein. It might seem odd that a minister of agriculture would favour a belligerent foreign policy, but then Tsarist Russia was something of an odd country.

Imposing in appearance – with her demographic and economic growth rates convincing the Germans that she was an unstoppable 'steamroller' – the empire of the tsars was, in reality, fragile and ramshackle, capable of cracking apart under pressure, as had very nearly happened in the Revolution of 1905, following her humiliating defeat in the Russo-Japanese war. Although Russian industrialisation continued apace, the peasantry still comprised 80 per cent of the population. Land reform was *the* key element of social policy, which gave outsized importance to the Agriculture Ministry. Krivoshein was the star protégé of Peter Stolypin, chairman of the Council of Ministers from 1906 to 1911, who had aimed, through reforming the laws of land tenure, to create a stable and prosperous class of peasant smallholders to serve as a bulwark against another anarchic social revolution. The 'Stolypin programme' required aggressive tariffs to block German wheat imports, French capital investment in Russian railways, and unimpeded access to grain export markets. Because most of Russia's wheat was grown in her southern regions abutting the Black Sea, and her Baltic and Arctic Sea ports were icebound most of the year (Vladivostok, on the Pacific, was too far afield to be a practical option), exporters desperately needed warm-water access to the Mediterranean for Russian grain exports, by way of the Ottoman Straits (the Bosphorus, Sea of Marmara, and Dardanelles). Through the Straits, in the other direction, flowed imported components critical to Russian industry, paid for by Russian grain exports. Any interruption of Russia's access to the Mediterranean would undermine the Stolypin land reform programme, on which everything else depended.

After Stolypin was assassinated in 1911, Krivoshein became the senior member of the Council of Ministers, considerably more senior than Sazonov. While Stolypin had famously advocated '20 years of peace' to complete Russia's economic modernisation, the Italian and Balkan Wars of 1911–1913 suggested to Krivoshein that Petersburg would not have so much time. In summer 1912, the beleaguered Ottoman government had briefly closed the Straits to commercial shipping, exposing the vulnerability of Russia's grain-export economy: the volume of her Black Sea exports dropped by one-third, and heavy industry in the Ukraine nearly ground to a halt. Even more worrisome was the 'Liman von Sanders affair' of December 1913–January 1914, when a German general had been appointed to command the Ottoman army corps in charge of defending the Straits. German officers had been training the Ottoman army since the 1880s, and relations between Berlin and Constantinople were usually warm, but this was something new: Liman's Straits command would leave Russia's access to the Mediterranean at the mercy of Germany, her most powerful enemy.[7]

Little wonder that Krivoshein was edgy in 1914. The agriculture minister was, anyhow, a temperamental Germanophobe: he was France's favourite Russian. Sazonov, to be sure, was a Francophile too, seeing the military alliance with France, which was concluded in 1894, as an essential part of Russia's foreign policy and France as something of a model for backwards Russia – not for her radicalism so much as for her passionate nationalism. Sazonov's was the Russian 'national liberal' position, which opposed the conservative or 'Germanophile' anti-war opposition, best represented by Sergei Witte, the statesman presiding over Russia's industrialisation drive since the 1890s, whose star had gone into eclipse after his fall from power in 1906.

Krivoshein and his French admirers did not really disagree with Sazonov's Francophile foreign policy, but they suspected him of being yellow, just as Conrad did not trust Berchtold's mettle. Austria's foreign minister, as we have seen, had been jolted out of his passive funk by the Sarajevo outrage. Would Sazonov likewise be nudged towards Krivoshein and the war party by the drama in the Balkans, or would he back down yet again when Austria made her move?

A great deal depended on the answer to this question in July 1914. And yet it remains just as difficult to answer today as it was for the Austrians then. Sazonov, unlike Berchtold, draws a veil over this entire period in his memoirs, skipping straight from a pro forma mention of the Sarajevo incident until July 24, revealing nothing about his thinking or intentions in between. Documents from the time are no help. After the war, the Bolsheviks, seeking to impugn the benighted 'imperialism' of the Tsarist Russian regime, published hundreds of volumes of secret diplomacy relating to the origins and course of the First World War. These volumes cover, in tremendous depth, events large and small from the nineteenth century to 1917 – everything except for the days following the assassination of Franz Ferdinand on 28 June 1914, when they fall virtually silent. Likewise, in the French diplomatic archives, the dispatches of Maurice Paléologue, France's ambassador to Russia, simply disappear between 28 June and 6 July 1914.[8]

Stranger still are the missing letters of Alexander Izvolsky, Sazonov's predecessor as foreign minister and, in 1914, ambassador to France, Russia's most important ally. Forced to resign as foreign minister after his humiliation in the First Bosnian Crisis, Izvolsky had been given the consolation prize of the Paris embassy, from which grounds he worked to avenge himself against Vienna. (When he learned that Russian mobilisation had been declared in July 1914, Izvolsky reportedly exclaimed,

'This is my war!') Some in Paris saw Izvolsky's hand in France's nationalist revival and her push towards rearmament in the years before 1914. As one Socialist leader asked, 'has [France] no other glory than to serve the rancors of M. Izvolsky?' After World War I, an entire 'black book' was published of Izvolsky's secret correspondence, which comes thick and fast: many days have five or more dispatches. But between 19 June and 22 July 1914, there is a single letter to Sazonov, and it concerns not Sarajevo or Russian foreign policy but French domestic affairs.[9]

Likewise, Britain's ambassador to Russia, Sir George Buchanan, in whom Sazonov rarely confided anyway, did not report on Russian reactions to Sarajevo until 9 July 1914, eleven days after Sarajevo. Even then he offered only a typically unsourced and unenlightening opinion that 'the general impression' in Petersburg was 'one of relief that so dangerous a personality [e.g., Franz Ferdinand] should have been removed from the succession to the throne.'[10]

Owing to the silence of Russian, French, and British sources, Sazonov's thinking in the days after Sarajevo must be puzzled out of reports from 'hostile' Austrian and German diplomats. These are more informative, although still ambiguous. Otto Czernin, the Austro-Hungarian legation secretary in Petersburg filling in for Ambassador Friedrich Szapáry in the latter's absence, reported to Berchtold on 3 July that Sazonov had expressed sincere and heartfelt condolences for the loss of the Habsburg heir. Slyly, however, Russia's foreign minister had also suggested that his own warm sentiments were not shared widely in Russia, where Franz Ferdinand was universally (and incorrectly) viewed as a 'Russia-hater.' The death of the archduke would not, Czernin concluded sadly, do anything to halt the 'extravagant anti-Austrian baiting Russian nationalists had been indulging in for years.'[11]

In a follow-up audience held over the weekend, Sazonov's sympathy evaporated quickly. After he warned Czernin that

Austrian press 'attacks' on Serbia were producing a 'disquieting irritation' in Russia, Czernin informed Sazonov that Austria-Hungary might indeed seek redress by bringing her investigation of the crime onto Serbian territory. Hearing this, Sazonov 'cut him off short' and unleashed a tirade. 'No country has had to suffer more than Russia from outrages prepared on foreign territory,' the Russian told Czernin. 'Have we ever claimed to employ against any country the procedure with which your newspapers threaten Serbia?' To ensure the Austrians got his point, Sazonov concluded the audience with a thinly veiled threat: 'Do not engage yourselves on that road; it is dangerous.'[12]

Sazonov spoke still more frankly with Germany's ambassador, Friedrich Pourtalès, shortly after the Sarajevo incident. As Pourtalès reported to Berlin on 13 July, Sazonov 'dwelt only briefly on his condemnation of the crime, while he could not find enough words to condemn the behaviour of the Austrian authorities, who had permitted excesses against the Serbs . . . and deliberately given free rein to popular fury [against Serbia].' Sazonov squarely denied that the murders could have resulted from some 'pan-Serbian plot'; rather it was the work of 'a few callow youths' in Bosnia-Herzegovina, a territory in which, Sazonov claimed in a seeming contradiction, 'only a few Muslims and Catholics were loyal to [Austria-Hungary].' The Serbian government was not merely innocent but behaving with 'perfect correctness.' When Pourtalès tried to win a familiar point by reminding Sazonov of the importance of monarchical principle for a country like Tsarist Russia, and how this was threatened by royal assassinations like the one in Sarajevo, he noted that 'Sazonov could not but agree to this remark but with less warmth than I usually find [on this subject].' Interpreting Sazonov's unsympathetic remarks about the slain Habsburg heir, Pourtalès told Berlin that the hostile tone could only be explained 'by the Minister's irreconcilable hatred of Austria-Hungary, a hatred which here more and more clouds all clear, calm judgment.' Overall, the attitude in Russian official circles vis-à-vis Vienna, Pourtalès concluded, was one of 'boundless contempt for the conditions prevailing there.' The German ambassador observed further that 'not only in the press, but also in society, one meets almost only with unfriendly judgments on the murdered archduke.' If Pourtalès was right, then it appeared that Sazonov, riding a wave of popular anti-Austrian indignation, had been jolted over to the war party no less dramatically than had Berchtold in Vienna.[13]

Coming as it does from the ambassador of a hostile country, and written nearly two weeks after the conversations it purports to describe, Pourtalès's 13 July 1914 dispatch would be easy to dismiss as a biased and unreliable report of Russian reactions to the Sarajevo incident. Filtered through the German ambassador's own fears and concerns, it may not accurately render what Sazonov truly said, any more than such a dispatch can tell us what the Russian was really thinking.

Whatever Sazonov and other officials may or may not have said after Sarajevo, we may still draw a picture of Russian intentions based on what they *did*. Actions speak louder than words, and Russia's actions, upon hearing the news about the assassination, were decisive.

Whether or not Serbia's government was behaving with 'perfect correctness' as Austria investigated the crime in Sarajevo, Pašić was preparing for the worst. Since February, he had been appealing to Petersburg, with increasing desperation, for arms and supplies to replenish stocks depleted in the Balkan Wars – aside from rifles, cannon, and ammunition, the Serbian army needed clothing for 250,000 soldiers, along with 'telegraphs, telephones and four wireless stations.' Sazonov had responded favourably in March, only to be overruled by V. A. Sukhomlinov, the imperial war minister, who did not want to deprive Russia's own army of needed supplies. By early June, when the plot to murder the archduke was being launched from Belgrade, Pašić's requests for arms became almost feverish. At last, on 30 June, two days after the Sarajevo incident, the General Staff, under pressure from Tsar Nicholas II, approved the dispatch of 120,000 three-line rifles, with 120 million rounds, to Serbia.[14]

On the same day, Sazonov dispatched a 'very secret and urgent' request to Russia's naval minister, I. K. Grigorevich, for information regarding the war-readiness of Russia's Black Sea Fleet. The context and content of this request were significant. Specifically, the foreign minister wanted to know what had been done so far to implement the measures ordered by a war-planning conference held in Petersburg on 21 February 1914 – a gathering of Russia's leading generals, admirals, and diplomats, which Sazonov had himself chaired. The February war council had originally been called at the end of December 1913, at the height of international tensions surrounding the Liman affair, but the conference was postponed until late February because of the illness of an important admiral, who had previously chaired the Naval Staff. On 13 January 1914, Sazonov had convened an emergency meeting of the Council of Ministers at which the war party, led by Krivoshein, had nakedly discussed the idea of provoking a European conflict over Liman and the Straits question. At one point, then-chairman of the Council of Ministers V. N. Kokovtsov asked Russia's war minister pointblank, 'Is a war with Germany desirable, and can Russia wage it?' Sukhomlinov answered without hesitation that 'Russia was perfectly prepared for a duel with Germany, not to speak of one with Austria.' Kokovtsov then asked Sazonov whether England and France would back Russia. Sazonov replied that France's departing ambassador, Théophile Delcassé, had told him that 'France will go as far as Russia wishes.' Of British intervention on Russia's behalf, Sazonov said he was personally confident, but less certain and unable to guarantee. With Sazonov leaning towards the war party but refusing, as usual, to take a strong stand, Kokovtsov had enough political cover to veto the idea of intervening, issuing a resolution to the effect that Russia would risk war over the Straits question only if 'the active participation of both France and England in joint measures were . . . assured.'[15]

By the time the war-planning conference convened on 21 February, the immediate danger posed by the Liman affair had passed. But there was still a sense of strategic urgency to the proceedings, not least because Kokovtsov, the man who had blocked the war party in January, had been ousted on 12 February and replaced by an elderly figurehead, I. L. Goremykin, widely seen as Krivoshein's creature. As the conference subject heading put it, Russia must reckon with the 'Possibility of the Straits Question Being Opened, Even Quite Possibly in the Near Future.' No one knew, of course, precisely *how* the Straits question would be opened, but opened it would be at some point, and Russia would have to be ready.[16]

As Sazonov recalled in his memoirs, everyone in attendance 'considered an offensive against Constantinople inevitable, should European war break out.' To this end, Sazonov, Sukhomlinov, and Grigorevich had drawn up a detailed plan for readying Russia to seize Constantinople and the Ottoman Straits in case of war. The plan covered the expansion of amphibious forces available on the Black Sea littoral; heightened artillery training in the Odessa military district; the acceleration of the mobilisation timetable, which would see the first day troops could put ashore at the Bosphorus speeded up from Mobilisation Day (M) + 10 to M + 5; the acceleration of dreadnought construction in (or their sudden importation into) the Black Sea, where Russia did not currently have any (two state-of-the-art British dreadnoughts, made to order for Turkey, were expected to arrive shortly in Constantinople, the first in July 1914); and finally the extension of rail lines in the Caucasus up to the Turkish Anatolian border. In May and June, Sazonov had fought a desperate rearguard campaign, via Russia's ambassador in London, to block delivery of the British dreadnoughts to Turkey, only to be rebuffed. Time was running out. After learning the news from Sarajevo, Sazonov asked Grigorevich to tell him how soon Russia's Black Sea dreadnoughts would be ready. More urgently, he wanted to know whether, in accordance with the measures ordered in February, the first Russian troops would now be able to land in the Bosphorus within 'four or five days' of mobilisation.[17]

Sazonov may really have believed that Serbia had nothing to do with the plot to assassinate Archduke Franz Ferdinand, as he protested to the German ambassador. He does seem, however, to have clearly appreciated how serious the news was and to have expected that Austria-Hungary was going to lash out in reaction. By sending arms to Belgrade, Russia was preparing her ally for war with Austria-Hungary. By readying the Black Sea fleet, Sazonov was preparing for a European war, in which Russia's key strategic objective was to seize Constantinople and the Straits.

If the Habsburg foreign minister Berchtold, despite his reputation for weakness, was, as the Hungarian minister-president Tisza feared, going to use Sarajevo as the pretext for a 'settlement of accounts' with Serbia, so was the beleaguered Sazonov rising quietly to Berchtold's challenge. The stage was being set for a diplomatic showdown.

3

Paris and London: Unwelcome Interruption

O N SUNDAY, 28 JUNE 1914, the better part of the French government, Europe's ambassadors to France, and much of Paris society, were enjoying a resplendent spring afternoon at the Longchamp racetrack in the Bois de Boulogne. Longchamp was France's answer to England's Ascot, the place to see and be seen. The flowers surrounding the track and its famous windmill were in full bloom. The sun shone down brilliantly on the elegant patrons, all dressed to the nines, as they enjoyed the races over a four-course Sunday dinner – this was France, after all. In between the third and fourth course, an army officer quietly approached the president, Raymond Poincaré, and informed him that 'the archduke heir to the throne of Austria and his morganatic wife were just assassinated in Sarajevo by a fanatic, believed to be of Serbian origin.' Although he was intrigued by the report, Poincaré did not leave his seat, not wishing to miss the finish of the race then underway. Certainly it was nothing to disturb his dinner over.[1]

Nor did the French papers think much of the story from the Balkans. The front pages that weekend were aglow with the incandescent Caillaux scandal, the most sensational cause célèbre to titillate France since the Dreyfus affair. Joseph Caillaux was the leader of France's centre-left Radical Party and a prominent part of the furniture of the French government in the years before 1914. He had been premier for nearly six months in 1911–1912 – a tenure that, in the election-mad Third Republic, almost qualified as legendary. Caillaux's real brief was finance, which ministry he had headed under most of the left-leaning cabinets of the past decade. Caillaux was finance minister again in early 1914, with new elections approaching in May, when Gaston Calmette, editor of the nationalist *Le Figaro,* launched a smear campaign against him.

Calmette had chosen his target well. Caillaux had inevitably dipped his hand in the till during the years he had overseen France's finances, and it was not hard to find opponents eager to stick in the knife. By rumour it was Caillaux's disgruntled servants who produced the most damaging material, which began to embarrass his political allies as well. It was when Calmette began publishing love letters between Caillaux and his mistress, Henriette, however, that the affair truly caught the public's attention.* The long-legged Henriette was now the second Mme Caillaux – but she had begun sleeping with him, it emerged, during his premiership, when he was still married to the first. Even this burning *scandale* might have grown stale eventually, had not Henriette Caillaux brought it to white-hot flame by taking matters into her own hands. At six PM on 16 March 1914, she called on Calmette in his *Figaro* office. 'You know why I have come?' she asked. 'Not at all, madame,' Calmette answered. Then, 'without a word,' Mme Caillaux drew a small brown pistol she had 'hidden amidst her expensive fur muffs' and pumped six shots into him at point-blank range.[2]

---

* It is not hard to see why. In one of Caillaux's letters to his mistress, intercepted by his wife, he signed off with 'a thousand kisses all over your adorable little body.'

Joseph Caillaux himself was not, most believed, guilty of abetting the crime. The stylish murder had, in effect, emasculated him: his wife had not trusted him to be man enough do his own fighting. Still, it was understood that Caillaux could not remain in office while his wife was prosecuted for a murder committed on his behalf. The trial of Mme Caillaux was scheduled to open in July, giving French news editors cause to run sensational headlines all spring, building anticipation for the trial of the century.

Adding political frisson to the scandal, the triumph of the Left in the May 1914 elections seemed to vindicate Caillaux's cause. Caillaux himself was easily re-elected to his parliamentary seat, but because of the scandal he remained ineligible to become premier as, by political right, he should have. Instead, Caillaux had to make do with forming a kind of shadow government, ready to take office if and when his wife's name was cleared. His shadow foreign minister was Jean Jaurès, leader of France's united Socialist Party (SFIO) and Europe's leading pacifist orator, who thundered against militarism at international socialist congresses, advocating a 'general strike' whereby labourers might stave off a European war if it ever came. Together, Caillaux and Jaurès had led the fight against Poincaré's Three-Year Service Law in 1913, which had improved war-readiness against Germany by enlarging France's army. Together, they planned, upon taking office, to 'press for a policy of European peace,' beginning with rapprochement with Germany. A Caillaux-Jaurès ministry, locked in battle with President Poincaré, must rank as one of history's greatest might-have-beens.[3]

After several weeks of intrigue, Poincaré at last summoned René Viviani, a Radical (and former Socialist) flexible, or weak enough, to form a government not explicitly hostile to him. Like Caillaux and Jaurès, Viviani had voted against the Three-Year Service Law. Unlike them, however, he had not lit the skies with rhetorical fireworks against Poincaré's militarism, had

A dramatic rendering of the assassination of Gaston Calmette by Mme Henriette Caillaux, from *Le Petit Journal. Source: Bibliothèque nationale de France.*

not accused him of being 'more Russian than Russia' (Jaurès), nor vowed to overturn the Three-Year Law and bring détente with Germany once in office. Viviani agreed to support the Three-Year Law as a condition of his taking office as both premier and foreign minister, as he did on 16 June 1914. Although he was respected inside the Radical Party for his earnest progressivism, Viviani had such a bland personality that most suspected his to be a caretaker government, which would step down for Caillaux as soon as Mme Caillaux was cleared.

By 1914, the rivalry between Caillaux and Poincaré was so explosive that Viviani would have been well advised to get out of the way once the trial ended. President Poincaré, founder of the centre-right Democratic People's Alliance, was a lawyer of middle-class origins, short, fastidious, and shy – the kind of man who preferred reading official documents in his study at night to socialising at banquets. A Lorrainer, born in territory lost to Germany in the Franco-Prussian War of 1871, Poincaré had reached the pinnacle of French politics because of the purity of his nationalist convictions,* his keen intelligence, and an extraordinary work ethic. Or, as critics believed, he had won the presidency in 1913 owing to Russian bribes – as much as two million francs a year were wired in from Petersburg – and the help of corrupt journalists such as Calmette. As Russia's ambassador, Alexander Izvolsky, boasted to Foreign Minister Sazonov after helping grease the wheels for Poincaré's triumph: 'We are therefore, for the period of his seven year term of office, perfectly safe from the appearance of such persons as Caillaux . . . at the head of the French Government.'[4]

Caillaux was everything the president was not: rich, well-connected, a dashing ladies' man-about-town. He had gone to the best schools, culminating in the Institut d'études politiques de Paris (Sciences Po), then as now a training ground for France's political elite. Despite their differences in background and temperament, Caillaux and Poincaré had once been close. In their bachelor days, they had cavorted around Italy together with their mistresses. Even here, however, the contrast in styles was striking. As Caillaux recalled, 'Mine I displayed, his he kept hidden.' Poincaré had always respected Caillaux as his equal in political stature – and unquestionably his superior in charisma.[5]

---

*'In all my years at school,' Poincaré once wrote, 'I saw no other reason to live than the possibility of recovering our lost provinces.'

In recent years, the two rivals had begun to clash sharply over foreign affairs. As prime minister, Caillaux's concessions to Germany in Africa had helped defuse the Moroccan crisis of 1911 while lighting a fuse under nationalists like Poincaré who believed in France's *réveil national*, a sort of national awakening in which there would be no more backing down to the Germans. The two had drawn political swords again over the Three-Year Law in 1913, when Caillaux had begun to sound almost as radical as Jaurès. By 1914, nationalists such as the *Figaro* editor Calmette viewed Caillaux as a pacifist menace to the republic's military readiness, if not an outright traitor taking bribes from Germany. *Le Figaro* was rumoured to possess documents linking Caillaux to German officials. Many believed that Caillaux, possessing compromising material of his own linking Poincaré to Izvolsky and the Russians, had blackmailed the president into suppressing them. Aside from rumours dogging him about Russian bribes, Poincaré had, as foreign minister, visited Russia in 1912 to strengthen military ties, a gesture seen as almost sacrilegious by the French Left, which viewed Tsarist Russia as the most backwards, anti-labour country in Europe, the land of the knout and the pogrom. Now, as president, Poincaré was planning an even grander sovereign summit with Tsar Nicholas II in July 1914: preparations for it had been underway since January.

In France, just as in Austria and Russia, foreign and domestic policy were intertwined in this era of constant international tension. At the time of the Sarajevo outrage, however, it was domestic, not foreign, affairs that were in the ascendant in Paris. The victory of the Left in the May polls threatened to ruin the upcoming summit in Petersburg, as Poincaré would have to bring along Viviani – a man who, despite his reluctant acceptance of the Three-Year Law, had no love for foreign or military affairs and thought about as ill of autocratic, labour-unfriendly Russia as did Caillaux and Jaurès. As Izvolsky reported to Sazonov, it was Viviani, not Poincaré, who was the man of the hour, and Viviani was bad news for the Russians (if not quite as bad as Caillaux would have been).[6]

Minister of education before he was plucked from obscurity by Poincaré, Viviani scarcely bothered to feign an interest in foreign policy, let alone in alliance obligations to Russia, on which subject President Poincaré was now trying, and largely failing, to enlighten him. If the assassination of the Habsburg heir was not enough to knock Mme Caillaux off the front pages, nor to rouse even Poincaré from his seat at Longchamp, it was certainly not going to turn the milquetoast Viviani into a warrior. At the first cabinet meeting held after the Sarajevo incident, one minister recalled afterwards, the murders were 'hardly mentioned.'[7] Viviani, no less than Poincaré and the French public, remained preoccupied with the Caillaux affair – to which he owed his recent promotion. Viviani's political fate, like Caillaux's, Jaurès's, and Poincaré's, would depend on the verdict of the Mme Caillaux trial in July. He would not want to miss any twist or turn in the story. Nor would the partisans of Caillaux and Poincaré, who were already, on occasion, brawling in the streets.

I N LONDON, THE READING PUBLIC, accustomed through long experience of empire to take an interest in incidents in far-off corners of the globe, was more likely to follow the latest Balkan imbroglio than were the domestic scandal–mad French. The *Times* was something like the paper of record for observers of global affairs and could hardly ignore the story. The paper's Sarajevo correspondent did not disappoint, providing colourful details on the assassinations (including the failed bombing attempt that preceded the shooting), noting the presence of multiple assassins, and concluding sensibly that the attacks were 'evidently the fruit of a carefully laid plot.' Other dispatches from Vienna rounded out the Austrian side of the story, weaving great drama out of the forlorn, doomed marriage of Ferdinand and Sophie and the (much exaggerated) grief of Emperor Franz Josef I. On Monday, 29 June, the Sarajevo outrage was front-page news in London, reported with all the verve and gusto one expected of Fleet Street. There was even a sharp downward blip in the London stock market that morning, reflecting investors' fears of European complications in the Balkans. By Monday afternoon, however, the City of London had fully recovered its footing. On Tuesday, even the globally minded *Times* had shunted Sarajevo back to page 7. The Balkan drama did merit an editorial that day, but its purpose was to explain why, even though the story must 'occupy the attention of all students of European politics,' it should not unduly concern anyone in Britain, where 'our own affairs must be addressed.' By the following Monday, a *Times* editorial wrote off the Sarajevo incident as old history: it was no longer a matter 'of European significance.'[8]

By 'our own affairs,' the *Times* meant Ireland. Just as France was consumed by the Caillaux affair, so was England convulsed with reverberations from the Curragh Incident of March 1914. By spring, Irish Loyalist Volunteers from Ulster (the 'Ulstermen') had put more than 100,000 men under arms to block any effort by the British government to impose Home Rule (that is, independence) on Ireland – on the northern counties of Ulster, anyway. In early March, the Liberal government in London had offered a 'compromise' exempting Ulster from Home Rule for six years and *only* six years. The offer was rejected, and documents turned up by army intelligence suggested that the Volunteers were planning a coup. Winston Churchill, first lord of the Admiralty, ordered the HMS *Pathfinder* and HMS *Attentive* to the Irish coast and vowed privately that, if the Ulstermen took up arms against the British army, 'he would pour enough shot and shell into Belfast to reduce it to ruins.' Churchill then gave an open-throated public speech on March 14, offering 'the hand of friendship' to Ulstermen if they desired it but a confrontation if they did not ('let us put these grave matters to the proof').

Fearing, with good cause, that the government was about to strike, on Friday, 20 March, 50 English cavalry officers at the Curragh barracks in Ireland announced that they would not take up arms against the Ulstermen – a sort of mutiny, as critics called it, although no orders had yet been given that they could have disobeyed. General Hubert Gough, the head 'mutineer,' then resigned with all his officers, which led Sir John French, chief of the General Staff, to resign, which in turn prompted the resignation of the secretary of state for war and the colonies, Colonel John Seeley. Just as the Caillaux affair divided Right and Left in France, Home Rule pitted pro-independence Irish Catholics against loyalist Protestants, pro–Home Rule Liberals against Conservatives and Unionists, and the Liberal/Irish Party–controlled House of Commons (which kept passing Home Rule bills, with a third reading scheduled in May 1914) against the more Conservative and Unionist-friendly House of Lords (which kept rejecting them). There was even a 'treason' angle, as it was widely reported that German firms, in late April, had sold arms to Ulster in the hope of provoking an Irish civil war. (The total haul was later confirmed at 35,000 Mauser rifles and three million rounds of ammunition.) The Curragh incident and all its echoes, said the *Daily Mail*, 'was the biggest story since the Boer War' of 1899–1902.[9]

While it lacked the sexiness of France's Caillaux affair, Britain's Irish crisis was more serious in nature. It was Prime Minister William Ewart Gladstone's attempt to pass the first Home Rule bill that had wrecked the Liberal Party in 1886, ushering in years of Conservative-Unionist dominance; his attempt to pass a second bill in 1893 had led to another thumping Tory-Unionist victory in 1895. So explosive was the issue that the Liberals, despite winning a landslide victory in 1905, had waited nearly seven years before introducing a Home Rule bill again in 1912. Many in the army wished that they had waited another decade. Sir Henry Wilson, an Irish Unionist major-general who was Britain's key liaison staff officer with the French high command, in charge of planning joint operations in case of a European war, thought that using the army to enforce Home Rule would split it 'from top to bottom.' This was hardly an unlikely scenario, considering that the mere rumour of impending Home Rule had nearly torn the army apart in March. Like Wilson, a large number of British officers hailed from Northern Ireland, and they tended, almost to a man, to be Unionists. If the Liberal government chose to enact and enforce Home Rule, many feared it would lead to a real mutiny or even civil war.

At the time of the Sarajevo incident, because of the fallout from the Curragh incident, Britain did not even have a secretary of state for war. This office was, in theory, occupied by the Liberal prime minister, Herbert Asquith, until a permanent replacement could be found, but Asquith had plenty else on his plate, beginning with Home Rule. Having been rejected by the House of Lords after its third reading in late May, the Home Rule bill was now eligible for enactment by royal assent, but Asquith was hardly going to tempt Gladstone's fate, and risk a civil war in Ireland, by doing so without negotiating a compromise. Secret talks were underway all through June over some kind of partition exempting Ulster from Home Rule – talks that threatened to enrage Asquith's Liberal and Irish nationalist supporters if they found out about them. In the House of Commons on 30 June, Asquith did set aside the burning Irish issue long enough to express 'indignation and deep concern' on behalf of the House over the Sarajevo outrage, which he called 'one of those incredible crimes which almost make us despair of the progress of mankind.' But this was all he had to say on the matter.[10]

With Asquith up to his neck in Irish affairs, and no secretary of war in the cabinet, foreign and defence policy was largely left to Sir Edward Grey, His Majesty's foreign secretary, and Churchill, the first lord of the Admiralty. While neither was as directly involved in the Home Rule business as was Asquith, it still dominated cabinet discussions; they could not afford to ignore it. Grey was also embroiled in another controversy that June. German newspapers, led by the *Berliner Tageblatt*, had got wind of ongoing naval talks between Britain and Russia, which they used to trumpet the nightmare of encircle- ment: the idea was that the British and Russian navies might team up against Germany's Baltic fleet. Germany's chancellor, Theobald von Bethmann Hollweg, had issued a formal protest to London, via his ambassador, Prince Karl Max Lichnowsky, on 24 June. Bethmann, whose entire foreign policy hinged on rapprochement with Britain – he saw this as a 'question of life and death for Germany' – was obviously disturbed. So was Grey when he learned how upset the Germans were. In conversa- tion with Lichnowsky, Grey dismissed the rumours about an Anglo-Russian naval convention, pointing out that Britain had no formal alliance 'committing us to action' with either France or Russia, although he conceded that 'we did from time to time talk as intimately as Allies.' This 'intimacy' was, Grey insisted, abso- lutely 'not used for aggression against Germany.' Lichnowsky, a notorious Anglophile, 'cordially endorsed' Grey's suspiciously vague assurance, but it was an open question whether less Anglophilic statesmen in Berlin would do so.[11]

What Grey told Lichnowsky was deeply misleading. While it is true that England's own 'Entente Cordiale' with France, first negotiated in 1904 over colonial questions in Africa, fell far short of a bilateral military alliance such as France had with Russia, over the years since, British naval and army officers had begun cooperating ever more closely with their French counter- parts in joint war-planning against Germany, without their superiors ever publicly owning up to this. Grey himself had personally worked out a secret naval agreement in 1912 with

France's ambassador to London, Paul Cambon, under which the French navy would 'cover' the Mediterranean, leaving France's northern and western coastlines undefended against Germany – with the understanding that the British fleet, covering the Channel, would defend them on France's behalf by interdicting the German navy.

Meanwhile, still-more-secret staff talks between the French and British armies had, by June 1914, reached the point where a top-secret liaison agreement specified that a British expeditionary force (BEF) of six divisions would be dispatched across the Channel if German armies violated Belgian territory in a European war, as Franco-British intelligence suggested they might do. All the powers, including Germany, had guaranteed Belgian neutrality by treaty, but the country, owing to its location alongside the Channel opposite the south of England, had outsized strategic importance for Britain. Indeed, the treaty creating an independent Belgium had been signed in London in 1839 under the watchful eye of one of Britain's greatest foreign ministers, Lord Palmerston. Not all British statesmen agreed that Belgian neutrality was worth a war: Lord Salisbury, the Tory titan of the 1880s and 1890s, would have preferred to water down the obligation because either France or Germany would inevitably have to violate Belgian territory if they went to war. But then not even Salisbury had succeeded in altering the London treaty.

Most ordinary Britons, and even most British members of Parliament, would have been astonished to learn that their country might go to war over a treaty obligation to uphold Belgian neutrality dating to 1839. And yet the staff work of recent years, along with Grey's shifty secret diplomacy, had made this scenario increasingly plausible. Sir Henry Wilson, the Irish Unionist general in charge of joint planning with the French in case the Germans violated Belgium, had done his work so thoroughly that the BEF deployment plan to France was now 'complete to the last billet of every battalion, even to the places where they were to drink their coffee.'[12] Curiously, by 1914 not only the French army but even German military planners, too, had a rough idea what to expect from the BEF (because the Germans knew their war plan required violating Belgian territory, they had to reckon with the possibility of British intervention), but Britain's own civilian government, including Grey, had been kept in the dark. Aside from lying about the Franco-British naval agreement with Cambon, Grey was therefore telling Lichnowsky the truth as he knew it, but then he did not know very much.

Much the same could be said of the Anglo-Russian naval talks. Despite German fears, discussions of joint manoeuvres had, by June 1914, barely got off the ground, which is why Grey felt no need to enlighten Lichnowsky about them. And yet serious naval talks were indeed afoot that spring between London and St Petersburg – not about Russia's Baltic fleet but about her Black Sea fleet. With their own Black Sea dreadnoughts-under-construction nowhere near completion, the Russians were terrified that the Turks were about to float their own state-of-the-art British dreadnoughts in the Bosphorus, which would effectively rule out any future Russian attempt to seize Constantinople and the Straits. Just as Germans like Liman von Sanders were helping train the Ottoman army, a British mission under Admiral Sir Arthur Limpus was modernising the Turkish navy. Skeleton crews were being trained to take over the first British-built dreadnought, scheduled to reach Ottoman territorial waters in July. This was the *Sultan Osman I*, which would mount more guns than any ship ever afloat – guns that were faster-firing and more accurate than the Russians'. And the inferior Russian dreadnoughts would not be completed before 1916, giving the Turks nearly two years to assert their dominance over a Russian Black Sea fleet rendered obsolete by the *Sultan Osman I*. Small wonder that Sazonov, via Russia's ambassador to Britain, Count Benckendorff, was requesting that the British government block, or at least delay, delivery of the *Sultan Osman I* – the first of no

Winston Churchill, Britain's first lord of the Admiralty in 1914, at 39 years old, in his explosive, high-energy prime. *Source: Getty Images.*

fewer than four dreadnoughts that British yards were building for the Ottoman navy. Alas for Russia, Grey and Churchill, on 12 June 1914, declined, on the classic Liberal grounds that the British government could not interfere with private business contracts.[13]

It is curious that neither Churchill nor Grey recalled anything of these momentous discussions in their memoirs. In Grey's case, the omission – and his general ignorance of what was going on around him in 1914 – may have been owing to faulty memory, in part caused by his failing health. All year he had suffered from deteriorating eyesight. In May, he was told that his condition was 'probably irreversible.' Having had no luck with English doctors, Grey was planning a trip to Germany to see an ocular specialist sometime that summer, if he could ever find the time. His failing eyes, along with the burgeoning

Home Rule crisis, preoccupied him to such an extent that Grey seems barely to have understood what Benckendorff was talking about when he issued his protests about the Turkish dreadnoughts in May and early June. Neither then, nor later, did Grey perceive the nature of Russia's strategic concerns over the Ottoman naval buildup. He was not unduly bothered by the Sarajevo incident, either – not enough for him to cancel a fishing trip that week. An avid outdoorsman and 'master of the complex art of fly-fishing' – he had written a book on the subject – Grey was keen to enjoy his favourite hobby while his failing eyes still allowed him to pursue it.[14]

In Churchill's case, it is not likely that poor memory accounts for his failure to recall the dreadnought discussions with Russia. Just 39 years old, Churchill was entering his explosive, high-energy prime in the spring of 1914. Grey, having failed to inform Churchill of what was going on all through May, had brought the first lord of the Admiralty in on the discussions with Benckendorff only at the last minute in early June, and even then he had done nothing to explain what the whole thing was about. Churchill's priority in June was not the Russian naval talks at all, but rather preparations for Fleet Week at Kiel, where the German and British fleets were staging joint manoeuvres as part of an ongoing détente between the rival navies. Churchill had helped kick off the opening ceremonies at Kiel on Wednesday, 24 June, before returning to England that weekend. On Monday, 29 June, he learned about the assassinations, like most Britons, from the morning papers, which he picked up at the ferry terminal in Portsmouth en route to London and the Admiralty. More imaginative than Grey, Churchill, in his book *The World Crisis*, recalled being overcome by 'a sudden and vivid feeling that something sinister and measureless had occurred. . . . I reflected that it would be nice to get our great vessels back from the Baltic soon.'[15] Intriguing as this suggestion of geopolitical prescience is, the remark has the unmistakable sound of literary licence.

In fact, there is no evidence that Churchill, after hearing the news from Sarajevo, ordered any precautionary naval measures or changed his daily routine any more than Grey did.

If Russia's clearly stated desire to prevent Britain from destroying her strategic position in the Black Sea by selling dreadnoughts to the Ottoman navy did not register in the minds of Churchill or Grey in June 1914, it is hardly surprising that neither man took much interest in the news from the Balkans. Prime Minister Asquith, preoccupied with Ireland, had little time for foreign policy at all. The failure of Britain's key policymakers to pay mind to the assassination of Archduke Ferdinand was understandable. It did not bode well, however, for their ability to master events in case the Sarajevo outrage snowballed into a real crisis.

4

Berlin: Sympathy and Impatience

K AISER WILHELM II WAS RACING HIS YACHT in a regatta at Kiel on Sunday afternoon, 28 June 1914, when he saw a small motorised launch steaming towards him at full speed. Anxious to complete the race, he gestured for the boat to change its course. The man captaining the motorboat, Admiral Georg von Müller, responded with a still more emphatic gesture, urging the yacht to slow down as he had an important message for the kaiser. When the launch came in range, the admiral folded his message into a cigarette case and tossed it on board the yacht. Seeing his messenger, Wilhelm could not have been pleased. Müller, chief of the German naval cabinet and one of Wilhelm's least favourite advisers, seemed to always bring him bad tidings. This time was no different. The kaiser opened Müller's case, unfolded the message, and turned pale as he read the news from Sarajevo. He then ordered his crew to come about and abandoned the regatta.

Wilhelm was deeply saddened to learn of the loss of his friend, whom he had just visited two weekends previously at his estate at Konopischt, and no less so by the loss of the archduke's wife. The kaiser, something of a social misfit himself despite his august lineage, had always had a soft spot in his heart for this earnest, loving couple cast out by the Habsburgs. To get around the problem of court rank during official banquets at Potsdam, the kaiser had come up with the clever solution of seating everyone at smaller tables of four, so that he and his wife, Auguste, could sit alone with Ferdinand and Sophie, without any archduchesses complaining that they should have been placed ahead of her. The kaiser had always made a point of calling on Sophie when visiting Vienna and of addressing her by her proper rank. The Duchess of Hohenburg could have asked for no greater respect from a sovereign, nor her husband for a better friend and supporter.

It was not mere sentiment that led the kaiser to indulge the archduke's morganatic marriage. With Franz Josef's health failing, Wilhelm had been expecting Franz Ferdinand to inherit the Habsburg throne in the near future, a prospect he welcomed, not least because the kaiser's relations with the aging emperor were far less cordial. The two friends had discussed far-reaching questions of European politics and diplomacy at Konopischt, reaching agreement on nearly all of them. The only real point of contention between them was over the Hungarian minister-president Tisza, whom Franz Ferdinand hated for Hungary's persecution of its minorities. The kaiser thought Tisza intelligent and worth humouring, not least because the Hungarian was, publicly at least, advocating closer relations with Romania, notwithstanding his persecution of Romanians inside Hungary. Even here, the two friends had reached a rough accord, after the kaiser proposed that the archduke popularise a slogan for hoisting Tisza on his own petard: 'But sir! Remember the Romanians!' The archduke, in turn, had tried to calm the kaiser's fears about Russian sabre-rattling, which he did not take seriously on account of Russia's internal problems.[1]

It was painful for the kaiser now to recall this amiable discussion. He and Franz Ferdinand would never again discuss

affairs of state together nor, indeed, be able to enact those policies they hoped, perhaps optimistically, might help to defuse
the Balkan powder keg. In a hostile international climate, Franz
Ferdinand had been Wilhelm's diplomatic anchor, the one man
he could always count on. Now his anchor was gone. Like
Berchtold and Conrad in Vienna, but unlike President Poincaré
in Paris and Grey and Churchill in London, Germany's sovereign was stopped cold by the news from Sarajevo. He called off
all further engagements at Kiel and returned to Berlin.

He found the city nearly empty of imperial officials. The
chancellor, Bethmann Hollweg, was at his country estate at
Hohenfinow. Helmuth von Moltke, Conrad's counterpart as
army chief of staff, was taking his annual cure at Carlsbad. The
naval secretary, Admiral Alfred von Tirpitz, was summering at
his estate in the Black Forest. Gottlieb von Jagow, state secretary
for foreign affairs, was on his honeymoon in Italy.

The kaiser was therefore initially left alone to react to the
news from the Balkans, without his usual coterie of advisers.
Constitutionally speaking, this was not inappropriate. Under
the German Imperial Constitution of 1871, the power to declare
war, or to make peace, rested solely with Germany's emperor
as 'supreme warlord,' not with the Reichstag. Only the upper
house of Parliament, the Bundesrat, had the power to veto a
declaration of war. In foreign policy more generally, there was
no countervailing power to the emperor whatever, beyond the
ability of the Reichstag to influence it by vetoing spending bills.
As sovereign of the country with the most powerful army – and
second most powerful navy – in Europe, the kaiser therefore
bore an awesome responsibility. Whether the Austrian-Serbian
dispute over the Sarajevo incident would spark a major European
war would depend largely, although not exclusively, on him.

Wilhelm II was one of the most fascinating, if often misunderstood, statesmen of his era. Born in the breech position
after a gruelling ten-hour labour his mother barely survived,

Kaiser Wilhelm II, striking an implausible warrior's pose. It was his strange misfortune to be supreme warlord of a country with a proud martial tradition, while being unable to use his left arm properly. *Source: Bain News Service, Library of Congress.*

he had suffered nerve damage that crippled his arm. By the time he reached adulthood, Wilhelm's left arm was six inches shorter than his right and all but useless. It was his peculiar misfortune to become supreme warlord of a country with a proud martial tradition, while being unable to cut his own meat at table, let alone handle weapons properly. Understandably, this led to an insecurity complex, a need for constant attention and acclaim. As one of his many critics put it, the kaiser needed to be 'the stag at every hunt, the bride at every wedding, and the corpse at every funeral.'[2]

Eager for praise, taking offence at the merest slight, the kaiser was a difficult man to work for. Bismarck had disdained to gratify Wilhelm II's fragile ego after he became emperor in 1888, which led to his sacking two years later. The only other chancellor serving under Wilhelm II to approach Bismarck in terms of accomplishment, Bernhard von Bülow, had likewise been fired in June 1909, in part because he had failed to defend his sovereign forcefully enough after an embarrassing interview with the kaiser was published in the *Daily Telegraph* in October 1908. In this disastrous interview, Wilhelm II had managed to insult the English, frighten the French, anger the Russians, and threaten the Japanese. The affair had so damaged Wilhelm II's reputation that many German papers had called for his abdication. Chastened, the kaiser had gone into hibernation for much of the winter, re-emerging only the following spring, when he pressed for Bülow's resignation.

The *Daily Telegraph* affair was emblematic of Wilhelm II's erratic statesmanship, but it was also misleading about his real character. In England, the kaiser had long been suspected of warlike tendencies due to his promotion of Germany's High Seas Fleet, which seemed so clearly aimed at upending British naval supremacy (it had not escaped the Admiralty's notice that Germany's own dreadnoughts had storage room for only enough coal to reach the North Sea, allowing more space for guns).[3] When the kaiser personally visited Tangier in March 1905, precipitating a diplomatic crisis over Morocco for what appeared to be no good reason, it seemed to French and English policymakers that his real aim was to start a European war before their nascent entente of 1904 had produced real military cooperation. The belligerent tone of his remarks during the *Daily Telegraph* interview crystallised Wilhelm II's reputation as a warmonger.

Nothing could have been further from the truth. As those who knew him best understood, the kaiser's bluster was a classic case of loud bark and little bite. The last thing he wanted was a war with England. As the grandson of Queen Victoria,

Wilhelm II longed for the approval of his English cousins and the English more generally. His enthusiasm for the High Seas Fleet, like his foolish outburst with the *Daily Telegraph*, was rooted in his craving for English respect, even if his provocative actions and reckless words tended to produce precisely the opposite effect on their intended audience. The kaiser was simply not subtle enough to realise that naval blackmail and thumping talk would annoy and frighten British policymakers, not impress them.

The Moroccan provocation of 1905 illustrates the disconnect perfectly. Its real author was not the kaiser who went to Tangier but the men who sent him there: Bülow and his key adviser, Friedrich von Holstein, who were hoping to break the Anglo-French entente through a show of force. Bülow and Holstein knew their blackmail was mere bluff, for their supreme warlord had no real stomach for war. As Bülow later explained, 'Wilhelm II did not want war, if only because he did not trust his nerves not to give way under the strain of any really critical situation. The moment there was actual danger His Majesty would become uncomfortably conscious that he could never lead an army in the field.'[4]

The kaiser's deep reluctance to take up arms was borne out clearly in the First Balkan War. By mid-November 1912, Serbia had already routed the Turks in Macedonia, reaching the Adriatic coastline via Albania; the Greeks had taken Salonica; and the Bulgarian army had raced across Thrace to the final Ottoman defensive lines at Çatalca, just 37 miles from Constantinople. Although a formal Turkish-German alliance had never been formed, the kaiser had loudly championed the Ottoman cause ever since first visiting Turkey in 1889. In Damascus in 1898, he had notoriously proclaimed himself the 'friend for all time' of the Muslim world. The Ottoman army had been trained by German officers; it fought with German weapons. It had been bested on all fronts by the Russophile armies of the Balkan League, which fought with French weapons of Creusot. If there was ever a time for Germany to intervene in the Balkans, this was it. But the kaiser, declaring a policy of 'free fight and no favour,' refused.[5]

There was, of course, a war party in Berlin, just as there was in Vienna and Petersburg. Moltke, the chief of staff, had made the case for intervention in the First Balkan War in a crisis meeting held in December 1912. Like Conrad – like, indeed, most high-ranking officers in both Austria and Germany – Moltke believed that time was not on the side of the Central Powers, with Russia growing stronger every year. A European war was, in his view, 'unavoidable, and the sooner the better.'[6] Naval secretary Tirpitz, recognising that Germany's construction of dreadnoughts lagged far behind Britain's, was less keen. The chancellor, Bethmann Hollweg, was also cautious, having invested much of his political capital in a rapprochement with England, which required slowing down the very dreadnought-building programme that Tirpitz was pushing (or even giving Germany's High Seas Fleet to Great Britain, as Bethmann suggested at one point – to the horror of both Tirpitz and Wilhelm II). In the end, the opinion that mattered most was the kaiser's, and he was dead set against going to war over Balkan issues unless Germany's hand were forced outright by a Russian invasion of Austria.

Thus, far from backing up his Austrian ally in the Balkans, Wilhelm had seemed almost to take Serbia's side. During the Second Balkan War of 1913, when Berchtold at last summoned up enough spine to demand that the Serbian army withdraw from Albania, it was the Russians – not wanting their Serbian client to become too powerful – who backed Austria, not the Germans. The kaiser called Vienna's efforts to block Serbian access to the Adriatic 'nonsense.' When, in March 1914, he heard Vienna opposed Serbian union with Macedonia, he retorted, 'Unbelievable! This union is absolutely not to be prevented. And if Vienna attempts it, she will commit a great stupidity, and stir up the danger of a war with the Slavs, which would leave us quite cold.' Berchtold and Franz Josef I were wholly, and deeply, committed to the 'stupidity' that left the kaiser cold. As Tisza warned his increasingly angry emperor, any Austrian move against Belgrade would run up against 'the Kaiser's preference for Serbia.'[7]

By the time of the Sarajevo outrage, the kaiser's growing hostility meant that Austria's diplomatic isolation was nearly complete. In a sense, this was what the Konopischt meeting of June 1914 had been about: Wilhelm II was looking forward to a change of regime, so that Austria, under its new emperor, would pursue a more sensible policy in the Balkans, winning over the Romanians and calming down the Serbs. Now, with the murder of his friend, apparently by Serbian terrorists, these hopes were dashed.

Knowing that his sovereign, along with Chancellor Bethmann, had long wanted to cool down tensions in the Balkans, Germany's ambassador to Austria-Hungary, Heinrich von Tschirschky, sensibly urged caution following the Sarajevo outrage. His first dispatch from Vienna, dated Tuesday, 30 June, reported Berchtold's ominous remark about how the 'threads of the conspiracy come together at Belgrade,' and that the prevailing view at the Ballplatz was that there 'must be a final settlement of accounts with the Serbs.' Tschirschky, evidently expecting the approval of Bethmann and the kaiser for his measured conduct, reported that he had felt compelled, 'calmly but very emphatically and seriously, to utter a warning against such hasty measures.'

Reading this report while still in shock over the loss of his friend, Wilhelm II lost his temper. 'Who authorised him to do so?' he scribbled on Tschirschky's dispatch, as he often did on official correspondence (the notorious 'marginalia'). 'That is utterly stupid! It is not his business . . . what Austria intends to do. Later on, if things went wrong, it would be said: Germany was not willing! Tschirschky will please drop this nonsense! Matters must be cleared up with the Serbs, and that *right soon*. That's all self-evident and the plain truth.'[8]

This was just the sort of reaction Berchtold had been hoping for. In a flash, Germany's nervous, hesitating, Serbia-sympathising Hamlet of a sovereign had been turned into a decisive Serb-hater ready to take up arms and fight – and the sooner the better, just as Moltke had long advised him. Of course, Wilhelm II was known for these kinds of outbursts, which often dissipated as quickly as they came over him. This is why Berchtold had hoped to corner the kaiser at the archduke's funeral in Vienna, so as to pin him down in his state of grief and rage, before he could change his mind.

It was Berchtold's rotten luck that Bethmann, fearing a copycat terrorist strike in Vienna, had intervened to cut off the trip. As he had no access to the scribbled marginalia on Tschirschky's dispatches to Berlin, for all Berchtold knew, Tschirschky's urging of caution represented the kaiser's own thinking on Sarajevo. And now, without the chance to make his case to the kaiser in Vienna, Austria's foreign minister had to assume it would be much harder to win the support of Germany's sovereign for a tougher line in the Balkans – support he desperately needed to overcome Tisza's opposition.

As usual, Berchtold would end up dragging his heels indefinitely in a crisis where decisive action was called for, cementing his reputation for cowardice and ineffectuality. Little did the Austrian know that his luck was about to turn around dramatically.

II

COUNTDOWN

5

The Count Hoyos Mission to Berlin

SUNDAY–MONDAY, 5–6 JULY

O N WEDNESDAY, 1 JULY, a prominent German journalist named Victor Naumann turned up at the Ballplatz, saying that he had urgent business to discuss. The man he wanted to talk to was Foreign Minister Berchtold's chief of staff, Count Alexander Hoyos. There were good reasons for Naumann's choice. As a subordinate in the Ballplatz, even if an exceptionally well-placed one, Hoyos could speak off the record, in the manner of back-channel diplomacy. In a sense he was Berchtold's alter ego, free to speak his mind in a way Austria-Hungary's careful foreign minister could not. Hoyos, 38 years old at the time of the Sarajevo incident, was energetic, highly motivated, and, by reputation, a hawk on Serbia. Hoyos had been sent to Berlin during the First Bosnian Crisis of 1908–1909 in order to win German support for the annexation of Bosnia-Herzegovina, so his hawkish views were well known to the Germans. Naumann, for his part, was known to be well connected in Berlin, a trusted confidant of high-ranking military and naval officers. He was also good friends with the state secretary, Jagow, and with

Wilhelm von Stumm, the political director of the German Foreign Office, who ran its day-to-day affairs. Hoyos therefore listened very carefully to what the German had to say.

Naumann opened the audience with remarks on the general outlook in Berlin. The Russian army's Great Programme was viewed with growing alarm, and her planned test mobilisation for fall 1914 seemed an ominous portent of a shift in the strategic balance. The idea of fighting a *Präventivkrieg*, or pre-emptive war, against Russia before the Great Programme was complete had long been discussed seriously in the army command. Now, Naumann told Hoyos, this idea was gaining influence even at the Wilhelmstrasse. The German naval command, meanwhile, although still viewing itself as overmatched by Britain, was feeling increasingly sanguine about the risk of war, owing to the success of Chancellor Bethmann Hollweg's rapprochement with England, as manifested recently at the Naval Week at Kiel. 'For this reason,' Naumann informed Hoyos that 'there was believed to be the certainty that England would not intervene in a European war.'

All this was interesting enough, but it did not necessarily herald a change in Germany's Balkan policy. The kaiser had pointedly refused to risk a European conflagration during the Balkan Wars and had been notably unsympathetic about Austria's concerns about Serbian aggrandisement. As yet, there was no indication from either Germany's Ambassador Tschirschky in Vienna, nor from Austria's own ambassador in Berlin, Count Ladislaus Szögyény, of a shift in German policy following the Sarajevo outrage. Hoyos therefore broached the subject carefully with Naumann. 'I let fall,' Hoyos reported to Berchtold, 'the remark that this state of affairs [e.g., German war-readiness] would not be unpleasing to us if we should ever find ourselves under the necessity of taking action against Serbia.' To Hoyos's pleasant surprise, Naumann told the

Austrian that a punitive war against Serbia 'was exactly what he had been going to suggest to me.' In Naumann's opinion, 'after the Sarajevo murder, it was a question of life or death for the Monarchy not to leave the crime unpunished but to annihilate Serbia. For Germany such a course would be the touchstone whether Russia meant war or not.'[1]

Here, it seemed, was an astonishing stroke of luck. Hoping for, at best, a declaration of support from the Germans for a tougher line on Serbia, Hoyos was instead treated to a display worthy of Austria's belligerent Chief of Staff Conrad. But who did Naumann really speak for? That Moltke and his colleagues in the German army command were keen for a test of strength with Russia was not news: it was their job to prepare for this, just as it was Conrad's job to plan for a war with Serbia. Naumann did claim to have spoken recently with Stumm, the political director of the German Foreign Office (although not also with Germany's Foreign Minister Jagow, who was still in Italy), which suggested there was a chance the Wilhelmstrasse had indeed come around to the German army's point of view. Chancellor Bethmann, though, was not mentioned at all.

As for Germany's sovereign, Naumann said he believed that the kaiser could be brought around, but only if everyone acted quickly to convince him. 'If, at the present moment,' the German emissary told Count Hoyos, 'when Kaiser Wilhelm is horrified at the Sarajevo murder, he is spoken to in the right way, he will give us all assurances and this time go to the length of war, because he perceives the dangers for the monarchical principle.' If the Austrians, that is, wanted a war with Serbia, the kaiser could give it to them – but only if they presented their case to him while he was still enraged by his friend's murder.

Naumann's report of the view from Berlin, whether reliable or not, gave Berchtold his first glimmer of hope that he could overcome the Hungarian minister-president's opposition to a war with Serbia. On Thursday, the foreign minister received more good news from Sarajevo. After he had been taken into custody following his murder of the archducal couple, Gavrilo Princip had initially denied any connection to a larger conspiracy. This took some courage, for Princip had been beaten badly by an angry mob after he fired off his volley. He was still vomiting and bleeding from his head when he arrived at the police station, so weakened that he was at first unable to speak. Once he regained his composure, Princip claimed to have come up with the idea entirely by himself and to have acted alone on the quai. Improbably, he denied any acquaintance with Chabrinovitch, the assassin who had thrown a bomb at the imperial motorcade only an hour before Princip had shot the archducal couple.

This transparent lie may not have held up for long in any case, but Princip was not helped by his fellow conspirators. Chabrinovitch himself admitted under questioning, on Monday, 29 June, that Princip was his friend, although – in a claim still more improbable than Princip's – he insisted that the two friends had both come up with the same idea to assassinate the archduke independently of one another; it was mere coincidence that they had tried to do so on the same morning and on the same Sarajevo road. When his interrogator pointed out how absurd this sounded, Chabrinovitch confessed at once that the two had planned the crime together, although still denying that they had help from others. Next to slip up was Ilitch, the main Sarajevo organiser, who, despite having slipped away from the quai on Sunday, had been arrested, along with his entire family, in a widening dragnet that eventually ensnared more than 200 Bosnian Serbs in Sarajevo alone. Because he, unlike Princip and Chabrinovitch, was over 21, Ilitch was eligible for the death penalty. To spare his life, on Wednesday, 1 July, Ilitch rolled over on the three other assassins he had recruited in Sarajevo (who all, like him, had run away on Sunday), fingering also

The arrest of bomb-thrower Nedjelko Chabrinovitch, Gavrilo Princip's co-conspirator, in Sarajevo on 28 June 1914. *Source: Getty Images.*

Grabezh, the third of the conspirators who had come in from Belgrade and who had likewise escaped the initial dragnet. The Austrian authorities were thus able to arrest six of the seven Serb assassins who had lined up on the Appelquai the previous Sunday, missing only Mehmedbashitch, the token Muslim, who had fled to Montenegro.

Princip himself finally gave in on Thursday, 2 July, independently of the others (he seems not to have known that Chabrinovitch and Ilitch had already confessed). In order to spare innocent men the grief of guilt by association, Princip offered to finger his fellow-conspirators so long as he was allowed to see Ilitch and Grabezh in person, in order to explain why he was confessing and encourage them to confess, too. Taking charge of the confessions just as he had taken charge on the quai, Princip then told Ilitch to let the Austrian authorities know 'among whom you divided the weapons and where the

93

weapons are.' He told Grabezh to 'confess everything, how we got the bombs, how we travelled and in what society we were, so that just people do not come to harm.'[2]

By owning up and trying to get the others to stick to the same story, Princip hoped to cut off the Austrian investigation before it reached Belgrade. But it was not terribly hard for investigators to follow the leads they were given as far as the Bosnian border, where Serbian officials had connived in the smuggling of the assassins, and their weapons, onto Austrian territory. With Ilitch, in particular, showing no signs of resistance under interrogation, it was only a matter of time before the Austrians would know who in Serbia, if anyone, had armed and trained the assassins. While falling well short of legal proof, the confessions were still excellent news for Berchtold.

There were other encouraging signs, too. Germany's ambassador, so cool on Monday to Berchtold's plan to punish Serbia, had begun to come around. Shortly before meeting the emperor on Thursday, 2 July, Tschirschky called on Berchtold and told him that 'only vigorous measures against Serbia' would do. Berchtold was not certain what accounted for the ambassador's change of attitude – he had no inkling that Tschirschky had been rebuked by the kaiser – but it was still a welcome development. Above all, Germany's ambassador told Berchtold, Vienna must this time develop a clear plan of action, ideally one that was 'bold and decisive,' in order to convince policymakers in Berlin that Austria was not going to back down again.[3]

This was exactly what Berchtold wanted to do. Just as he was beginning to see a way out of the impasse with Tisza, however, Emperor Franz Josef I threw up another obstacle. The Habsburg sovereign, after his own meeting with Germany's ambassador on Thursday, felt obliged to call Berchtold in to discuss their conversation. Despite his own feelings on the matter, which were closer to Berchtold's than Tisza's – Franz Josef agreed that some kind of 'powerful response to Serbia' was necessary – the emperor was worried that events were moving too quickly. With Tisza so resolutely opposed, he was not yet ready to speak of war. Berchtold and Conrad, Franz Josef said, must wait.[4]

All day Friday, Berchtold mulled over his options. Some kind of approach must be made to Berlin, but how and on what pretext? Tisza was still insisting on his 24 June 'peace plan' for winning over Bulgaria and Romania to the Central Powers. The Hungarian surely would not object if this plan were presented to Berlin. But if the Austrians sent Tisza's memorandum off as is, it would hardly impress the Germans as, in Tschirschky's words, a 'bold and decisive' course of action. So Berchtold decided to write a postscript to Tisza's text, informing the Germans that 'the above memorandum had only just been completed, when the terrible events at Sarajevo happened.' Offering the murders as proof 'that the gulf between the monarchy and Serbia was beyond bridging over,' Berchtold concluded that Austria must 'tear asunder with a determined hand the threads which its enemies are weaving into a net over its head.'[5] For good measure, Berchtold composed a letter to the kaiser for Franz Josef to sign, informing Wilhelm II that 'the crime of Sarajevo is not the deed of a single individual, but the result of a well-arranged plot whose threads reach to Belgrade.' So long as the 'source of criminal agitation in Belgrade lives on unpunished,' Berchtold's royal letter continued with an eye to the kaiser's strong feelings on the monarchical principle, 'the peace policy of all European monarchs is threatened.' The danger, the letter concluded, would only pass 'when Serbia . . . is eliminated as a political power-factor (*politische Machtfaktor*) in the Balkans.' While careful not to let slip the word 'war' lest Tisza object, Berchtold wanted to leave the Germans in little doubt as to what Austria really intended to do.[6]

The next question was how to send the diplomatic notes to Berlin. Berchtold could simply use a courier as usual, but this might not be enough to convince the Germans of how serious he was. Nor was Ambassador Szögyény an ideal candidate to announce a change in policy. Having served at his post since 1892, he was a part of the furniture of Embassy Row in Berlin, closer, in some ways, to the Wilhelmstrasse than to the Ballplatz, where his long tenure was resented, not least because Szögyény was untouchable, protected by Emperor Franz Josef himself. Moreover, he was Hungarian. Berchtold had long wanted the aging Szögyény, now 73 and in poor health, to retire so he could replace him with a loyal German-Austrian, Prince Hohenlohe-Schillingfürst. Szögyény's retirement was expected in August, but in the current crisis that might not come soon enough.

Of course, Berchtold could simply go himself. Such a high-level mission, however, would invariably attract unwanted attention from the other powers – and from Tisza. Finally, on Saturday morning, 4 July, Hoyos had an inspiration: perhaps he could go in Berchtold's stead. The foreign minister trusted Hoyos, and so evidently – based on Naumann's approach earlier that week – did the Germans. No one in Berlin would doubt his ability to represent the views of the Ballplatz. Better still, as a vigorous young hawk, Hoyos could counteract any impression of indecisiveness left by the aging Hungarian ambassador. A Hoyos mission was, Berchtold agreed, the perfect solution.

Events now moved rapidly. Saturday afternoon, Berchtold wired to Szögyény, asking him to arrange an urgent appointment with the kaiser for the following day. Shortly before Hoyos left the Ballplatz, Berchtold furnished him with oral instructions that went further than his textual glosses. Hoyos was, Berchtold later recalled telling him, to 'explain to Ambassador Szögyény that we believe the moment has come for a final reckoning with Serbia. We must obtain from the government in Belgrade specific guarantees for the future, the refusal of which will result in military action.' Szögyény's task, Berchtold explained, was to 'see if such a course of action [by Austria] would be supported . . . by official circles in Berlin.'[7] Armed with these instructions, Hoyos boarded the night train for Berlin. Berchtold then returned to his estate at Buchlau, to cultivate the appearance that little was happening.

Tisza knew nothing of these momentous decisions. Following his audience with the emperor at Schönbrunn on Wednesday, Hungary's minister-president had returned to Budapest, where urgent domestic business awaited him. Having made his opposition to punitive action against Serbia clear to both the emperor and Berchtold, he did not suspect that any significant change in the foreign policy of the dual monarchy would be made without him. Tisza was therefore shocked when, on Sunday morning, he received a phone call from the Ballplatz, informing him that a diplomatic note had just been dispatched to Berlin, outlining Austria's new Balkan strategy in light of the Sarajevo incident. Tisza demanded at once to be shown a copy of the text of the note, which was duly wired to Budapest. Recognising at once the importance of Berchtold's additions, which changed the entire meaning of his Balkan peace memorandum, Tisza called back the Ballplatz and demanded that he be allowed to delete objectionable passages – especially the one about 'eliminating Serbia as a political power-factor in the Balkans,' obvious shorthand for war. It was too late: Hoyos, with Berchtold's unedited texts in hand, was already in Berlin.[8]

Upon his arrival in the German capital Sunday morning, 5 July, Hoyos went straight to the Austro-Hungarian embassy, where he briefed Szögyény on the two diplomatic notes and on Berchtold's unwritten instructions. There was little time to waste, as Szögyény was expected at the Neues Palais for lunch with the kaiser. After the briefing was finished, the ambassador set off for Potsdam, while Hoyos headed over to the Wilhelmstrasse to meet with his contacts in the German Foreign Office.

Count Szögyény, despite his frailty, had developed valuable skills during his extra-long tenure in Berlin. Above all, he was good at handling Wilhelm II. He knew the kaiser's likes and dislikes, his capricious moods, and how to manipulate them. Szögyény began the lunchtime audience by telling Wilhelm II how strongly Franz Ferdinand had admired him. Serbian terrorism, both men readily agreed, was a threat to sovereigns everywhere. As the conversation shifted onto the always-favourable ground of the 'monarchical principle,' Szögyény unveiled the sovereign-to-sovereign note signed by Franz Josef I (although actually written by Berchtold), along with the accompanying diplomatic note on the Balkans. The kaiser read both notes, he reported, 'with the greatest attention.' This was the moment Berchtold and the Austrians had been waiting for. A week to the day after the Sarajevo incident, Wilhelm II would weigh in on Austria's plans to demand satisfaction from Serbia. What would he say?

Somewhat to Szögyény's disappointment, Germany's sovereign did not at first assent to the general thrust of the Austrian notes. His anger over the murder of his friend having apparently subsided over the course of the week, the kaiser told Austria's ambassador calmly that 'he had expected some serious step on our [i.e., Austria's] part towards Serbia, but that at the same time he must confess that the detailed statement of His Majesty made him regard a serious European complication as possible.' Wilhelm was no less fooled than Tisza had been by Berchtold's language in the sovereign-to-sovereign note: 'eliminating Serbia as a political power-factor in the Balkans' clearly meant punitive war. The kaiser had been burned before for loose, bellicose talk, most famously in the *Daily Telegraph* affair of 1908. He was not about to stick his neck out so recklessly again. On a question of this magnitude, the kaiser told Szögyény, he 'could give no definite answer before having taken council with the Imperial chancellor,' Bethmann Hollweg. The ambassador quietly dropped the subject.[9]

Szögyény knew the kaiser too well, however, to let the matter rest there. It was well to let Berchtold's diplomatic notes percolate in Wilhelm's mind, which was never fixed for long. Having let his host relax over dessert and coffee, the ambassador tried once more in the early afternoon. 'When I again called attention to the seriousness of the situation,' Szögyény reported later that day to Vienna, 'the Kaiser authorised me to inform our gracious Majesty that we might in this case, as in all others, rely upon Germany's full support.' Wilhelm insisted once more that he must speak with Bethmann, but this time he assured the ambassador that he was certain the chancellor would go along with his declaration of support.

This should have been the end of the conversation, and, in the hands of a more seasoned statesman than Wilhelm II, it would have been. Having now twice told Szögyény that he could not say anything further without consulting his chancellor, the kaiser proceeded to do just that. It was 'his opinion,' he offered, that

> our action against Serbia . . . must not be delayed. Russia's attitude would no doubt be hostile, but to this he had been for years prepared, and should a war between Austria-Hungary and Russia be unavoidable, we might be convinced that Germany, our old faithful ally, would stand at our side. Russia at the present time was in no way prepared for war, and would think twice before it appealed to arms.[10]

This would be more to Berchtold's liking. The kaiser's incandescent rage over the Sarajevo outrage may have dissipated, but his recklessness remained. Even if Wilhelm changed his mind later, Szögyény, and through him Berchtold, now had the kaiser's belligerent remarks (even though made only in oral conversation) on the record: these remarks might prove invaluable in a policy tussle with Tisza. While Germany's loose-lipped sovereign did remember to summon Bethmann from Hohenfinow to Potsdam for consultation, as far as Szögyény was concerned, the kaiser had said enough. He returned to the Austrian embassy that afternoon to report to Vienna on his promising conversation with the kaiser, expecting to speak to Bethmann the following day.

In addition to the chancellor, Wilhelm also summoned to the Neues Palais those of his military advisers to be found in Berlin. These included his own adjutant, General Hans von Plessen; General Moritz von Lyncker, chief of the military cabinet; General Erich von Falkenhayn, the Prussian minister of war; and, to represent the navy in Tirpitz's absence, a Captain Zenker. Once everyone had arrived, shortly after five PM, the kaiser read out the diplomatic notes Szögyény had presented him, and briefly summarised his conversation with the ambassador. He then opened the floor for discussion.

There is no precise transcript of what was said at this historic 5 July audience in Potsdam, but several of the participants wrote accounts shortly afterwards, which give a good idea of what was – and was not – decided. First, General Plessen wrote in his diary that night that the gist of the Austrian diplomatic notes, as presented by the kaiser, was that 'the Austrians are getting ready for a war with Serbia and want first to be sure of Germany.' Everyone was agreed, Plessen recalled, that 'the sooner the Austrians make their move against Serbia the better.' The 'prevailing opinion' in the room, he observed, was that 'the Russians – though friends with Serbia – will not join in.' There was thus no need for extraordinary military preparations, and the kaiser would proceed with his annual July Baltic cruise as normal.[11]

Falkenhayn's recollection of the audience was somewhat different. In his report to Moltke – the chief of staff was still taking his spa cure at Carlsbad – the Prussian war minister said that the kaiser's somewhat 'hurried' presentation made it difficult to figure out exactly what the Austrians were up to. Unlike Plessen, Falkenhayn seems to have taken Berchtold's two notes literally, noting that neither of them 'speaks of the need for war, rather both expound "energetic" action such as the conclusion of a treaty with Bulgaria, for which they would like to be certain of the support of the German Reich.' Overall, he told Moltke, 'these documents did not succeed in convincing me that the Vienna government had taken any firm resolution.' Chancellor Bethmann, he added, 'appears to have as little faith as I do that the Austrian government is really in earnest, even though its language is undeniably more resolute than in the past.'[12]

Berchtold, it seemed, had outsmarted himself. By camouflaging his appeal for German support for a war with Serbia inside Tisza's Balkan peace plan, he had allowed doubt to creep into German minds that Austria really intended to punish Belgrade. His oral instructions to Hoyos, passed on verbally to Szögyény, had been enough to convince the kaiser of the warlike intentions of the Ballplatz. The kaiser had even given oral – though not written – support for this policy. When forced to justify himself before the chancellor and military advisers, however, Wilhelm had apparently hedged. Plessen, who as the kaiser's adjutant may have understood his sovereign's manner of speaking better than the others, was able to intuit what the Austrians were about. Falkenhayn and Bethmann were not. So far as they knew, the Austrians were still full of empty talk.

Count Hoyos had been sent to Berlin precisely to dispel any doubts about Austrian intentions. He did his utmost to do so. While Szögyény lunched with the kaiser on Sunday, Hoyos met with Arthur Zimmermann, the undersecretary of state, who, as Jagow's top assistant, was something like Hoyos's equivalent as chief of staff to Berchtold – and a good friend. Zimmermann, like Hoyos, was hawkish, which in the German case meant he was a proponent of 'preventive war' against Russia. Seeking to impress his friend, Hoyos laid out a position even more aggressive than Conrad's, telling Zimmermann that Austria was considering a 'surprise attack [on Serbia] without preliminary preparation,' which would lead to a 'partition of her territory among Austria-Hungary, Bulgaria, and Albania.' Zimmermann, Hoyos claimed in his report, merely smiled at this and offered no objections. As the two men parted, Hoyos told his friend, as if in triumph, 'you could not have believed that Austria-Hungary would quietly accept the murder of the heir apparent and do nothing about it.' Zimmermann, in his reply, pithily summed up the feelings of the German war party: 'No, but we were a little afraid you might.'[13]

Satisfying as this conversation must have been for Hoyos and Zimmermann, they were, after all, both subordinates in policymaking. The next day, they were summoned to a more serious audience with the chancellor, with Ambassador Szögyény also present. Bethmann, not unlike Berchtold in Vienna and Sazonov in Petersburg, was distrusted by his country's war party. His policy of rapprochement with England was acceptable to German hawks, so long as it kept the British navy off Germany's back in case of war. But the very priority Bethmann put on relations with England suggested a certain softness, as did his periodic efforts to derail Tirpitz's naval building programme. Hawks referred to the chancellor and his neurotic sovereign as 'the two old women.'[14] Foreign Secretary Grey and his English colleagues shared this opinion of Bethmann, seeing him as a voice for peace in Berlin – a view that hardly commended Bethmann to the generals. Moltke could not stand him. The chancellor had been a cipher during the Balkan wars, allowing the kaiser's naturally feckless instincts to prevail. Wilhelm himself liked and trusted

Bethmann Hollweg, Germany's brooding chancellor. A pessimist at the best of times, he was in an even deeper funk than usual in summer 1914, following the death of his wife, Martha, in May. *Source: Bain News Service, Library of Congress.*

Bethmann, whom he had known since childhood, but at times Bethmann's opposition to armaments spending – especially on the navy, a pet cause of the kaiser's – annoyed even him.

A temperamental pessimist at the best of times, Bethmann was in an even deeper depression than usual that July. His beloved wife, Martha, whose natural sociability and good cheer had nicely balanced out the chancellor's solitary tendencies, had died of internal hemorrhaging on 11 May after a protracted illness. Martha's death dealt Bethmann a crushing blow. He was having trouble sleeping, was putting on weight, and was generally ill at ease. Bethmann had taken a long leave of absence at Hohenfinow after his wife's death to recover his morale and would have preferred to spend the entire summer there if he could. First the press hysteria over the Anglo-Russian naval talks, then the Sarajevo outrage, and now the Hoyos mission had interrupted what might have been a prolonged country convalescence. A new Balkan crisis was the last thing Bethmann wanted.

Arriving at the last minute to the audience with the kaiser on Sunday, Bethmann probably had been too exhausted from his trip to perceive quite how acute the situation was. Recovering his faculties after a good night's sleep, Bethmann was sharper on Monday afternoon when he received Count Hoyos, Ambassador Szögyény, and Zimmermann. With Szögyény present, Hoyos could not be as blunt as he had been with Zimmermann the previous day, but together the two of them were able to convince Bethmann that Austria was serious. Because Bethmann left no record of the conversation, we have to follow Szögyény's version of what the chancellor said – which, if accurate, suggested a dramatic shift in German policy. 'With regard to our relations towards Serbia,' the ambassador reported to the Ballplatz, 'the German government is of the opinion that we must judge for ourselves what is to be done. . . . Whatever we decide, we may reckon with certainty, that Germany will stand by our side as our ally.' As for Bethmann's own view, Szögyény informed Berchtold that 'the chancellor, like the kaiser, believes that immediate action on our part against Serbia offers the best and most decisive solution to our difficulties in the Balkans.' From the 'international standpoint' – that is, the prospect of a European war – Bethmann also 'considers the present moment as more favourable than some later time.'[15] Better now than later: this was what Moltke and Conrad had been saying for years. Now, for the first time, Bethmann was saying it too.

In this way first Kaiser Wilhelm II and then Chancellor Bethmann Hollweg furnished Austria with a blank check for immediate military action against Serbia. In doing so, they remained unaware that Tisza stood resolutely opposed to Berchtold over this very policy, which might put a serious damper on the 'immediate' part. Had they known of Tisza's opposition, the chancellor, at least, might have been more circumspect in offering such blanket support for an uncertain policy course to be pursued in Vienna, but it is hard to be certain about this. As far as we know, Bethmann's shift towards support for a dangerously aggressive Austrian line against Serbia was genuine, although tinged as always with his natural pessimism. 'Better now than later' did not necessarily mean that things *would* get better – only that, if the Central Powers waited any longer before confronting the Entente with a test of strength, things were sure to get worse.

As the kaiser prepared to leave on Monday morning, he summoned Germany's top-ranking active-duty army and navy officers. With Moltke and Tirpitz still absent, he spoke instead with Admiral Eduard von Capelle, the acting chief of Naval Staff, and General Hermann von Bertrab from the General Staff. He informed them of Austria's plans to take action against Serbia. To Bertrab, he emphasised that he did 'not think that Russia will intervene, particularly in view of the cause [e.g., a regicide], the Tsar . . . will hardly ever decide to do so. His Majesty therefore regards the affair as in the first instance a purely Balkan concern.' To Capelle, the kaiser said that 'Russia and France were not prepared for war.' Significantly, he did not mention England as something about which the German navy should be concerned. No preparatory military measures, the kaiser concluded, needed to be undertaken.[16]

At nine fifteen AM, Wilhelm II left Berlin en route for his Baltic cruise. Monday night, Bethmann returned to Hohenfinow. Both men, satisfied with their declaration of support, were content to let Austrian policy take its course.

6

War Council in Vienna (I)

TUESDAY, 7 JULY

EVEN AS AUSTRIA'S AMBASSADOR was winning over the kaiser in Potsdam on Sunday afternoon, 5 July, Conrad was making the case for war at Schönbrunn Palace. By now, the chief of Army Staff claimed, Emperor Franz Josef had come to agree with him that a war with Serbia was unavoidable. 'How, though, will you fight this war,' the emperor asked, 'if everyone takes up against us, especially Russia?' Conrad replied with a question of his own: 'Do we have Germany's backing?' Here the emperor hedged, saying he was not sure. He informed the chief of staff about the dispatch of the royal note to Berlin, saying that he expected a reply shortly. Conrad saw his opening. 'If the answer is that Germany stands by our side,' he asked his sovereign, 'do we then make war on Serbia?' 'In that case,' the emperor replied, 'yes.'[1]

Meanwhile, also on Sunday, Oskar Potiorek, the military governor of Bosnia-Herzegovina, produced the first real 'smoking gun' from the interrogation of Ilitch, confirming the involvement of Serbian army major Tankositch in training the three principal assassins (Princip, Chabrinovitch, and Grabezh) in Belgrade. This confession would make it harder for Tisza to make his case opposing war with Serbia, especially now that the emperor was – conditionally – on board.[2]

Monday afternoon, 6 July, Conrad visited the Ballplatz to report on his audience at Schönbrunn. Berchtold thus learned for the first time that Austria's emperor would support a war against Serbia, if it were backed by Germany. The foreign minister, in turn, informed Conrad that the kaiser had already promised this support on Sunday afternoon, although he was not yet sure about the chancellor, whom Wilhelm II had told Ambassador Szögyény he still needed to consult. Berchtold informed Conrad that he expected an answer from Chancellor Bethmann the next morning. Meanwhile, Berchtold dashed off a quick note to Tisza, informing the Hungarian minister-president that Kaiser Wilhelm II had promised that 'Austria could count on the full support of Germany in any eventual action . . . against Serbia.' Germany's sovereign, Berchtold further told Tisza in a slight exaggeration of what Wilhelm had actually said, had added that Austria 'must not let the current favourable moment go unused,' and that 'Russia was not ready for war.' Berchtold did not let Tisza know that the German chancellor had not yet been heard from.[3]

Monday evening, Berchtold received Szögyény's report of his promising conversation with Bethmann. Tuesday morning, 7 July, Hoyos returned to Vienna on the overnight train and set off for the Ballplatz at once. Having witnessed the German chancellor's verbal declaration of blanket support on Monday afternoon in person, he was able to confirm the veracity of the ambassador's report for Berchtold – and for Conrad, who had gone to the Ballplatz as soon as he heard the envoy was back from Berlin. Hoyos also passed on the gist of his Sunday conversation with Zimmermann. Berchtold, buoyed by Hoyos's encouraging report, assured Conrad that 'Germany will stand by our side unequivocally, even if our operations against Serbia will bring about the great war. Germany advises us to strike at once.'[4]

This was exactly what Conrad wanted to hear. Without wasting a minute, the chief of staff rushed over to military headquarters. His first telegram went off to Archduke Friedrich, who, following the death of Franz Ferdinand, was slated to take over as Austria-Hungary's commander in chief in wartime. Conrad told the archduke to cut off his planned trip to Hamburg and await urgent developments. Next, he called in Colonel Josef Metzger of the operational branch of the army to discuss the preliminary measures that would be undertaken in a mobilisation against Serbia. With Berchtold and Emperor Franz Josef I fully on board, the signs pointed clearly to war this time, and Conrad wanted the army to be ready.[5]

Berchtold, too, went right to work. Pursuant to Tisza's request, an emergency Ministerial Council was to convene at three PM Tuesday afternoon to discuss the German reply to the diplomatic notes. In part to make amends for having kept Tisza out of the loop over the weekend, Berchtold summoned him to the Ballplatz for a full debriefing on Hoyos's mission, along with the German ambassador, Tschirschky, and the Austrian minister-president, Count Stürgkh. Hoyos read out Szögyény's two telegrams from Berlin and then repeated what he had told Berchtold about his conversation with Zimmermann. He did not hide anything, laying out the whole scenario of a surprise attack on Belgrade and the partitioning of Serbian territory. Tisza was horrified: he insisted that Hoyos's remarks be regarded as solely the latter's 'personal opinion.' Berchtold, awkwardly, was forced to disavow his own chief of staff's stated views on the record. A surprise attack was thus ruled out, along with the goal of partitioning Serbia. Tisza had won his first point, and it was a big one.[6]

Nevertheless, the odds were stacked heavily against him that afternoon. Tisza was not merely outnumbered by the ever-expanding war party; he stood essentially alone. In addition to Berchtold, who chaired, and Hoyos, who kept the meeting protocol, the men arranged against Tisza included Biliński, the minister for Bosnia-Herzegovina, keen to avenge the act of terrorism committed on his watch; Count Stürgkh, who had been urging war all along; War Minister Krobatin, a hawk of Conrad's ilk; and Conrad himself, who, everyone knew, wanted to mobilise as soon as possible.

Berchtold began the meeting by bringing everyone up to speed on the Hoyos mission to Berlin. The 'discussions with Germany,' he informed those not already in the know, 'brought about a most satisfactory result, since Kaiser Wilhelm as well as Herr von Bethmann Hollweg solemnly promised the unconditional support of Germany in case of a warlike complication with Serbia.' The German government, he continued, was fully aware that 'an armed encounter with Serbia might lead to war with Russia.'* Despite the risks, however, Berchtold believed that showing weakness in the current crisis would be fatal. Only a 'timely settlement of accounts with Serbia,' he concluded, could halt the disintegration of the dual monarchy.

Tisza now took the floor. Having been sidelined by the dispatch of Hoyos to Berlin with instructions he had not approved, he had every right to cry foul. Berchtold's envoy had all but confessed that he was a loose cannon, letting slip unauthorised

---

* There is some debate as to whether Berchtold revised the meeting protocol here, having originally said that the Germans believed that 'war with Russia would be the *likely* consequence' of an Austrian war against Serbia. This statement may have reflected the views of Zimmermann, as passed on by Hoyos. It would not, however, have accurately represented the views of either the kaiser or Bethmann Hollweg, who both clearly told Austria's ambassador that they did not think Russia would intervene.

scenarios at the Wilhelmstrasse about an Austrian war of conquest against Serbia. Displaying an open mind, Tisza graciously
admitted that 'the facts revealed by the inquiry in Sarajevo'
showed that he had initially been 'mistaken' about Serbian
involvement in the assassination.[7] In light of the dramatic
developments 'of the past few days,' the Hungarian said that
he now saw 'the possibility of military action against Serbia
as less remote' than he had a week ago. Nevertheless, Tisza
expressed regret that Hoyos had spoken in Berlin of 'a surprise
attack on Serbia without preliminary diplomatic preparation.' If
Austria attacked without sufficient diplomatic cause, he warned,
she must 'count on the enmity of the entire Balkans, except for
Bulgaria' – and Bulgaria, prostrate following her comeuppance
in the Second Balkan War, could offer Austria little help on
the battlefield. An opportunistic Romania would in that case
surely come in alongside Serbia, and quite possibly Russia too.
Austria-Hungary would then have a three-front war on her
hands.

To prevent such a nightmare scenario, Tisza proposed a
careful diplomatic strategy to precede any war against Serbia.
First, the dual monarchy must draw up unequivocal demands
on Serbia; if she rejected them, an ultimatum could be prepared,
with a threat of armed intervention. If Belgrade then accepted
Austria's demands, Tisza promised, 'we would have won a
resounding diplomatic success and our prestige in the Balkans
would rise.' If, on the other hand, the Serbs said no, then Tisza
would agree to 'warlike action' – if, and only if, Austria's war
aims were limited to a 'reduction in the size of Serbian territory,' but not any kind of partition. Tisza warned that Russia
would regard the 'full annihilation of Serbia as a struggle of
life and death.' Moreover, as Hungary's minister-president,
Tisza declared himself resolutely opposed to any annexation
of Serbian territory by the dual monarchy, preferring that any
post-war border changes benefit smaller Balkan states instead.

On the question of 'now or later,' Tisza stated a clear preference for 'later,' on the grounds that the low French birthrate
meant that Germany's relative strength was increasing. Finally,
Tisza distanced himself from the Hoyos mission, declaring that
it was 'not for Germany to decide whether we ought to go to
war with Serbia or not.' The question of war or peace was, in
Tisza's view, up to Austria-Hungary alone – meaning, in effect,
it was up to him.

It was quite a performance. Having declared himself willing, for the first time, to consider taking 'warlike action' against
Serbia in retaliation for Sarajevo, Tisza then hedged his support for such action with so many diplomatic preconditions
that there was almost no way the foreign minister could satisfy
them. Still, Berchtold tried his best. While conceding Tisza's
point that Romania's attitude was important, he argued that
any intervention by Bucharest would depend on the attitude
of Bulgaria, however weakened she was by the Second Balkan
War, and that Romania did not want to fight a two-front war
any more than Austria did. Echoing the view of German military planners, Berchtold noted that 'the reduction of the growth
of the population of France was more than balanced by the
increasing number of inhabitants in Russia.' Coupled with
the Great Programme enacted in 1913, which would speed up
Russia's mobilisation, the demographic data suggested that the
Central Powers were growing relatively weaker, not stronger,
over time.

The others quickly rallied around Berchtold. Stürgkh took
up Tisza's point about not letting the Germans decide when
Austria went to war, arguing sensibly that the Germans had
not only offered 'unreserved loyalty' in Austria's time of need,
but had also insisted on immediate action. 'Count Tisza,' he
warned, 'should take into account that if we pursue a weak
and hesitating policy we may not be able to count on German
support in the future.' Krobatin said that even Tisza's best-case

scenario, that of a 'diplomatic triumph' against Serbia, would be 'worthless.' 'We have already lost two opportunities for solving the Serbian question,' the war minister reminded everyone, with an eye on the Balkan Wars. 'If we do this again,' he chided Tisza, 'this will be taken as proof of our weakness.' Diplomatic niceties, he argued, impressed no one – the Japanese had not declared war on Russia in 1904, nor had the Balkan aggressors of 1912 or 1913. From the military point of view, it was best to mobilise sooner, and secretly, so as to take full advantage of surprise, rather than telegraphing Austria's intentions to everyone.

All this was logical enough. By seeking to refute the Hungarian's talking points, however, the other ministers were, in effect, conceding the ground of debate. Slowly, at first imperceptibly, Tisza succeeded in moving things in his direction by sheer stubbornness. The others budged on essentials; he did not. At last, after two hours of discussion, the council declared itself 'prepared to accept [Tisza's] view according to which mobilisation will not take place until after concrete demands have been addressed to Serbia and, after being refused, an ultimatum has been sent.' As a sop to majority opinion, the council also stipulated that 'all present except [Tisza] hold the belief that a purely diplomatic success, even if it ended with a glaring humiliation of Serbia, would be worthless.' But then this hardly mattered, as Tisza had already won the point about preparing the ground diplomatically, through two stages, before mobilising.

The same dynamic was at work over the nature of the demands to be levied on Serbia. 'Count Tisza,' the transcript reads, 'remarked that he was anxious to meet the others halfway and was prepared to concede that the demands addressed to Serbia should be harsh.' But the Hungarian did not really meet the others halfway. 'All but Tisza,' we read on, agreed unanimously that 'such stringent demands must be addressed to Serbia, that will make a refusal almost certain.' To this, Tisza objected that the terms given to Belgrade could 'be very harsh, but not so [harsh] that everyone will clearly understand that we mean them to be rejected.' The key detail was this: Tisza would have to read and sign off on the text. Having been burned over the weekend by Berchtold and Hoyos, Tisza was not about to let it happen again.

Berchtold tried to put a brave face on things as he closed the fractious meeting. 'Although there are still differences of opinion between Count Tisza and the others,' he declared, 'we have still come closer together, as the propositions of the Hungarian minister-president will, in all probability . . . lead to a declaration of war with Serbia.'[8] If Berchtold played his cards right, that is, Hungary's minister-president might eventually support a war against Serbia that met his strict conditions. Meanwhile, Tisza had all but declared veto power over Berchtold's diplomacy, insisting that he approve the text of any diplomatic note sent to Serbia. Moreover, by insisting on the sending of a note in the first place – with the implication that its rejection, too, be followed not by war but by another ultimatum – Tisza had badly routed Conrad and Krobatin, who both wanted to mobilise as rapidly as possible. In this way the stubborn Magyar had ruined Austria's prospects of taking the kind of 'decisive action' the Germans had insisted on. The kaiser and his chancellor, by offering carte blanche support, were now wedded to Austria's new Balkan policy – no matter how dilatory and incompetent it might turn out to be.

7

Radio Silence

8–17 JULY

Tisza's tactical victory put Berchtold in a difficult position. The Hungarian had thrown sand in the gears of any swift action against Serbia; meanwhile, the Germans continued to press the need for speed. The kaiser and Bethmann were still on leave, but the policy they had outlined was clear enough. When German ambassador Tschirschky visited the Ballplatz on Wednesday, 8 July, to learn of the result of the previous day's conference, he told Berchtold that 'he could not emphasise enough, that Berlin expects the [dual] monarchy to take action against Serbia and that Germany would not understand if we let this opportunity pass without striking a blow.' That same day in Berlin, Austrian ambassador Szögyény visited the Wilhelmstrasse, where he was told by Undersecretary of State Zimmermann and 'other authoritative figures' that 'everyone here awaits with impatience our decision on what to do, for they have the view, that now is the right moment to move against Serbia – a moment this favourable will not easily repeat itself.' State Secretary Jagow, having at last returned from his Italian honeymoon, backed up the hawkish Zimmermann, telling Szögyény 'in a most emphatic manner' that 'the proposed action against Serbia must be taken without delay.'[1] Delay, of course, was exactly what Tisza was insisting on.

Some kind of delay was also all but mandated by the Austrian army's recent institution of summer 'harvest leave' for troops from rural areas. Conrad, the chief of staff, had signed off on the policy, although reluctantly, in order to appease powerful landowners in the dual monarchy. On Monday, 6 July, after rushing over to military headquarters from the Ballplatz, Conrad discovered, to his horror, that seven of his sixteen army corps had just been furloughed for harvest leave. Of these, five (the III, IV, V, XIII, and XIV) would return to active duty on 19 July, with the final two (VI and VII) on leave until 25 July. Unless Conrad wanted to telegraph Austria's warlike intentions to Europe, he could not cancel harvest leave early. Therefore the army, too, would require two weeks to pass before mobilisation was possible. Two weeks was far too slow for the Germans, but it might be enough to satisfy Tisza's conditions.[2]

In Conrad's first meeting with Berchtold after the Tuesday war council, at six PM on Wednesday, 8 July, the chief of staff insisted firmly that an ultimatum to Serbia be dispatched with a 24- or 48-hour time limit, so as not to give the Serbs time to mobilise while Austria waited for the expected refusal, which would be the signal for war. In view of the harvest leave issue – and the need to convert Tisza – both men agreed that the ultimatum could not be dispatched until 22 July at the earliest. It would be up to the foreign minister to win over Tisza in time to send a note to Belgrade by that date. Meanwhile, Berchtold suggested that Conrad and War Minister Krobatin each take vacation leave from Vienna, 'to leave the impression that nothing was going on.' The chief of staff did as he was told, heading off Wednesday night to his estate, the Klammschlössel at Innichen, where he would stay for two weeks.[3]

Berchtold now did everything he could to break Tisza's resistance. He told Tschirschky on Wednesday afternoon that the Hungarian was 'the one slowing things down,' so that the Germans would know he himself was doing all he could to move quickly. He then sent Tisza, who had returned to Budapest, a note outlining Tschirschky's remarks on how keen Berlin was on speed, concluding from them that 'the Germans would regard any reconciliation with Serbia on our part as a sign of weakness,' which would call into question Austria's status as an ally. Berchtold informed Tisza that he was en route for an audience with His Majesty Franz Josef I at Bad Ischl, and 'begged' the Hungarian to telegraph the palace with his response to the German ambassador's remarks.[4]

Tisza did not take the bait. He had already composed a memorandum for the emperor outlining conclusions from Tuesday's conference, and he was not about to revise them. 'If war were to result after all,' he argued, 'it must be demonstrated before the eyes of all the world that we stand on a basis of legitimate self-defence.' Absent thorough diplomatic preparation – meaning a two-step ultimatum process – before a declaration of war on Serbia, he warned the Habsburg sovereign, Romania, Russia, and possibly Italy would take up arms against Austria-Hungary – a four-front war! Because of these risks, he concluded, 'Serbia should be given the opportunity to avoid war by means of a severe diplomatic defeat.'[5]

Since Tisza refused to budge, Berchtold would have to tell his sovereign, again, that there was no agreement yet on what to do. He arrived at Bad Ischl at seven AM on Thursday morning, 9 July, and met Franz Josef two hours later. Together they read over Tisza's memorandum. Although it presented, on the surface, a roadblock to immediate action, they gradually began to see some room for manoeuvre. Tisza was obviously expecting the Ballplatz to make severe demands on Serbia, even if he wanted them to be less obviously harsh than the other ministers would have preferred. Why could Berchtold not simply go ahead and draw up an ultimatum? It would take time to win

Tisza's approval, but so long as he took Conrad's advice and gave a 'strict time limit' of 48 hours or less, it would increase the chances of the desired rejection by Serbia. While Berchtold and Franz Josef understood the need to keep Tisza on board, they were now agreed on the need to levy 'concrete demands on Serbia,' as Berchtold told the German ambassador the next day. More fundamentally, the emperor decided that the time had come for a reckoning with Serbia, saying that 'there was no going back.'[6]

Based on this informal verbal mandate from the emperor, Berchtold ordered his staff to begin preparing an ultimatum to Serbia. On Friday, 10 July, Tschirschky reported to Berlin, with evident satisfaction, that the Austrians were finally getting their act together. True, Berchtold had admitted to him that Tisza wanted to water down the terms offered Serbia – to, as Tschirschky put it contemptuously, 'proceed *gentleman-like*' (he used the English phrase for emphasis). Tisza's opposition notwithstanding, the facts were these: Berchtold was writing up an ultimatum to Belgrade with a 'strict time limit, at most 48 hours.' Austria's foreign minister, along with Emperor Franz Josef I and everyone in the government except for Tisza, hoped that the terms would be rejected. For good measure, Tschirschky also reported to Berlin that Krobatin and Conrad were taking vacation leave so as to 'guard against any impression of alarm.'[7]

That evening, a terrible scene transpired in Belgrade. Baron Giesl von Gieslingen, Austria's minister to Serbia, had returned to town on Friday after a long sojourn in Vienna. The absence of the ranking Habsburg diplomat in early July had allowed Russia's minister to Belgrade, Nikolai Hartwig, a useful excuse not to condole with the Austrians. It was now nearly two weeks since the Sarajevo outrage, however, and even Hartwig's stubbornness had its limits. He therefore visited the Austrian legation to clear the air. Arriving at 9 PM, Hartwig expressed to Giesl his 'personal and sincere condolences for the atrocious outrage.' He then denied having held a bridge party the evening of the murders and claimed it was untrue that he had refused to fly the flag at half-mast during the archduke's memorial service. Anxious to believe in the Russian's good intentions, Giesl accepted these assertions. A reconciliation of sorts was thus affected between Austria and Russia, but it was not of long duration. At 9:20 PM, Hartwig collapsed of a heart attack in the Austrian legation. Within minutes he was dead.

Hartwig's sudden and shocking demise turned a delicate moment in high-stakes diplomacy into a crime scene. Seeking to deflect suspicion that the Russian had died of unnatural causes, Giesl sent a carriage to pick up Hartwig's daughter Ludmilla, his nearest of kin. When she arrived in the legation to see the body, however, Ludmilla made it clear that she already suspected foul play. Her manner, Giesl reported to Vienna, 'was cold and hostile.' Hartwig's daughter inspected the room 'thoroughly,' 'rummaging around in some large Japanese vases,' and taking particular interest in a bottle of cologne that she suspected might have contained poison. After composing herself, Ludmilla asked if Hartwig had eaten or drunk anything from the legation kitchen. Giesl assured her that he had not – the Russian had arrived after dinner and died scarcely 20 minutes after his arrival. Hartwig had, however, smoked two cigarettes. The Austrian offered the butts to Ludmilla, who 'carefully put them in her purse,' to guard as evidence. Shortly after she left, a Serbian policeman showed up to investigate, only for Giesl to turn him away on the grounds of extraterritorial diplomatic immunity. While Giesl was perfectly within his rights to do so, his denial of access to local police led most Serbs to believe the Austrians were hiding something.[8]

The Serbian press had a field day with the story. All weekend, lurid stories circulated about the alleged Austrian murder of Hartwig. So widespread was belief in Giesl's guilt that Giesl heard himself accused of the crime while visiting (incognito, luckily) a local barber. The story had, by this point, been embellished to the point where the Austrian was not simply a murderer but a kind of mass executioner. One Serb, Giesl reported, calmly told another that 'Giesl has brought an electric chair from Vienna which causes the immediate death of anyone who sits down on it and leaves not the slightest trace.'[9]

Hartwig, already a hero to Serbian nationalists for his support during the Balkan Wars, was now celebrated as a martyr against Austrian tyranny. He was given a 'magnificent' funeral worthy of a head of state. A prominent Belgrade street was named after him, and sculptors began work on a monument in his honour to be erected in the centre of town. On Sunday, 12 July, anti-Austrian demonstrations were organised all over Belgrade to capitalise on popular rage over Hartwig's death. On top of the celebration of the murder of Franz Ferdinand that took place at Kossove Polje on Vidov Dan, and the unfounded murder accusations levelled at Giesl in the Serbian press, the weekend hullabaloo over Hartwig seemed deliberately calculated to insult Austrian pride. While Paris and London continued to slumber on, oblivious to the unfolding drama in the Balkans, Belgrade already felt like a city at war.

Any sympathy the Austrians might have felt for Russia or Russians following Hartwig's death dissipated quickly. Sunday afternoon, the Italian chargé d'affaires, called in by Giesl to clear up the rumours about Hartwig's behaviour, confirmed that the story about the Russian flag not being lowered during the funeral requiem was true. So, too, was the story about the bridge party. So Hartwig had lied to Giesl. The late Russian's 'sincere condolences for the atrocious outrage' were phony after all.[10]

The news from Berlin was more positive. That Sunday, Ambassador Szögyény reiterated that the Germans wanted Austria to move quickly against Serbia. This time, though, he was more explicit, saying that 'both H. M. Kaiser Wilhelm and all other responsible personages' wanted Austria to 'make a clean sweep of the revolutionary conspirators' nest [in Serbia] once and for all.' The Germans wanted Vienna to realise that 'it is by no means certain that . . . Russia would resort to arms' in support of Serbia, and, more significantly, that 'the German government further believes it has sure indications that England at the present moment would not join in a war over a Balkan country, even should this lead to a passage of arms with Russia and eventually even with France.'[11] This was more than a blank check: the Germans were all but demanding that Austria attack Serbia immediately.

Monday brought more welcome news for the war party in Vienna. On Friday, the chief counsel at the Ballplatz, Dr Friedrich Wiesner, had been sent to Belgrade to prepare a legal dossier on the crime. On Monday, 13 July, he filed his initial report. While Wiesner all but ruled out actual Serbian *government* complicity in plotting the crime, he did declare it 'beyond reasonable doubt' that the plot had been hatched in Belgrade with the assistance of Major Tankositch, who had provided the assassins with 'bombs, Brownings, ammunition, and cyanide of potassium' to swallow after their deed. It was also clear that 'Princip, Chabrinovitch, and Grabezh [had been] secretly smuggled across the frontier by Serbian officials.' While Wiesner's report did not go far beyond what Potiorek had already discovered, his careful, lawyerly prose reassured Berchtold that a proper dossier outlining Serbian guilt would be ready in time to make Austria's case for war.[12]

On the basis of Szögyény's latest telegram, the weekend outbreak of Serbian chauvinism in Belgrade, and the Wiesner report, Berchtold called a meeting with Tisza, believing he had the stubborn Hungarian cornered at last. As he told Tschirschky on Monday afternoon, 13 July, he 'hoped to agree with Tisza tomorrow on the text of a note to be delivered to Serbia.' Assuming success, Berchtold would then travel to Bad Ischl on Wednesday, 15 July, to present the note to the emperor for approval. A 48-hour ultimatum could then be delivered to Belgrade that evening, a week ahead of the original plan for 22 July (Berchtold, keen to impress the German ambassador, seems to have forgotten about the harvest leave issue).[13] If everything came off as planned, Berchtold could at last shed his reputation for dithering indecisiveness. How pleased the Germans would be!

There was another important reason why Berchtold would have liked for the ultimatum to go out that week (as opposed to the following one, as mandated by the harvest leave timetable). Wednesday, 15 July, was the day French president Poincaré would embark at sea aboard the *France*, en route for his summit with Tsar Nicholas II in St Petersburg. While Berchtold had succeeded in keeping the French and the Russians in the dark until now about Austrian plans, the dispatch of an Austrian ultimatum to Belgrade would at once precipitate a diplomatic crisis. The last thing he wanted was for this to happen while France's president was in Petersburg; Poincaré and the tsar could then coordinate a military response to Austria's action in the heat of the moment, quite possibly while toasting each other's health at an official banquet. If, by contrast, Berchtold could somehow send off the ultimatum before Poincaré's departure, the president might call off the trip, which would make it far more difficult for him to coordinate policy with the Russians. A steamer journey from France's Channel coast to the Russian capital usually took about five days, which would put Poincaré in Petersburg on Monday, 20 July. So Berchtold could also win a trick if he sent the ultimatum off on Thursday or Friday, which would ensure that the 48-hour window for Serbia's answer would be blanketed with the 'radio silence' of a long sea voyage. France's president could still, in this case, coordinate a response with the Russians after his arrival in Petersburg on Monday, 20 July, but if Austria (again, disregarding the harvest leave problem) began mobilising following

121

Serbia's rejection of the ultimatum on Saturday or Sunday, it would be too late to make much difference to the outcome of the war. The Germans could then have their fait accompli.

W HEN TISZA RETURNED to Vienna on Tuesday, 14 July, he knew that Berchtold was expecting a decision. His resistance worn down by the constant pressure coming at him from all sides, Tisza began at last to draw down his guard. He conceded that the anti-Austrian attacks of the Serbian press had become intolerable. Reluctantly, Tisza said that each day since the crisis had begun unfolding had 'strengthened him in the conviction that [Austria-Hungary] must come to a bold resolve to demonstrate its vitality and put an end to the unendurable state of affairs in the southeast' (a euphemism for Serbia). Tisza had been particularly impressed by 'the unconditional manner in which Germany has ranged herself at the side of the [dual] monarchy.' While it 'had not been easy to take the decision of advising war,' he was now 'convinced of its necessity.'[14] Berchtold appeared to have won. Tisza had, however, exacted a heavy price for his conversion. More than two weeks had passed since the Sarajevo outrage, two weeks during which Austria had not begun mobilising her army as Conrad wished to (although doing so would have been possible only in the first week, before harvest leave began), nor even prepared an ultimatum to serve as a casus belli against Serbia. The passage of time had helped to deflect international scrutiny away from Vienna, as most of Europe had begun to forget about the Balkan crisis. But it also helped ensure that, when this scrutiny finally came, the Austrians would appear to be acting out of cool, cynical calculation, rather than in the first flush of rage following the assassination of the Habsburg heir. Conrad's plan to mobilise on 1 July (before the harvest furlough was underway), for all its bluntness, would have been diplomatically sound: while some statesmen would have been shocked, no one could have doubted Austrian sincerity or resolve. Now, as a result of Tisza's delaying tactics, the Austrians were forced to operate in the shadows, camouflaging their intention to wage war on Serbia inside an insincere diplomatic note to Belgrade. Berchtold had conceded this when he told the German ambassador that he wished to send off the ultimatum while France's president was at sea – as if he were afraid the ultimatum would not stand the light of day. This was the sort of dishonest, baldly cynical diplomacy that Tisza's stubbornness had reduced Berchtold to.

In one final gesture of defiance, Tisza made even this plan impossible. Staying true to his vow at the 7 July council that he would have to approve the text of any note sent to Serbia, Tisza informed Berchtold that the ultimatum must pass muster at a full Ministerial Council, which could not convene before Sunday. The ultimatum could therefore be dispatched, at the earliest, on the evening of 19 July – just hours before Poincaré arrived in Petersburg. There was no way that Berchtold was going to allow the French president and the Russian tsar to learn of Austria's ultimatum while 'swearing brotherhood under the influence of champagne.' As he put it drily to Tschirschky, 'it would be good if the toasts were all over before the note is delivered.'[15] The new plan was thus to wait until the night the French delegation would leave Petersburg, which Berchtold expected (incorrectly) to be Saturday, 25 July – nearly a month after Sarajevo and three days after the date that he and Conrad had agreed to, owing to the harvest leave issue.

Despite the latest delay occasioned by Tisza, the new plan had much to recommend it. 25 July was a bit later than Conrad wanted, but by that date even the last two furloughed army corps, the VI and VII, would be back on duty. Moreover, 'radio silence,' as Berchtold realised once he had thought it over, would work better on the return than on the outward voyage. By waiting until Poincaré left before showing its hand, Austria could deny France and Russia any chance to coordinate during the summit. Poincaré, by well-deserved reputation the most belligerent statesman in either Paris or Petersburg, would miss his chance to put steel into Sazonov and the tsar when they learned of the Serbian ultimatum. Austria would then lay down her fait accompli when Poincaré was at sea, unable to react. It was a cynical plan – but also brilliant.

Brilliant but not foolproof. If the French or the Russians got wind of the Austrian ultimatum early, they could coordinate a response to it over champagne toasts – with the added, enraging motivation that Berchtold had tried to snooker them. The ultimatum would therefore have to be handled in the strictest possible secrecy (aside from keeping the German ambassador more or less in the loop): any leak picked up by a hostile power could be fatal. With London engulfed in the Irish crisis and Paris consumed by the Caillaux affair, it would not be that difficult to keep the English and the French off the scent. The Russians, of course, might be more suspicious. Still, the Austrian embassy in Petersburg was able to inform the Ballplatz on Tuesday, 14 July, that Sazonov had left the capital for his country estate near Grodno. Russia's foreign minister would not return to his office until Sunday – the very day the Ministerial Council would approve the final text of the ultimatum. If Berchtold could keep things under wraps until then, the 'radio silence' plan might succeed. It was a big if.

8

Enter Sazonov

SATURDAY, 18 JULY

A USTRIAN EFFORTS TO KEEP THE ULTIMATUM secret were thorough. Sending Chief of Staff Conrad and War Minister Krobatin out of town on 'vacation leave' was a clever smokescreen, which seems to have taken in even the Russian ambassador, Nikolai Shebeko, who reported this without evident suspicion in a 16 July dispatch to Foreign Minister Sazonov.[1] But for a 24-hour visit to Vienna for the Ministerial Council on Sunday, 19 July, the über-belligerent Conrad remained at Innichen, a south Tyrolean resort town near the Italian border, from Tuesday, 14 July, until Wednesday, 22 July, which had the important side benefit of preventing him from talking to anyone. Harvest leave continued for enlisted men, and vacationing officers, too, remained undisturbed.

Meanwhile, Berchtold instructed his diplomats to take a conciliatory tone in their discussions with representatives of foreign powers, while avoiding all mention of the Sarajevo outrage in his own utterances. Perhaps not entirely trusting himself, Berchtold called off his usual weekly reception for foreign ambassadors, meeting with them only privately and on request. Luckily, the Austrian Reichsrat was out of session in July, which meant that the foreign minister would not have to answer any awkward questions there. The Hungarian Diet was meeting in Budapest, but in that house it was Tisza who had to run the gauntlet. 'The government,' Hungary's minister-president replied in the Diet to a barrage of questions on the Balkan crisis, 'is fully conscious of all the weighty interests in favour of the maintenance of peace . . . [and] is not of the opinion that the clearing up of the [Serbian] question will necessarily involve warlike complications.' Tisza conceded that 'every state . . . must be in a position to carry on war as an *ultima ratio*,' but then declared cryptically that he would not 'indulge in any prophecies' as to whether war with Serbia was imminent.[2] Berchtold could not have said it better himself – in fact, he probably could not have said this at all. Tisza, simply by being his usual cautious, war-wary self, was able to dispel a good deal of suspicion about Vienna's intentions regarding Serbia.

Still, the general air of frenzied activity at the Ballplatz was hard for Berchtold to hide, no matter how hard he tried. Diplomatic professionals across Europe had been expecting some kind of response from the dual monarchy ever since the Sarajevo outrage. Spies and informants were crawling over Vienna, hoping to tease out the truth about what Berchtold was up to. Ordinary journalists, too, were chasing down every source they could find to pick up the slightest hint about Austrian intentions. A single leak, from any source, that reached the ears of a hostile ambassador might ruin Berchtold's plans by allowing France and Russia to coordinate a response to the forthcoming ultimatum during the Petersburg summit.

In the end, it was Berchtold himself who slipped. As early as Monday, 13 July, the foreign minister had invited an old friend, Count Heinrich von Lützow, to sit in on his discussions with German ambassador Tschirschky and Count Johann Forgách, chief of section in the Ballplatz. Lützow, now 62 years old, had served as Austro-Hungarian ambassador to

Italy from 1904 to 1910, but had thereafter been sent into early retirement. Because he was senior to Berchtold, the foreign minister treated the retired Lützow as a kind of 'wise man' elder, outside the chain of command in the Foreign Ministry, who could offer him blunt advice without worrying about upsetting the chief. During the Monday audience, Lützow had warned Berchtold that the idea of 'localising' a conflict with Serbia was a 'fantasy.'[3]

So concerned was Lützow by what he had heard of Berchtold's plans that he resolved to tell someone about it. The old diplomat left Vienna on Tuesday for his country estate, where, it happened, one of his closest neighbours was Britain's ambassador to Vienna, Sir Maurice de Bunsen, with whom Lützow often dined. Over luncheon on Wednesday, 15 July, Lützow recounted for his British friend the conversation he had just had with Berchtold regarding the Balkan crisis. Lützow, de Bunsen recalled, 'put on a serious face and wondered if I knew how grave the situation was.' The dual monarchy, Lützow warned de Bunsen, 'was not going to stand Serbian insolence any longer. . . . A note was being drawn up and would be completed when the Sarajevo enquiry was finished. . . . No futile discussion would be tolerated. If Serbia did not at once cave in, force would be used to compel her.'[4]

Britain's ambassador wasted no time returning to Vienna to share this stunning coup with London. On Thursday, 16 July, de Bunsen reported to Foreign Secretary Sir Edward Grey that 'a kind of indictment is being prepared against the Serbian Government for alleged complicity in the conspiracy which led to the assassination of the Archduke.' De Bunsen's source, he informed Grey, was 'language held by the Austrian Minister for Foreign Affairs to a friend of mine.' This 'friend,' Grey learned, had further informed de Bunsen that 'the Serbian Government will be required to adopt certain definite measures in restraint of nationalist and anarchist propaganda, and that Austro-Hungarian Government are in no mood to parley with Serbia, but will insist on immediate compliance, failing which force will be used. Germany is said to be in complete agreement with this procedure.'[5] De Bunsen's 'friend,' he confessed the next day, was Lützow.

Astonishingly, Berchtold does not seem to have told his adviser to keep his mouth shut when speaking with de Bunsen. As far as we can glean from Lützow's memoirs, his own intention was to frustrate Berchtold's designs by warning the British about what was brewing, in the hope that they might act to restrain Serbia, France, and Russia. If so, then he had committed an act of gross insubordination – except for the fact that, as a retired diplomat, he was not bound by the foreign minister's instructions. As Berchtold's senior, moreover, Lützow may not have felt the need to hew to a policy he clearly disagreed with. Whatever the truth about Lützow's motivations, it does not speak well of Berchtold's discipline that he spoke so freely with a retired diplomat, however senior, without expressly forbidding him from betraying his confidence to foreigners.

De Bunsen sought out Berchtold on Friday to enquire further. Seemingly unaware that his colleague had just spilled the beans, the foreign minister put on an impressive display of insouciance. Berchtold had been utterly 'charming,' de Bunsen reported happily to London. He promised to visit de Bunsen's estate in the country shortly and invited the Briton to visit his own estate at Buchlau. Berchtold 'never mentioned general politics or the Serbians.' Mostly, the Austrian seemed exercised by an upcoming horse race he had thoroughbreds running in. Showing characteristic British reserve, de Bunsen did not interrupt this amiable discussion to demand clarification on Lützow's revelations about Austrian plans to send an ultimatum to Serbia. Nor did Grey, after receiving de Bunsen's explosive dispatch from Vienna, press his ambassador for more information on the matter. In a follow-up dispatch sent on Saturday, 18 July, de Bunsen all but endorsed Berchtold's protestations of innocence, reporting that the Italian ambassador had told him that he 'does not believe that unreasonable demands will be made on Serbia' because neither the timid Berchtold nor the cautious Emperor Franz Josef 'would sanction such an unwise proceeding.' De Bunsen then dropped the matter, at least in his correspondence with London.* British incuriosity, it appeared, had saved Austria's foreign minister from the consequences of Lützow's undisciplined tongue.[6]

WITH THE RUSSIANS, Berchtold would not be so lucky. Foreign Minister Sazonov was in the Russian countryside, incommunicado, until Saturday, but during his absence his ambassador to Vienna, Nikolai Shebeko, would display much greater curiosity – and suspicion – than did his British counterpart. While Shebeko, as a 'hostile' ambassador, was not favoured with the confidence of Lützow, much less Berchtold's, he was favoured with that of the British ambassador, who passed on the gist of Lützow's story to the Russian. As Shebeko later recalled, on Thursday afternoon, 16 July, he learned from de Bunsen that 'there had been a discussion' earlier that week at the Ballplatz, between Berchtold and Forgách, 'on the terms of a note which, when the inquiry would have terminated, the Austrian Government had decided to present to the Serbian Government. This note was drafted in extremely

---

* Curiously, on the evening of Saturday, 18 July, shortly after the British ambassador had parroted Berchtold's confession of innocence without objection, de Bunsen's wife recorded in her diary: 'A strong note with ultimatum Lützow told M[aurice de Bunsen] is to be sent in the next week probably not acceptable to Serbia.'

stiff terms and contained demands unacceptable to any independent State.'[7] Although he was not able to confirm this independently, Shebeko was confident enough of his source to inform the Russian Foreign Ministry that 'information reaches me that the Austro-Hungarian government at the conclusion of its inquiry intends to make certain demands on Belgrade, claiming that there is a connection between the question of the Sarajevo outrage and the pan-Serb agitation within the confines of the monarchy.' Unlike his British counterpart, Shebeko was in no doubt as to the gravity of the moment. He asked Sazonov urgently to inform 'the Vienna cabinet' as to 'how Russia would react to the fact of Austria's presenting demands to Serbia such as would be unacceptable to the dignity of that state.' The Habsburg ambassador to Russia, the Hungarian Count Friedrich Szapáry, Shebeko further informed Sazonov, had left Vienna the previous evening (Wednesday, 15 July), and would arrive in Petersburg shortly.[8]

Britain's ambassador had first picked up the hint of Austrian intentions from Lützow, but it was the Russians who would make use of the information. Russian cryptographers had, over the past several years, broken many of Austria's diplomatic codes. While Berchtold had been careful to forbid the sending of cables to Petersburg mentioning the ultimatum itself, he had been less careful regarding its timing. On Tuesday, 14 July, Berchtold had wired directly to the Austro-Hungarian embassy in Petersburg, demanding to know when the French delegation would leave town following Poincaré's summit with the tsar. This suspicious telegram had been decoded by Russian cryptographers by Tuesday evening. Knowing now what to look for, the Russians then intercepted two more reply telegrams on Thursday and Friday, 16–17 July, which informed Berchtold that Poincaré would embark at sea on his return voyage to France on the evening of Thursday, 23 July.[9] From Shebeko (via de Bunsen and Lützow) the Russian Foreign Ministry was able to learn – roughly at least – what Berchtold intended to do. From their own cryptographers, the Russians learned exactly when he planned to do it. When Sazonov returned from the country, he would have a great deal to catch up on.

The man working the wires in Sazonov's absence was his chief of staff, Baron Moritz Schilling. Equivalent in rank and function to Zimmermann in Berlin and Hoyos in Vienna, Schilling would play a role no less important than they in the unfolding diplomatic drama. Even before reading Shebeko's ominous Thursday dispatch from Vienna, Schilling had begun to have his own suspicions about Austrian intentions based on a conversation he had that very night with the Italian ambassador to Russia, Marquis Carl Carlotti di Riparbella. Carlotti had told Schilling that 'it was his impression that Austria was capable of taking an irrevocable step with regard to Serbia based on the belief that, although Russia would make a verbal protest, she would not adopt forcible measures for the protection of Serbia.' Schilling himself felt that Russia was 'firmly determined not to permit any weakening or humiliation of Serbia,' but he thought it best if Italy, as an ally (nominally, at least) of Austria-Hungary, or better still Germany, put this warning to Vienna on Russia's behalf. If the Russians themselves 'made such a declaration in Vienna,' Schilling explained to Carlotti, 'it would perhaps be regarded as an ultimatum, and so render the situation more acute.' Then, too, Schilling, as a mere chief of staff, was not authorised to stipulate as to Russian policy. He would, however, immediately upon his return to town, inform Russia's foreign minister of Carlotti's warning.[10]

On Friday, 17 July, Schilling learned of Shebeko's Thursday dispatch and of the decoded messages to and from Vienna regarding the timing of Poincaré's departure from Petersburg. As if to crystallise Schilling's worst suspicions about Austrian intentions, Ambassador Szapáry, fresh in from Vienna, called at Chorister's Bridge and 'expressed a desire to see Sazonov as soon as possible.' Szapáry did not say why he urgently needed to see Russia's foreign minister, but it was not hard for Schilling to guess. Sazonov, Schilling informed the Austrian ambassador, was still at his country estate near Grodno, although he was expected back early next morning. Schilling penciled Szapáry in for an eleven AM meeting at Chorister's Bridge.[11]

Sazonov returned to Petersburg on schedule Saturday morning. To get him up to speed on the latest developments before his audience with Szapáry, Schilling met him right at the train station. En route to the Foreign Ministry, Sazonov's chief of staff read out for him the contents of the Thursday dispatch from his ambassador in Vienna. It was not hard to draw the connection between Shebeko's warning that Austria was about to 'present demands to Serbia such as would be unacceptable to the dignity of that state' with Szapáry's urgent demand for an audience with him. After all, Shebeko's telegram linked the two implicitly by asking Sazonov urgently to inform Vienna 'how Russia would react,' before informing Sazonov that Szapáry was on his way to Petersburg. Schilling also recounted for his boss the gist of his conversation with Carlotti, which seemed to confirm the worst. Sazonov, Schilling wrote later that day in a diary he kept for the Foreign Ministry, 'was troubled by this information, and agreed with Baron Schilling as to the necessity of forewarning Austria regarding the determination of Russia on no account to permit any attempts against the independence of Serbia.' Russia's foreign minister, Schilling continued, 'formed the resolve to express himself in the most decided manner to [Szapáry] regarding this matter.'[12]

When Sazonov received the Austro-Hungarian ambassador at eleven AM, however, he seemed to backtrack on his vow to stand firm. The Russian, Szapáry reported to Vienna, 'carefully avoided raising the subject of Austria's relations with Serbia.' Szapáry himself was under strict orders from Berchtold not to give any hint of the upcoming ultimatum, and so Sazonov's reticence to bring it up naturally put a damper on the conversation. Seeking to draw the Russian out, Szapáry tried gamely to invoke the 'monarchical principle.' While Sazonov 'made no effort to contradict' him, Szapáry was not able to lure the Russian into any belated expression of sympathy for the Sarajevo outrage. Instead, Sazonov changed the subject, warning Szapáry that 'the latest news from Vienna had disquieted him,' without spelling out what news he was talking about. Gingerly, Sazonov tried to draw Szapáry out by declaring that 'Vienna would never be able to establish proof of Serbian tolerance for machinations,' such as those that produced the Sarajevo incident. To this, Szapáry replied carefully that, while the final results of the Austrian investigation were not yet in, 'every government must be held responsible, to a certain degree, for acts emanating from its territory.' Knowing that Sazonov had opposed this very proposition in previous conversations with Czernin, the Austrian legation secretary, Szapáry tried to corner him into a firm declaration of policy, but the Russian simply changed the subject again.

Overall, Szapáry reported to Vienna, Russia's foreign minister 'gave no impression' of having settled on a firm policy. Meanwhile, Sazonov himself, shortly after the meeting, told Schilling that Szapáry had been 'as docile as a lamb.'[13] Circling each other like wary adversaries careful not to expose their flanks, the two diplomats had somehow made it through the awkward encounter without once losing their tempers – and without, it seemed, revealing a thing.

Because Szapáry, not Schilling or Sazonov, had called for the Saturday meeting, the whole thing was clearly the Austrians' idea. The intention is not hard to fathom: Berchtold wished to find out whether the Russians knew what he was up to. A corollary motive was probably for Berchtold to put Sazonov off his guard, lulling the Russian to sleep so as to snuff out any possibility that he might get wind of the Serbian ultimatum before, or worse still during, the summit with French president Poincaré, which would begin on Monday. In both aims, Ambassador Szapáry had apparently succeeded. Sazonov had not confronted the ambassador with any serious allegation about Austrian intentions, nor raised his voice, nor indeed done anything to suggest that he had the faintest clue of what Berchtold was up to. Sazonov's 'docile as a lamb' remark, although unknown to the Austrians, suggested that Berchtold's plan had worked perfectly.

All was not, however, quite what it seemed to be in this dance of diplomatic misdirection. Sazonov was being as cagey as Szapáry. Just as Berchtold wanted to be sure the Russians did not know what he was up to, so did the latter not want the Austrians to know that they were cottoning to the game. Later Saturday afternoon, Sazonov spoke more frankly to Britain's ambassador, Sir George Buchanan, of the 'great uneasiness which Austria's attitude towards Serbia was causing him.' When the British ambassador asked him to clarify what he meant, Sazonov responded that 'anything in the shape of an Austrian ultimatum to Belgrade could not leave Russia indifferent, and she might be forced to take some precautionary military measure.'[14] Within eight hours of his return to Petersburg from holiday, and little more than 24 hours before he would host President Poincaré and Premier Viviani at a high-level summit of the Franco-Russian alliance, Russia's foreign minister was already contemplating a military response to the expected Austrian ultimatum to Serbia.

Sunday morning, Sazonov went to Peterhof Palace to debrief the tsar on the unfolding crisis. Significantly, he had

Nicholas II read over the text of Shebeko's 16 July telegram, alerting Russia's sovereign that some kind of ultimatum to Belgrade was being worked up in Vienna. Following his conversation with Sazonov, the tsar scribbled in the margins of Shebeko's telegram: 'In my opinion a State should not present any sort of demands to another, unless, of course, it is bent on war.'[15] That very morning, Berchtold was convening the Ministerial Council in Vienna to draw up the terms of Austria's ultimatum to Serbia.

9

War Council
in Vienna (II)

SUNDAY, 19 JULY

AFTER TISZA CONVERTED to the war party on Tuesday, Austria's foreign minister had been forced to wait five agonising days before his plan could be put into motion. Keeping a secret of this magnitude was not easy for a sociable man like Berchtold, who had never been known for message discipline. He remained unaware that Lützow, an old friend, had betrayed him to the British ambassador (and via him, to the Russians). As far as Berchtold knew as he awoke on Sunday morning, Austria had kept the other powers entirely in the dark – even the Germans, who had been told nothing more since Berchtold had informed Ambassador Tschirschky of Tisza's conversion on Tuesday, 14 July. So long as Tisza stayed true to his word, on Sunday the Ministerial Council could finally draft the text of a 48-hour ultimatum to Serbia, behind which the imperial government would stand united. The note could then be dispatched to the Austrian legation in Belgrade anytime in the next four days, so long as it was under seal, with strict instructions not to be opened until Thursday, 23 July.

Despite the appearance of success so far, Berchtold was taking no chances on Sunday. To keep the gathering secret from foreign ambassadors, the foreign minister had ordered elaborate security measures. With the Hungarian Diet still in session in Budapest, Berchtold invented a cover story to explain Tisza's presence in Vienna. The press was told that the Hungarian minister-president had been tasked by the Diet with getting more information on the latest Balkan developments – not an implausible scenario. Chief of Staff Conrad, on vacation in the South Tyrol, had returned late Saturday evening in order, he told anyone who asked, to visit a son who was ill and bedridden. The other ministers – Biliński, Krobatin, Stürgkh – were all based in Vienna, and so no explanation of their being in town was needed. To further allay suspicions, the meeting was held at Berchtold's private residence in Vienna, the delightfully named Strudelhof, rather than at the Ballplatz. In true cloak-and-dagger style, everyone arrived in unmarked cars so as not to tip off the neighbours.[1]

At ten AM, the top-secret war council began in the House of Strudel. Berchtold, chairing, opened the session by laying out the basic timeline. The 48-hour ultimatum – technically termed a 'note with a time limit' (*befristete Démarche*) – would be dispatched by five PM on Thursday, 23 July, the night Poincaré would leave Petersburg. The other powers would then be told of it on Friday morning. While it was theoretically possible that the French delegation would learn of the note before departing Petersburg on Thursday night, Berchtold thought this unlikely (the military chiefs were insisting on five PM). Assuming Serbia's rejection, the ultimatum would expire the same time that Saturday, allowing mobilisation to begin by midnight Saturday–Sunday, 25–26 July. To pre-empt possible objections to this timetable (that is, from Tisza), Berchtold informed the ministers that 'the Germans were getting nervous,' which militated against any further postponement.[2]

The military chiefs, predictably, were wholly in favour of Berchtold's plan, wishing only that things could move faster still. Conrad repeated, for what must have seemed like the thousandth time, his view that 'from the military standpoint, the speediest possible commencement of mobilisation was desirable.' His only concession to caution was to allow that martial law would not be proclaimed anywhere in Austria-Hungary until mobilisation was formally underway, even in Bosnia-Herzegovina, from which operations against Serbia would be launched. War Minister Krobatin promised to begin writing up mobilisation orders on Wednesday, 22 July, so that everything would be ready by the weekend. Judging by these matter-of-fact disquisitions, the war with Serbia was basically a done deal, which would begin as soon as the ultimatum expired on Saturday.

Tisza, of course, did not see things quite that way. Although he had come over – more or less – to the war party on Tuesday, he was still a reluctant convert, beset with doubts. From the Hungarian perspective, the greatest danger in any Balkan war would come from Romania, over the Transylvanian Alps. Bucharest was scarcely a hundred miles from Kronstadt (today's Braşov), the first and greatest of the Hungarian-Transylvanian Siebenbürgen, or 'Seven Cities,' settled by Saxons in medieval times. Sinaia, Romania's summer capital in the Transylvanian Alps, was only 30 miles from Kronstadt and closer still to the Hungarian border. A Romanian incursion across that border would immediately threaten the prosperous Siebenbürgen, and thereby Hungarian control over Transylvania. Tisza had already taken what measures he could, as minister-president, to strengthen the local gendarmerie in the Seven Cities, but this was hardly enough to deter a Romanian invasion. Before consenting to the final ultimatum plan, Tisza wanted Conrad to explain what was being done to defend Transylvania.

Conrad, anticipating this very question, had a ready answer. Martial law, he promised Tisza, would be proclaimed in Transylvania as soon as mobilisation commenced. While the demands of the Serbian invasion plan, and the need to defend Galicia against a possible Russian intervention, prevented the army from concentrating its forces against Romania, Conrad had created special Landsturm battalions for the Siebenbürgen: a kind of expanded militia, under the command of actual military officers. It was true, he confessed to Tisza, that these irregular formations would not suffice if it came to war with Bucharest, but their conspicuous staging should be enough to deter Romanian aggression. As an added precaution, Conrad had made certain that the Transylvanian formations contained 'only a small percentage of Romanian nationals.'

Tisza declared himself satisfied with Conrad's assurances, but he was still not done. Because no one else was playing devil's advocate, the Hungarian minister-president, as usual, raised every objection himself, whether or not they affected Hungary directly. What about Italy? he asked next, reminding his fellow ministers that Austria's nominal ally coveted Trieste and the South Tyrol, and that if she took advantage of a war against Serbia to invade, Austria would face a two-front war even if Russia and Romania stayed out. Berchtold promised him straightaway that Italian intervention was 'not likely' and that he would undertake every diplomatic measure to work against it.

Here, at last, Tisza saw his opening. With Berchtold conceding that diplomatic finesse would be required to assure even the neutrality of Austria's nominal Italian ally, the Hungarian minister-president laid down the non-negotiable terms under which he would consent to the dispatch of an ultimatum to Serbia. In order to ensure the support, or at least the indifference, of powers such as Italy, Romania, and Russia, Tisza insisted that the ministers agree 'unanimously, that no plans of conquest by the [dual] monarchy were connected with the action against Serbia, and that, with the exception of rectifications of the frontier necessary for strategic reasons, Austria did not wish to annex a single piece of Serbia.' Failing this, Tisza would withdraw his support for the dispatch of the 48-hour ultimatum.

Berchtold could accept Tisza's condition, he told the Hungarian, 'only with a certain reserve.' While he agreed that Austria-Hungary should not herself annex territory, he was still adamant that she 'should seek to reduce [Serbia's] size so that she would no longer be dangerous, by ceding as large parts of Serbian territory as possible to Bulgaria, Greece, Albania, and possibly to Romania also.' Whether or not Berchtold really wished for Austria to conquer Serbia and then turn over her gains to greedy Balkan powers, Tisza had forced him to say that he would do this – which was something. Count Stürgkh, Austria's minister-president, insisted that even if Serbia's territorial integrity were respected, she might still be placed in a relation of dependence on Vienna by means of 'the deposition of the dynasty, a military convention, and other appropriate measures.' Krobatin was more explicit still, declaring that 'frontier rectifications' must include control of the bridgeheads of the river Sava in Serbia's Sabaç district – across which district, he did not need to add, Gavrilo Princip and the Sarajevo assassins had crossed into Bosnia-Herzegovina.

Still, Tisza stood tall. His opposition to dismembering Serbia, he explained, 'was not simply on grounds of domestic politics, but rather because he was personally convinced that Russia would be forced to offer resistance *à outrance* if we were to insist on the complete annihilation of Serbia.' Not trusting the ministers at their word, Tisza insisted not only on their unanimous acceptance of a no-annexation pledge but also that it be made public. The final resolution of the Ministerial

Council stipulated, 'on the proposal of the Hungarian minister-president,' that 'immediately on the outbreak of war a declaration shall be made to the foreign powers that the monarchy is not waging a war of conquest, and does not intend to incorporate the Kingdom [of Serbia].' Still, the other ministers insisted (although this part would not be made public) that 'this vote naturally does not preclude rectifications of the frontier strategically necessary, nor the diminution of Serbia for the benefit of other states, nor the temporary occupation of parts of Serbia which may eventually be necessary.'

Just as in the earlier war council on 7 July, the policy differences between Tisza and the others had been patched over in a 'unanimous' resolution that resolved nothing. The first clause, mandating a public vow not to dismember Serbia, was flatly contradicted by the second, which implied that Serbia would be dismembered after all (although not, supposedly, by Austria-Hungary herself). The cynicism with which the other ministers viewed their promises to Tisza was nicely captured in a remark Conrad made to Krobatin as they left the Strudelhof: 'Well, we shall see. Before the Balkan War the powers also talked about [preserving] the status quo – after the war nobody bothered himself about it.'[3]

Reading the transcript today, the most striking thing about the 19 July Ministerial Council – which, at Tisza's insistence, had been called to iron out the final terms of the Serbian ultimatum – is that there was no discussion of the terms of the ultimatum. Berchtold had written it himself, without consulting Tisza, although the Hungarian was apparently shown the text on Sunday. Nor, despite Berchtold having explicitly promised on Tuesday, 14 July, to run it by Tschirschky before sending it off, was the German ambassador allowed to see it on Sunday, 19 July, nor on Monday, nor on Tuesday. Nor was Emperor Franz Josef I allowed to vet the ultimatum. Astonishingly, given the historic importance of the document, not a single minister of Austria-Hungary's imperial government, nor her sovereign, nor the ambassador of her only real ally, signed off on Berchtold's text before he sent it off, under seal, to Minister Giesl in Belgrade on Monday, 20 July.

The reason for Berchtold's secrecy is not hard to fathom. The ultimatum was so draconian that the Germans were unlikely to have approved it. Some of the clauses, to be sure, were reasonable and unsurprising, dealing with such matters as suppressing the smuggling of weapons and explosives into Austrian territory. Others, however, were almost deliberately insulting. Serbia's government was to 'dissolve immediately the society styled "Narodna Odbrana,"' despite the fact, well-known to Berchtold and the Austrians, that much of that government consisted of dues-paying members of that society. Serbia's prime minister, Pašić, would also be required to fire all Serbian military officers and government officials 'guilty of propaganda against the Austro-Hungarian monarchy,' with Vienna herself making up the list of offending individuals. Most onerous of all were clauses 5 and 6, which would force Belgrade to 'accept the collaboration in Serbia of representatives of the Austro-Hungarian government for the suppression of the subversive movement directed against the territorial integrity of the dual monarchy' and require that Austrian officials 'take part in the investigations relating thereto.'[4] No sovereign state could reasonably be expected to turn over the operation of her police and justice systems to representatives of an outside (and hostile) power – certainly not when many of her own officials might be found guilty of aiding and abetting the crime. These draconian clauses gave the game away: Berchtold wanted the ultimatum to be rejected.

Given that the Germans had learned, from Ambassador Tschirschky as early as 10 July, that the Ballplatz intended that Belgrade refuse her terms, no one in Berlin should have been surprised by the uncompromising terms of the ultimatum. Nevertheless, the extremely harsh tone of Berchtold's 'note with a time limit' was far from what the Germans had wanted. Berchtold himself implicitly admitted this when, after finally showing the text to the emperor at Bad Ischl on Tuesday, 21 July, he wired the Ballplatz with instructions to tell Ambassador Tschirschky that 'he cannot be given the Note until early tomorrow morning [Wednesday, 22 July] since some corrections are still to be made to it.'[5] Given that the final text of the ultimatum had already been sent off under seal on Monday, it is clear that Berchtold was lying outright about 'corrections . . . still to be made.' Suspecting that Tschirschky would not approve the text, Berchtold was trying to delay showing it to him until shortly before it would be submitted to Serbia on Thursday – by which time it would be too late for the Germans to do anything about it.

Germany's foreign minister had just as much cause for grievance as her ambassador in Vienna. In the days before the Ministerial Council, Jagow had expressly advised Berchtold to come to terms with Italy before submitting the ultimatum – even, if necessary, offering Rome territorial compensation in exchange for neutrality. He had further stipulated that a dossier outlining Serbian complicity in the Sarajevo outrage should be published *before* the ultimatum was sent to Belgrade, so as to neutralise diplomatic opposition in Rome and the Entente capitals.[6] All this was sensible advice. Berchtold had not followed a word of it. No agreement of any kind with Italy had been reached, and the long-awaited dossier on Sarajevo remained unfinished. Instead, Berchtold had instructed his diplomats to inform the powers on Friday, 24 July, when they presented the note to them, that such a dossier would be made available at a later date.[7]

Of course, Berchtold could easily have justified his high-handed methods in view of the Germans' repeated insistence on a 'bold and decisive' course of action. And yet Berlin had pressed for speed back at the beginning of July, when the hope was that Austria would invade Serbia in retaliation for the Sarajevo murders – a military fait accompli ideally so speedy that the powers would not have time to react. Unable to offer this to the Germans because of Tisza's opposition (and the harvest leave programme), Berchtold had instead waited three weeks and then given Berlin a take-it-or-leave-it diplomatic fait accompli. The resulting policy was a diplomatic disaster in the making that combined the worst aspects of German bludgeoning (the sharp tone and strict time limit) with Austrian prevarication (the note dispatched nearly four weeks after Sarajevo, with the dossier outlining Serbian complicity still not complete). Foolishly, Kaiser Wilhelm II and Bethmann had written a blank check for an Austrian war against Serbia, while having no control over the war's timetable or the terms in which the war would be justified to Europe. The Austrian noose, rigged up by the Germans themselves, was slowly tightening around Germany's neck.

10

Poincaré
Meets the Tsar

MONDAY, 20 JULY

A T TWO PM ON MONDAY, 20 JULY, the battleship *France*,
accompanied by an escorting dreadnought, the *Jean Bart*,
laid anchor at Kronstadt, the Russian naval base in the Gulf of
Finland that guards the approaches to St Petersburg. Aboard
were France's president, Raymond Poincaré, and her premier
and foreign minister, René Viviani, who had set sail from
Dunkirk at dawn the previous Thursday.

It had not been a happy passage. While the seas had
remained relatively calm for the four-and-a-half-day voyage,
the political atmosphere was more stormy. Jean Jaurès, the
great Socialist orator, had made a show of voting against fund-
ing the trip in Parliament. The anti-war crowd in Paris saw
Poincaré's effort to shore up the Franco-Russian alliance as dangerously provocative, especially now that a new Balkan crisis threatened the European equilibrium. Reluctantly, Viviani
had agreed to accompany Poincaré as part of the duties of his
new office, but he made it clear that he would have preferred
not to go. All through the voyage, Poincaré had badgered the

quasi-pacifist former education minister about the importance of France's three-year military service law, the need to be 'very firm' with the Germans, and the vital strategic importance of the Russian alliance. Viviani, to the president's consternation, seemed scarcely to be listening. Poincaré found him 'extraordinarily ignorant of foreign affairs, which do not interest him at all and which he does not even seem to understand.' To his dismay, Viviani was wholly preoccupied by the upcoming trial of Mme Caillaux, scheduled to open on Monday, 20 July – the very day they would arrive in Russia to meet the tsar. As the French delegation docked at Kronstadt that afternoon, Viviani was surprised to feel a 'murderous heat' beating down upon them. He had thought he was travelling to the north country but instead found the climate worse than that of 'tropical Africa.' Clearly ill at ease, France's premier was overheard asking an aide, 'What are we doing here?'[1]

Poincaré, by contrast, was a man on a mission. He had set up the summit in January, at the height of the Liman von Sanders crisis, the last serious European war scare before the Sarajevo outrage. That month, Poincaré had also dispatched a new ambassador to Petersburg, Maurice Paléologue, who shared his own views on the importance of the Russian alliance. Only if French officials convinced Petersburg of their own firmness of purpose in serious international crises could they trust that the tsar's armies had France's back against Germany. Or, as then-premier Gaston Doumergue had instructed Paléologue prior to his departure for Russia, 'War can break out from one day to the next. . . . Our [Russian] allies must rush to our aid. The safety of France will depend on the energy and promptness with which we shall know how to push them into the fight.'[2]

Poincaré, like Doumergue, had long believed that a bit of 'pushing' would be needed to get the Russians to stand firm against the Central Powers. His doubts about Viviani were of a piece with those he harboured about Sazonov. Not unlike Hartwig and other Russian nationalists, France's president had pointedly criticised the Russian foreign minister's submissive attitude during the Balkan Wars. Steeling up Sazonov was one of Poincaré's key goals at the summit.

The tsar, too, remained something of an enigma to the French. Nicholas II had never – publicly, at least – expressed any distaste for Russia's alliance with an 'atheistic' republic like France, nor complained when forced, at summits, to listen to her national anthem, 'The Marseillaise,' a blood-curdling masterpiece of revolutionary lèse-majesté. Then again, he had never displayed any particular passion for the alliance, either. The tsar did have good French, although, because his German wife, Alix, spoke little Russian, he spoke English more often (and wrote it, as in his famous letters to 'his dear friend Willy,' Kaiser Wilhelm II). More important than all this was the issue of the tsar's will, or lack thereof. In theory an autocrat in the long Romanov tradition who had sidelined the Duma from policy-making shortly after it was first elected in 1906, Nicholas II was, many in Paris feared, a weak-willed man easily manipulated by his subordinates.

The truth was that no one outside Russia really knew for sure who ran things in the imperial government. Krivoshein, the agriculture minister, and not Council of Ministers chairman Goremykin, was believed by the French to be the most influential policymaker in St Petersburg, but this was a guess – an optimistic one, as Krivoshein was the government's most passionate Germanophobe. Going to Petersburg in person was the only sure way of figuring out where the Russians stood.

T SAR NICHOLAS II WAS LUNCHING with Sazonov and Paléologue aboard his imperial yacht, the *Alexandria*, when the

French delegation arrived at Kronstadt. Also present at the luncheon were Alexander Izvolsky, Russia's ambassador to France, and General Pierre de Laguiche, the French military attaché to Russia. The subject of conversation was the upcoming summit, particularly the thorniest problem on the agenda: how to douse growing tensions between London and Petersburg over the zones of influence accorded Britain and Russia in the Anglo-Russian Convention of 1907. While it was too soon to discuss details, the tsar agreed on the importance of winning over London. 'Unless she has gone out of her mind altogether,' he told Paléologue, 'Germany will never attack Russia, France, and England combined.' Coffee had just been served when the signal was heard announcing the arrival of France's president. 'For a few minutes there was a prodigious din in the harbour,' Paléologue wrote of the dramatic scene: 'the guns of the ships and the shore batteries firing, the crews cheering, the *Marseillaise* answering the Russian national anthem, the cheers of thousands of spectators who had come from St Petersburg on pleasure boats.'

Honouring France's head of state, the *Alexandria* travelled out to meet the *France*. The tsar himself mounted the gangway to welcome Poincaré aboard the Russian imperial yacht, before it set sail for Peterhof Palace. 'Seated in the stern,' Paléologue observed, 'the Tsar and the President immediately entered into a conversation, I should perhaps say a discussion, for it was obvious that they were talking business, firing questions at one another and arguing. As was proper it was Poincaré who had the initiative. Before long he was doing all the talking, the Tsar simply nodded acquiescence.'[3]

Of the two heads of state, France's president was the stronger personality. It was the Russians, however, who held the cards. In any Balkan crisis, military measures against the Central Powers would be initiated by Russia, not France. The reason was simple geography. While Russia and France both bordered

Germany – this, indeed, was why they had teamed up in the first place – France shared no border with Austria-Hungary. Nor did Germany, unlike Austria, border any Balkan countries. Any Balkan affair must therefore involve Austria and Russia primarily, such that a European war would begin with Austrian and/or Russian mobilisation, with Germany then responding to Russian mobilisation, and France to Russian and German (after which, the Entente Powers hoped, Britain would come in, too). Because everyone expected Russia's mobilisation to be the slowest of all the powers', with Germany's the quickest (and expected to be focused on her western front), any war breaking out over Balkan issues would paradoxically put France in the first line of German attack. This is what Doumergue had meant when he said that 'the safety of France' depended on how quickly she could 'push [Russia] into the fight.'[4]

Of course, no one was sure yet whether the powers would come to blows in the Balkans. Poincaré had been at sea when the leaks from the Ballplatz about Austria's ultimatum to Serbia had reached the ears of Russian Shebeko and then Sazonov. With Poincaré's reputation for bellicosity, it was not hard to predict how he would react when he learned what the Austrians were up to.

All this, though, would have to wait until the morning. The main event Monday evening was the welcome banquet. When the *Alexandria* docked at the Peterhof at three PM, Poincaré recalled, the French delegation was greeted by 'a posse of Grand Dukes.' They and the tsar's entourage then completed the short zigzag journey through the palace gardens in horse-drawn carriages, 'riding at a sharp trot.' Poincaré was less than impressed by the park, which he found 'a rather *fadé* replica of Versailles.' His 'heavily gilt,' white satin–lined suite, too, he found overdone, 'being somewhat of a piece with the over-decorated galleries and the great saloons, the gorgeousness of which seems rather to run riot.'

Poincaré was more impressed with the hall where the gala dinner was held. It was 'lighted by a dozen gorgeous crystal candelabra,' he recalled. 'The wax candles [were] infinitely more becoming than the electric light, which has not yet been installed.' Paléologue, too, despite having lived in Petersburg for months, could not help being overwhelmed by 'the brilliance of the uniforms, superb toilettes, elaborate liveries, magnificent furnishings and fittings, in short the whole panoply of pomp and power, the spectacle was such as no court in the world can rival.' The ladies were still more striking, with a 'dazzling display of jewels on the women's shoulders.' Glancing around the banquet table, his eyes were struck by 'a fantastic shower of diamonds, pearls, rubies, sapphires, emeralds, topaz, beryls – a blaze of fire and flame.' 'In this fairy milieu,' the ambassador observed, Poincaré's 'black coat was a drab touch.'[5]

France's president, of course, had not come to Petersburg to impress or flatter archduchesses. The business of the evening was the mutual toasts he and Nicholas II would give to cement the Franco-Russian alliance. The tsar went first, assuring France's president that he would find the 'warmest welcome' in Russia, owing to the 'mutual sympathies and common interests' of the two peoples, now bound together as allies for 'almost a quarter century.' The alliance, Nicholas II proclaimed, had worked to safeguard 'the equilibrium and the peace of Europe.' Expressing the hope that 'the ties which bind us will grow ever tighter,' Russia's tsar raised his glass to the health of France's president and to 'the glory and prosperity of France.'[6]

Poincaré, in his reply, seconded the tsar's sentiments but went further. True to his reputation for plain-speaking, France's president noted that the alliance was 'founded on a community of interests' – that is, fear of Germany – and 'supported by armed forces on land and at sea which know and value one another and have become accustomed to act as brothers.'

'Your Majesty may rest assured,' he promised Tsar Nicholas II, 'that France in the future, as always in the past, will, in sincere and daily cooperation with her ally, pursue the work of peace and civilisation.' Poincaré then raised his glass to 'Your Honourable Majesty, Your Majesty the Empress, Your Majesty the Emperor-Mother, His Imperial Majesty the heir to the throne and the entire imperial family.' Viviani raised his glass too, but with little enthusiasm.[7]

11

Sazonov's Threat

TUESDAY, 21 JULY

AT TEN AM TUESDAY MORNING, Tsar Nicholas II called on Poincaré in his suite at the Peterhof. They went straight to business. The first item on the agenda was Anglo-Russian relations. British diplomats had informed Poincaré that 'several Russian consuls in Persia had broken the terms of the Anglo-Russian Convention of 1907, and had behaved themselves as if they were in a conquered country.' To his pleasant surprise, as the Frenchman recorded in his memoirs, the tsar conceded 'frankly that England was perfectly justified in her complaints, and he assured me that there would be no recurrence of what were very regrettable incidents.' On the matter of an impending Anglo-Russian naval convention, which would help assuage French concerns about being left in the lurch by London in a conflict with Germany, the tsar promised to 'speed things up.' '*The* thing,' he assured Poincaré, 'is that no problem should present itself which might jeopardise good relations between England and Russia, and this I am as keen about as you are.'

The Russian sovereign had good reason to improve relations with England. Although Poincaré remained unaware of Austrian intentions, Nicholas II had learned about Berchtold's plan to issue a Serbian ultimatum over the weekend, when Sazonov had shown him Shebeko's telegram from Vienna. His conclusion, as he had written in the margins of the document, was that Austria intended to make war on Serbia. A European war might thus be on the near-term horizon, and British belligerence was essential to the Franco-Russian cause. As Poincaré observed that morning, 'the Tsar's liveliest preoccupation was with Austria. He wanted to know what she was preparing in response to the assassination at Sarajevo.' Without spelling out what it was that he feared, Nicholas II told Poincaré with conviction that 'in the current situation, the complete accord between our two governments was more necessary than ever.'

The tsar then took his leave, and Poincaré dressed for a trip into town, where he was to be formally welcomed by the diplomatic community at the Winter Palace. Nicholas II had offered the president the use of his imperial yacht for the trip but did not accompany him to St Petersburg. Poincaré was perplexed as to why 'I could not see myself,' he thought, 'receiving a crowned head at Versailles and letting him go alone to Paris.' 'Does he fear,' Poincaré wondered, 'or does he disdain a crowd?'[1] Ambassador Paléologue, in his own memoirs, offers a possible explanation: on Monday a series of industrial strikes had broken out all over town, and there were 'collisions with police at several points.' At any rate, Poincaré and Prime Minister Viviani were going in the safety of the tsar's yacht (at least until they reached town). For the tsar to have called off the day's programme would have put a serious damper on the summit.

At about one thirty PM, Paléologue met Poincaré as he disembarked on the quai near Nicholas Bridge. 'In accordance with the old Slav rites,' the ambassador recalled, 'Count Ivan Tolstoy, the Mayor of the Capital, offered him bread and salt.' The president was then shown the nearby fortress of St Peter and St Paul, where he laid a wreath on the tomb of Tsar Alexander III, to honour the father of the Franco-Russian alliance. The party was then escorted by an honour guard of Cossacks along the banks of the Neva in a horse-drawn carriage as far as the French embassy, where Poincaré formally 'received the deputations of the French colonies in St Petersburg and throughout Russia' – many from as far away as Odessa, Kiev, and Tiflis. Thus far there was no sign of labour unrest in the streets, and there was much cheering from the crowds, although as Paléologue noticed, these often consisted of 'poor wretches' who 'cheered loudly under the eye of a policeman.'[2]

At four PM, the French delegation arrived at the Winter Palace to meet the diplomatic community. It was a full-dress occasion, following strict protocol. Paléologue was to introduce each ambassador in turn to France's president for a one-on-one conversation, with Viviani attending to Poincaré's left (but not participating in the conversations). As the doyen of the diplomatic corps, Germany's ambassador, Friedrich Pourtalès, went first. In view of the scarcely concealed hostility between his country and the president's, this could have been an awkward audience, but it proved anything but. Pourtalès was part French by descent and spoke the language perfectly. He was planning a road trip later in the summer through Provence, where he would visit his relations in Castellane. The two men discussed the area and its sights. Poincaré found the German ambassador 'an agreeable person with a pretty knack for evasive phrases and well-turned compliments.'

More significant was the encounter with the British ambassador, Sir George Buchanan. While Franco-British relations were fairly cordial at the moment, those between London and Petersburg were fraught with tension over Persia, which threatened to destroy the Triple Entente of French dreams before it would ever coalesce on the battlefield. While discussing the thorny Persian issue, Buchanan was 'exquisitely courteous if a little cold,' Poincaré recalled afterwards, noting the Briton's anxiety on the subject. Buchanan thought that the

Anglo-Russian Convention of 1907 needed to be modified to fit new conditions on the ground, and he hoped that the Russians would parley. Poincaré was able to report the tsar's avowal of good faith intentions, given just that morning. Buchanan was 'very pleased' to hear it.

Up to this point, matters had been fairly routine, as befitted a formal ceremony among professional diplomats trained to be polite. But then Buchanan let slip a confidence that alarmed Poincaré. Although the British ambassador had not received his colleague de Bunsen's reports from Vienna (Foreign Secretary Grey, astonishingly, had not forwarded them to Petersburg), he had heard Sazonov discuss the expected Austrian ultimatum to Serbia on Saturday. Earlier Tuesday, Buchanan had spoken with the Serbian minister, who told him that he was expecting Austria to 'create some incident that would furnish her with . . . a pretext for attacking [Serbia].' Putting these bits of information together, Britain's ambassador painted a dark picture. 'He has gathered,' Poincaré recalled learning, 'from the Serbian Minister that some violent Austrian note may be sent to Belgrade.'[3]

The protocol order now took on ominous significance. Right after Buchanan had put Poincaré on guard about Austrian intentions, the president received the Habsburg ambassador, Count Friedrich Szapáry. Seeking to draw out Berchtold's man in Petersburg, France's president asked straightaway, 'Have you any news from Serbia?' Szapáry replied coldly that 'the judicial enquiry is advancing.' When Poincaré noted that previous investigations of this sort had always increased tensions in the Balkans, Szapáry retorted, more coldly still: 'Monsieur le Président, we cannot suffer a foreign Government to allow murderous attacks against our sovereignty to be prepared on its territory.' Poincaré responded by gently warning the Hungarian 'that in the present state of public feeling in Europe every government should be twice as cautious as usual.' Changing tack ever so slightly, the president said that 'this Serbian business' could still be settled 'with a little good will.' Poincaré could not resist, however, getting in the last word of the argument. 'Serbia,' Poincaré warned Szapáry, 'has very warm friends in the Russian people. And Russia has an Ally, France. There are plenty of complications to be feared!'[4]

Like hunters catching a first, fleeting glimpse of their prey, the two men left this encounter energised and primed for battle. Szapáry reported the conversation to Vienna in sharp tones. The French president had been 'tactless'; his so-called reassurances of cooperation had 'sounded like a threat.' The ambassador contrasted Poincaré's aggressive behaviour with the 'reserved and cautious attitude' taken by Sazonov on Saturday (when the Russian foreign minister had found Szapáry 'docile as a lamb'). All in all, the unpleasant encounter in the Winter Palace confirmed Szapáry's 'expectation that M. Poincaré will have anything but a calming effect here.'[5]

Szapáry had read Poincaré perfectly. 'I'm not satisfied with this conversation,' France's president told Paléologue shortly after speaking with Szapáry. 'The Ambassador has obviously been instructed to say nothing. . . . Austria has a *coup de théâtre* in store for us. Sazonov must be firm and we must back him up.'[6]

The president, accompanied by Viviani and Paléologue, left the Winter Palace at six PM to visit the French hospital before arriving at the French embassy for another banquet. Outwardly everything seemed fine, with the programme proceeding smoothly. In their minds, however, both Poincaré and Paléologue (if not also Viviani, who continued sleepwalking through the summit) knew that some kind of Rubicon had been crossed at the Winter Palace. In addition to Buchanan's revelation that a 'violent Austrian note' was to be dispatched to Belgrade, Poincaré had received a report during the day that Léon Descos, France's minister to Serbia, had suffered a mental breakdown nearly a week ago, on Wednesday, 15 July – shortly before the French delegation had embarked at sea from Dunkirk. While insignificant in itself, Descos's collapse meant that Paris had no up-to-date reports on Serbia. Buchanan's revelation therefore stood out even more starkly: the first news of Serbian affairs that France's government had received for over a week was that Serbia expected shortly to be attacked by Austria. Louis de Robien, the French embassy attaché in Petersburg who had been accompanying Poincaré on his tour, wrote in his diary on Wednesday morning, 22 July, that 'already, in the discussions one sensed that the atmosphere had changed overnight. We were speaking overtly about a war which no one had imagined possible only a few days previously.'[7]

The most important result of the run-in between Poincaré and Szapáry at the Winter Palace Tuesday afternoon, however, was what happened after the president told Sazonov about it. From Ambassador Shebeko and his chief of staff, Schilling, Russia's foreign minister already knew, more or less, what the Austrians were up to. Now, steeled up by French support and Poincaré's example of firmness, Sazonov was loaded for bear. Not wanting to provoke an acute diplomatic crisis, however, he avoided confronting Szapáry directly but would vent his fury at Germany's ambassador instead.

Sazonov began the Tuesday night audience by reminding Pourtalès of Russia's position on the Sarajevo outrage. It was an isolated deed of 'a few individuals,' for which 'an entire state' – Serbia – 'could not be made responsible.' For the Austrians to demand redress from Belgrade, he argued, was akin to Russia threatening Sweden because so many Russian revolutionaries took refuge there. Even the 'greater Serbia' propaganda emanating from Belgrade, Sazonov argued, was Austria's own fault because of the way it misgoverned Serbs.

Pourtalès answered these provocative arguments as carefully as he could, but he could do little to slow down Sazonov's momentum. Clearly the Russian had got wind of Austria's intentions, for he was now talking not only about the issue of responsibility for the Sarajevo murders but also about actions he expected Vienna to take. 'If Austria-Hungary was determined to break the peace,' Sazonov warned Pourtalès, 'she should realise that this time she would have to reckon with Europe.' (Opposite this passage, Kaiser Wilhelm II, reading it about a week later, scribbled 'No! But with Russia, yes!') 'Russia could not,' Sazonov continued, 'regard any step taken at Belgrade, which was intended to humiliate Serbia, with indifference.' Pourtalès, seeking to calm the Russian's fears, promised that Serbian rights would be respected; there would be no 'humiliation' (*Erniedrigung*) of Belgrade. Unimpressed, Sazonov warned that 'Russia would not be able to endure it if Austria-Hungary issued threatening language to Serbia or undertook military measures [against her].' Russia's policy, he declared, 'was pacific but not passive.' To ensure that Pourtalès – and through him, Berlin and Vienna – got the message, Sazonov now issued a threat of his own to Vienna: 'whatever happens *there must be no talk of an ultimatum.*'[8]

Russia's foreign minister had drawn a line in the sand, daring Berchtold to cross it. According to plan, Berchtold would do so exactly two days later.

12

Champagne Summit

WEDNESDAY–THURSDAY, 22–23 JULY

WEDNESDAY MORNING, 22 JULY, Poincaré was invited to visit the imperial family at the Villa Alexandria, a modest (by Romanov standards) brick cottage not far from the Peterhof. He found the four young archduchesses – Olga, Tatiana, Maria Nicolaevna, and Anastasia – 'delightful in their perfect simplicity.' The tsarevich Alexis, ten years old, was pale in complexion and much shier than his sisters, although considering his hemophiliac condition, this was hardly surprising. While cruising the fjords of Finland with the tsar the week before aboard the *Alexandria*, Alexis had stumbled on the bottom rungs of a ladder. The resulting swollen ankle had caused him acute pain. His mother, Alexandra, was also in poor health, suffering from heart trouble and also neuropathia, which resulted from a displacement of her uterus. Because of these well-known maladies, Poincaré was half-expecting to encounter the tsarina's notorious peasant faith-healer in the household. But Rasputin, as it turned out, had recently been stabbed in the stomach by a young woman while visiting his village at Pokrovskoie, and no one in the family knew where he was or how he was doing. (It later emerged that a surgeon had been sent from the capital to operate on him in a hospital in Tiumen; Rasputin's rapid recovery would add to his growing legend as a healer.)

Poincaré's call was a welcome distraction for the ailing tsarina and her afflicted son. As a visiting head of state from the world capital of luxury goods, it was not hard for the president to please the girls with gifts of diamond watch-bracelets from Paris, which left them 'open-mouthed with delight.' But it was Alexis who received the greatest honour, being presented with the Cordon of the Grand Cross, 'duly measured for his childish figure' – the first foreign decoration the tsarevich had ever received. Tsar Nicholas II thanked the president profusely (although the gift was actually Paléologue's idea). Poincaré also gave the boy furniture for his future library, as would befit a sovereign. It was well that the president had come prepared to please Alexis in the imperial villa, for the fragile tsarevich, still recovering from his swollen ankle, would not be able to join the delegation for the train journey to the military parade ground at Krasnoe Selo that afternoon.[1]

Following the presentation of the gifts, Poincaré, accompanied by the tsar, headed back to Peterhof for a luncheon on the terrace with officers of the French squadron, Foreign Minister Sazonov, Russia's ambassador to France Izvolsky, and Goremykin, chairman of the Council of Ministers. Among the honoured guests was Count Fredericks, a general of cavalry who was also chancellor of the Imperial Orders, among many other honorifics relating to his role dispensing 'all favours and gifts, all the reproofs and punishments' among the high Russian aristocracy. A man of legendary charm, Fredericks took it on himself to cheer up Viviani, whose sense of discomfiture was obvious to everyone. In addition to homesickness and anxiety over Mme Caillaux, the premier was having digestive difficulties and was worried about his liver. The Russians feared he was having some sort of nervous breakdown. Unlike the tsarevich, however, Viviani could not opt out of the afternoon programme. He would have to endure it as best he could.

At three thirty, the party boarded the imperial train at the Peterhof station for the half-hour journey to Krasnoe Selo. For all but Viviani, leaving the capital behind brought an easing of mood. The diplomatic business had been completed; now it was time for military parades and toasting. As Paléologue described the scene, 'a blazing sun lit up the vast plain, tawny and undulating . . . bounded on the horizon by wooded hills. . . . The elite of Petersburg society were crowded into some stands. The light toilettes of the woman, their white hats and parasols made the stands look like azalea beds.' Led by Tsar Nicholas II on horseback, the imperial carriage carrying France's president along with the tsarina and the four archduchesses proceeded through what seemed to Poincaré like 'an interminable lane of troops.' The soldiers all greet their emperor with 'the traditional shout.' The progress lasted, in all, about an hour and a half, during which time poor Viviani had to stand in front of the imperial tent. The only consolation was that, when the tsar and the president finally arrived, they, too, were forced to stand for the grand finale, which saw warplanes fly overhead as the military band played a series of French and Russian marches. A triple salvo of artillery blasts then announced the evening prayer. As the 'sun was dropping towards the horizon in a sky of purple and gold,' Paléologue wrote in his diary, 'a non-commissioned officer recited the *Pater* in a loud voice. All those men, thousands upon thousands, prayed for the Tsar and Holy Russia.' By the time the long ceremony was over, Viviani looked so sickly that Paléologue called a specialist doctor from town to inspect the suffering Frenchman.[2]

From the parade field, the party then proceeded to the nearby estate of Grand Duke Nicholas Nikolaevich, inspector-general of cavalry. Grandson of Tsar Nicholas I, his namesake,

Grand Duke Nicholas was a prince of the blood, whom many Russians wished had been in line for the imperial succession (his father was the third son of Nicholas I, rendering the father third in line, and his son, in turn, still further back). Although wholly loyal to Nicholas II, the grand duke was a stronger personality who, at six foot six inches tall, literally towered over other men (after he took over as commander in chief of Russia's armies, he had aides put signs above the door at headquarters, reminding him not to bump his head).[3] A fervent Francophile, Grand Duke Nicholas was happy to host the French delegation for a dinner banquet, just as he had on Poincaré's earlier visit in 1912.

Paléologue was one of the first to arrive. 'Three long tables,' he observed, 'were set in half-open tents around a garden which was in full flower. The beds had just been watered and from them the fresh scent of flowers . . . rose into the warm air.' As he was admiring the scene, France's ambassador was 'given a boisterous welcome' by the two 'Montenegrin Princesses,' Anastasia Nicolaievna, wife of Grand Duke Nicholas, and her sister, Militiza, as they put the final decorations on the tables. It was Anastasia and Militiza who had first introduced the tsarina to Rasputin. Their influence at court was considerable.

The two princesses were happy to see Paléologue. As soon as they finished sprucing up the banquet tables, they both rushed over to the ambassador and all but drooled over him with compliments. One princess carried around a box of soil from 'occupied' German Lorraine, which she had visited two years earlier; the other, Paléologue learned, had decorated the tables with thistles – also from Lorraine (apparently she had planted her garden with sacred plants from its Teuton-occupied soil). 'We are passing through historic days, blessed days!' the princesses exclaimed, before informing France's ambassador that, during the military review the grand duke would put on for them tomorrow, 'the bands will play nothing but the *Marche Lorraine* and *Sambre et Meuse.*'

When the champagne started flowing, the mood grew more euphoric still. Grand Duchess Anastasia, as if taking Paléologue into confidence, told France's ambassador that 'there's going to be war. There'll be nothing left of Austria. You're going to get back Alsace and Lorraine. Our armies will meet in Berlin. Germany will be destroyed!' She may have been just warming up, but a 'stern gaze' from Tsar Nicholas II cut off this belligerent reverie. Anastasia was, after all, married to the host, a possible commander in chief of the Russian armies. 'I must restrain myself,' she told Paléologue with a hint of conspiracy. 'The Emperor has his eye on me.'[4]

Poincaré, occupied most of the time in conversation with the tsar, had a less interesting evening than his ambassador. The president, too, however, noticed the Montenegrin princesses – and not just their beauty. Before and after the dinner, they 'plied [him] unceasingly with questions' about Austria and the Balkan crisis. Regretfully, Poincaré told them, he had no answers, assuring them only that he was equally as anxious as they. He did not tell them that earlier that day, he had received a disquieting report from his ambassador in Rome, passing on Italian intelligence that 'Germany will make no effort to restrain Austria. In Vienna, they believe that Russia will let Serbia be violated.'[5] Lending credence to this report of Austrian arrogance in the face of expected Russian passivity, Anastasia and her sister whispered warnings in the president's ear about Sazonov, whom they believed to be cowardly and weak. These suggestions dovetailed well with Poincaré's own concerns. In part because he had spent so much of the summit speaking with the tsar, the president had come to believe that Russia's sovereign was 'more decided' than his foreign minister on a course of defending Serbia.[6] Poincaré and the princesses were unaware that Sazonov had, the preceding evening, issued an explicit threat to Vienna, via Pourtalès, that 'there must be no talk of an ultimatum.'

The burgeoning atmosphere of belligerence in the Franco-Russian camp was given an even sharper jolt after the French delegation awoke in their tents the next morning. Even Viviani, invigorated by the country air, was feeling better on Thursday. The military review to be held that morning was, in a sense, the point of the whole summit: a demonstration of the might and unity of the alliance. Anastasia had not misspoken when she promised Paléologue that the band would play nothing but French marches. As the ambassador recorded in his diary,

> Review at Krasnoïe-Selo this morning. Sixty thousand men took part. A magnificent pageant of might and majesty. The infantry march past to the strains of the *Marche de Sambre et Meuse* and the *Marche Lorraine*.
>
> What a wealth of suggestion in this military machine set in motion by the Tsar of all the Russias before the President of the allied republic, himself a son of Lorraine!
>
> The Tsar was mounted at the foot of the mound upon which was the imperial tent. Poincaré was seated on the Tsaritsa's right in front of the tent. The few glances he exchanged with me showed me that our thoughts were the same.[7]

Following the review, everyone retired to the tsar's tent for a grand luncheon of Russian *zakuski* and caviar. Russia's sovereign insisted that Grand Duke Nicholas introduce the president to 'several of the more important generals' in Russia's army, which he did, before the party returned to the Peterhof for a brief rest. At six PM, Nicholas II took the French delegation aboard his yacht, the *Alexandria*, which would escort them out to the *France*, harboured at Kronstadt for the return voyage.

President Poincaré and Tsar Nicholas II, inspecting a Russian Naval Guard of Honour at the Franco-Russian summit in July 1914. *Source: Getty Images.*

This time it was Poincaré who hosted the tsar for a farewell dinner banquet, aboard the *France*.

The setting was spectacular. Although a 'momentary squall' had damaged the floral arrangements, the tables were still laid out with all the elegance the French crew could muster. The deck, Paléologue observed, 'had a kind of terrifying grandeur with the four gigantic 304 mm guns raising their huge muzzles above the heads of the guests.' As if to remind the ambassador of their conversation of the previous night, 'the Grand Duchess Anastasia raised her champagne glass towards me more than once,' Paléologue noticed, 'indicating with a sweep of her arm the warlike tackle raised all about us.' As usual, the tsar and the president were engrossed in conversation all night, both at dinner and afterwards on the bridge, where they remained alone for 'what seemed like an eternity.' No one could be sure of what they were talking about, but it was clearly something important.

In between the first and second courses, Viviani had a message delivered to Paléologue. Having evidently recovered his morale – or remembered his brief as foreign minister – Viviani ordered his ambassador to draw up a communiqué for the press, summarising the conclusions of the summit. Paléologue did what he was told, scribbling a short draft on his dinner menu, to the effect that 'the two governments have discovered that their views and intentions for the maintenance of the European balance of power, especially in the Balkan peninsula, are absolutely identical.' Viewing this as the kind of 'neutral and empty phraseology suitable for documents of this kind,' the ambassador was taken aback when Viviani objected to the last phrase, stipulating that French and Russian interests in the Balkans were not 'absolutely identical.' Paléologue wrote up another draft, which asserted that the two allies were in 'entire agreement in their views on the various problems which concern peace and the balance of power in Europe . . . particularly in the East' (few could have doubted that this meant Serbia). This bland, yet suggestive, communiqué was heartily approved by the president, the tsar, Viviani, Sazonov, and Izvolsky. Poincaré's own farewell toast, which declared that France and Russia 'have the same ideal of peace in strength, honour, and self-respect,' was equally bland but, delivered with his customary forcefulness, was received by the Russians with 'thunderous applause.'[8]

As the Imperial Guard shouldered arms for the tsar's exit onto the waiting *Alexandria*, prior to the departure of the *France* at eleven PM, all seemed well in the Franco-Russian alliance. While Poincaré still harboured doubts about Sazonov, he was now confident that the tsar would remain firm in the face of whatever the Austrians threw at him. The Russians, meanwhile, were assured of France's full support for any strong stand they might take against Vienna. The next move was up to Berchtold.

13

Anti-Ultimatum
and Ultimatum

THURSDAY, 23 JULY

AT THE TIME POINCARÉ and the tsar were saying their good-
byes aboard the *France* Thursday evening, Berchtold's
'radio silence' appeared to be working. Sazonov's cagey act in
his weekend audience with Szapáry suggested that Lützow's
leak to the British ambassador had not reached Russian ears,
at least not by Saturday, 18 July. Berchtold had learned of the
dramatic confrontation between Szapáry and Poincaré at the
Winter Palace on Tuesday, 21 July, which suggested that the
French, at least, had a rough idea of what was coming – but then
Szapáry had pointedly contrasted the French president's belligerent posture with the 'reserved and cautious attitude' taken
by Sazonov on Saturday. True, Szapáry had warned Berchtold
that the French president's presence in Petersburg would 'have
anything but a calming effect,' but Poincaré had a reputation as
a hothead. His warning to Vienna that Russia had a 'friend' in
France may not have reflected more than Poincaré's own wish
for the Russians to stand firm; whether they would do so was
another question. Meanwhile, Sazonov's own threat that 'there

must be no talk of an ultimatum,' issued later Tuesday evening to Pourtalès, remained unknown to the Austrians: Pourtalès's report, sent by post, was not received in Berlin until the morning of Thursday, 23 July, and forwarded on to Tschirschky, in Vienna, only a week after that. So far as Berchtold knew, then, the Russians were still in the dark.

He was wrong. Even while the Montenegrin princesses had been questioning Sazonov's manhood at Krasnoe Selo on Wednesday evening, the Russian foreign minister had rushed back to town to send off a strong message to Ambassador Shebeko in Vienna, wired off at four AM on Thursday, 23 July. Earlier on Wednesday, Sazonov had received a disturbing report from Rome, passing on the belief of Italy's foreign minister 'that Austria was preparing a great blow and aims to annihilate Serbia.'[1] Informing Shebeko that he had credible information that 'Austria was planning to undertake measures against Serbia,' Sazonov instructed his ambassador to warn Vienna 'cordially but firmly' of the 'dangerous consequences which must follow any such measures incompatible with the dignity of Serbia.' Giving this warning stronger diplomatic point, Sazonov informed his ambassador that 'from my discussions with [Poincaré] it clearly emerges that also France . . . will not tolerate a humiliation of Serbia.' Russia's foreign minister may not yet have convinced Poincaré – or Berchtold – of his own firmness, but France's president had left Sazonov in no doubt about his own. The French ambassador to Austria, Sazonov told Shebeko, would shortly make an identical warning to the Ballplatz. He said he also hoped that Britain's ambassador to Vienna, de Bunsen, would 'speak in the same sense,' although he did not yet have confirmation of this.[2]

Sazonov was not speaking alone when he issued this warning. Sometime during the summit – neither he nor Poincaré ever revealed when – Russia's foreign minister had agreed with France's president on the terms of an 'anti-ultimatum ultimatum' to Vienna. Poincaré's version was almost identical to Sazonov's – only, true to the Frenchman's reputation, his language was still stronger. Alfred Dumaine, France's ambassador to Vienna, was instructed that 'no avenue must be neglected to prevent an [Austrian] demand for retribution or any set of conditions foisted [on Serbia] which might . . . be considered a violation of her sovereignty or her independence.' As we might expect, the unequivocal language of this veiled threat was not to the liking of Viviani, who, as foreign minister, agreed to send it to Dumaine 'only with reluctance' (*avec peu d'empressement*). Send it off Viviani did, however, from the switchboard of the *France*, shortly after its departure from Kronstadt, in the wee hours of Friday morning.[3] (Sazonov and Poincaré apparently had decided to stagger the delivery of their joint anti-ultimatum ultimatum, so as to avoid the impression that they were 'ganging up' on Berchtold.)[4]

In their dithering over the Serbian ultimatum, the Austrians had outsmarted themselves, allowing France and Russia to coordinate a joint response to it during a highest-level government summit. Owing to Berchtold's trick of waiting until the French delegation departed, the timing of the dispatch of France's warning – sent off before France's government had been formally notified of the ultimatum – proves that Poincaré and Viviani had prior knowledge of Austrian plans, contrary to their later protestations. It also meant, however, that the French warning would not arrive in Vienna until Friday, 24 July, the day after the actual ultimatum was given to Serbia. It could thus have had no deterrent effect on Berchtold.

Sazonov's own warning arrived sooner than this – it was deciphered by the Russian embassy in Vienna at three PM on Thursday, 23 July – but not soon enough. With Shebeko out of town, the Russian chargé d'affaires rushed over to the Ballplatz in his stead to present Sazonov's 'anti-ultimatum ultimatum' to the Austrian foreign minister. Berchtold's secretary, alas, brushed off the Russian, telling him the foreign minister was busy and could not see him that afternoon. Might the Russian come back at eleven the next morning?[5]

The timing is suggestive. By eleven Friday morning, the ultimatum would have been delivered to Belgrade on schedule Thursday evening, and Europe's governments would have been formally notified of it (the plan was to tell them at ten AM Friday). Berchtold may have told his staff not to allow any representatives from 'hostile' powers to see him before Friday morning. Whether or not he knew how much the Russians knew, the excuse his secretary gave Shebeko's chargé d'affaires was not entirely disingenuous: Berchtold *was* busy that fateful afternoon. The ultimatum time bomb was furiously ticking away, scheduled to detonate in Belgrade scarcely an hour after the Russian envoy arrived at the Ballplatz. The plan was for Minister Giesl to present it to the Serbian government between four and five PM, so as to ensure the deadline would expire by five PM on Saturday, 25 July, in time to allow Austria to begin mobilisation by midnight. Giesl had therefore demanded an audience with Serbia's prime minister at four thirty PM. Thursday morning, however, Berchtold had learned that the *France* would not lift anchor until eleven PM, nearly five hours later than expected.[6] Even given the hour and a half time difference between Petersburg and Central Europe, this meant that, if Giesl turned over the note at four thirty, it was almost certain that news of the démarche in Belgrade would reach Petersburg before Poincaré left Kronstadt at eleven, which might allow him to coordinate a response with Sazonov and the tsar. Learning this, Berchtold altered the schedule at the last minute, sending Giesl an urgent telegram to postpone delivery until six PM.[7] Any later than this, and Conrad would be furious that the 48-hour deadline would expire too late on Saturday evening for mobilisation orders to go out overnight. It would be a close-run thing: even six might be too early to prevent news of the ultimatum from reaching Petersburg Thursday evening. Still, given the hour-and-a-half time difference (and the time needed for telegrams to be composed, encrypted, sent, and deciphered), the news would, Berchtold hoped, not reach the Russian capital until the farewell banquet had already begun on board the *France*.

Adding to Berchtold's headaches was a disquieting conversation he had with the chief of staff early Thursday afternoon. With the prospect of an actual war now staring him in the face within two days, the foreign minister was finally mulling over the worst-case scenarios he should have been thinking about before putting the ultimatum plan into action. What if, he asked Conrad, Serbia complied after the 48-hour deadline had passed – that is, after Austrian mobilisation had begun – but before hostilities had commenced? The chief of staff, unlike the foreign minister, had already considered this possibility, although he did not think it likely. If this transpired, a solution was simple: 'Serbia will [be required to] pay the costs of [our] mobilisation.' Conrad was taken aback, however, by Berchtold's second question. For days the Ballplatz had been receiving disquieting reports from Rome suggesting that the Italians knew what Berchtold was up to. On 10 July, Italy's foreign minister, Antonio di San Giuliano, had even named a quid pro quo for Austrian gains in a Balkan war: Vienna must surrender the entire Italian-speaking South Tyrol (including, not incidentally, Innichen, where Conrad had his country estate). The Germans had been warning Berchtold for weeks that he needed to nail down Italian support, or at least neutrality, but so far nothing had been done. Now, out of the blue, he asked Conrad: What if Italy intervenes against us? In that case, Conrad answered, Austria-Hungary, facing a two-front and possibly three-front war, 'should not mobilise at all.'[8] It was Berchtold's job to ensure Italian neutrality. If he had not succeeded, it was rather late to be telling the army chief of staff.

Conrad would have been even more worried had he or Berchtold known that news of the ultimatum had leaked not only to the British, French, Italians, and Russians but to Belgrade. Back on Wednesday, 15 July, the first serious warning from the Serbian minister at Vienna of impending diplomatic action had reached Belgrade. On Friday, 17 July, the Serbian minister in London informed his government that 'the way is being prepared for diplomatic pressure upon Serbia which may develop into an armed attack.' Prime Minister Pašić was sufficiently alarmed by this news that, later that day, he had informed the Austrian minister Giesl, 'in unofficial conversation,' that 'the Serbian Government are prepared to comply at once with any request for police investigation and to take any other measure compatible with dignity and independence of State.' However, Pašić had also informed Britain's minister to Belgrade (although not Giesl), in a manner that suggested he had excellent intelligence on Austrian intentions, that 'a demand on the part of Austro-Hungarian Government for appointment of a mixed commission of inquiry, for suppression of nationalist societies and for censorship of press, could not be acceded to, since it would imply foreign intervention in domestic affairs and legislation.'[9]

Compounding the unfavourable augurs for the Austrians, Giesl, on demanding an audience with Pašić to deliver his ultimatum Thursday evening, 23 July, learned that the prime minister was not even in town; he was at Nish, campaigning for re-election. Had the Serbians not known what was coming, Pašić's absence would have been unremarkable. Because they did, however, there may have been gamesmanship involved. The Austrians were half-expecting Pašić to resign as soon as he saw the text of the ultimatum, so as to avoid the opprobrium of having to comply with it. To forestall this possibility, Berchtold had instructed Giesl, in the case of such a resignation, to deny its relevance vis-à-vis the ultimatum period on the grounds that 'it is well-known that a Government after resigning still has entire responsibility for the conduct of affairs until the formation of a new Ministry.' The Austrians were not about to let Pašić wiggle out of replying to their ultimatum. Pašić, for his part, was just as keen to wiggle out. As if anticipating imminent action from Austria, on Wednesday, 22 July, Pašić had expressly deputised Serbia's little-known finance minister, Dr Laza Paĉu, to act on his behalf while he was outside Belgrade the next few days. When Paĉu, after receiving Giesl's demand Thursday morning for an urgent audience that night, asked the prime minister to return to Belgrade, Pašić refused and ordered the finance minister to 'receive him in my place.'[10]

By the time Giesl arrived at the Serbian foreign ministry shortly before six PM on Thursday, 23 July, the Austrian ultimatum to Serbia was the worst-kept secret in Europe. True, only the Austrians and Germans had seen the actual text of the note Giesl now carried with him in a sealed envelope. But the Serbs – like the Russians, French, British, and Italians – were in no doubt that it was coming and that the terms would be so harsh as to make their acceptance difficult, if not impossible. Berchtold may not have known how badly his plans had leaked to the chancelleries of Europe, which could only ruin his hope of a localised Balkan fait accompli. Or he may not have wanted to know. Gazing into the abyss of a broader war that might ensue from his failed diplomatic gambit, Berchtold jumped right in.

When Giesl arrived, he was unpleasantly surprised to learn that Paĉu, cynically deputised as head of Serbia's government, did not speak a word of French, the language in which the 'note with a time limit' was written. Luckily, the Serbian foreign ministry did have at least one man on hand, Secretary General Slavko Gruić, who could translate the conversation, if not also provide an instantaneous translation of the note for the benefit of the acting head of Serbia's government. Wasting little time, Giesl displayed a copy of the ultimatum, a two-page annex, and a brief letter addressing Paču as a representative of Prime Minister Pašić. He informed the finance minister that the time limit would expire at six PM on Saturday, 25 July, and that if a satisfactory reply were not received by then, he would leave Belgrade with the entire staff of his legation. Paču scarcely needed an interpreter to figure out what this meant: war.

Still, there was no reason for the Serb to acknowledge that he understood this. Showing that there was method to Pašić's absence, Paču refused to take the documents in hand, objecting that he was unqualified to receive the Austrian note on Serbia's behalf. Without even glancing at the ultimatum (which he could not have read anyway), the acting prime minister protested to Giesl that, because 'there were elections on and many of the ministers were absent, he was afraid that it would be physically impossible to convene a full cabinet meeting in time to decide on a matter of such evident importance.' Giesl, expecting just such an excuse, replied that 'the return of the ministers [to Belgrade] in the age of railways, telegraph, and telephone in a land the size [of Serbia] could only be a matter of a few hours.' He reminded Paču that he had given many hours' notice of the current meeting and that it was Pašić's own choice not to return to Belgrade, as he easily could have. The issue of cabinet meetings and their convocation was, moreover, 'a private matter for the Serbian government in which he [Giesl] had nothing to say.'[11]

Gamely, Paču resisted even this barrage: he simply would not accept the ultimatum on behalf of Serbia's government. After a long, uncomfortable pause, Giesl decided simply to leave it on the table, saying that Paču, and Serbia, 'could do what they liked with it.' Giesl then turned and left. There was nothing more for him to do.[12]

In this way the Austrians, after ruining the surprise of the ultimatum through careless leaks, botched its delivery, too. Having sniffed out the ultimatum early – as did all the other powers – Serbia's government had nearly neutralised it on technical grounds. At the least, Pašić had deprived Giesl and Berchtold of the satisfaction of cornering him.

Meanwhile, dropping his fool's mask the moment Giesl left the room, Paĉu shared the contents of the ultimatum with two other ministers who had been hiding in the next room. They, in turn, passed on the news to friendly diplomats. Naturally, it was the Italians, kingpin gossips of European diplomacy, who had the story first – before passing it on to the Russians. At around nine (Russia time) Thursday evening, an attaché at the Italian embassy in Petersburg, having arrived late to the fare-well banquet on board the *France*, quietly informed K. E. Bützow, acting head of the Russian Foreign Ministry's Near Eastern Department, that 'Austria-Hungary has given a completely unacceptable ultimatum this day to Serbia.' Confirming the veracity of the Italian report, secretaries at Chorister's Bridge received an urgent request almost simultaneously from Count Szapáry for an hour-long morning audience with Russia's foreign minister.[13] Berchtold was about to find out what Sazonov was made of.

14

Sazonov Strikes

FRIDAY, 24 JULY

NEWS OF THE AUSTRIAN ULTIMATUM reached Petersburg soon after Giesl presented it in Belgrade Thursday evening. Berchtold had delayed its delivery for as long as possible, but a bombshell of this kind was hard to suppress once it went off. Sazonov was too wrapped up in the diplomatic niceties of sending off Poincaré to be bothered with the news while still on board the *France*, but he was informed of the Italian attaché's report about the delivery of an ultimatum to Serbia, and of the Austro-Hungarian ambassador's demand for an urgent audience, before he turned in Thursday night. At seven AM, Schilling, Sazonov's chief of staff, received further confirmation about the ultimatum in a telegram from the Russian consulate in Belgrade.[1] By the time Sazonov arrived at the Foreign Ministry around ten AM on Friday, 24 July, he was primed and ready.

'C'est la guerre Européenne!' – This means European war! – Sazonov exclaimed to Schilling as soon as he saw him. While his remark has become justly famous, it is usually mistaken for a spontaneous interjection, in reaction to shocking news (that is, his receipt of the Austrian ultimatum). It was far from this. Sazonov had known an ultimatum of some sort was coming for days, and he had learned of its actual delivery in Belgrade nearly ten hours before saying this. It is true that he had not seen the actual text of the Serbian ultimatum before it was delivered, but then neither had he seen it now: he uttered his bon mot about 'European war' before, not after, Ambassador Szapáry arrived to present him the ultimatum. So if the remark is not apocryphal, it cannot have been spontaneous. It was closer to a declaration of policy.[2]

This interpretation is buttressed by Szapáry's report of his brief and fractious encounter with Russia's foreign minister that morning. Nothing in Sazonov's demeanour suggested surprise or shock. While the ambassador showed him the text of the ultimatum to Serbia, with accompanying commentary, Sazonov remained 'quite calm.' The Russian objected firmly and unambiguously to two clauses of the ultimatum. The Serbs, he said, would never consent to the dissolution of Narodna Odbrana, nor could they allow the participation of Austrian agents in the investigation of the Sarajevo crime on Serbian territory. To Szapáry's claim that Austria-Hungary, in making its demands to suppress terrorist agitation against the dual monarchy, 'stood as one with all civilised nations,' Sazonov replied that 'this was erroneous' (*dies sei ein Irrtum*). 'You,' the Russian insisted, 'are setting Europe ablaze.' With a level of conviction that took Szapáry aback, Russia's foreign minister warned him 'to consider the impression [the ultimatum] would make in Paris, London, and perhaps elsewhere,' where it would be 'considered as unjustified aggression.' When the ambassador, desperate for a sign of goodwill, invoked that old theme the monarchical principle, Sazonov simply swatted it away: 'the monarchical idea has nothing to do with this.'[3] With these words, he concluded the audience, leaving Szapáry in no doubt where Russia stood.

Sazonov's cool and calculated tone with the Austro-Hungarian ambassador suggests that he had already made up his mind on a policy line after learning the news from Belgrade Thursday night. As he had told Britain's ambassador after getting wind of Berchtold's plans the previous Saturday, if Austria delivered an ultimatum to Serbia, Russia 'might be forced to take some precautionary military measure.' True to his word, scarcely had Szapáry left his office Friday morning at ten thirty AM than Sazonov summoned the Council of Ministers to meet at three PM, with urgent notice of required attendance sent to the chief of Army Staff, N. N. Yanushkevitch, and the naval minister, I. K. Grigorevich. Sazonov also ordered Yanushkevitch to make 'all arrangements for putting the army on a war footing,' and to have a 'partial mobilisation' plan written up and ready for consideration by three PM.[4] Sazonov then recalled all Foreign Ministry officials of the Diplomatic Chancellery and the Near East Section from leave, ordering them to report at once.

Russia's finance minister, Peter Bark, was the first to respond to Sazonov's summons, arriving at Chorister's Bridge at eleven AM. The foreign minister had stepped out, so Bark spoke to Schilling instead. 'Was there any likelihood of war?' he asked. Schilling answered without hesitation that '*Sazonov considered war unavoidable.*' In view of this, Bark asked if he might be informed 'whether . . . matters would move quickly since, in that case, I should have to take immediate steps to ensure the transfer of the Russian Treasury funds deposited in Berlin.' Again without hesitation, Schilling told Bark to do just this. Moving with almost Germanic speed (the finance minister, though Russian, had worked a long stint at the German House of Mendelssohn), Bark wired Berlin before the Council of Ministers convened, ordering his agents there to transfer balances held in German banks – 100 million rubles' worth in all, more than $20 billion in today's terms – to Paris and Petersburg.[5]

While Bark was repatriating Russian funds from Germany, Sazonov was discussing mobilisation plans with the army chiefs. In late November 1912, as the First Balkan War was heating up, Sukhomlinov, the war minister, had drawn up a 'partial mobilisation plan' against Austria-Hungary alone, his idea being to threaten Vienna without alarming Germany into mobilising on Austria's behalf pursuant to her alliance obligations. A key corollary was that the Warsaw district – that is, Russian Poland – would *not* be mobilised, so as not to alarm the commanders of the German 8th Army in East Prussia. Just as he had later blocked the war party during the Liman von Sanders crisis in January 1914, chairman of the Council of Ministers Kokovtsov had vetoed Sukhomlinov's 'partial mobilisation' plan in November 1912 on the grounds that 'no matter what we chose to call the projected measures, *a mobilisation remained a mobilisation*, to be countered by our adversaries with actual war.'[6] With the gun-shy Kokovtsov having been removed from the council in February 1914, Sazonov now was ready to try Sukhomlinov's plan. Shortly after eleven AM on Friday, 24 July, he brought Yanushkevitch up to speed on the situation and asked him to draw up a partial mobilisation directive. The chief of staff agreed.

Yanushkevitch then summoned the chief of the Russian Army's Mobilisation Section, General Sergei Dobrorolskii, who arrived at headquarters just before noon. Showing that he had been thoroughly briefed by Sazonov on the diplomatic situation, Yanushkevitch informed Dobrorolskii that Russia would shortly announce publicly that it could not 'remain indifferent' regarding Vienna's 'wholly unacceptable ultimatum' to Serbia. An even more aggressive, though less official, notice would also be posted in *Russkii Invalid*, the official newspaper of the Russian War Ministry, proclaiming that Russia would 'not remain inactive if the dignity and the integrity of the Serbian people, our blood brothers, are threatened with danger.' 'Have you everything ready for the proclamation of the mobilisation of our army?' Yanushkevitch asked his mobilisation chief. Dobrorolskii said yes. 'In that case,' the chief of staff continued, 'in an hour bring me all the documents relative to the preparing of our troops for war, which provide, in case of necessity, for proclaiming partial mobilisation against Austria-Hungary alone. This mobilisation must give no occasion to Germany to find any grounds of hostility to herself.'

Hearing this, Dobrorolskii was perturbed. Mobilising against Austria-Hungary alone and not Germany, he told his boss, was 'folly.' The army's current Plan 19 required mobilisation against Germany and Austria simultaneously, with no variant separating the two. Moreover, Dobrorolskii explained, it was 'physically impossible' to mobilise effectively against Austria without extensively using the Warsaw railway hub. Were a mobilisation to exclude Poland, it would be possible to attack Austria only via a tiny sliver of Galicia or by way of Romania, which was clearly out of the question. Deploying against Austria via the Warsaw hub was unavoidable, but doing so would inevitably alarm German commanders in East Prussia, defeating the point of a 'partial' mobilisation.[7] Just as Kokovtsov had said in 1912, 'a mobilisation remained a mobilisation,' no matter what Sukhomlinov or Sazonov wished to call it. Yanushkevitch, a recent appointee as chief of staff, may not have understood this fact. Still, as a subordinate officer, Dobrorolskii agreed to do what he was told, in so far as it was possible.

Because Sazonov was a civilian, it is possible that he was just as ignorant as Yanushkevitch about the strategic implications of 'partial' mobilisation. There is evidence, however, that suggests otherwise. The foreign minister had been present at the emergency Ministerial Council meeting in November 1912, when Sukhomlinov had presented his partial mobilisation plan. He had heard the war minister explain it, and he had then heard Kokovtsov dismiss it on the grounds that, because the Germans would see through it ('a mobilisation remained a mobilisation'), it could not but lead to a European war.

Sazonov, true to his reputation for hesitation, had voted with the chairman. He had even chimed in that Russia should never order even a partial mobilisation without consulting first with France. This crucial exchange, prefiguring the current policy dilemma with uncanny precision, had taken place less than two years ago. Unless his memory had failed him completely, Sazonov must have been thinking of it now, as he asked the army to order partial mobilisation against Austria. This time, unlike in November 1912, Sazonov had personally consulted with France – indeed with her entire civilian government – the previous day and in the three days before that. He therefore felt confident of French support in case Russia's 'partial mobilisation' led to war, a prospect that, judging by Schilling's remark to Bark, Sazonov viewed as unavoidable.

Still, to make extra sure of France, the foreign minister visited the French embassy to lunch with Paléologue and Britain's Ambassador Buchanan, who was keen to learn what France and Russia were up to. Sazonov declared unequivocally, Buchanan reported, that 'the step taken by Austria meant war.' He informed the Briton of the full agreement on Balkan questions reached by France and Russia at the summit. Paléologue affirmed this heartily, promising that 'France would not only give Russia strong diplomatic support, but would, if necessary, fulfil all the obligations imposed on her by the alliance,' shorthand for mobilising against Germany. Would His Majesty's government, Sazonov asked Britain's ambassador, 'proclaim their solidarity with France and Russia'? Buchanan, to the Russian's disappointment, was unable to do so. Britain, he declared, 'had no interests in Serbia, and public opinion in England would never sanction a war on her behalf.' To this, Sazonov objected that 'the Serbian question was but part of [the] general European question and that we [i.e., the British] could not efface ourselves.' Seeking clarification as to what the

Russian meant by this, Buchanan asked Sazonov point-blank: 'If [Austria-Hungary] took military action against Serbia, did Russia propose to declare war on her?'

Here Sazonov hedged. Nothing, he assured Buchanan, would be decided until the Council of Ministers met that afternoon. In turn, no policy would be formally enacted until the ministers presented their recommendations to Tsar Nicholas II at Tsarskoe Selo the next morning. But there was no doubt where Sazonov stood. The foreign minister himself, Buchanan reported to Grey, 'thought that at any rate Russia would have to mobilise.' This was not what anyone in London wanted to hear.

Trying to slow down the doomsday machine, Buchanan asked that France and Russia help pressure Vienna into extending the ultimatum deadline, before Russia took any warlike measures. Revealingly, it was France's ambassador, and not Sazonov, who shot down this idea as a fantasy. 'Either Austria was bluffing,' Paléologue opined, 'or had made up her mind to act at once.' So belligerent was the 'French Ambassador's language,' Buchanan informed Grey, 'that it almost looked as if France and Russia were determined to take a strong stand even if we refused to join them.' Sazonov's tone he found somewhat milder than Paléologue's, but no less worrying. Russia's foreign minister, Buchanan reported, warned him 'that if war did break out, we [i.e., Britain] would sooner or later be dragged into it, but if we did not make common cause with France and Russia at the outset we should have rendered war more likely, and should not have played a *beau rôle*.' With these forceful words, Sazonov returned to Chorister's Bridge, leaving Britain's ambassador in little doubt as to Russia's seriousness of purpose.[8]

A T THREE PM, the Council of Ministers convened for a special session that lasted nearly two hours. With Kokovtsov out of the picture, and the new chairman, I. V. Goremykin, largely a figurehead, it was Sazonov's show. If Agriculture Minister Krivoshein and the other belligerent 'Germanophobes' had any doubts that the foreign minister would stand firm against Austria, he dispelled them immediately. The current crisis, Sazonov told everyone, was a long time in the making. 'There were deep-seated causes of conflict,' he said, 'between the Central European powers and those of the Entente.' Russian weakness in recent years had provoked Germany's aggressive behaviour. Austria's ultimatum to Serbia was only a 'pretext that would enable her [i.e., Germany] to prove her superiority by the use of force.' Russia, Sazonov concluded,

> could not remain a passive spectator whilst a Slavonic people was being deliberately trampled down. In 1876 and 1877 Russia had fought Turkey for the liberation of the Slavonic peoples in the Balkans. We had made immense sacrifices with that end in view. . . . If Russia failed to fulfil her historic mission, she would be considered a decadent State and would henceforth have to take second place among the Powers. . . . If, at this critical juncture, the Serbs were abandoned to their fate, Russian prestige in the Balkans would collapse utterly.

Krivoshein was impressed. Supporting Sazonov's line, he declared that 'public and parliamentary opinion would fail to understand why, at this critical moment involving Russia's vital interests, the Imperial Government was reluctant to act boldly.' If Russia did not take a strong stand this time, the government – if not the whole Tsarist regime – would collapse in the face of public contempt for her weakness.

Krivoshein's argument, recalled Bark, 'made a profound impression on the Cabinet.' The ministers resolved to issue a stern public warning to Vienna that Serbia's fate 'could not leave Russia indifferent.'[9]

The real business, however, had been conducted beforehand by Sazonov. The ministers were presented with five policy resolutions. The first two were fairly innocuous, although cleverly contrived. In the first, Russia promised to work with the other powers to request that Austria extend the ultimatum deadline – notwithstanding the fact that Sazonov and Paléologue had just told Buchanan that this was impossible. In the second, Russia advised Serbia to announce that she would not resist any Austrian invasion, but would rather entrust her fate to the Powers. Considering that Russia had just shipped arms to Belgrade at Pašić's express request, this was curious advice – but it made good diplomatic sense. So long as Britain and other neutral powers believed Russia – and Serbia – to be acting in moderation, they would see Austria-Hungary and Germany as the powers disturbing the peace.

The last three resolutions, all secret, were more serious. The third said that the army and navy chiefs, Yanushkevitch and Grigorevich, would ask the tsar, at a formal Crown Council at Tsarskoe Selo the next day, to approve 'in principle' the mobilisation of the four military districts of Kiev, Odessa, Moscow, and Kazan (a partial mobilisation 'against Austria alone'), along with the Black Sea and Baltic fleets (interesting, in that Austria-Hungary bordered neither body of water). The fourth resolution authorised the army to begin stockpiling supplies necessary for war. Finally, the fifth resolution stipulated that state funds were to be repatriated from Germany and Austria-Hungary.[10]

Although these resolutions were, formally, put up for vote in the Council of Ministers and then subject to a possible veto from the tsar at the Crown Council, Sazonov would not have written them up if he was not confident they would be approved. Yanushkevitch, indeed, had already begun preparing a 'partial mobilisation' directive before the ministers met – on the foreign minister's direct orders. Bark, too, had already begun repatriating funds from Germany simply on Sazonov's say-so. To no one's surprise, Sazonov's resolutions passed unanimously, making their approval by the tsar a foregone conclusion.

Having won over the ministers to a secret 'partial mobilisation,' Sazonov returned to his office around six PM. Serbia's minister to Russia, M. Spalaiković, was waiting for him, first in line to learn what had been resolved by the Council. Spalaiković's instructions from Pašić (still campaigning at Nish) were to inform Sazonov that the Serbian army was in no state to resist an invasion by Austria-Hungary and to ask, in light of this information, what Russia advised Belgrade to do. In a telegram to the tsar, Serbia's Prince-Regent Alexander had been more submissive still, promising that Serbia would agree to all terms of the ultimatum 'whose acceptance shall be advised by Your Majesty.' Whatever the truth about the war-readiness of Serbia's army, the stance in Belgrade was clear: Serbia would do whatever Russia advised.[11]

Sazonov's advice was firm. Somewhat to Spalaiković's surprise, Russia's foreign minister told him not to comply with the ultimatum. As a show of good faith, he advised that Serbia declare acceptance of the more inoffensive clauses. She must not, however, accept articles 5 and 6, which related to the participation of Austrian officials 'in the suppression of the subversive movement' and in the prosecution of accessories to the Sarajevo crime. These clauses, Sazonov told Spalaiković, infringed on Serbian sovereignty. Publicly, as resolved in the Council of Ministers, Russia's foreign minister advised that Serbia 'make a declaration and allow the Austrians to enter Serbia without putting up any resistance.' Privately, however, Sazonov assured Spalaiković that 'Serbia may count on Russian aid.' While we do not know how explicit Sazonov was in conversation with the Serbian minister about the form this 'aid' to Serbia might take – whether, that is, he informed Spalaiković about the impending partial mobilisation – Sazonov's message to Belgrade was still clear:* Serbia should make a show of moderation but not yield. If it came to war, Russia would fight on her behalf.[12]

At seven PM, Spalaiković left Sazonov's office, making haste for the telegraph office so he could report to Belgrade. On his way out, the Serb ran into Count Pourtalès. Since the morning, Germany's ambassador had been demanding an audience to discuss Russia's response to the Austrian ultimatum; he had been put off on the grounds that Sazonov was busy assembling the Council of Ministers. Now, to his consternation, Pourtalès learned that the foreign minister had met with Spalaiković first. He would have been more disquieted still had he known that Sazonov had lunched with the French and British ambassadors. Seeking an indication as to Russia's response to the ultimatum, Pourtalès told Spalaiković that Germany hoped to 'localise' the Austro-Serbian dispute. 'Localisation' was a loaded word, of course: the German line, established by Foreign Minister Jagow and Chancellor Bethmann, was that Austria should have a free hand to settle accounts with Belgrade without the other powers butting in. Spalaiković would have none of this. The Austrian ultimatum, he warned Pourtalès, was already a 'European question.'[13]

Germany's ambassador had little more luck with Russia's foreign minister. Despite what must have been an exhausting day, Sazonov was sharp. Rejecting the case Pourtalès presented for 'localisation,' the Russian pointed out that the Austrian ultimatum began by invoking the promise Serbia had made to recognise Austria's annexation of Bosnia-Herzegovina in a declaration of 31 March 1909, the idea being that this solemn promise had been broken. This Serbian declaration, however,

---

* A number of Spalaiković's crucial 24 July dispatches to Belgrade have gone missing, but at least one survives, which contains the passages cited here.

had been made 'in deference to the advice of the Great Powers' – not simply to Austria-Hungary. Moreover, just that morning Austria's ambassadors had presented the ultimatum to all signatory powers of the 1878 Treaty of Berlin, which had underwritten Serbia's 1909 declaration (because the annexation of Bosnia-Herzegovina revised that treaty). Sazonov had not pointed this out to Ambassador Szapáry during their morning audience, in part because he had not yet had time to read through the text of the ultimatum. Now that he had, he was able to poke a large hole in the Austrian case for localisation. Szapáry recognised as much as soon as Pourtalès reported his conversation to him. Sazonov, Szapáry informed Berchtold in an urgent telegram sent later that evening, 'had unfortunately found grounds for his objection in our own note.'[14]

The Russian was still not finished. He was unconvinced, he told Pourtalès, by the so-called proofs that Vienna had linking Serbia to the Sarajevo crime. He dismissed the German's invocation of the monarchical principle, saying that 'it had absolutely nothing to do with the present case.' Working himself into a rage, the Russian began 'indulging in the most extravagant accusations and imputations against the Austro-Hungarian Government.' At last Pourtalès interrupted him, objecting that the Russian 'was speaking under the sway of his blind, relentless hatred of Austria.' Without losing his temper, Sazonov replied that 'hatred was not in my character. It is not hatred I feel for Austria, but contempt.'

The Russian then came to the point. He was now firmly convinced, he told Pourtalès, 'that Austria-Hungary was looking for a pretext to "swallow up" Serbia.'* 'In that case,

---

* The French word Sazonov used was *avaler* ('to absorb or swallow'). Pourtalès rendered this in German as *verschlingen*, with roughly the same sense. Szapáry, reporting to Vienna, retranslated this back into French as *dévorer* ('to devour').

however,' he told the German ambassador, 'then Russia will make war on Austria.'

Pourtalès was shocked. Although Sazonov had talked tough during their Monday audience, this was something else. Never before had he heard the word 'war' cross Sazonov's lips. At first, he did not quite believe it. To give Sazonov room to back down, Pourtalès tried to reassure the Russian that the ultimatum would only lead, even in the 'worse-case scenario,' to 'a punitive Austrian expedition against Serbia,' and that 'Austria was far removed from any contemplation of territorial acquisitions': there would be no 'swallowing up' of Serbia. At this, Pourtalès reported, 'Sazonov shook his head incredulously and spoke of far-reaching Austrian plans. First Serbia would be devoured (*verspeist werden*), then it would be Bulgaria's turn and then "we shall have them [i.e., the Austrians] at the Black Sea."' Pourtalès refused to humour such 'fantastic exaggerations,' seeing them as 'not worthy of serious discussion.' But he did not forget what the Russian had said. The only explanation for the use of such extreme language, Pourtalès believed, was Sazonov's 'passionate national and especially religious hatred for Austria-Hungary,' which, as a Catholic power, he viewed as fundamentally hostile to Orthodox Serbia.[15]

There are differing accounts of how this confrontation at the Russian Foreign Ministry ended. In a telegram he sent to the Wilhelmstrasse shortly after midnight, Pourtalès reassured Jagow that, despite Sazonov's strong language, his real goal was likely to 'Europeanise' the ultimatum question. 'Prompt Russian intervention,' he predicted, 'was not to be expected.' Szapáry, passing on to Vienna what Pourtalès told him that night, reported that the audience had been 'friendly' and that Sazonov had concluded it by appealing to Pourtalès that 'Germany might work together with Russia to preserve peace.' In a longer letter to Jagow sent the next day, Pourtalès likewise reported that Sazonov's real goal was to 'temporise' and delay, not to force matters to a head. 'Despite the agitation reigning in Russian governing circles,' Pourtalès concluded, 'such rash steps as this [i.e., Sazonov's threat to make war on Austria] were not to be expected.'[16]

Other sources, however, suggest that the meeting did not conclude as amicably as this. The Russian Foreign Ministry logbook reports that 'those who saw Count Pourtalès as he left the Ministry state that he was very agitated, and did not conceal the fact that S. D. Sazonov's words, and especially his firm determination to resist the Austrian demands, had made a strong impression on him.'[17] Lending credence to this report, Pourtalès himself recorded in his diary that night – perhaps not wishing to alarm Jagow or to give cause to the German war party, he did not report this to Berlin – that Sazonov's remarks 'gave him the impression' that the Council of Ministers must have 'seriously eyed the eventuality of a break with Germany and Austria-Hungary' and 'resolved not to hang back from an armed conflict.'[18]

Scarcely had the German ambassador left Sazonov's office, at around eight PM, than his French counterpart arrived.* The Russian foreign minister, Paléologue observed, 'was still agitated over the dispute in which he has just been engaged. He has quick, nervous moments and his voice is dry and jerky.' Casting aside the diplomatic assurances he and the German had both just exchanged, Sazonov told France's ambassador that 'Germany wholeheartedly supports the Austrian cause. Not the

---

* Paléologue claims in his memoirs that he saw Pourtalès leaving Sazonov's office, 'his face purple and his eyes flashing.' According to Schilling, however, the French ambassador deliberately avoided Pourtalès by waiting in the anteroom, to which the German, as a 'hostile' ambassador, was not allowed access.

slightest suggestion of conciliation. So I told Pourtalès quite bluntly that we should not leave Serbia to settle her differences with Austria alone.' (Sazonov may not have told the Frenchman just how 'blunt' he had been, threatening to make war on Austria.) With revealing candour, the Russian told Paléologue of the German's accusation that he 'hated' Austria, claiming that he retorted, 'No, of course we don't like Austria. . . . Why should we like her? She has never done us anything but harm.' Sazonov then 'promptly informed [Paléologue] of the decisions come to by the Council of Ministers' – including the partial mobilisation against Austria.[19]

It had been quite an evening at Chorister's Bridge. In less than three hours, Russia's foreign minister had (1) instructed Serbia's minister not to comply with Austria's ultimatum and promised that 'Serbia may count on Russian aid' (although it is unclear whether he also spelled out what form this 'aid' would take); (2) warned Germany's ambassador that Russia would go to war with Austria if she 'swallowed up' Serbia; and (3) informed France's ambassador about Russia's impending mobilisation measures. Making the performance still more remarkable, before making these moves Sazonov had not consulted with any of the three statesmen most directly involved with Russian policy. Tsar Nicholas II was sailing his yacht off the Finnish coast while most of this took place (although he had been ordered to return to Tsarskoe Selo in time for the next morning's Crown Council). President Poincaré was cruising the Baltic aboard the *France*. Serbia's prime minister, Pašić, had not even returned from the campaign trail to Belgrade. When these men awoke on Saturday, it would be in a different world.

15

Russia, France, and Serbia Stand Firm

SATURDAY, 25 JULY

A S DAWN BROKE ON SATURDAY, the streets of St Petersburg were already beginning to simmer. All through July the heat wave had been building. Now it reached its terrible peak. The train stations were packed with vacationers desperate to escape the swampy heat of the capital. In the working-class districts, the situation had steadied somewhat since Wednesday, when many strikers had been injured in clashes with Cossacks. Still, the heat was doing nothing to improve the mood in the factories and cramped housing quarters. Police feared that a new explosion was imminent.

On the parade ground at Krasnoe Selo, a better-heeled crowd had gathered to observe the annual summer review of imperial troops. The manoeuvres were to have been held in the late morning, before the midday sun had ascended over the baking-hot plain. Unfortunately for the overdressed spectators, they would not be this lucky. Although at first no one was told why, the review was postponed until early afternoon.

THE REASON, IT SOON EMERGED, was that an emergency session of the Council of Ministers had been convened at nearby Tsarskoe Selo to ratify the decisions made in Petersburg the previous afternoon. While Petersburg high society was gathering for a lazy Saturday at the parade ground, Sazonov had been furiously making the rounds. He had spent the night at Tsarskoe Selo, risen early, and gone to his office at Chorister's Bridge to pick up the evening's telegrams before returning for the council. This session, unlike yesterday's, was presided over by Tsar Nicholas II himself. The historic resolutions went even further than those taken on Friday.

First, Russia's sovereign approved the previous day's decision 'in principle' to undertake a 'partial mobilisation' of the four military districts of Kiev, Odessa, Moscow, and Kazan, along with the Black Sea and Baltic fleets. The idea was to telegraph a limited mobilisation 'against Austria alone,' although even this would not be announced publicly until Austria moved against Serbia. Mobilising these four districts would prime for war a substantial force of 1.1 million men, not including naval forces.

Second, all troops were to return to standing quarters. As at Tsarskoe Selo, most of the army was at summer quarters instead, engaging in seasonal manoeuvres and drills. Standing quarters were the permanent bases where arms and other war matériel were stored – equipment soldiers must have in hand before they could be mobilised. While not tantamount to mobilisation itself, this measure would rapidly put troops into motion across the vast reach of the Russian Empire – not just the 1.1 million men who were to be mobilised in the four districts 'against Austria,' but the entire army. It was given the highest priority. On Chief of Staff Yanushkevitch's orders, Dobrorolskii sent out secret cipher telegram no. 1547 at 4:10 PM:

PREPARE QUICKLY TRANSPORT PLANS AND PROVISIONS FOR THE RETURN OF ALL TROOPS TO STANDING QUARTERS. TIME FOR THE COMPLETION OF THIS WORK: 24 HOURS.[1]

Third, army cadets were immediately promoted to officers. Russia's army was notably inferior to the German one in the strength of its subalterns and non-commissioned officers. This measure would go some way towards closing the gap. It not only enlarged the officer corps in absolute terms but also freed for active service many mature officers previously engaged in training recruits.

Four, a 'state of war' (that is, martial law) was proclaimed in Moscow, St Petersburg, all towns in European Russia containing fortresses, and 'in the frontier sectors facing Austria and Germany.'[2]

Finally, and most important, the council issued top-secret orders to inaugurate the 'Period Preparatory to War in all lands of the empire,' beginning at midnight. This was a pre-mobilisation directive akin to the Germans' own *Kriegsgefahrzustand*, which immediately preceded mobilisation (which, in the German case, also meant war). The Russian version was no less portentous than the German. As a secret military commission had reported to War Minister Sukhomlinov in November 1912, 'it will be advantageous to complete concentration without beginning hostilities, in order not to deprive the enemy irrevocably of the hope that war can still be avoided. Our measures for this *must be masked by clever diplomatic negotiations*, in order to *lull to sleep as much as possible the enemy's fears.*'[3] According to the final statute signed into law by the tsar on 2 March 1913, the Period Preparatory to War

> means the period of diplomatic complications which precedes the opening of hostilities in the course of which all Government departments must take the necessary measures for the preparation and smooth execution of the mobilisation of the Army, the Navy and the Fortresses, as well as for the deployment of the army at the threatened frontier.[4]

The gravity of these decisions was felt immediately on the parade ground at Tsarskoe Selo. Scarcely had the review of the imperial guard troops begun than it was cut short. As General Oskar von Chelius, Germany's aide-de-camp to the tsar, reported to Berlin, 'during the afternoon review it was announced . . . that manoeuvres would be called off for tonight, and that troops must return [to base].' Showing that the orders applied to the top rank of the army too, General Adlerberg, the military governor of St Petersburg, next 'broke off' a conversation with Chelius, announcing that '*he had to go to attend to the "mobilisation."*'[5]

Sazonov, too, returned to his own base – at Chorister's Bridge – as soon as the review concluded at Krasnoe Selo. His first item of business was to inform the French and British ambassadors about what had been resolved at Tsarskoe Selo. To enhance the impression that the Entente Powers should work together as a team, he called them both in together. With Britain still on the diplomatic sidelines, Sazonov had to be very careful with Buchanan. So he discussed only the first resolution of the morning: the decision 'in principle' to mobilise the four military districts against Austria (and even here, the Russian neglected to mention that the Baltic and Black Sea fleets would be mobilised as well). Sazonov, Buchanan reported to Foreign Secretary Grey, insisted that the imperial *ukase* 'ordering mobilisation of 1.1 million men' would 'only be published when Minister for Foreign Affairs [Sazonov] considers moment come for giving effect to it.' When the Briton 'expressed [his] earnest hope that Russia would not precipitate war by mobilising before you [i.e., Grey] had had time to use your influence in favour of peace,' Sazonov assured him 'that Russia had no aggressive intentions, and she would take no action until it was forced on her.' In a seeming contradiction, however, Sazonov also told Buchanan and Paléologue that 'necessary preliminary preparations for mobilisation would, however, begin at once' – an allusion to the 'Period Preparatory to War,' although the Russian did not spell this out.

Paléologue, speaking for France, endorsed the council's decisions, Buchanan reported to London, 'without the slightest sign of hesitation.' When Sazonov asked Buchanan whether Britain, too, would make a statement backing Russia, the answer was no. At best, the Briton was able to promise to 'play the role of mediator at Berlin and Vienna.' Hearing this, Sazonov grew frustrated. Germany's attitude towards war, he tried to convince Buchanan, depended on her view of what London would do. 'If we [Britain] took our stand with France and Russia,' Buchanan said Sazonov argued, 'there would be no war.' If, by contrast, 'we failed them now, rivers of blood would flow and we would in the end be dragged into war.'

To this veiled warning Buchanan replied with a warning of his own. Unable to give Russia the unequivocal endorsement she wanted, the Briton 'said all he could to impress prudence on [Sazonov].' If, however, 'Russia mobilised,' Buchanan warned Russia's foreign minister, 'Germany would not be content with mere mobilisation or give Russia time to carry out hers, but would probably wish to precipitate a conflict.' Since neither Austria nor Russia looked like blinking, war now looked increasingly likely. The position, Buchanan concluded in his report to Grey, was 'perilous.' Because Russia was now 'secure of support of France, she will face all the risks of war.' Before long, Britain 'shall have to choose between giving Russia our active support or renouncing our friendship.'[6]

Paléologue had no such qualms. Poincaré and Viviani were still at sea. He had received no messages either from the *France* or from the acting director of foreign affairs at the Quai d'Orsay, Jean-Baptiste Bienvenu-Martin, urging any sort of caution (he may have agreed on a policy line with Poincaré before the president left). Paléologue therefore felt justified in assuring Sazonov that 'France placed herself unreservedly at Russia's side.'

Unlike Buchanan, France's ambassador was under no illusions about what the Period Preparatory to War meant. In a telegram sent to Bienvenu-Martin at 6:22 PM, following his afternoon audience with Buchanan and Sazonov, Paléologue reported not only Russia's 'partial' mobilisation, to be announced if and when Austria-Hungary attacked Serbia, but also that 'meanwhile secret [Russian military] preparations will begin today.'[7] In the same telegram, Paléologue informed Paris that France's military attaché, General Pierre de Laguiche, had been posted liaison at Krasnoe Selo to Russia's War Minister Sukhomlinov and her future commander in chief, Grand Duke Nicholas. Laguiche, for his part, received secret instructions from the French General Staff this day to treat with the Russians on the assumption that 'European war could no longer be avoided.'[8] Thus even while her civilian government was at sea, France's diplomatic and military liaisons in Petersburg would be fully in the loop – and in contact with Paris – as Russia's secret mobilisation proceeded.

A BOARD THE *FRANCE*, Poincaré and Viviani remained unaware of the momentous decisions made at Tsarskoe Selo on Saturday. Although the ship's wireless was working, the signal strength was often weak. Thus the *France*'s wireless operator was able to decode Paléologue's Saturday morning telegram announcing Friday's decision at the Council of Ministers to advise Serbia not to resist an Austrian invasion but not the telegram he sent at 6:22 PM announcing Russia's impending partial mobilisation and that 'secret military preparations will begin today.' Poincaré, unaware that Sazonov was taking a carrot-and-stick approach, thus thought it was all carrots. He was apoplectic on hearing that Russia wanted Serbia to submit. In his diary Saturday evening, Poincaré called Russia's advice to Belgrade an 'abdication of the tsarist empire' that would mark a 'sinister day in world history.' The French, he lamented, 'can certainly not be more pan-Slavic than the Russians. Poor Serbia will thus likely be humiliated.'[9] Had the *France* decoded Paléologue's second telegram, Viviani almost certainly would not have approved. Poincaré, by contrast, would have danced a jig in joy.

Meanwhile, in Belgrade, the ultimatum deadline was fast approaching. While Berchtold had told his colleagues, and the Germans, to expect a rejection, the signals coming from Belgrade were ambiguous. Somewhat to everyone's surprise, Pašić's initial response, given Saturday morning to foreign legations in Belgrade – including Austria's – suggested that Serbia would comply with the ultimatum with only minor reservations. As Britain's chargé d'affaires in Belgrade, Dayrell Crackanthorpe, reported to Grey, the reply 'will be drawn up in the most conciliatory terms and will meet Austrian demands in as large measure as possible.' The key public demand, that Serbia publish in its official gazette a statement of apology and condemnation of anti-Austrian propaganda, would be met in full. The ten points of the ultimatum, Crackanthorpe continued, 'are accepted with reserves.' Serbia would 'agree to suppress Narodna Odbrana' and to 'dismiss and prosecute those officers whose guilt can be clearly proved.' Apis's right-hand man, Major Tankositch, whose apprehension for helping organise the assassination plot was demanded in point 7, was already under arrest. Even the onerous points 5 and 6, which demanded that Austro-Hungarian officials collaborate in the 'suppression of the subversive movement' in Serbia and 'take part in the investigations relating thereto,' were accepted conditionally, so long as the appointment of such a 'mixed commission of enquiry . . . can be proved to be in accordance with international usage.'[10]

France's new minister to Belgrade, Jules August Boppe, added in his own report that Pašić had agreed to 'dissolve the societies of national defence [i.e., Narodna Odbrana] and all other associations which might agitate against Austria-Hungary,' and to 'modify the press law, to dismiss from the army, public instruction and other administrations all officials whose participation in the propaganda shall be proved' – Pašić telling Boppe, helpfully, that Austria-Hungary might provide her own list of guilty officials. As to points 5 and 6, Boppe said that Serbia would 'ask for explanations' and 'only agree to that which is consonant with international law or to relations of good neighbourliness.'[11] If this was the only objection Pašić would raise, Vienna would be hard-pressed to find fault with his reply.

Sometime Saturday afternoon, however, the draft presented to the legations in Belgrade that morning was scrapped and replaced by something quite different. The final text of Serbia's reply to the Austrian ultimatum, which Pašić presented to Giesl in person at six PM, reneged on many of the promises made earlier, beginning with the public apology. Rather than expressing regret 'that Serbian officers and officials have participated in the above-mentioned propaganda,' as demanded in the ultimatum, Serbia expressed 'regret that, *according to the communication from [Austria-Hungary]* certain Serbian officers and functionaries participated.' Rather than regretting an action, that is, Serbia regretted being accused of an action. Likewise, the Serbian reply note agreed that Narodna Odbrana would be dissolved but insisted that Serbia's government 'possess no proof, nor does the note of [Austria-Hungary] furnish them with any, that the *Narodna Odbrana* and other similar societies have committed . . . any criminal act.' Four other clauses were accepted in principle, but with enough conditions and camouflage as not to suggest compliance in practice.

As to the crucial clauses 5 and 6, Pašić's final draft split the difference. The first – collaboration of Austrian officials in suppressing the subversive movement – was accepted, as Boppe and Crackanthorpe had informed Paris and London it would be, insofar as this 'agreed with the principle of international law, with criminal procedure, and with good neighbourly relations.' The second, however, was shot down firmly. 'As regards the participation in this inquiry of Austro-Hungarian agents or authorities,' Pašić's reply read, Serbia 'cannot accept such an arrangement, as it would be a violation of the Constitution and of the law of criminal procedure.'[12] There was no camouflaging this one: it was a blanket refusal.

Had Pašić changed his mind? Because so many of the relevant Serbian documents have disappeared, it is difficult to determine exactly when, and why, Serbia's prime minister decided not to comply with the Austrian ultimatum. One possibility is that he never meant to comply at all but told allied ministers such as Boppe and Crackanthorpe that he would in order to win British and French backing (Russian support was taken for granted). Buttressing this explanation, the final reply presented to Giesl at six PM, unlike the morning draft, was not presented to the other powers until days later (it was not sent by telegraph), by which time events had overtaken it and no one paid it much attention – with the curious exception of Kaiser Wilhelm II, who, on reading Pašić's reply on 28 July, believed it to constitute acceptance.

Another explanation is that Pašić resolved to take a firmer line after reading Spalaiković's report from Petersburg, in which Sazonov had advised him not to accept points 5 and 6 and that 'Serbia may count on Russian aid.' This report arrived in Belgrade before midnight on Friday and was probably decoded Saturday morning and then given to Pašić, who had returned from Nish overnight. It must have been welcome news. Were Pašić to comply with all or even most of the ultimatum, the faction of extreme nationalists in the Black Hand led by Apis would have an excellent pretext for overthrowing his government. On Friday, the German minister at Belgrade, Julius Griesinger, had reported to Berlin that the Serbian military 'categorically demand the rejection of the note and war' and that in the event a Serbian public apology were published in the official Serbian gazette, as demanded by Austria, 'a military uprising is feared.'[13] Lending further credence to this version of events, Slavko Gruić, the secretary general of the Serbian Foreign Office charged with translating the reply note, recalled endless hassles over the text. All Saturday afternoon, Pašić and his advisers badgered poor Gruić with suggested changes, to the point where the running draft was 'was so full of crossings out and additions as to be almost incomprehensible.'[14] The prime minister clearly sweated over his draft until the last minute, trying to make it sound as conciliatory as possible to allies and neutrals, while still making a strong enough stand on point 6 such as he knew could not be acceptable to Austria-Hungary, thus protecting his political flank against Apis. Pašić may have wanted to reject the ultimatum anyway, but until he was sure of Russian backing, he could not risk doing so. Sazonov's pledge thus saved him from the horns of a very serious dilemma – and, possibly, from a coup d'état.

Whatever the reason for the revisions, Pašić knew that the Austrians would not accept his reply. He seems not to have minded if the Austrians knew, too. By one PM on Saturday – five hours before Giesl was to accept Pašić's reply – Giesl reported to Vienna that Serbian preparations for war had already begun. 'The reserves of the National Bank, along with the archives of the Foreign Ministry,' he informed Berchtold, 'are being removed from Belgrade to the interior.' Serbian troops garrisoned in the capital were returning to field bases in the country. Munitions depots near Belgrade were likewise being evacuated. At the train station, 'strong military traffic' was observed. At three PM on Saturday, 25 July, Serbian mobilisation against Austria-Hungary was ordered (although it was not yet made public). While Giesl did not learn this until later that evening, an informant from the cabinet told him around the same time that the government would not accept Austria's demands unconditionally. Serbia meant war.[15]

When Pašić arrived at the Austrian legation at around 5:55 PM, then, Giesl already knew what to expect. There would be no such melodrama as occurred on the same premises two weeks previously, when Hartwig dropped dead. Pašić handed over the note to Giesl, informing him (in broken German) that 'part of your demands we have accepted. . . . For the rest we place our hopes on your loyalty and chivalry as an Austrian general.' Giesl looked over the reply with equal lack of ceremony and promptly decided – whether based on the document itself or on Pašić's terse remark – that it did not fulfil Berchtold's conditions of unconditional acceptance within 48 hours. He then handed Pašić his own note, informing Serbia's government that, having not received a satisfactory reply, he would leave Belgrade that evening along with the entire Austro-Hungarian legation.[16]

Giesl was not bluffing. With truly Germanic efficiency, his staffers burned the diplomatic codebooks in a matter of minutes. Giesl, his wife, and the entire legation staff evacuated the premises by 6:15 PM, aiming to make the 6:30 train to Vienna. Giesl later reported that en route he 'found the streets leading to the station and the station itself occupied by the military.' Serbia's army did not, however, detain him. Giesl made his train, which crossed the Austrian frontier at 6:40 PM on Saturday, 25 July, thus establishing what the American historian Sidney Fay called 'the speed record for the rupture of diplomatic relations.'[17]

As per Berchtold's instructions, Giesl stopped in the border town of Semlin and wired the news immediately, en clair, such that Tisza, in Budapest, learned of Serbia's rejection even before 7 PM. For good measure, Giesl telephoned Tisza and personally informed him that Serbia had begun mobilising at 3 PM. Tisza passed on Giesl's reports to the Ballplatz by telephone at 7:45 PM. At Bad Ischl, Franz Josef I, anxious all afternoon, got the news even sooner than this, via an aide-de-camp at the War Ministry who phoned directly. Berchtold and Krobatin, the war minister, were already at Bad Ischl. Together they convinced the emperor that he must mobilise. The order was dispatched at 9:23 PM.[18] Chief of Staff Conrad could not have complained. His timetable was being adhered to almost perfectly.

Just as the elaborately designed Austrian war plan seemed to be coming together, however, notes of hesitation crept in. In part to appease opinion in England, in the last few days Berchtold had begun insisting publicly that a rejection by Serbia did not necessarily mean war. As he had instructed Giesl on Thursday, 'fruitless expiry of time limit will be followed only by breaking off diplomatic relations, not by immediate commencement of state of war. State of war will begin only with declaration of war or Serbian offensive.'[19] On Friday, Berchtold had spoken along similar lines with the Russian chargé d'affaires, Prince N. A. Kudashev, insisting that the only immediate result of a rejection would be that 'our minister and the legation staff would depart.' The Russian was not convinced. 'Then it is war' (*Alors c'est la guerre*), Kudashev told Berchtold before leaving the Ballplatz. And yet Berchtold, as late as Sunday morning, 26 July, hours after mobilisation had been decreed, insisted to Giesl that it 'still does not mean war.'[20]

Did it? Juridically speaking, Berchtold was right: a state of war would exist only when either war was declared or hostilities were commenced by either side. Even Conrad, despite his haste, framed up his Saturday night directive to the army such that Austria-Hungary's actual mobilisation against Serbia would not begin until Tuesday, 28 July, even though Serbia's own had begun on Saturday. No one expected the Serbs to attack, and it was not inconceivable that Pašić would change his mind before Austrian mobilisation began on Tuesday – although, as Giesl informed Berchtold as soon as he arrived in Vienna, this was unlikely, given the fact that the Serbs had learned they had Russian backing. Unlike Russia's mobilisation Plan 19, Conrad's own plans *did* include a realistic 'partial' option – plan 'B' or Balkans, as against 'R' for Russia. In fact the plans were all but mutually exclusive, as the frontiers were located in opposite directions. It was mobilisation plan B, against Serbia, that was to begin on Tuesday – unless, of course, Russia mobilised before then, which would make an invocation of only plan B dangerous. For all his bellyaching and hesitating, Berchtold not only had produced a casus belli with his rigid instructions to Giesl but had convinced the emperor to mobilise following Serbia's rejection. If Austria-Hungary backed down now, Berchtold would be the author of her humiliation.

AT KRASNOE SELO, the drama of the afternoon had given way to a mood of quiet anxiety at the evening banquet. There had been no official explanation as to why the review had broken off early, although rumours about the onset of some kind of Russian mobilisation were rife, not least because of loose-lipped officers such as General Adlerberg, who had told General Chelius, the German aide-de-camp, that he had to 'go attend to the mobilisation.' With Adlerberg gone, at dinner Chelius sat instead next to his friend Baron Grünwald, the court equestrian officer – another of the German nationals so prominent in the upper-ranks of aristocratic tsarist army regiments, who tended naturally towards Germanophilia. Grünwald, obviously disquieted by the events of the afternoon, told Chelius confidentially that 'the situation is very serious; I am not allowed to tell you what was decided earlier today, but you will soon learn of it by your own accord.' In any case, Grünwald continued, Chelius should 'assume . . . that the outlook is grave.' The two friends then toasted one another as if in farewell: 'hopefully we will meet again in happier times.'[21] On the streets of the Russian capital, the first outward signs of Russia's secret pre-mobilisation were already visible. At seven PM, France's ambassador went over to the Warsaw station to see off Izvolsky, who was returning to his post in Paris 'in hot haste' now that war seemed imminent. 'There was a great bustle on the platforms,' Paléologue observed. 'The trains were packed with officers and men. *This looked like mobilisation.* We rapidly exchanged impressions and came to the same conclusion: "It's war this time."'[22]

In a curious coda to the drama of the day, Sir Edward Grey made his first appearance on the European diplomatic scene in weeks. Despite the flurry of alarming reports from Vienna, Belgrade, and Petersburg, Grey, like everyone else in the British cabinet, had remained preoccupied with Ireland until Austria's ambassador, Count Albert Mensdorff, presented him the ultimatum Friday morning (and he was distracted even afterwards, as the cabinet convened a long meeting Friday afternoon to discuss the Irish crisis). Upon reading the 'note with a time limit,' Grey informed his ambassadors that he thought it 'the most formidable document I had ever seen addressed by one State to another that was independent.' Still, he also instructed them that the Austro-Serbian dispute was 'not our concern.' What worried Grey was the attitude taken by the other powers – especially that of Russia regarding Austria.[23]

To this end, Grey called in France's ambassador, Paul Cambon, to discuss the crisis and let Cambon know that he would speak next to Lichnowsky, the German ambassador. Viewing the Austro-Serbian conflict as hopeless and anyway none of England's business, Grey's initial proposal was for the 'outside powers' – meaning Britain, France, Germany, and also Italy – to mediate at St Petersburg in case Russia responded with hostility to Austria's ultimatum, so as to prevent the Balkan conflict from escalating. That is, he proposed mediation between Austria and Russia. Cambon did not like the idea at all. Mediating with Russia would be mostly France's responsibility, and it was hardly the kind of task a close ally could take up without it seeming like a betrayal. Instead, Cambon proposed that the Germans help mediate at Vienna, between Austria and Serbia. This was not what Grey himself had meant, but he promised to mention Cambon's idea to Lichnowsky.[24]

Germany's ambassador had his own idea – or rather, that of Bethmann and Jagow – which he presented to Grey Friday afternoon. The German proposal was localisation: that is, that everyone simply stay out of the Austro-Serbian dispute. In a sense this was not far from what Grey was himself proposing, although the spirit was considerably different. Grey, seeing the Balkan imbroglio as none of Britain's business, would have loved for it to remain 'localised,' but in view of the sharp tone of the ultimatum, he did not think this was possible. Instead, expecting trouble between Austria and Russia, he wanted the four other great powers to mediate between them. While this was not quite Germany's own ideal scenario, it was far closer to it than was Cambon's idea of mediation between Austria and Serbia – a literal negation of localisation. So Lichnowsky responded more positively to Grey's suggestion than did Cambon.[25]

On Saturday, Grey proposed his 'four-power mediation' idea to Russia's ambassador, Count Benckendorff, while also sending copies to his ambassadors in Berlin and St Petersburg. (Cambon, for his part, had returned to Paris overnight to report to Bienvenu-Martin, so he should, in theory, have presented Grey's proposal personally.) The responses were revealing. Germany's State Secretary Jagow, in Berlin, declared himself 'quite ready to fall in with [Grey's] suggestion as to the four Powers working in favour of moderation at Vienna and St Petersburg.'[26] By contrast, Russia's ambassador rejected Grey's proposal straightaway, on the grounds that four-power mediation in St Petersburg 'would give Germany the impression that France and England were detached from Russia.' Cambon, meanwhile, did not inform anyone in Paris about Grey's proposal, which had struck him as so repugnant as to be beneath consideration. To Grey's consternation, no reply of any kind was received in London on Saturday from the Quai d'Orsay, nor from aboard the *France*.[27]

Still, to Grey, there seemed no reason for undue alarm. So long as Austria and Russia refrained from mobilising against one another, war could still be averted. Even if they did mobilise, meanwhile, the Germans had offered to help mediate between Vienna and St Petersburg. Buoyed by this reassuring logic, Grey left London Saturday evening for his country estate at Itchen Abbas, where he hoped to clear his mind with a spot of fly-fishing. Churchill, first lord of the Admiralty, also left London, for the beach, where he looked forward to a lazy Sunday morning playing with his children. Once news of the day's events in Belgrade and Petersburg would reach London, however, neither Grey nor Churchill would be able to relax for long.

16

Russia Prepares for War

SUNDAY, 26 JULY

IN THE WEE HOURS of Sunday morning, Russia's Period Preparatory to War took effect. While the measure theoretically applied across 'all the lands of the empire,' the focus was on European Russia, where it was expected that hostilities would commence. Contrary to what Sazonov had told Buchanan and Paléologue officially, however, military measures were not limited to the 'four military districts' facing Austria. Nor would they begin only after Austrian mobilisation against Serbia, as Sazonov had implied to Buchanan. At 1 AM Sunday, the Warsaw military district – that is, Russian Poland, sandwiched in between Austrian Galicia and German East Prussia – was 'placed in a state of war,' and 'ordered to begin with the works which are indicated in Lists 1 and 2 attached to the Regulation Concerning the Period Preparatory to War.' At 3:26 AM, Chief of Staff Yanushkevitch wired Warsaw command that the Period Preparatory to War was now in force 'across the whole territory of European Russia,' comprising six (not four) military districts: Warsaw, Vilnius (i.e., the Baltic area), Kazan, Kiev, Moscow, and Odessa.[1]

Phase 1 of the Period Preparatory to War saw the calling up of reservists, a measure that required only the signature of the war minister (Sukhomlinov), not the tsar. 'Out of the territorial reserve,' the regulation stipulated, 'will be formed troops for securing the frontiers, the lines of communication, the telegraph system, and other objects of military importance.' While not all reservists were called up immediately, a special provision was also made for 'call-up of the three youngest classes of reserves in areas threatened by enemy action' – which in the current case meant all Poland west of the Vistula River. The border districts facing Germany and Austria-Hungary thus saw the call-up of reserves immediately.[2]

Other measures in Phase 1 concerned the return of naval vessels to harbour and their provisioning for war; the suspension of furloughs (rather as Conrad had wished, but failed, to cut off harvest leave for Austrian troops); the reshoeing of horses; the arrest of espionage suspects; and the removal of 'money and valuable securities' from frontier areas to the Russian interior. Crowning Phase 1 was the manning and arming of frontier posts and the instruction of frontline troops 'as to the uniforms and probable dispositions of the enemy.'[3]

Phase 2 extended the call-up of reservists. Then would begin the mining of Russian harbours; the buying of extra horses and wagons for baggage trains; the transport of officers' families away from the frontier, to safety; and the commandeering of small-gauge rolling stock (which met the European width of four feet, eight and a half inches, as against the Russian gauge of five feet). All these secondary measures, too, required only Sukhomlinov's signature. Overlaying the Period Preparatory to War, a strict censorship would descend across Russia, with mention of the ongoing war preparations strictly forbidden in the press.

Censorship, of course, could never be absolute in practice. If the ultimate aim of Russia's Period Preparatory to War was to premobilise against Austria and – especially – Germany without them knowing it, then it was a failure from the start. After returning to town Saturday evening, General Chelius had gone over to the German embassy to report the substance of his alarming conversations with Adlerberg and Grünwald to Ambassador Pourtalès. He was accompanied by Germany's military attaché in Russia, Major Bernhard von Eggeling, who also had witnessed the breaking off of manoeuvres at Krasnoe Selo and heard similar rumours of mobilisation. Germany's ambassador thus knew something of the outlines of Russia's impending pre-mobilisation even before it happened.

Pourtalès might have been more anxious still had he not chanced to run into Sazonov on the railway platform at Tsarskoe Selo Sunday morning.[4] A peculiarity of Petersburg diplomacy in summertime was the frequent to-and-froing between the tsar's summer palace (and the nearby parade ground of Krasnoe Selo) and the capital. Not only Sazonov, but most of the major ambassadors took up summer residence at Tsarskoe Selo, much as the foreign colony in British India escaped the heat of Delhi every summer for the Himalayan hill station of Simla, and the European ambassadors in Constantinople left their grand Pera embassies for their only slightly less grand summer houses up the Bosphorus at Therapia. The difference in Petersburg was that, because the rail connection was so swift and sure, actual diplomatic business was still conducted in town, even as everyone lived at Tsarskoe Selo.

It was thus a happy accident that Pourtalès and Sazonov met at the station this morning, although not that unusual an occurrence. Their two previous meetings, on Tuesday and Friday, had taken place at Chorister's Bridge. Both formal audiences had been marked by abnormal tension, as the Russian berated the German over the reckless behaviour of his Austrian ally. Now, on Sunday morning, in the open country air on the rail platform, Sazonov was all smiles as he invited Pourtalès to accompany him for the short trip to town.

The foreign minister's tone, Pourtalès reported to Berlin after arriving at the embassy, was 'far more calm and conciliatory' than previously. Sazonov, he continued, 'insisted with great warmth that Russia was as far from possible from wanting a war.' Pourtalès told the Russian that Germany felt the same way, assuring him that Austria, too, had no desire to spark a conflagration over the Balkan affair and would respect Serbia's sovereignty. Moreover, the German pointed out, if the Austrians were really seeking 'a pretext to come to blows with Serbia, we would already be hearing now of military action.' The ultimatum had expired the previous evening, after all; as yet no sign was seen of Austrian military action. Perhaps there was still a way out. Pourtalès urged Sazonov to begin direct talks with Szapáry, the Austrian ambassador, immediately, once the train arrived in Petersburg. The Russian agreed.[5]

Despite the ominous events of the past 24 hours, there were grounds for optimism as the Austrian ambassador arrived at Chorister's Bridge Sunday afternoon. A curious aspect of the ongoing crisis was that, despite his overheated rhetoric about Austrian perfidy, Sazonov had thus far been on friendlier terms with 'docile as a lamb' Szapáry than with Pourtalès. In part this was because of the need to route complaints via a third party so as to avoid direct accusations between Austria and Russia that could ratchet up the Balkan crisis towards war. But Sazonov, despite his misgivings about Austria, also seemed genuinely to like Szapáry, a refined diplomat of the old school. Certainly the foreign minister did not blame this well-mannered Hungarian count for the policies of his government.

The audience at Chorister's Bridge went as well as everyone could have hoped. Sazonov received Szapáry 'very cordially' and even made a point of apologising for briefly losing his temper when the Austrian ambassador had presented him the ultimatum Friday morning. More importantly, he actually listened to what Szapáry had to say without interrupting, something Sazonov had conspicuously failed to do in his tense recent audiences with Pourtalès. Austria-Hungary, Szapáry insisted, contrary to the suspicions of Russian nationalists, was quite far from 'wishing to push forward into Balkan territory and to begin a march to Salonica or even to Constantinople.' Her aim, rather, was one of 'self-preservation and self-defence.' Nevertheless, Szapáry understood that complications might follow from the ultimatum to Serbia. 'If a conflict between the Great Powers arose,' he told Sazonov, 'the consequences would be fearful, and then the religious, moral, and social order of the world would be at stake. In glaring colours I set forth a notion of what might follow if a European war broke out.' Sazonov, Szapáry reported to Berchtold, 'agreed with me thoroughly and seemed uncommonly pleased with the purport of my explanations.'

Sazonov then spoke with similar frankness. He not only conceded 'that in Russia there were old grievances against Austria,' but 'admitted that he had them too.' Still, 'this belonged to the past' and should not interfere with the current situation. As for Serbia, Sazonov surprised the ambassador by claiming that 'he had no sympathy at all for the Balkan Slavs,' who had become 'a heavy burden for Russia.' The Russian was even willing to consider the justice of Austria's case regarding Serbian complicity in the Sarajevo outrage, although, Szapáry reported to Berchtold, the Russian 'considered the path we were pursuing to attain it was not the safest way.' Having had several days to study the 'note with a time limit,' Sazonov had become convinced that seven out of the ten points could have been accepted by Serbia 'without great difficulty.' Point 4, which demanded the firing of certain Serbian officials, could become acceptable with some amending.

The key sticking point for Sazonov was still points 5 and 6, relating to the collaboration of Habsburg officials inside Serbia.

Were Belgrade to accept this, he told Szapáry, 'King Peter [of Serbia] would run the risk of being killed at once' (that is, by the Black Hand or extreme nationalist officers). Taking a clever tack, Sazonov threw the 'monarchical principle' back in Berchtold's face, warning Szapáry that another nationalist coup, following the violent upheaval of 1903, would destroy what little legitimacy the Karageorgevitch dynasty still possessed in Serbia, setting up on Austria's frontier 'an anarchistic witches' cauldron.'

Getting back to the Serbian ultimatum, Sazonov assured Szapáry that the problem was not substance but 'phraseology.' Even in the matter of points 5 and 6, there might be wiggle room – perhaps Austrian involvement could be limited to 'consular intervention at legal proceedings'? Or, failing this, would Austria accept outside mediation from Italy or England? At this, Szapáry had to stop. He was not authorised to express an opinion on the text of the ultimatum, much less alter it himself. Besides, he reminded Sazonov, 'matters had already begun to move' – not least Serbia's own mobilisation against Austria, begun at three PM on Saturday. He would happily report Sazonov's remarks and suggestions in detail to Vienna, but he could not promise the Russian anything. On this amicable note the conversation concluded. 'Sazonov,' Szapáry reported, 'again in the warmest words expressed his pleasure at the explanations which I had given and which had materially calmed him. He would also, he said, make a report of our conversation to Tsar Nicholas, whom he would see the day after tomorrow [Tuesday, 28 July].'[6]

Had Sazonov changed his mind since pushing Russia to mobilise on Friday and Saturday? In their initial response to the Russian's change of tone Sunday, both Szapáry and Pourtalès thought so. 'Russian policy,' the Austrian ambassador opined to Berchtold, 'has travelled a long distance in two days – from the first rude rejection of our procedure and from the proposition for a judicial investigation of our *dossier*, making a European question out of the whole affair; and from that point on again to a recognition of the legitimacy to our claims and to a request for mediators.'[7] Pourtalès, on hearing Szapáry's account of the audience, reported to Berlin at once that he 'had the impression that Sazonov, perhaps owing to communications from Paris and London, has lost his nerves somewhat and is now looking for a way out.' It was Grey, after all, who had insisted the previous day on direct talks between Vienna and Petersburg. Benckendorff, in London, had rejected the idea, but perhaps Sazonov had thought it over and taken up the idea himself.[8] That this might be true is suggested by the fact that Sazonov sent a telegram Sunday evening to Shebeko in Vienna, instructing him to ask Berchtold to authorise Szapáry to discuss, and possibly revise, the ultimatum to Serbia.[9] Or, as Sazonov told Paléologue, he had admonished the Austrian ambassador: 'Withdraw your ultimatum; modify the wording; and I will guarantee you the result.'[10]

It would be natural if Sazonov, a diplomat by training and inclination, was having cold feet now that war was staring him in the face. Still, in trying to interpret the signs at Chorister's Bridge, Szapáry and Pourtalès had also to consider the reports they were receiving about the onset of some kind of large-scale secret mobilisation in Russia. At around three PM, just before Szapáry arrived to debrief him on the promising audience with Sazonov, Pourtalès forwarded to Berlin the following report from Eggeling, the German military attaché: 'Can confirm with certainty, that mobilisation has been ordered in Kiev and Odessa. Warsaw and Moscow possibly, the other [districts] probably not yet.'[11] Hearing similar reports from his own consuls and attachés, Szapáry cautioned Berchtold, at the end of his report on the audience with Sazonov: 'We must not overlook the fact that along with this backing-water policy on the part of the diplomats, there is setting in a lively activity on the part of the militarists.'[12] Had Pourtalès and Szapáry known that it was Sazonov himself who had set the wheels of Russia's pre-mobilisation in motion, they would have been more disquieted still.

WHATEVER THEIR ORIGIN AND INTENT, Russia's military preparations were viewed with understandable alarm in Vienna and Berlin. Reports coming in were still unclear about the details, but by Sunday afternoon there was no doubt that *some* kind of mobilisation was underway. So confident of this were the Germans that, late Sunday afternoon, Ambassador Lichnowsky lodged a formal complaint about hostile Russian mobilisation measures near the German frontier with Whitehall. Foreign Secretary Grey was still in the country at Itchen Abbas (although he was able to receive telegrams there), and so the ambassador met with His Majesty's permanent undersecretary of state, Sir Arthur Nicolson, instead. As Nicolson reported to Grey, 'Prince Lichnowsky called this afternoon with an urgent telegram from his Government to say that they had received information that Russia was calling in "classes of reserves," which meant mobilisation.' Trying to make the most favourable case possible for Germany's protest, the German ambassador even allowed that Germany 'would not mind a partial mobilisation say at Odessa or Kieff – but could not view indifferently a mobilisation on the German frontier.' The geographical details therefore mattered greatly. 'If this mobilisation took place on the German frontier,' Lichnowsky continued, 'Germany would be compelled to mobilise – and France naturally would follow suit.' A European war would then be at hand. He thus requested that Britain 'urge the Russian Government not to mobilise.'

Nicolson listened politely but dismissed the German's complaints. 'I told Prince Lichnowsky,' he reported to Grey at Itchen

Abbas, 'that we had no information as to a general mobilisation or indeed of any mobilisation immediately.' In parenthesis, he justified this assertion by alluding to Buchanan's telegram of the previous evening, which had reported Sazonov's (in fact misleading) remarks about the decisions made by the Council of Ministers. 'The Ukase mobilising 1,100,000 men,' Nicolson declared to Lichnowsky as if stating a fact, 'has not been issued.' While this was literally true, in that Russia's 'partial mobilisation' against Austria had not yet been announced, in fact considerably more than 1.1 million men were by now being made mobile – if not officially mobilised – according to the regulations of the Period Preparatory to War.

After denying that any kind of mobilisation was underway in Russia, Nicolson then compounded Lichnowsky's frustration by telling him that Britain could not tell Petersburg not to mobilise, as doing so would be 'difficult and delicate for us . . . when Austria was contemplating such a measure – we [i.e., the British] should not be listened to.' The main thing, Nicolson insisted, was 'to prevent, if possible, active military operations.' He then informed Lichnowsky of a new proposal Grey had concocted overnight, that of a 'meeting *à quatre*,' in which the four powers least directly interested in the Balkan imbroglio (Britain, Italy, France, and Germany), would mediate between Russia, Austria, and Serbia, while the latter three countries would 'suspend active military *operations* pending results of Conference' (mobilisation, presumably, was another matter).[13]

Filling in for the absent Grey, Nicolson had conducted a remarkable – and unfortunate – diplomatic performance. Believing himself to be acting neutrally and with great circumspection, the undersecretary had managed to provoke Germany on no fewer than four grounds. First, he issued a blanket denial of Russian mobilisation measures actually underway, a denial he would have known to be untrue had he or Grey bothered to enquire of Britain's ambassador in Petersburg. Second, Nicolson

refused point-blank to exercise the slightest restraining influence on Russia, despite Britain's public posture as a neutral,
uninterested party in the current crisis. Third, he adopted the
extremely biased position that, even if Russia *were* mobilising
against Germany, this was not a matter of concern for Britain, as
only 'active military operations' threatened the peace. He made
this statement despite Germany's ambassador having just told
him that Germany would have to counter a Russian mobilisation on its frontier by mobilising against Russia, which would
lead France to mobilise against Germany. (Nicolson's astonishing insouciance about the critical mobilisation issue reflected
Grey's own ignorance. In fact the foreign secretary, far from
discouraging Russia from mobilising, had told Benckendorff
on Saturday, as if in passing, that he fully expected Russia to
mobilise against Austria, a matter on which Grey expressed no
opinion – this lack of opinion naturally being interpreted by the
Russians as tacit approval.)

Finally, by introducing Grey's new proposal for a four-
power conference to mediate between Russia, Austria, and
Serbia equally, Nicolson had unceremoniously scuttled Grey's
proposal for outside mediation in Petersburg (between Austria
and Russia alone, not including Serbia) issued just the previous day – a proposal to which the Germans had responded
positively – and replaced it with a new initiative inherently
biased against the Central Powers. As everyone except Grey
and Nicolson seemed to know, Italy, despite being nominally allied to the Central Powers, was fundamentally hostile to Austria. With Britain herself semi-allied to France and
Russia – and clearly taking Russia's side by summarily dismissing Germany's protest at her mobilisation measures – this
meant Germany would be outnumbered three to one. Such, it
appeared, were the wages of British 'neutrality.'

Lichnowsky was too much of a gentleman to take umbrage
at this. Himself possessing no more information on Russian

mobilisation measures than had been forwarded from Berlin, he was in no position to press the point harder, nor did he really want to. In fact Lichnowsky's Anglophilia ran so deep that he was willing to go in with Grey's new four-power conference idea in order to prevent a breach in relations between England and Germany, a prospect he viewed with horror (not least because it would mean that he would have to give up his beloved post in London). 'The localisation of the conflict hoped for in Berlin,' Lichnowsky reported to Jagow following his audience with Nicolson, 'is entirely impossible and must be ruled out as a practical policy.' As soon as Austrian troops crossed the Serbian frontier, he lamented, 'all would be lost' – Russia would be forced to mobilise, and Europe would be at war.[14] To prevent such a catastrophe, Lichnowsky sent a telegram to Grey at Itchen Abbas announcing – prematurely, as he had not yet received authorisation for this from Berlin – that 'my government accepts your suggested mediation à quatre.'[15]

Lichnowsky's Anglophilia was not widely shared in Berlin. At the Wilhelmstrasse, where report after report was pouring in Sunday about Russia's secret mobilisation, Nicolson's brush-off of German protests was both surprising and disturbing. Could the British really not know what was going on in Russia? Or were they deliberately covering for their ally's warlike manoeuvres?

The signals coming from St Petersburg were, in any case, mixed. If Sazonov was losing his nerve, as Pourtalès had suggested in his report of the foreign minister's afternoon audience with Szapáry (a report that arrived in Berlin shortly after midnight), then perhaps localising the Austro-Serbian conflict was still possible after all. The key for the Germans, as it had been all along, was speed: the Austrians must strike Serbia so rapidly as to make Russian countermeasures irrelevant. As Jagow had instructed Germany's diplomats in an 18 July circular, 'the more boldness Austria displays, the more strongly we support her, the more likely Russia is to keep quiet.' Despite mounting evidence from Petersburg undermining the logic of this claim, Jagow, backed by Bethmann (still summering at Hohenfinow), stuck to this line. In a Saturday afternoon audience with Austria's ambassador conducted before the ultimatum deadline passed, Jagow had emphasised that the Germans expected and hoped that a Serbian refusal would be followed by an 'immediate declaration of war' by Austria-Hungary. 'Any delay in the commencement of military operations,' the state secretary warned, 'would bring the great danger of intervention by outside powers' (i.e., Russia). Ambassador Szögyény was thus enjoined to urge Vienna, in the strongest possible terms, to declare war now and thereby 'present the world with a fait accompli.'[16]

Sunday afternoon, Berchtold summoned to the Ballplatz the German ambassador, Tschirschky, along with Chief of Staff Conrad, to discuss Szögyény's telegram. Tschirschky wholeheartedly endorsed Bethmann's urging of speed in launching the war against Serbia; indeed he could not have done otherwise, as this was stated German imperial policy. Berchtold, too, agreed. Together, the two diplomats pressed the case with Conrad, fully expecting that the notoriously bellicose chief of staff would give Berlin what it wanted. 'When,' Berchtold asked Conrad, 'do you want the declaration of war?' Conrad replied that it would be needed 'only at the stage when operations can begin at once – say on 12 August.'[17]

The Austrians had done it again. After weeks of prevarication, Vienna had finally put the 48-hour ultimatum plan in motion, had received the expected rejection from Belgrade on schedule, and had even received the unexpected gift of unilateral Serbian mobilisation before the ultimatum deadline was up. The casus belli was there. Europe was expecting (even if not necessarily approving) an Austrian attack. What was Conrad waiting for?

He was waiting for Austria's mobilisation to proceed according to its normal schedule. Sensibly, the chief of staff saw no reason to declare war before Austria was ready to fight. Why, indeed, give Russia and her allies a diplomatic pretext against the Central Powers by declaring war now, when Austrian troops would not be able to invade Serbia for another two weeks? Curiously, Conrad was the one thinking like a diplomat, while Berchtold had taken on the role of army hothead, warning his chief of staff that Austria could not wait two weeks, as 'the diplomatic situation will not hold so long.'[18]

Berchtold was almost certainly right that the 'diplomatic situation' – that is, the Austro-German desire for localisation – would not last until 12 August. Nevertheless, his argument for declaring war immediately made no diplomatic sense, considering that Conrad had told him Austria could not invade Serbia in strength for another two weeks. The Austrian army chief of staff had, in effect, already ruled out a military fait accompli as impossible, which should have invalidated the entire fait-accompli strategy. To admit this, however, would be to disappoint the Germans again. And so Berchtold hedged. Ambassador Tschirschky was informed that Austria was not going to declare war on Serbia yet. Still, Berchtold informed Jagow and Bethmann, she might do so very soon, if Serbia undertook hostile manoeuvres on the Bosnian border.[19]

Berchtold might have hesitated further had he known of Szapáry's promising audience with Sazonov, which took place almost simultaneously with his own meeting with Conrad and Tschirschky. But the Petersburg ambassador's report, filed just after midnight, would not arrive in Vienna until late Monday afternoon. Sazonov's own report of the encounter, sent to Shebeko Sunday evening, would arrive sooner than this, but Shebeko would not be able to see Berchtold before Monday at the earliest.[20] Shebeko's own Sunday dispatch to Sazonov, meanwhile, was just as ominous as Sazonov's was reassuring. In it Russia's ambassador reported on Austria's own pre-mobilisation measures against Serbia, which had already begun.

These measures were broadly similar in outline to Russia's Period Preparatory to War, involving the immediate promotion of officers, the selective call-up of reserve divisions, the strengthening of border posts, and the onset of a strict military censorship.[21] By the time the Ballplatz would learn of Sazonov's proposal to allow Szapáry to negotiate modifications in the note to Serbia, it would have been made largely moot by events, whether or not Berchtold was interested.

Sazonov may have been sincere in his desire to defuse tensions by negotiating directly with Austria. Whatever the foreign minister's true intentions, however, his conciliatory stance vis-à-vis Pourtalès and Szapáry Sunday morning and early afternoon was belied by the acceleration of Russia's mobilisation measures during the day. At 1:55 PM, France's liaison officer at Russian military headquarters, General Laguiche, had reported to the War Ministry in Paris:

> Yesterday at Krasnoe Selo the war minister confirmed to me the mobilisation of the army corps of the military districts Kiev, Odessa, Kazan and Moscow. The endeavor is to avoid any measure likely to be regarded as directed against Germany, but nevertheless the military districts of Warsaw, Vilna, and St Petersburg are secretly making preparations. The cities and governments of St Petersburg and Moscow are declared to be under martial law. . . . The minister of war has reiterated to us his determination to leave to Germany the eventual initiative of an attack on Russia.[22]

German and Austrian intelligence on Russia's Period Preparatory to War was necessarily less solid than this inside account from an allied liaison officer. Nevertheless, by nightfall Sunday it was thorough enough that Pourtalès felt the need to confront Sazonov at Chorister's Bridge, notwithstanding their friendly morning conversation on the train. At around nine PM, the German ambassador put in a formal protest with Russia's foreign minister about 'the news widely reported among the circles of foreign military attachés, according to which several Russian army corps have been sent towards the western border in accordance with a mobilisation directive.' Sazonov, Pourtalès reported to Berlin, 'replied that he could guarantee that no mobilisation order had been given, and that none could be expected until Austria-Hungary undertook hostile measures against Russia.' Nevertheless, in an important caveat that seemed to contradict his first statement, the Russian conceded that 'certain military measures . . . had been taken.'[23]

At about the same time Sunday evening, Russia's war minister summoned Major Eggeling for an urgent audience. Evidently aware of German suspicions, Sukhomlinov sought to defuse them by offering the German military attaché 'his word of honour that no mobilisation order had yet been issued.' Certain preparatory measures were, he conceded, underway, but Sukhomlinov insisted that 'not a horse was being requisitioned, not a reservist called up.' This was a bald-faced lie, although, lacking hard evidence, the German would have been hard-pressed to prove this. Instead, Eggeling confined his own comments to warning Sukhomlinov that even Russian 'mobilisation against Austria alone must be regarded as very dangerous.' Overall, the military attaché reported to Army Chief of Staff Moltke of his frustrating audience with the Russian war minister: 'I got the impression of great nervousness and anxiety. I consider the wish for peace genuine, military statements so far correct, that complete mobilisation has probably not been ordered, but preparatory measures are very far-reaching.' The Russians, he concluded, 'are evidently striving to gain time for new negotiations and for continuing their armaments.'[24]

Time was exactly what the Germans did not have. The clock was already running out on the prospect of an Austrian fait accompli against Serbia. With Russia having begun her own war preparations – as it appeared, against both Austria and Germany – the clock was also beginning to tick on Germany's own strategy in case of war, which required striking a decisive blow against France before Russia would be ready to invade East Prussia. Earlier Sunday, Moltke, architect of Germany's latest mobilisation plan, had returned to Berlin after a month-long spa holiday at Karlsbad. Tirpitz, naval secretary, was expected back on Monday from Switzerland – against the orders of Bethmann, who wanted to avoid the impression that Germany was taking any steps toward war. Kaiser Wilhelm II, likewise disregarding Bethmann's request to remain with Germany's Baltic fleet off the Norwegian coast, had just docked at Kiel, en route for Potsdam on the overnight train. As they awoke Monday, Bethmann and Jagow would have some quick thinking to do. News was flooding in from Belgrade, Vienna, Petersburg, Paris, and London. Almost none of it was what anyone in Berlin wanted to hear.

17

The Kaiser Returns

MONDAY, 27 JULY

Considering the prominent role that Germany's leaders had played in encouraging Austria to pursue her aggressive course in the Balkans, it is remarkable how insouciant they remained as that course grew more and more dangerous later in July. When Army Chief of Staff Moltke, Naval Secretary Tirpitz, and the kaiser returned to Berlin on Monday, 27 July, after long absences, they were expecting the chancellor to bring them rapidly up to speed. And yet Bethmann himself had been at his country estate at Hohenfinow until late Saturday afternoon. Earlier that day it had been Foreign Minister Jagow, not Bethmann, who had urged Vienna, via Austrian ambassador Szögyény, to declare war immediately. True, Bethmann was firmly behind the fait-accompli policy, but this did not mean that he was abreast of all the latest developments. Indeed the chancellor had not seen the text of the Austrian ultimatum before it was sent to Belgrade on Thursday. Nor had he yet seen the text of the Serbian reply – nor even, it appears, requested that he be apprised of it. It was as if the author of Germany's blank check to Austria was not interested in how the check was filled in, so long as she cashed it. Having helped to unleash the

Austrians in all their blustering incompetence, Bethmann may also have been wary of examining too closely the consequences of his folly.

By the time he returned to Berlin Saturday night, those consequences were beginning to come into focus. Serbia and Austria had mobilised against each other, while Russia had backed Belgrade with some kind of secret military preparations of her own. French and British intentions were murky, but there were no especially positive signs from either of those directions. Localisation looked to be hanging by a thread. Not trusting the nerves of his erratic sovereign, Bethmann played down the seriousness of the situation in his first dispatches to the kaiser. While he did inform Wilhelm II on Saturday night that Serbia's reply had been deemed unsatisfactory and that Austria's minister, Giesl, had left Belgrade, Bethmann made no mention of Russia's early steps towards mobilisation, nor that Serbia had mobilised against Austria even before the ultimatum deadline expired.[1]

In a Sunday afternoon telegram, the chancellor did pass on General von Chelius's report from Petersburg that the Saturday military review at Krasnoe Selo had broken off and that regiments were returning to quarters (which report, he knew, the kaiser would have heard about from his military advisers). Still, Bethmann insisted that, Chelius's report aside, 'there was still no authenticated news on the Russian posture.'[2] At around eight PM Sunday evening, just before Germany's Ambassador Pourtalès and Military Attaché Eggeling issued formal protests at Russia's secret mobilisation, Bethmann wired the kaiser that the Russians were 'visibly hesitating' (although he gave no source for the claim). There was thus no need to return home, much less dock the fleet at Kiel, as he had heard Wilhelm proposed to do.[3]

The kaiser was having none of this. As supreme warlord he had his own sources of information, via the Admiralty and the army, which allowed him to see through Bethmann's sugarcoating of the situation. In the kaiser's marginal notes on these telegrams, we can trace a mounting exasperation with Bethmann that finally broke on Sunday. What angered Wilhelm most was that he had finally learned that day of the text of Austria's Thursday ultimatum to Belgrade – not from Jagow or Bethmann, but from the Wolff news agency. The kaiser then ordered Germany's Baltic fleet to return to Kiel, ostensibly taking this precautionary measure – the Admiralty reported to Berlin – in reaction to the 'Wolff telegram.' When Bethmann, citing this rumour back to the kaiser, 'ventured most humbly to advise that Your Majesty order no premature return of the Fleet,' Wilhelm exploded, writing on the margins of his chancellor's telegram:

> Unbelievable assumption! Unheard of! It never entered my mind!!! [The return of the fleet to Kiel] was done on report of my minister about the mobilisation at Belgrade! This may cause the mobilisation of Russia; will cause mobilisation of Austria. In this case I shall keep my fighting forces by land and sea collected. In the Baltic there is not a single ship! Moreover, I am not accustomed to take military measures on the strength of one Wolff telegram, but on that of the general situation, and that situation the Civilian Chancellor does not yet grasp.[4]

Wilhelm II often adopted exaggerated poses playing All-Highest Warlord, but in this case his chiding of his 'civilian' chancellor was not far from the mark. Bethmann, whom everyone knew to be a habitual pessimist, was fooling no one with his pose of affected calm, his reassurances that localisation was working. When the chancellor sent a second message urging the kaiser to return to his Norwegian cruise and disperse the fleet – this is the telegram in which he claimed that Russia was 'visibly hesitating' – Wilhelm underlined the word 'hesitat-ing' (*schwankend*) twice, asking rhetorically in the margins, 'and from where do you infer this? Not from any of the materials laid before me.' Besides, as the supreme warlord informed his civilian chancellor, 'There exists a Russian fleet! In the Baltic now on exercises there are five Russian torpedo boat flotillas, all or part of which could in sixteen hours be in a position . . . to cut [German naval] communications.' 'My fleet,' the kaiser admon-ished his chancellor, 'has orders to proceed to Kiel, and to Kiel it shall go!'[5]

With impressive stubbornness, Bethmann responded to this hectoring by sending his sovereign one last, deliberately misleading telegram before he had to greet him Monday after-noon (the kaiser had insisted that the chancellor meet him at Potsdam's Wildpark Station). In a remarkably optimistic read-ing of the diplomatic situation, Bethmann reported that 'Austria seems not to be able to begin war operations until 12 August,' as Conrad had informed Germany's Ambassador Tschirschky on Sunday; that Serbia 'seems to intend to stand entirely on the defensive,' while also having offered what was reported to be a fairly conciliatory reply to the ultimatum (but which Bethmann had not yet read); that England and France were 'desirous of peace'; and, most important, that 'Russia on the latest reports seems not yet to be mobilising and to be will-ing for negotiations with Vienna.'[6] While none of these state-ments was literally untrue, taken together they were far from the whole truth, as anyone who had read even a few recent dispatches would have known. Small wonder that Bethmann, upon greeting his sovereign at Wildpark Station at one PM Monday afternoon, appeared 'pale and wretched.' 'How did it all happen?' the kaiser asked him. Bethmann, recalled Count August Eulenberg, one of Wilhelm's confidants, 'utterly cowed, admitted that all along he had been deceived and offered the kaiser his resignation.' His Majesty answered: '*You've cooked this broth and now you're going to eat it.*'[7]

Of course, Kaiser Wilhelm II himself was hardly devoid of responsibility for Germany's disastrous diplomacy in July. It was he, not Bethmann, who had first offered the Austrian ambassador a blanket promise of support on Sunday, 5 July; he who, just like Bethmann, had all along urged speedy, decisive action against Serbia; and he who, like Bethmann, had failed to take the slightest interest in the text of the Austrian ultimatum before it was too late to revise it. In fact, so far from wishing that Austria modify its terms to make them acceptable to Belgrade, when one of Wilhelm's ambassadors (Baron Schoen in Paris) had suggested that Austria do this to win international sympathy, the kaiser had furiously scribbled in the margins: '*Ultimata* are either accepted, or they are not! There is no discussion! That is why they have the name!' (Wilhelm may have been unaware of just how much effort the Austrians had put into denying that their 'note with a time limit' *was* an ultimatum.)[8] In truth the kaiser, Bethmann, and (after he returned from his honeymoon) Jagow had cooked up the broth together. They, along with Germany's military service chiefs, would now eat it.

S HORTLY AFTER THREE PM on Monday afternoon, Moltke and Jagow arrived in Potsdam to meet with the kaiser and the chancellor. Although Tirpitz was not called in, Admiral Müller, chief of the naval cabinet, attended in his stead. In view of the momentous developments of recent days, this should have been a council of decisive importance. With Austrian and Serbian mobilisations underway, Germany's civilian and military leaders needed urgently to decide what posture to take regarding a prospective war between Austria-Hungary and Serbia. Next in importance was how to respond to reports of a secret early mobilisation in Russia. There was also British foreign secretary Grey's four-power conference proposal; whether or not Germany would play along fully, she needed at least to finesse the issue so as to prevent an open breach with Britain. While input from everyone was needed, it was up to Bethmann to get everyone on the same page and devise a sensible policy course. No one else had access to all the reports pouring into Berlin; no one else had the urgent duty, as head of government, to make sense of them. The chancellor, alas, was not up to the job. Unless it entirely escaped everyone's recollection afterwards, neither Bethmann nor Jagow seems to have mentioned Pourtalès's report of his dramatic Sunday evening confrontation with Russian foreign minister Sazonov, deciphered in Berlin just past ten PM, nor Eggeling's report of his frustrating encounter with War Minister Sukhomlinov, which reached the Wilhelmstrasse at two thirty AM on Monday. Instead the basis for discussion remained Pourtalès's earlier, more optimistic Sunday telegram in which he had surmised that Sazonov was 'losing his nerve.' Bethmann seems also to have seized on a Sunday night report from Ambassador Schoen, in Paris, that Prime Minister Viviani was going to try to exercise a moderating influence in St Petersburg (how the French premier would do this from the Baltic Sea was left unsaid).[9] Meanwhile Grey's four-power proposal, however unattractive to the Germans' localisation policy, could be and was interpreted as a sign that England was keen to prevent a European war, even if her method of doing so was questionable. Then, too, the rumour that Serbia's reply to the Austrian ultimatum had been mild – agreeing on 'nearly all points,' as Bethmann had wired the kaiser Monday morning – suggested that there might be a way out of the diplomatic impasse (strangely, however, Bethmann had still not bothered to read the actual reply, although a copy had arrived at the Wilhelmstrasse late Sunday evening).[10] Put together in this selective fashion, the documents available as of early Monday afternoon, 27 July, were reassuring enough as to lull Bethmann into a posture of complacency.

He was not alone in adopting this attitude. Before heading to Potsdam, Moltke had written to his wife that 'the situation continues to be extremely obscure. . . . It will be about another fortnight before anything definite can be decided.'[11] While no transcript of the Potsdam meeting survives, the evidence we do have suggests that nothing transpired there that jolted Moltke or the others awake. As General Plessen, the kaiser's adjutant, recorded in his diary afterwards: 'The Austrians are not nearly ready! It will be the beginning of August before operations can begin. It is hoped to localise the war! England declares she means to remain neutral. I have the impression that it will all blow over.'[12] Müller, likewise, wrote after the meeting that 'the tenor of our policy is to remain calm. To allow Russia to put herself in the wrong, but then not to shrink from war if it were inevitable.'[13] The Potsdam council of Monday, 27 July, resolved nothing. The Germans would wait and see.

Viewed in the context of what was going on elsewhere in Europe on that very day, the passive posture of Germany's leaders seems astonishing. Monday morning at seven AM, the British First and Second Fleets, fortuitously concentrated at Portland Harbour off Dorset, had been scheduled to disperse following a test mobilisation. On Sunday, Churchill, first lord of the Admiralty, had ordered them to stay in Portland. This 'holding together' of the fleet fell well short of actual mobilisation, but it was still a serious measure that kept Britain's main naval forces facing Germany together.[14] Russia's secret mobilisation was also gathering steam on Monday. A full Russian artillery division was observed marching westwards from Kiev. From Riga, German intelligence reported that the Düna (Dvina) River had been mined; all rolling stock had been commandeered for the army. Closer still to Berlin, the German consul in Warsaw telegraphed at three forty-five PM on 27 July:

> ALL TROOPS HAVE BEEN RECALLED FROM MANOEUVRES STOP
> MUCH INFANTRY INCLUDING ALSO CAVALRY UNITS WERE
> SENT VIA THE BREST STATION TOWARDS LUBLIN AND KOVEL
> STOP THE ENTIRE NIGHT HUNDREDS OF MILITARY VEHICLES
> WENT UP AND DOWN THE AVENUE OF BREST-LITOVSK . . .
> YESTERDAY THE ARTILLERY STORES IN THE CITADEL BLEW
> SKY HIGH.[15]

Finally, and most significantly, Ambassador Tschirschky reported Monday afternoon from Vienna that, contrary to the previous day's report that Berchtold was going to wait before declaring war, the Austrians, 'in order to cut the ground out from any attempt at intervention,' would 'make an official declaration of war [on Serbia] tomorrow, or at the latest the day after tomorrow.'[16]

Rarely has a statesman been so far off the mark in reading the international situation as Bethmann was on Monday afternoon, 27 July. How could he have been so wrong? One possibility is that, just as he had sugarcoated his dispatches to the kaiser on Saturday and Sunday, he wanted to keep Wilhelm in the dark on Monday, so as to prevent his nervous sovereign from intervening to restrain the Austrians from invading Serbia. Buttressing this theory is the fact that Jagow, shortly after the Potsdam meeting, called in Britain's ambassador, Sir Edward Goschen, to reject Grey's mediation proposal.[17] There is also Bethmann's strange incuriosity about the text of the Serbian reply, which he neither read nor presented at the Potsdam meeting. The text would not finally be dispatched to Potsdam until nine thirty PM Monday, and even then not by wire but by private courier. By the time it reached the Neues Palais,

Wilhelm was in bed. Germany's sovereign would thus not see Serbia's reply until Tuesday, 28 July – nearly three days after it had been handed over to Giesl in Belgrade. Some of the delay can be attributed to difficulties in transcribing and decoding the text (a Wilhelmstrasse log entry says the telegram from Vienna containing it was 'somewhat illegible').[18] But it is also likely that Jagow and Bethmann deliberately delayed its delivery to the kaiser, whom they expected might be impressed by its moderate wording and then seek to call off the Austro-Serbian war.

Some or all of this may be true. Following the fait-accompli policy, neither Bethmann nor Jagow was inclined to put the brakes on Vienna. They also had good motivation to hide the worst news from the kaiser. This does not explain, however, why they would have kept Moltke, too, in the dark; he was hardly one to shrink from a challenge. Nor was there any reason to conceal bad news from the other military leaders. In the end, the simplest explanation is the most convincing. Bethmann did not lay out the full picture of the international situation in Potsdam on Monday afternoon because he did not have it. Having to play catch up after returning to Berlin on Saturday, he had not yet digested all of Sunday's dispatches by the time he met the kaiser at Wildpark Station at 1 PM Monday – nor, of course, any of Monday's key dispatches, which began arriving in the late afternoon. Tschirschky's report announcing that Austria was about to declare war on Serbia was deciphered at the Wilhelmstrasse at 4:37 PM, about the same time the Potsdam meeting was concluding. The reports from Russia announcing Monday's alarming mobilisation news began arriving only after 7 PM. So desperate was Lichnowsky, Germany's Anglophilic ambassador to London, to cling to his hopes for peace, meanwhile, that he failed to mention the critical news about the holding together of the British fleet in any of his three Monday dispatches. It may be, of course, that Lichnowsky had not yet learned of Churchill's action; in any case he did not report it.*[19] Bethmann therefore remained unaware of the day's three key pieces of news while at Potsdam, in part because the kaiser himself had insisted on being briefed immediately on his return. Had everyone waited three or four hours, the meeting might have taken on a very different air.

Of course, Bethmann had given the kaiser a selective, self-serving reading of the weekend's confusing dispatches, and he might have done the same with Monday's more unambiguously negative ones. So wedded was the chancellor to localisation, and more broadly to the English rapprochement on which he had staked his entire foreign policy, that he seemed to be regarding the whole unfolding crisis through rose-coloured glasses. By Monday night, however, not even Bethmann could ignore the signs, which all pointed towards a general conflagration. True, Austria's plan to declare war immediately on Serbia, reported by Tschirschky, was ostensibly good news – the Germans had been demanding this for weeks. But the belated timing could not have been worse. With more disturbing news coming in every hour about far-reaching Russian mobilisation measures, the hoped-for localisation of the Austro-Serbian conflict looked like a mirage.

On top of this, Serbia's cleverly crafted reply to the Austrian ultimatum, initially lost in the flurry of weekend events, was now receiving serious attention in Europe's capitals – especially

---

* That news of the holding together of the British fleet reached Berlin on Monday, 27 July, is asserted by nearly all historians of the July crisis, although it is not confirmed by any contemporary source. Lichnowsky's three dispatches from London sent this day do not mention it. According to the German official history, two telegrams were received from the German naval attaché in London on English naval preparations – on *Tuesday*, 28 July.

at the Foreign Office in London, where Grey had returned Monday from Itchen Abbas. Already sceptical of Austrian intentions, the foreign secretary was floored by the Serbian reply, which he thought had met the Austrian demands 'to a degree which he would never have thought possible.' Lichnowsky had found Grey 'in a bad temper' on Monday. The foreign secretary was clearly losing patience with the Austrians – and with the Germans, whom he thought were doing nothing to hold them back. 'The key to the situation,' Grey emphasised, 'is Berlin and if Berlin seriously means peace, Austria can be restrained from pursuing a foolhardy policy.'[20] He therefore requested that the Germans mediate at Vienna, working towards some kind of 'agreement between Vienna and St Petersburg on the basis of the Serbian note.' If no such agreement was reached and there was 'an Austrian passage of arms with Serbia,' Grey told the German ambassador, then he would hold Berlin responsible.[21] Taking an uncharacteristically sharp tone, Lichnowsky therefore warned Jagow and Bethmann that 'if war comes in these conditions, we shall have England against us.'[22]

Bethmann's ultimate nightmare, a breach with Britain that left Germany opposed by three major powers in a European war, now stared him in the face. Encouraging the Austrians had all along been what the chancellor called a 'calculated risk,' a kind of colossal bluff. As Bethmann had told his private secretary, Kurt Riezler, at Hohenfinow shortly after giving Vienna her blank check, there were three possible scenarios. The first was localisation: a punitive Austrian strike that would erode Serbian prestige and lead to a favourable Balkan realignment, with Bulgaria and Romania falling in with the Central Powers. It is not that Bethmann necessarily expected that this would come to pass. He saw the second scenario, a 'continental' war pitting Germany and Austria against France and Russia, as about as likely. Such a conflict posed manifest dangers, but it could also allow Germany to 'break the iron ring of encirclement,' if it could humiliate France, weaken Russia, and strengthen Austria. The last possibility was the worst of all: Britain would join France and Russia, turning the conflict into a world war. The odds against Germany winning the latter would be almost insurmountable. Urging on the Austrians against Serbia thus constituted, the chancellor had warned Riezler in a flourish of his characteristic fatalism, a 'leap in the dark.'[23]

Riezler's diary entries following Bethmann's return to Berlin suggest a similar fatalism, as the beleaguered chancellor was rapidly overwhelmed by bad news. Bethmann, Riezler recorded on Saturday, 'sees a fate greater than human power hanging over Europe and our nation.' At other times, he saw this 'fate' not as supernatural but as outside his own control. It was not Germany, he kept repeating to himself and to Riezler, but rather Russia 'on which the European peace solely depends.' On Sunday, Bethmann insisted that 'only compelled by dire necessity will we unleash the sword, but then *with the clear conscience that we bear no guilt* for the nameless misfortune which war must bring to Europe's peoples.'[24]

This was a rationalisation, as Bethmann would have realised if he were thinking clearly. If he truly enjoyed a clear conscience, he would not have been so wracked with doubts as the crisis hurtled towards war. While neither Bethmann nor the kaiser was solely to blame for the war clouds now darkening Europe's horizon, Grey was not wrong to point to Germany as the focal point for war or peace on Monday, 27 July. True, Russia was secretly mobilising, almost certainly with French connivance and British – well, indifference. But the power about to actually declare war on another sovereign state was not Russia but Austria-Hungary. And the Austrians would never take this fateful final plunge without approval from Berlin. Why else had Berchtold directed Tschirschky to inform Bethmann about the impending declaration of war on Serbia, if not to ask for German permission? With localisation evidently a fantasy, with Britain all but lost to the Entente, with the Germans' fait-accompli stratagem rendered effectively obsolete by weeks of delay in Vienna, the time to take a step back and call off the Austrians was that moment – Monday night. The next day would be too late.

It must have been an evening of excruciating tension. As Riezler recorded in his diary, there was 'immense commotion at the Wilhelmstrasse. Nobody sleeps. I see the chancellor only for seconds.'[25] Bethmann's dilemma was acute. If he called off Austria's war with Serbia now – after Vienna had finally given the Germans the fait accompli they had been demanding for weeks – the chancellor might well rupture the alliance with Austria-Hungary, Germany's only true ally. If, however, he allowed the Austrians to declare war as planned on Tuesday, then the long-feared breach with London might result, turning Britain from disinterested neutral into likely enemy in a European war.

Faced with such unappealing options, Bethmann, unsurprisingly, chose a third. Rather than call off the Austrians, he passed on to the Ballplatz Grey's new proposal for German mediation in Vienna 'on the basis of the Serbian note,' while signalling that he was passing it on under duress. 'After our having declined an English proposal for a conference' (Grey's four-power idea, targeting Austria, Russia, and Serbia equally), Bethmann informed Tschirschky, Germany's ambassador to Austria, in a telegram dispatched from the Wilhelmstrasse just before midnight, 'it is impossible for us to reject this English suggestion *a limine*. By a rejection of all mediatory action we should be held responsible for the conflagration by the whole world and be represented as the real warmongers.' Germany's position, the chancellor continued, was 'all the more difficult as Serbia has apparently yielded so much. We cannot therefore reject the role of mediator and must submit the English proposal to the Vienna cabinet for consideration.' For good measure, Bethmann asked that Tschirschky also remind Berchtold of 'M. Sazonov's desire to negotiate directly with Vienna,' of which he had learned from Pourtalès. In this way the chancellor covered his British flank, furnishing evidence that Germany was not opposed to mediation, while still not quite pulling the rug out from under Austria's impending war with Serbia (which subject he did not mention at all).[26]

More quietly still, Jagow (presumably with Bethmann's tacit approval, if not outright connivance) sought to reassure Berchtold, in off-the-cuff remarks made to the Austrian ambassador in Berlin, that Germany would not really hold Austria to account over England's mediation proposals. Jagow, Ambassador Szögyény reported to the Ballplatz at nine fifteen PM, told him 'in a strictly confidential form that in immediate future mediation proposals from England will possibly (*eventuell*) be brought to Your Excellency's knowledge by the German government.' Jagow did not indicate which of Grey's proposals was meant: the four-power conference or the idea of German mediation at Vienna on the basis of the Serbian reply (in the event, it was the latter that Bethmann passed on to Tschirschky several hours later). He did not really need to, as his real purpose was to assure Berchtold that 'the German government . . . tenders the most binding assurances that it in no way associates itself with the proposals, is even decidedly against their being considered, and only passes them on in order to conform to the English request.' The reason was straightforward. 'It is of the greatest importance,' Jagow explained to Szögyény, 'that England at the present moment should not make common cause with Russia and France.'[27] The Germans, that is, wanted plausible deniability with London, but meanwhile, Austria could go ahead in her war with Serbia.

The cynicism with which Bethmann forwarded Grey's mediation proposals to Vienna has come in for well-deserved opprobrium among historians.[28] And yet it is not entirely clear what the chancellor's manoeuvre proves, beyond that he was trapped in an impossible policy dilemma and tried, clumsily, to climb out. As his critics point out, Bethmann could indeed have pulled back from the brink and forced the Austrians, against their will, to negotiate. Conrad, Austria's army chief of staff, might even have gone along with this, knowing that Austria's cumbersome mobilisation meant that he could not invade Serbia until 12 August anyway. It was not Conrad, though, who was insisting on declaring war immediately; it was Berchtold. Were Bethmann to rebuke him now, Berchtold would be humiliated. So, too, would Bethmann himself; the fait accompli was, after all, *his* policy (and the kaiser's, although the nature of German court politics meant that Bethmann alone would be blamed if the policy went wrong). For the chancellor to unwind it now would all but necessitate his resignation – a resignation he had in fact offered on Saturday. Instead, Bethmann was now eating the broth he had cooked, just as the kaiser had ordered him to.

Bethmann's critics also fault him for being dishonest with Grey, by pretending that he was sincerely trying to pressure the Austrians to negotiate. But what else could Bethmann have done? Having chosen a policy course requiring Germany to back Vienna, he stuck to it now. If he was trying to deceive Grey about this, it was for the obvious reason that Grey had made an impossible demand of him. Why, indeed, was an ostensibly neutral England demanding so forcefully that Germany mediate at Vienna, but not that France mediate at St Petersburg? When Grey had demanded the latter back on Saturday – mediation between Austria and Russia, in which France was expected to pressure the latter – the French and Russian ambassadors had both rejected the proposal outright, and yet Grey had not responded to their rejection by threatening them with war, as he now implicitly threatened Germany. Indeed, France and Russia had not responded to Grey's four-power proposal on Sunday either (Bienvenu-Martin did accept it on Monday afternoon, but only on the condition that the Germans intervene at Vienna first).[29] The Germans had rejected Grey's second, four-power conference proposal just as publicly and frankly as they had accepted his first, for outside mediation between Austria and Russia. If they were now treading more carefully around the third (Grey's idea of using the Serbian reply note as the basis for German mediation at Vienna), it was for good reason.

No matter whether the Germans said yes or no, Grey had concluded – as he told Lichnowsky – that Germany alone would decide the question of war and peace, while exonerating France and Russia, despite their not yet having accepted *any* of his proposals! In the same conversation, Grey had 'confirmed' to Lichnowsky that 'no Russian call-up of reserves has taken place.'[30] This statement was not only blatantly untrue; its very formulation signalled bias to the Germans. (How could Grey possibly have 'confirmed' something in a faraway country *not to have happened*? Only by taking Russian denials at face value.) Declaring himself, and by implication Britain, impervious to any evidence of Russia's warlike intentions, Grey had already taken sides, despite his pose of disinterestedness. Small wonder that Bethmann resorted to deceit. Grey had rigged the diplomatic game over Britain's belligerence in such a way that Germany could not possibly win if she played it straight.

Of course, Grey did not believe himself to be lying when he kept denying that Russia was mobilising. He had little to go on beyond the reports of his ambassador, and these were about as ill-informed as diplomatic dispatches could be. Buchanan had reported, on Sunday evening at 8 PM, that the 'Governments of St Petersburg and Moscow have been placed in a "state of extraordinary protective activity."' But he qualified this report immediately by claiming that this had been done 'ostensibly in view of strikes' (this is what Sazonov must have told him). All he offered Grey in the way of critical acumen was that the measure *might* have been connected to 'intending mobilisation.'[31] But then even this watered-down interpretation was undercut when Buchanan failed to follow up on the matter. In a dispatch filed from Petersburg on Monday night at 8:40 PM, by which time dozens of reports on Russia's secret mobilisation measures had arrived in Berlin and Vienna, Buchanan did not so much as mention a single rumour about mobilisation.[32] So far as Grey knew, he was therefore acting in good faith. He *thought* he was averting an unnecessary war by making a reasonable demand for German mediation in Vienna, as Austria appeared to be the only power threatening the peace of Europe. In reality, he was putting the screws exclusively on Germany while ignoring Russia's threatening moves on the Austrian and German frontiers.

Grey was just as ignorant, apparently, of Britain's own war preparations. After ordering the fleet at Portland not to disperse as planned, on Monday night Churchill had gone further still, wiring to all of Britain's naval commanders:

EUROPEAN POLITICAL SITUATION MAKES WAR BETWEEN TRI-
PLE ENTENTE AND TRIPLE ALLIANCE POWERS BY NO MEANS
IMPOSSIBLE. BE PREPARED TO SHADOW POSSIBLE HOSTILE
MEN OF WAR AND CONSIDER DISPOSITIONS OF H.M. SHIPS
UNDER YOUR COMMAND FROM THIS POINT OF VIEW. MEASURE
IS PURELY PRECAUTIONARY. NO UNNECESSARY PERSON IS TO
BE INFORMED. THE UTMOST SECRECY IS TO BE OBSERVED.[33]

Churchill, by sending this secret message without approval from the cabinet, had committed an act of insubordination. Yet his behaviour was more honest about British intentions than that of Sir Edward Grey, who, against the logic of his own biased diplomacy, continued denying that such a thing as a

Triple Entente existed. Grey's desire for peace was genuine, but it was hardly helped along by his flimsy pose of neutrality.

Good intentions in diplomacy avail little without good intelligence. In his knowledge of Russian military preparations, Grey was two full days behind events, and falling further behind. France's peace-minded premier, stuck on board the *France*, was no better off. Germany's Ambassador Schoen was not wrong to inform Berlin that Viviani intended to influence Petersburg, but Bethmann was deeply mistaken if he really believed that the premier's efforts would amount to anything. Viviani did succeed in getting one official message to his ambassador, Paléologue, on Monday, reaffirming France's support for Russia in the current crisis – though adding, in a personal touch (this phrase was not in the original Quai d'Orsay draft), that she was offering this support 'in the interests of general peace.'[34] Whether or not this message was intended to stiffen or weaken Russia's posture vis-à-vis Germany and Austria, it was certainly not going to convince Sazonov to rescind mobilisation measures Russia had already taken, about which Viviani seems to have been just as oblivious as Grey.

On the German side, Kaiser Wilhelm II, as a result of Bethmann's dithering, was also two or three days behind. He had seen the text of the Austrian ultimatum only on Sunday and had still not seen Serbia's reply when he went to bed Monday night. All three men, though for different reasons, would dearly have loved to prevent the European war that now seemed imminent. The lack of up-to-date information rendered them impotent in the face of onrushing events.

18

'You Have Got Me into a Fine Mess'

TUESDAY, 28 JULY

THE KAISER ROSE AT DAWN in the Neues Palais on Tuesday morning, 28 July. At seven thirty AM, he went for a ride with his adjutant, General Plessen. Neither man was aware of the previous evening's critical dispatches to and from Vienna. There was thus little to disturb the pleasant early morning exercise. 'H[is] M[ajesty],' Plessen recorded in his diary, 'tells me England thinks the Serbian answer to the Austrian ultimatum such that in essence all the demands are conceded and therewith all reason for war is gone.' While Plessen saw no reason to disagree, he did tell his sovereign that he 'thought Austria must at least lay hands on some gauge which should serve as a guarantee for the carrying out of [Serbia's] concessions.' The kaiser thought that Austria had missed her chance for a punitive war, but this was by no means a bad thing, if a diplomatic triumph over Serbia was still on offer.[1]

It was in this state of mind that Wilhelm sat down, at long last, to read the Serbian reply to Austria's ultimatum after he returned to the palace shortly after nine. Delivered from the Wilhelmstrasse by courier, the decrypted French-language text had arrived in Potsdam shortly before midnight, long after the kaiser had turned in. While he already suspected that the tone of the reply would be reasonably conciliatory, Wilhelm was floored when he read it. 'A brilliant achievement in a time limit of only 48 hours!' he scribbled, declaring Serbia's near-total compliance 'more than one could have expected!' and 'a great moral success for Vienna.' With Prime Minister Pašić's reply, he deduced, 'all reason for war is gone, and Giesl ought to have quietly stayed on in Belgrade!' Receiving such a reply, he wrote, 'I should never have ordered mobilisation.'[2]

The kaiser often responded impulsively when he scribbled marginalia, but this time he meant what he said. By ten AM, he had composed a formal memorandum to Foreign Minister Jagow, requesting that Germany ask the Austrians to use the Serbian reply as a basis for negotiation – precisely as Grey had suggested to Ambassador Lichnowsky on Monday. 'The few reservations made by Serbia on single points,' he wrote, 'can in my opinion well be cleared up by negotiation. But capitulation of the most humble type is there proclaimed *urbi et orbi* and thereby *all reason for war* falls to the ground.' It was true, Wilhelm conceded, that the reply was 'a mere scrap of paper,' the text of which meant little unless it was 'translated into *deeds*.' After all, as the kaiser argued, 'the Serbs are Orientals, therefore liars, deceitful, and master hands at temporising.' To turn their 'fine promises' into 'truth and fact,' he proposed that Austria carry out a temporary occupation of Belgrade, 'as *security* for the enforcement and execution of the promises and remaining there until the demands are *actually* carried out.' This solution would also satisfy honour for the Austrian army, which had once again, just as during the Balkan Wars, 'been mobilised *to no purpose*.' On the basis of this temporary occupation plan, the kaiser declared himself 'ready to *mediate* for *peace* in Austria.'[3]

In light of this dramatic reaction, it is interesting to reflect on what might have happened had Germany's sovereign been shown Serbia's reply to Austria during the Potsdam council on Monday afternoon or even on Monday evening, before he went to bed. Had the kaiser come up with his mediation-in-Vienna plan on Monday – a plan very close to what Grey was demanding, aside from the part about a temporary occupation of Belgrade to save Austrian face – Chancellor Bethmann and Jagow would have been forced to promote Grey's plan seriously to Vienna, even if in the kaiser's modified form, rather than signalling that they wanted Vienna to reject it. More important, with the kaiser now favouring negotiation, they could never have approved Foreign Minister Berchtold's plan to declare war on Tuesday. They would have been forced, at the least, to inform Wilhelm of Austria's impending declaration of war, of which they learned early Monday evening, and this would have occasioned the kaiser's furious objection. Matters would then have come to a head on Monday night, quite possibly with a confrontation between Bethmann and his sovereign. The chancellor would almost certainly have backed down, as he always did when the kaiser rebuked him. Without authorisation from Berlin, Austria-Hungary would then not have declared war on Serbia on Tuesday. Some kind of negotiations over modifying Serbia's reply would have begun, whether the initiative was taken by Grey, the kaiser, or even Russian foreign minister Sazonov. Berchtold would have been crushed, of course, but, absent Germany's backing, he would have had to go along.

But the kaiser did not read Serbia's reply before going to bed on Monday night, almost certainly because Bethmann and Jagow, knowing how he would react, had instructed their courier not to wake him. Still, had Wilhelm's letter reached Jagow on Tuesday morning, it still might have been in time to call off the Austrians, who planned to declare war on Serbia at noon.

Had the kaiser read the reply immediately on rising – rather than going riding with his adjutant – his response might have reached the Wilhelmstrasse, and through it the Ballplatz, with an hour or two to spare. Even composed at ten, as it was, it might have had effect had Wilhelm sent it off with instructions that the text be wired immediately to Vienna. But the kaiser, not having any idea that Austria was about to declare war, and not someone accustomed to the telephone, sent the message to Berlin by courier, such that Jagow could not have received it before eleven or eleven thirty AM at the earliest.[4] On top of this, Wilhelm stipulated that, because of its sensitive nature, he wanted his proposal forwarded to Vienna by private courier. So, even had Jagow received the letter before noon, there was no chance the Austrians would have got the message in time.

Rendering this drama moot, at 11:10 AM Tuesday morning, Austria-Hungary formally declared war on Serbia (the telegram was deciphered by the Serbs at 12:30 PM). 'The Royal Serbian Government not having answered in a satisfactory manner the note of July 23, 1914, presented by the Austro-Hungarian Minister at Belgrade,' the note declared, 'the Imperial and Royal Government are themselves compelled to see to the safe-guarding of their rights and interests, and, with this object, to have recourse to force of arms. Austria-Hungary consequently considers herself henceforward in a state of war with Serbia.'[5]

It was Berchtold's final fait accompli. It was he who had decided on Monday, against Chief of Staff Conrad's advice and contrary to German expectations, to declare war immediately. It was Berchtold who had, on Tuesday morning, made a final pitch to Franz Josef I at Bad Ischl, convincing the emperor that only prompt action could stave off the threat of Entente intervention (for added measure, citing specious evidence, Berchtold had told Franz Josef that Serbian troops had fired on Austrian positions on the Danube). It was Berchtold who had written and signed the French-language text sent to Serbia

– a novel act in itself, as the Italian journalist Luigi Albertini observed: 'for the first time in history a declaration of war was made by telegram.' Finally, and strangest of all, Berchtold's telegram was unaccompanied by any military action, which appears to have left the Serbians in doubt as to its veracity. Pašić, indeed, thought it was a hoax, not least because the direct telegraphic line to Austria had been cut off and he was not sure how the telegram had reached Serbian territory. Serbia's prime minister went so far as to wire to Petersburg, Paris, and London to inform friendly powers 'of the strange telegram he had received and to ask whether it was true that Austria had declared war on Serbia.'[6]

Berchtold had logical reasons for proceeding in this way, but this did not make them sound ones. Just as he had informed the Germans on Monday, his goal in declaring war on Serbia was not so much to actually begin a war – Conrad had said this would not happen until 12 August – as to obviate further mediation efforts. By Monday evening, Berchtold had learned from both Russian ambassador Shebeko and Vienna's ambassador in Petersburg, Szapáry, of Sazonov's proposal for direct talks between Austria and Russia, as well as of Grey's proposal for a four-power conference. Later that night, he received the messages from Berlin reporting on Grey's newer idea for German mediation on the basis of the Serbian note. Europe's diplomats were clearly gearing up for action to stave off a Balkan war. In a kind of perverse anti-diplomacy, Berchtold wanted to start the Balkan war (on paper, at least) before they could stop it. When more mediation offers came in on Tuesday, as he knew they would, Berchtold now had his answer ready: they were no longer relevant, as Austria and Serbia were already at war, even if there was no actual fighting between them.

It is hard to think of a policy more inept than this. The original Austro-German plan was for a military first strike against Serbia so quick and decisive that the powers would be unable to react. Berchtold's final version, a kind of fait accompli ad absurdum, now offered the world a rapid-fire declaration of war – but without the actual war, which would only come two weeks later. As diplomacy for the Central Powers, it was suicidal; as strategy, it was nonsensical. The only advantage of any kind that it offered was to allow Berchtold to ignore the entreaties of European diplomats – in effect, not to have to answer his phone. The Germans, forced to defend the reckless behaviour of their ally in order to fend off diplomatic encirclement, would not be so lucky.

Berchtold's upside-down diplomacy played right into Sazonov's hands. With Austria speaking loudly and brandishing a soft stick, the Russians could offer carrots all around – while accelerating their secret preparations for war.

By Tuesday, 28 July, Russia's preliminary mobilisation was so far advanced that only the willfully ignorant, like Britain's ambassador Sir George Buchanan, failed to notice it. On Monday, Chief of Staff Yanushkevitch had wired Tiflis command that the Period Preparatory to War was now also in force for the military districts of Omsk, Irkutsk, Turkestan, and the Caucasus, expanding the scope of Russia's pre-mobilisation across nearly the entire Russian Empire, from central Europe to Siberia, from the Arctic Circle to the Persian border.[7] By Tuesday, dispatches reporting these alarming developments were pouring into Vienna and Berlin. In Odessa, the German consul observed the call-up of reserves.[8] Warsaw's train station, Consul Brück reported, was a beehive of activity, with troop trains setting off in all directions – including towards the German border.[9] The intelligence summary of the German General Staff that day concluded that the Russians were 'apparently conducting at least a partial mobilisation' and that the Period Preparatory to War had 'probably' been declared in all of Russia.[10] The gist of these German reports was confirmed by an Entente observer. As Serbia's military attaché in Berlin recalled,

On July 28, in company with several Serbian officers, I arrived at Warsaw [from Berlin]. As far as the German frontier, not the slightest indication was seen of military measures. But immediately after crossing the frontier [into Russian Poland], we noticed mobilisation steps being undertaken on a grand scale (assembly of freight cars in several stations, military occupation of the railway stations, massing of troops in several cities, transport of troops, mobilisation signalling). When we arrived at Brest-Litovsk, July 28, the state of siege had already been proclaimed.[11]

As against such energetic and detailed reporting, as late as eight thirty PM on Tuesday, 28 July, Buchanan had picked up only a single vague rumour of 'forces of infantry leaving Warsaw for frontier' – without explaining which forces or which frontier.[12]

Only Buchanan himself knew whether it was laziness or malice that produced dispatches that so signally failed to inform London about what was going on in Russia. The Briton's obliviousness was perfectly captured in a series of conversations he had with Sazonov and French ambassador Paléologue at Chorister's Bridge on Tuesday afternoon. Buchanan met with Russia's foreign minister around three PM, before either man had learned of Austria's declaration of war on Serbia. Still entertaining hopes that he could mediate between Austria and Russia as Grey desired, Buchanan asked Sazonov what he thought of Austria's public pledge to respect 'Serbia's independence and integrity.' 'His Excellency,' Buchanan reported to Grey, 'replied at once that no engagement that Austria might take on these two points would satisfy Russia.'[13] With the clear intention to mislead, Sazonov then promised Britain's ambassador that 'the order for [Russian] mobilisation against Austria would be given on the day that the Austrian army crossed the Serbian frontier,' implying that Russia would not even so much as 'partially mobilise' for days, if not weeks. So far from suspecting the Russian of deceiving him, Buchanan instead earnestly 'urged him to refrain from any military measures which might be construed as a challenge by Germany.'[14] Such measures had, unbeknownst to Buchanan, been underway for three full days already.

On his way out of Sazonov's office, Buchanan ran into Paléologue in the antechamber. 'I have just been begging Sazonov,' he informed his French counterpart, 'not to consent to any military measure which Germany could call provocative. The German Government must be saddled with all the responsibility and all the initiative. *English opinion will accept the idea of intervening in the present war only if Germany is indisputably the aggressor.* . . . Please talk to Sazonov to that effect.' France's ambassador, stifling any urge to relieve Buchanan's ignorance, cleverly responded: 'That's what I'm always telling him.'[15] It does not seem to have occurred to Buchanan, either then or later, that Paléologue and Sazonov were deliberately deceiving him about Russia's 'provocative' military measures, precisely in order to manipulate 'English opinion' into supporting the Franco-Russian side in the European war that now seemed imminent.

Imminent, but not quite inevitable. At the time of these exchanges, the die for war was not yet firmly cast. Far-reaching as Russia's Period Preparatory to War was, threatening as it appeared to the Germans and the Austrians alike, on 28 July it still fell short of actual mobilisation. The red placards announcing general mobilisation had not been posted, not even in the four districts that were to be 'partially mobilised' against Austria. The Germans could protest all they liked, but until those placards went up, Sazonov still had plausible deniability that Russia had 'mobilised' – especially in Britain, where he was protected by further layers of ignorance and incuriosity. Moreover, although Austria and Serbia had both been mobilising for several days, until hostilities commenced between them, there was still an outside chance that the powers could intervene in Vienna. It was, indeed, expressly to cut off this possibility that Berchtold had composed his 'strange telegram' announcing that Austria was at war with Serbia. In doing so he not only cut the legs out from his own diplomatic position but also gave Russia a clear-cut casus belli against Austria (if not also against Germany), handing Sazonov a priceless diplomatic gift.

In response to Berchtold's toothless declaration of war, which he learned of around four PM on Tuesday afternoon, Sazonov at last admitted that Russia had inaugurated 'partial mobilisation' of four military districts against Austria-Hungary (Odessa, Kiev, Moscow, and Kazan) – notwithstanding the fact that Russia's preliminary mobilisation had long since expanded well beyond those districts to encompass all of European Russia plus Siberia and the Caucasus, the Baltic and Black Seas, and Russian Poland. Even this disingenuous announcement, meanwhile, was passed on not in a public declaration à la Berchtold, but in a secret dispatch to Russian diplomats abroad.[16] Sazonov even took special care *not* to report this news to Sir George Buchanan, or even to his own ambassador in London, Count Benckendorff, who was informed only that 'in consequence of the Austrian declaration of war on Serbia, direct discussions on my part with the Austrian ambassador are obviously useless.'[17] Whereas Berchtold seemed resolved to paint the worst possible picture of Austro-German intentions in London by declaring war on Serbia two weeks before Austria would be ready to fight, Sazonov perceived that the key diplomatic question in July 1914 was British belligerence or neutrality. Grey, the cabinet, and above all the British public still had no idea that Russia was mobilising against the Central Powers, and Russia's foreign minister saw no reason to disabuse them of their ignorance.

IN LONDON, AS SAZONOV MUST HAVE KNOWN, Ireland was still dominating the news cycle. On Sunday, following the arrival of a shipment of Mauser rifles in Dublin harbour, a melee had developed that saw British troops fire into a 'crowd of stone-throwing Dubliners'; the clash had left three dead and 36 wounded. This was far bigger news on Fleet Street than the unfolding Balkan crisis or murky events in distant Russia, about which even Britain's government remained unaware. As the *Times* reported on Monday, 'there can no longer be the slightest doubt that the country is now confronted with one of the greatest crises in the history of the British race' – the possibility of a civil war over Home Rule, that is, not a European war breaking out. To the extent that Prime Minister Asquith gave thought to the Balkan crisis at all, he saw it as possibly 'a good thing,' as it had the potential to distract the public from Ireland. He seems first to have suspected that it might *not* be a good thing on Tuesday evening, 28 July, when he was told by officials from the House of Rothschild that the French government was dumping her London securities. While he found the news 'ominous,' Asquith apparently did not bother to enquire about why France's government was doing this.[18] Sir Edward Grey, in charge of foreign policy, was of course following the crisis as closely as he could, but it was still not closely enough. As late as four PM on Tuesday, he instructed Sir Edward Goschen, his ambassador in Berlin, to promote 'the direct exchange of views between Austria and Russia,' not realising, because of the sloth of his diplomats, that (1) Austria was already at war with Serbia, and (2) Russia had begun pre-mobilising secretly against both Austria-Hungary and Germany three days previously and would begin at least 'partial' mobilisation as soon as Petersburg learned that Austria was at war with Serbia. Five hours after a Balkan war had begun, Grey was still telling Goschen that 'as long as there is a prospect of that [peaceful mediation] taking place, I would suspend every other suggestion.'[19] Goschen was not enjoined to exert any pressure on the Germans to restrain Austria (nor, it goes almost without saying, did Grey expect Buchanan to restrain the Russians). Grey would learn only around eight PM on Tuesday evening that Austria had declared war on Serbia, and he would remain in the dark about Russia's ongoing mobilisation measures through the night. Another day had come and gone, this one the most decisive yet – and Grey's dawdling diplomacy had left Britain impotent to influence events.

The only official in London who seems to have sensed the mounting danger was Churchill. Without consulting Grey, much less his even less belligerent Liberal colleagues in the cabinet (although he did inform Asquith, from whom he received 'a sort of grunt' implying approval), at five PM on Tuesday Churchill ordered the First Fleet to proceed northwards to its war station at Scapa Flow, passing through the Straits of Dover under cover of darkness. Even this measure, however, was not taken until the early hours of Wednesday morning.[20] It thus could have had no deterrent effect on Germany or Austria on Tuesday.

In Paris, the general public remained just as oblivious to ongoing events in the Balkans – and Russia – as were the British. On Tuesday, everyone was far more preoccupied with the conclusion of the trial of Mme Caillaux. Caillaux's lawyer laid his case on temporary insanity and lack of premeditation. In a curious closing argument, he admonished the courtroom to 'save [y]our anger for the enemy outside. . . . War is at the gates. . . . Acquit Mme Caillaux.' The jury agreed: innocent! It was this stunning verdict, along with the 'ferocious melee of shouts' on the streets that followed ('Vive Caillaux!' 'Death to Caillaux!') – not Austria's declaration of war on Serbia, much less Russia's accelerating mobilisation measures, that would dominate French headlines on Wednesday morning.[21]

In Potsdam, meanwhile, Bethmann was humbled once again by his sovereign, who was livid when he learned of Austria's declaration of war. Summoning his chancellor to the palace after hearing the news on Tuesday afternoon, Kaiser Wilhelm issued another stinging rebuke: 'You have got me into a fine mess.' Seeking to undo the damage wrought by Austrian recklessness, he ordered Bethmann to lean on Vienna to negotiate with Russia, even if it was necessary that the Austrian army occupy Belgrade to satisfy her honour.[22]

Bethmann was in a foul mood when he returned to Berlin on Tuesday evening. Lichnowsky's latest depressing dispatch from London was on his desk. While this one, at least, contained no new, biased, British mediation initiatives, the news was still not good. Even while Lichnowsky, carrying out standing instructions from Berlin, was reassuring Grey that Austria had no territorial designs on Serbia, Austria's ambassador to Britain, Count Mensdorff, was telling Lichnowsky that Austria was resolved on war so that Serbia could be 'flattened' (the German word Mensdorff used was the colourful *niedergebegelt*) and then 'carved up' by the Balkan jackal states (if, that is, Austria did not take her share). As Bethmann knew, by the time he read this that Austria had gone ahead and declared war, this revelation crystallised his frustrations with Vienna. 'The ambiguity on the part of Austria,' he scribbled on Lichnowsky's report, 'is intolerable. To us they refuse information about their programme and expressly say that Count Hoyos's remarks about a partitioning of Serbia were purely personal; in St Petersburg they are lambs without evil intentions and in London their embassy talks of giving away Serbian territory to Bulgaria and Albania.'[23]

It is easy to sympathise with the chancellor's exasperation. When he (following the kaiser's lead) had signed the blank check, he could not have imagined the unpredictable, self-defeating twists and turns that Austrian policy would take. As Bethmann wrote at ten fifteen on Tuesday night to

Ambassador Tschirschky in Vienna, Pašić's conciliatory reply to the ultimatum 'met the Austrian demands in so considerable a measure that a completely intransigent attitude on the part of the Austro-Hungarian government would bring about a gradual revulsion of public opinion all over Europe.' Berchtold, by declaring war unilaterally, had taken just such an 'intransigent attitude.' And for what purpose? Conrad himself, Bethmann reminded Tschirschky, had informed Berlin that 'active military measures against Serbia will not be possible before 12 August.' Germany had thus been 'placed in the extraordinarily difficult position of finding itself exposed to proposals for mediation and conferences from the other cabinets, and if it persists in its previous reserve towards such proposals, the odium of having caused a world war will fall on [Germany] *even in the eyes of the German people.*' It was thus imperative, Bethmann told Tschirschky, that Austria begin negotiating with Russia and assure Sazonov as unequivocally as possible that 'territorial gains in Serbia are remote from its thoughts and that its military measures are aimed purely at a temporary occupation of Belgrade and other definite points on Serbian territory in order to force the Serbian government into full compliance (*völliger Erfüllung*) with Austrian demands. . . . As soon as Austrian demands are met, evacuation will follow.'[24] If Russia did not go along with this, then she, and not Germany, would be perceived as the power disturbing the peace – or so Bethmann hoped.

There was an element of desperation about this 'Halt in Belgrade' proposal, as the German initiative soon came to be known. While Bethmann and the kaiser both bore heavy responsibility for having encouraged Austrian recklessness, there is no reason to doubt the sincerity of their dismay at learning that Austria had declared war on Serbia two weeks before she was ready to fight her. In signing the blank check, both men had known that they were *risking* war if Russia intervened on

Serbia's behalf, and yet neither man had wished, or intended, for this intervention actually to come to pass. They had unquestioningly trusted in their ally's diplomatic competence, only to watch Berchtold make one wrong move after another. It was getting late, but perhaps it was not too late to rein Austria in.

There was a crucial difference, however, between the way the kaiser and his chancellor wanted to go about doing this. In his letter to Jagow written at ten AM Tuesday morning, Wilhelm had made clear that he thought 'the few reservations made by Serbia on single points' in Pašić's reply to the ultimatum 'can in my opinion well be cleared up by negotiation.' This would be asking a great deal of the Austrians, of course: although Conrad and the army might still satisfy honour with a 'temporary' occupation of Belgrade, Berchtold would be forced to swallow his pride and back down on a major point of principle. By contrast, Bethmann's instructions to Tschirschky stipulated that the Austrian occupation 'force the Serbian government *into full compliance with Austrian demands,*' implying that it was Pašić, not Berchtold, who would have to back down. Whether or not Bethmann understood this, the distinction was fundamental. Any small chance that the Russians would acquiesce in a 'temporary' occupation of Belgrade would surely vanish once Sazonov learned that there would be no real negotiation over the terms of Serbia's compliance with the Austrian ultimatum.

Russian acquiescence was rendered more improbable still by Bethmann's strange decision not to issue any warnings to Russia on Tuesday about her ongoing mobilisation measures, as Berchtold had requested him to do on Monday, hoping that the threat of German countermeasures would put the fear of God in Sazonov. Perhaps wishing to spite the Austrians for putting Germany in such an impossible position, Bethmann informed Vienna that 'a categorical declaration at St Petersburg would seem today to be premature' and made no effort to follow up on the disquieting reports of Pourtalès and Eggeling from Petersburg.[25] The chancellor did let the Russians, French, and British know – via a telegram to his ambassadors sent off at nine PM – that he now favoured direct talks between Austria and Russia, hoping that this assurance, coupled with his muffling of German protests against Russia's mobilisation measures, would convince Sazonov to parley. Why Sazonov would want to do so after Austria had already declared war – and on the basis of a subsequent Austrian occupation of Belgrade, without any hint of Austrian concessions on the terms of Serbia's reply to the ultimatum – was left unclear.

In fact Bethmann did not even spell out the terms of his 'Halt in Belgrade' plan in his nine PM telegram circular; rather he spoke only in the vaguest sense of Austrian-Russian talks and claimed speciously that Vienna's declaration of war 'changes matters not at all' (*ändert hieran nichts*).[26] This was hardly the way to impress Grey – much less Sazonov or the French – that Bethmann was serious about mediating at Vienna. Thus Bethmann in Berlin, not unlike Berchtold in Vienna, settled on the most incompetent policy possible: demanding concessions from Russia rather than offering them himself, while undermining his own leverage by refusing to warn Petersburg that Germany would respond to Russia's secret mobilisation. He had got his carrots and sticks backwards.

Unaware of his chancellor's latest policy blunders, Kaiser Wilhelm II sat down in the Neues Palais on Tuesday evening to edit an urgent telegram to Tsar Nicholas II. Although addressed from 'Willy' to 'Nicky,' in the familiar style in which the sovereigns addressed one another, the message was actually drafted first by Wilhelm von Stumm, the political director at the Wilhelmstrasse, under Bethmann's supervision. Mildly suspicious as to what his chancellor was up to, the kaiser did insist on several changes that softened the tone. He rewrote the key line personally: 'I am exerting my utmost influence,' Willy promised Nicky, 'to induce the Austrians to deal straightly to arrive at a satisfactory understanding with you.' He signed off, 'your very sincere and devoted friend and cousin Willy.'[27]

Unbeknownst to the kaiser, Nicky was writing his own sovereign-to-sovereign telegram almost simultaneously. The tsar had been having second thoughts ever since inaugurating the Period Preparatory to War on Saturday. On Monday, he had come up with his own mediation idea, proposing to Sazonov that the Austrian-Serbian dispute be submitted to arbitration by the Hague Tribunal. Sazonov had simply ignored the tsar's suggestion, hoping that his simple-minded sovereign would forget about it. Nevertheless, Sazonov was unable to prevent the tsar from intervening in his own way, appealing directly to Willy to pull back the Austrians. 'An ignoble war,' Nicholas wrote, 'has been declared to a weak country. The indignation in Russia shared by me is enormous. I foresee that very soon I shall be overwhelmed by the pressure brought upon me and be forced to take extreme measures which will lead to war. To try to avoid such a calamity as a European war, I beg you in the name of our old friendship to do what you can to stop your allies [e.g., Austria-Hungary] from going too far.'[28]

Just at the moment when Russia's tsar was demanding that the kaiser do what he could to stop his Austrian ally from 'going too far,' Willy was promising Nicky that he was 'exerting his utmost influence' to do just that. Although neither sovereign was a man of strong will or keen intelligence, each did possess moral imagination. Both men clearly felt a grave responsibility about unleashing a war sure to kill thousands, if not millions, of their subjects. As that war loomed ever more closely on the horizon, Willy and Nicky were searching desperately for a way out. Were their sovereign authority as absolute in practice as it appeared on paper, they might even have succeeded.

It was not. Bethmann, as we have seen, undermined his sovereign's desire to mediate in Vienna by reconfiguring the kaiser's

'Halt in Belgrade' proposal into a form sure to be rejected by the Russians. In Petersburg, meanwhile, Sazonov and the military chiefs were proceeding over (or around) the tsar's head with important decisions that would render his personal mediation efforts dead on arrival. In doing so they had strong French encouragement. Poincaré and Viviani were still at sea on Tuesday, but in their absence France's ambassador, along with her army chief of staff, General Joffre, and her war minister, Adolphe Messimy, had begun to take matters into their own hands. On Tuesday, even as crowds were milling about Paris awaiting the Mme Caillaux verdict, Russia's military attaché to France reported to Petersburg that Joffre and Messimy had assured him of France's readiness to fulfil her alliance obligations. Joffre himself requested (via the Quai d'Orsay) that Ambassador Paléologue 'endeavor through all possible means to make sure that, if hostilities broke out, *the Government of St Petersburg would immediately take the offensive in East Prussia*, as had been agreed upon in our conventions.' Messimy wired similar instructions to Petersburg, 'urg[ing] with all my might that, in spite of the slowness of Russia's mobilisation, the tsar's armies should as soon as possible take the offensive in East Prussia.' Just as then-premier Gaston Doumergue had instructed Paléologue upon his appointment to Petersburg, 'the safety of France will depend on the *energy and promptness* with which *we shall know how to push them into the fight*.' It was now up to Paléologue to start pushing.[29]

Paléologue did not disappoint Joffre and Messimy. Shortly after Sazonov learned of Austria's declaration of war at four PM Tuesday, Paléologue had returned to Chorister's Bridge for another audience with the foreign minister. While Paléologue does not discuss this second meeting in his memoirs, the logbook of the Russian Foreign Ministry kept by Schilling confirms that it took place. We do not know everything that was said between the two men, but Schilling's log gives a capsule summary. 'On the instructions of his Government,' the entry reads, 'the French Ambassador acquainted the Foreign Minister with the complete readiness of France to fulfil her obligations as an ally in the case of necessity.'[30]

Schilling's logbook leaves unstated on whose 'instructions' this critical declaration was given – they may have been Joffre's, Messimy's, or even Poincaré's, issued informally while he was still in Petersburg. Almost certainly they did not come from Viviani. The log entry also leaves unclear the context, as there is no mention of Austria's declaration of war on Serbia or of Russia's response.

There is no doubting, however, the critical nature of Paléologue's blanket declaration of support for Russia on 28 July. Its significance was confirmed in a telegram Sazonov sent the next morning to Izvolsky in Paris (copied to London, Vienna, Rome, and Berlin), in which Russia's foreign minister asked his ambassador to pass on 'our sincere gratitude for the declaration, which the French ambassador made to me in his government's name, that we may count in full measure on the support of France under the alliance. In the present circumstances,' Sazonov continued, 'this declaration is of especial value to us.'[31]

Buoyed by Paléologue's declaration of France's unconditional support in the wake of Austria's declaration of war on Serbia, Sazonov moved decisively to speed up Russia's war preparations. His first stop was Peterhof Palace, where Nicholas II was waiting for him – in order, the tsar thought, to discuss his Hague arbitration idea. At about six PM Tuesday, Sazonov informed Russia's sovereign that Austria had declared war on Serbia. He also requested the tsar's permission to have Chief of Staff Yanushkevitch draw up two mobilisation *ukases* for the Russian army, one for partial and the other for general.

The tsar consented – or at least, so Sazonov claimed Russia's sovereign had done when he ordered Yanushkevitch to draw up the orders. It may be that the tsar agreed to have the orders drawn up on the understanding that they would not take effect until he signed them. Whether or not the tsar fully understood what he had consented to, Yanushkevitch promptly drew up two mobilisation *ukases*.[32] Interestingly, the principal documents we have from Tuesday night both mention general, not partial, mobilisation, which suggests that Sazonov and Yanushkevitch were already leaning that way. Paléologue, too, was likely in the loop, as the first such document is his own telegram sent off at 7:35 PM, in which he informed Paris – as if hypothetically – that 'in case of general mobilisation, two officers will be delegated to be sent to my embassy.' He then named his preferences (Messrs. de Ridder and de Sèze) and suggested that they proceed to Russia via Stockholm, rather than by the more direct route via Germany.[33] That Russia's impending general mobilisation was more than hypothetical is suggested in a telegram dispatched later Tuesday night by Yanushkevitch to the commanders of all Russia's military districts, informing them that '30 July will be proclaimed the first day of our general mobilisation. The proclamation will follow by regulation telegram.'[34]

Even as Willy and Nicky were exchanging their 'peace' telegrams, Russia had begun the countdown to European war. The Austrian noose on German necks was now taut. Russia's generals (although not yet her sovereign) had even determined the date of execution.

19

'I Will Not Be Responsible for a Monstrous Slaughter!'

WEDNESDAY, 29 JULY

J UST AFTER MIDNIGHT on Wednesday, 29 July, Britain's First Fleet left Portland harbour, heading south at first before proceeding along a 'middle Channel course' to the Straits of Dover. The squadrons, First Lord of the Admiralty Churchill had instructed, were 'to pass through the Straits without lights during the night and to pass outside the shoals on their way north.' As Churchill himself imagined the scene as the fleet steamed slowly out of harbour, 'scores of gigantic castles of steel wending their way across the misty, shining sea, like giants bowed in anxious thought. We may picture them again as darkness fell, eighteen miles of warships running at high speed and in absolute blackness through the Narrow Straits, bearing with them into the waters of the North the safeguard of considerable affairs.'[1]

On the other side of the English channel, at eight AM the battleship *France* sighted land after more than five days at sea, interrupted only briefly by stopovers at Stockholm and Christiana (Oslo). Prime Minister Viviani, who had been reluctant to go to

Russia in the first place, was ecstatic. 'At last!' he remarked, ' a twinkling light beneath a roof, a house, dockyards, masts, a gradually emerging skyline – Dunkirk!'[2]

After their ship laid anchor in the harbour, Viviani and President Poincaré were transferred onto a smaller steamer and piloted into port, where they were surprised by crowds shouting, *'Vive la France!'* and *'Vive Poincaré!'* While he ordinarily enjoyed such displays of patriotism, Poincaré was surprised by the intensity of the public mood. 'What struck me,' he recalled later, 'was that many people here seem to think war imminent.' Crowds showed up at every station along the three-hour train trip to Paris and at many points in between. 'We saw the inhabitants massed on both sides of the way,' he observed, 'shouting without ceasing the same public greetings, the same cheers, the same vows of peace, the same promises of courage and resignation.'[3] If war would come, it seemed that the French people were ready, whether or not France's government had decided what to do.

Poincaré and Viviani were a bit behind events because of the vagaries of wireless communication at sea. There remains some controversy as to whether the German Admiralty deliberately jammed the *France*'s signals while it was off Germany's Baltic coast, as the French always claimed.*[4] Poor signal strength, along with interference among wireless messages transmitted at similar frequencies across well-trafficked sea channels, may account for the difficulties of reception aboard the *France*. Still, it is clear that not all messages from Paris and Petersburg got through. On Tuesday evening, 28 July, Ambassador Paléologue had told Foreign Minister Sazonov that he could not reach the

---

* German naval intelligence did intercept two encrypted wireless transmissions from aboard the *France*. This does not prove that the signal was jammed, however; in fact it suggests the opposite, that the Germans were trying to listen in, not to block communications.

France – with the corollary that, because his superiors were out of touch, 'they cannot send me any instructions.' He thus left the Russians in doubt about whether his endorsement of the acceleration of Russia's mobilisation measures that day ('the complete readiness of France to fulfil her obligations as an ally') really had been given 'on the instructions of his Government,' as he told Sazonov.[5] To this day, we do not know for sure whether Paléologue was acting on orders from his president or premier, or exceeding them.

Almost certainly, Poincaré and Viviani knew less than did their ambassador in Petersburg when they returned to France. Still, they knew more than they made out in post-war memoirs. Viviani's latest communication from on board the *France* to Bienvenu-Martin, acting director of the Quai d'Orsay, on Tuesday, had taken up British foreign secretary Grey's three-days-old proposal for a four-power conference, not the more urgent recent ones for direct Austrian-Russian talks on the basis of Serbia's reply.[6] This suggests he was running behind on mediation efforts. Poincaré and Viviani probably had not heard yet of Austria's declaration of war on Serbia on Tuesday (although they would learn of it after docking at Dunkirk), nor of the drawing up of mobilisation *ukases* in Petersburg on Tuesday night. They may or may not have known about the inauguration of Russia's Period Preparatory to War: the Paléologue and Laguiche telegrams discussing it were sent directly to Paris, and there is no proof that these messages ever reached the *France*.

Still, as against their later claims to have known nothing of Russian war preparations, we can confirm that Viviani was informed by Bienvenu-Martin on Sunday, 26 July, that Russia planned to 'partially mobilise' thirteen army corps against Vienna 'if Austria were to bring armed pressure to bear on Serbia,' and that 'Russian public opinion affirms its determination not to let Serbia be crushed.'[7] In response to this telegram,

Viviani had instructed Paléologue, on Monday, 27 July, to tell Sazonov that France was 'ready . . . wholeheartedly to second the action of the [Russian] imperial government' (although Viviani, significantly, had inserted the clause 'in the interests of general peace' to the original Quai d'Orsay draft, in between 'ready' and 'wholeheartedly').[8] Neither Viviani nor Poincaré was up on all the latest developments. But they had left Russia in no doubt as to French resolve and support.

On the train to Paris, Poincaré and Viviani were further debriefed by Abel Ferry, the French undersecretary of state, who had assembled 'an enormous pile of telegrams' for them. They learned, among other things, that French Algeria and Morocco had been mobilised: a hundred thousand 'crack troops' were assembling on the coast, ready to be shipped to the French mainland. French and other European civilians were being evacuated into the African interior for safety. Even Poincaré was taken aback by this news. Still, Ferry did not know everything. He informed the president neither of Russia's far-reaching Period Preparatory to War, underway by now for four days, nor that Joffre, Messimy, and Paléologue had urged the Russians to go further still.[9]

Poincaré would not remain ignorant for long. Messimy met him as soon as the president's train pulled into the capital. 'Monsieur le Président,' the minister of war said by way of greeting, 'you are going to see Paris; it is magnificent.' Indeed it was. Only the previous day the Caillaux trial had concluded, after dividing the French public for months. It was a kind of exorcism: France's inner demons seemed to have dissolved into a nationalist frenzy against the Germans. 'As I came out of the station,' Poincaré recalled,

I was greeted by an overwhelming demonstration which moved me to the depths of my being. Many people had tears in their eyes and I could hardly hold back my own. From thousands of throats arose repeated shouts of: Vive la France et Vive la République! Vive le Président! . . . From the station to the Elysée the cheering never stopped. . . . Here was a united France. Political quarrels were forgotten. . . . How far away the [Caillaux] affair seems now! What different matters now claim public attention![10]

For a man himself involved in the affair on the side of the nationalist publisher murdered by Caillaux's wife, who had legitimate concerns that Russian subsidies routed via Ambassador Izvolsky to his presidential campaign in 1913 would be exposed, Poincaré saw the outpouring of patriotism as something of a personal vindication.

Once the cheering subsided, it was time to go to work. At eleven fifteen that morning, Izvolsky arrived at the Quai d'Orsay to debrief Viviani and Poincaré. He shared with them Sazonov's telegram, sent on Tuesday evening, announcing Russia's partial mobilisation in response to Austria's declaration of war on Serbia, along with the vaguer one to Ambassador Benckendorff in London, in which Sazonov spoke only of Austria's declaration of war on Serbia (but not Russia's response to it) and requested that his ambassador ask Grey 'with all speed to take action in view of mediation and for Austria at once to suspend military measures against Serbia.' Izvolsky did not acquaint the president – or at least not the premier – with his recent discussions with Messimy and Joffre regarding the acceleration of Russian mobilisation measures.[11]

Izvolsky's briefing was a classic red herring. According to the terms of the Franco-Russian military convention, reaffirmed as recently as 1913, neither country could mobilise without first informing the other. If Russia were to order general mobilisation without clearing this with France (or without prior German mobilisation, which would trigger both French and Russian mobilisations), it would violate one of the fundamental conditions of the alliance.[12] This, and not Sazonov's loaded request for Austria to suspend military measures against Serbia (even while Russia accelerated her own), should have been the first order of business between Izvolsky and France's government. By Wednesday, Russia's war preparations had already begun to resemble a general mobilisation, whatever she chose to call them. We can get an idea of their scope – and intent – in a report filed that day by Germany's consul in Warsaw:

> Russia is already fully in a state of preparation for war. . . . The troops ranged against Germany are assembling between Lomza and Kovno along the Niemen, while those ranged against Austria are assembling at Lublin and Kovel [in Ukraine]. . . . The Warsaw-Kalish line [to the Prussian border] and the Warsaw-Vienna tracks have been blanketed with infantry and sappers, who are laying mines under the roadbeds.[13]

Unaware of all this – and with Izvolsky doing nothing to enlighten him – Viviani agreed to telegraph his ambassador in London, Paul Cambon, to tell him that he should support Sazonov's request that England get Austria to 'suspend military measures.'[14] While the request was reasonable on the surface, in terms of diplomatic priorities it made little sense. There was little that France, much less England, could do to influence Vienna directly, especially as Austrian military measures thus far targeted Serbia, not Russia. France did, however, have an interest – a legal obligation, even – to sign off on Russian military measures, which had already taken on threatening overtones on both the Austrian and the German borders. It was the

strategic-alliance implications of Russia's own military measures, underway since Saturday night, that Viviani should have
been focusing on. France's premier was rushing to get up to
speed on Austria. When it came to his own ally, however, he
was running nearly four days behind.

THE GERMANS WERE NOT DOING MUCH BETTER. By Tuesday,
28 July, Chancellor Bethmann had, more or less, caught up
to events following his return from Hohenfinow, but, whether
by accident or design, he had done a very poor job of keeping
his sovereign and the military service chiefs informed. The kaiser remained unaware for most of Wednesday that Bethmann
had effectively gutted his proposal to mediate at Vienna by rul-
ing out any negotiations over the terms of Serbia's reply. Chief
of Staff Moltke, responsible for the mobilisation of Germany's
armies in case the crisis spiraled into war, had awakened to
the seriousness of the situation only towards Tuesday evening,
when he began composing a policy statement for the chancellor. Given to Bethmann Wednesday morning, Moltke's memorandum made for depressing reading. It would be suicidal, he
argued, for Austria to send her armies into Serbia without also
mobilising against Russia – otherwise the tsarist armies could
seize Austrian Galicia without a fight. 'The instant Austria
mobilises her whole army,' Moltke continued,

> the clash between her and Russia will become inevit-
> able. Now that is for Germany the *casus foederis*. Unless
> Germany means to break her word and allow her ally
> to succumb to Russia's superior strength, she must
> also mobilise. This will lead to the mobilisation of the
> remaining Russian military districts. . . . The Franco-
> Russian agreement . . . comes thereby into operation,

and the civilised states of Europe will tear each other to
pieces. . . . This is the way things will and must develop,
unless, one might almost say, a miracle takes place at the
last hour, to prevent a war that will annihilate the civilisation of almost all of Europe for decades to come.[15]

Although tinged with his habitual pessimism, Moltke's
statement was a fairly accurate representation of where things
stood on Wednesday. Austria had not yet mobilised her whole
army, nor Russia hers, although both were far along in 'partial' mobilisation measures, and in the Russian case this clearly
included the areas of Poland bordering Germany. Nor had
France mobilised – although, as Moltke pointed out, she had
already begun a few pre-mobilisation measures on the frontier,
as reported by German army intelligence. On the orders of Erich
von Falkenhayn, the Prussian minister of war (not Moltke), the
German army had undertaken a few precautionary measures
of her own on Tuesday, keeping troops in garrison by calling
off planned manoeuvres, purchasing grain, and heightening
security on the railways. This fell far short of pre-mobilisation,
much less mobilisation. So long as the powers refrained from
accelerating war preparations, therefore, there was still a slim
chance of staving off war – but, as Moltke suggested, it would
require a diplomatic miracle. Any further perturbation in the
delicate dance of mobilisation timetables could be fatal.

After reading over the memorandum, Bethmann summoned Moltke and Falkenhayn to the Wilhelmstrasse. We have
no transcript of this Wednesday morning audience, but it seems
to have been a difficult one. Falkenhayn, having ordered precautionary measures on Tuesday, wanted to take things to the
next level by proclaiming *Kriegsgefahrzustand*, or 'the Imminent
Danger of War,' a stage akin to Russia's Period Preparatory
to War, although in the German case still more serious, as,

barring contrary orders, general mobilisation would follow automatically after just two days. Bethmann, hoping that the kaiser's 'Halt in Belgrade' plan might still work, refused. He was backed by Moltke, who, Falkenhayn complained, 'would not go further than giving military protection to important railway key points.'[16]

Still, Moltke had his own concerns about Bethmann's dithering. Germany's latest mobilisation plan, which he had modified significantly from the design of Count Alfred von Schlieffen, his predecessor as chief of staff, dating to 1906,* required the German armies to achieve a major victory on the western front within six or seven weeks of mobilisation, so as to give Moltke enough time to wheel them around to fend off Russia's expected offensive on Berlin. Every passing day, during which France and Russia were mobilising (or pre-mobilising) threatened Moltke's timetable. It was thus imperative, he told Bethmann, to clarify French and Russian intentions immediately.[17]

The chancellor agreed. At 12:50 PM Wednesday, Bethmann sent off wires to his ambassadors in Paris and Petersburg. Baron Schoen was instructed to inform the French government that, in response to France's preliminary mobilisation preparations, Germany would have to proclaim *Kriegsgefahr* ('Danger of War,' not quite 'Immediate Danger of War'), which, Schoen was to insist, fell well short of mobilisation.[18] More ominously,

---

* Moltke had weakened the German right wing in the north and strengthened the left in the south, which faced the French in Alsace-Lorraine. In Schlieffen's conception, the northernmost German army would have violated not only Belgian but even some Dutch territory, ultimately enveloping the French armies from behind. Moltke, concerned about German access to world markets in the case of a long war, had eliminated the Dutch option, weighted the German deployment further south overall, and allowed for some operational flexibility depending on what the French would do. The German war plan of 1914 was nowhere near as rigid as the Schlieffen plan of legend; 'Paris by day 40' was a myth. Still, speed of deployment mattered greatly.

Pourtalès was asked to 'please impress on M. Sazonov very seriously that further progress of Russian mobilisation measures would compel us to mobilise and that European war could then scarcely be prevented.'[19]

Bethmann had once again blundered into the most counterproductive policy imaginable. Having failed to follow his kaiser's instructions on Tuesday to mediate seriously in Vienna, he had lost what was probably his last realistic chance to lure Austria, and with her Russia, back from the precipice. Bethmann had also failed to give point to his ministrations in Petersburg by refusing to declare *Kriegsgefahrzustand*, which might have put a scare into Sazonov – and the French. Instead of quietly preparing for war, the chancellor issued two clumsy *threats* to undertake retaliatory mobilisation measures – and in his threat to Russia, Bethmann vowed explicitly that German mobilisation would lead to 'European war.' In doing so, he undermined his own 'Halt in Belgrade' initiative, which he had committed to (however selectively) on Tuesday night. France and Russia, though speaking softly – especially in London – continued priming their fists for war. The Germans were loudly proclaiming their warlike intentions – but doing little to prepare for the fight.

Meanwhile, the Austrians were serving up another fait accompli, without bothering to inform the Germans. Wednesday afternoon, while Pourtalès was mulling over how to issue Bethmann's veiled threat to Sazonov without it sounding like a threat, the Austrian army began shelling Belgrade, conveniently located on the Austrian border, directly opposite the Danube. The attack was mostly symbolic, doing little actual damage. It petered out quickly and was not followed by any hint of a ground offensive. Still, it gave the lie to any expectation that the Austrians might accept mediation with Serbia – or that the Germans would force them to.

B Y WEDNESDAY EVENING, Bethmann's contradictory policies had borne evil fruit in St Petersburg.

At around eleven AM, Pourtalès had called on Sazonov to reassure him that Berlin was working to rein in Austria, as promised in the kaiser's 'Nicky' telegram – although (lacking clearer instructions from Bethmann) he was not able to spell out how, exactly, the Germans were restraining their ally. The ambassador also requested that the Russians not make things harder by undertaking a 'premature mobilisation' against Austria (apparently Sazonov had not yet informed Pourtalès about the 'partial mobilisation' against her that was ordered on Tuesday). Sazonov replied that Austria should halt her own mobilisation measures – no fewer than eight corps, he told Pourtalès, had been mobilised (this was true, but it was also true that, at Chief of Staff Conrad's insistence, all eight had been mobilised against Serbia, not Russia). Sazonov then called in his advisers to discuss whether the Germans were sincere or were merely using delaying tactics. An answer, of sorts, was offered at around five PM, when Sazonov learned of the Austrian bombardment of Belgrade.[20] At six PM, Pourtalès returned, carrying Bethmann's veiled warning, so contrary in spirit to what he had said that morning (although the ambassador gamely insisted to Sazonov that 'it was not a threat, but a friendly opinion').[21]

The effect on the Russian foreign minister was electric. After being told – shortly after hearing that Austria had begun shelling the Serbian capital – that Germany would be 'compelled' to mobilise if Russia continued her military preparations, Russia's foreign minister 'sharply replied, "I no longer have any doubt as to the real cause of Austrian intransigence." At this, Count Pourtalès jumped up from his seat, and also sharply exclaimed, "I protest with all my power, Mr Minister, against this injurious assertion."' Sazonov, Schilling recorded, 'drily replied that Germany still had an opportunity for proving the erroneousness of what he had said.' The two men then parted 'coolly.'[22]

In a week of mounting tension between Pourtalès and Sazonov, this was their most disastrous encounter yet.

The next hours in Petersburg were packed with incident. Shortly before 8 PM, the tsar phoned Sazonov to share with him the previous night's telegram from the kaiser, which he had just finished reading. Sazonov, in turn, informed his sovereign about Bethmann's warning and the resulting unpleasant confrontation with the German ambassador from which he had just emerged.[23] The tsar was perplexed by the seeming contradiction and sent an urgent telegram to Willy at 8:20 PM, demanding clarification:

THANKS FOR YOUR TELEGRAM CONCILIATORY AND FRIENDLY, WHEREAS OFFICIAL MESSAGE PRESENTED TODAY BY YOUR AMBASSADOR TO MY MINISTER WAS CONVEYED IN A VERY DIFFERENT TONE. BEG YOU TO EXPLAIN THE DIVERGENCY. IT WOULD BE RIGHT TO GIVE OVER THE AUSTRO-SERBIAN PROBLEM TO THE HAGUE CONFERENCE. TRUST IN YOUR WISDOM AND FRIENDSHIP. YOUR LOVING NICKY.[24]

As if wishing to surpass the Germans in the 'divergency' of his own signals, the tsar, shortly before composing this plea for peace and while still on the phone, had, according to Schilling's diary, extended 'permission to S. D. Sazonov to discuss the question of our mobilisation at once with the Minister of War and the Chief of the General Staff.' Sazonov promptly summoned Sukhomlinov and Yanushkevitch to Chorister's Bridge. The three men met in Yanushkevitch's office at the ministry, with supporting staff waiting in the next room to carry out urgent orders. Earlier that day, the tsar had signed both partial and general mobilisation orders, although neither had yet been made operative. Yanushkevitch had carried both orders around all day in his pocket, although he was personally confident that, the tsar's hesitation aside, general mobilisation was inevitable. In fact, Yanushkevitch had gone so far as to wire Tiflis command to mobilise Russia's Army of the Caucasus on the basis of 'variant 4' of 'a war with a coalition,' in which the participation of both Britain and France was assured and in which 'Turkey does not *at first* take part.'[25]

Sazonov and Sukhomlinov saw things the same way. Although the three men 'examined the situation from all points,' their discussion did not last long. Shortly after nine PM, Sazonov phoned Tsar Nicholas II – less than an hour after the latter had requested that the kaiser submit his Austrian ally to international arbitration at the Hague – to ask his sovereign's permission to order general mobilisation against both Austria-Hungary and Germany (variant 4, as Yanushkevitch had specified). The tsar agreed at once. His decision, quickly relayed to everyone at Chorister's Bridge, was, according to Schilling, 'received with enthusiasm.'[26] General Dobrorolskii, chief of the army's Mobilisation Division, headed over to the Central Telegraph Office of St Petersburg to issue the fateful order. 'In my presence,' Dobrorolskii recalled, the switchboard operators proceeded 'to click off the telegram on several typewriters in order to send it at the same moment by all the wires which connected St Petersburg with the principal centres of the Empire. . . . There existed a special instruction for the sending of the mobilisation telegram. During the transmission no other telegrams of any sort could be sent.'[27]

Even while the mobilisation orders were being typed up, however, a dramatic scene was transpiring at the Peterhof. At 9:40 PM, a second 'Willy-Nicky' telegram was delivered, replying to the tsar's first (not his second, about the Hague, which the kaiser had not yet received when he wired this one from Potsdam at 6:30 PM). The tsar, understandably, thought Willy was replying to the telegram he had sent just an hour previously, rather than the one he had sent the night before. 'I share your wish,' the kaiser informed Tsar Nicholas II, 'that peace should be maintained.' Although he disputed the tsar's description of Austria's initiation of hostilities against Serbia as an 'ignoble war,' the kaiser agreed on the need for 'a direct understanding between your Government and Vienna' and 'readily accepted' the tsar's appeal, on his friendship, that he would act as mediator (there was no mention of the Hague, which should have tipped off the tsar that his second message had not yet been received). The kaiser's said his role as mediator, however, would be 'jeopardised' if Russia continued her military preparations, which might easily 'precipitate a calamity we both wish to avoid.'[28]

Russia's sovereign was moved (and also confused: he really did think the kaiser had responded within minutes to his urgent telegram sent off an hour earlier). Calling in the minister of the imperial court, the tsar told his aide, 'in extreme agitation,' that 'everything possible must be done to save the peace. I will not become responsible for a monstrous slaughter.' The tsar then phoned Chorister's Bridge and asked that Sukhomlinov be put on the line. Horrified that his nervous sovereign would gum up the works of Russia's general mobilisation, Sukhomlinov tried to dissuade him. 'Mobilisation,' the war minister argued, 'is not a mechanical process which one can arrest at will, as one can a wagon, and then set in motion again.' The tsar then asked for Yanushkevitch, who offered the same opinion. Summoning all his strength, Tsar Nicholas II asserted his sovereign control over the army and demanded that the general mobilisation order be rescinded.[29]

Back at the telegraph office, Dobrorolskii, still waiting for the typed copies of the general mobilisation order to be transmitted throughout the empire, was summoned to the telephone. Yanushkevitch was on the line, telling him to call off the orders because the tsar had changed his mind. At the last possible moment – around ten PM on Wednesday, 29 July – European war was averted.[30] For the moment.

V. A. Sukhomlinov, Russia's forceful war minister, who pressed for mobilisation in November 1912, January 1914, and July 1914. *Source: Tsentralnyi gosudarstvennyi fotoarkhiv kinofotofonodokumentov, St Petersburg, Russia.*

IN BERLIN, BETHMANN'S NERVES were breaking. On Wednesday afternoon, he had been summoned to Potsdam, along with Chief of Staff Moltke, Minister of War Falkenhayn, and Naval Secretary Tirpitz. Everyone, it seemed, agreed on one thing: the chancellor was to blame. The kaiser, Tirpitz recalled, 'expressed himself without reserve regarding Bethmann's incompetence.' Time was running out on a diplomatic solution. If such a solution were impossible, then Germany's army – and her navy – were running out of time to prepare for war. Still, however inept the chancellor's policies may have been so far, the military chiefs (but for Falkenhayn) agreed that, so long as the 'Halt in Belgrade' initiative endured, it was too soon to proclaim *Kriegsgefahrzustand*. Desperate to keep Britain out of the

European war that stared him in the face, the chancellor 'proposed that, in order to keep England neutral, we should sacrifice the German fleet for an agreement with England.' Tirpitz was horrified, although not surprised – Bethmann had mooted the idea of turning over Germany's entire navy to the British Admiralty in the past, in order to split England apart from the Entente.[31] To Tirpitz's relief, the kaiser, reluctant to sacrifice his beloved high-seas navy, refused. Bethmann was foiled again. After wolfing down dinner in ten minutes, he left the Neues Palais in a serious funk, appearing to witnesses as if he had 'completely collapsed.'[32]

Reaching the Wilhelmstrasse sometime between seven and eight PM, the chancellor was in for a new series of shocks. A telegram from Pourtalès had been decoded around three PM, reporting Russia's partial mobilisation. Just minutes later a wire had come in from Chelius, the military attaché in Petersburg, stating that, since Austria's declaration of war on Serbia, 'in the tsar's entourage, a general war was regarded as almost inevitable.'[33] At around four PM, the German General Staff passed on to the Wilhelmstrasse a report of intimidating length on Russian military preparations, citing 'troop concentrations near the border of all arms in up to multi-regimental strength, the recall of reservists and the preparation of rail rolling stock.'[34] This was accompanied by the disquieting news that Belgium had called up three classes of reservists, strengthened frontier defences, armed fortresses, and prepared bridges for demolition in case French or German troops came in.[35] Meanwhile two telegrams from Lichnowsky painted a disturbing, if ambiguous, picture of British intentions. In the first he reported that British diplomats were certain that Italy would never fight alongside Austria and Germany.[36] In the second, Lichnowsky passed on the impression 'that there is a firm conviction here . . . that, failing readiness on the part of Austria to enter into a discussion of the Serbian question, world war will be unavoidable.'[37]

This new batch of bad news heaped yet more pressure on Bethmann. Because even 'partial mobilisation' in Russia had grave implications for Germany's mobilisation timetable, the chancellor had to call in the military chiefs, along with foreign minister Jagow, for an urgent meeting at the Wilhelmstrasse. War now looked likelier than ever, which put the question of British neutrality front and centre. It was imperative, Bethmann argued, to put the onus of starting the conflict on Russia. Sazonov had claimed, when Pourtalès confronted him, that Russian mobilisation 'did not mean war.' Whatever the truth of the Russian's claim – Falkenhayn, for one, thought it 'a direct lie' – Bethmann wanted to test it out with an eye to British opinion. 'England,' he argued, 'would not be able to side with Russia if Russia unleashed a general war by an attack on Austria and thus took on her shoulders the guilt for the whole smash-up (*Kladderadatsch*).' For this reason the chancellor urged that *Kriegsgefahrzustand* still not be proclaimed, so as to make clear to London that Russia, not Germany, was starting the war. Moltke and Falkenhayn, reluctantly, agreed to wait.[38]

Bethmann was staking a great deal on his hope of British neutrality. Having based his foreign policy for years on rapprochement with England, having just told his military chiefs to hold off on war preparations so as not to prejudice English opinion, Bethmann was ready to go all in. Despite the worrying tone of Lichnowsky's afternoon dispatches, there were some grounds for optimism. At Potsdam, the chancellor had learned of an encouraging declaration made several days earlier by King George V to the kaiser's brother, Prince Heinrich, that 'we shall try all we can to keep out of this, and shall remain neutral.' The prince had arrived in Potsdam on Wednesday afternoon; he assured the kaiser that this statement had 'been made in all seriousness' and that England would almost certainly be neutral at the start of the war, with her future attitude depending on the fate of France.[39] It was only the secondhand sentiment of a sovereign, but, since the kaiser had refused to allow Bethmann to barter Germany's fleet for British neutrality, the English king's vow was all the chancellor had.

Clinging to this thin reed of hope, Bethmann ventured out on a dangerous limb. At ten thirty Wednesday night, the chancellor called in Britain's ambassador, Sir Edward Goschen. Bethmann may not have been entirely of sound mind, following an exhausting day during which he had been chastised by his sovereign in front of the military chiefs and then received a depressing litany of bad news,* which had forced him to face the disapproving glares of Falkenhayn and Moltke again. Still, Bethmann's opening was sensible. Although he 'was continuing his efforts to maintain peace,' the chancellor told Goschen that, if Germany was forced to mobilise owing to a 'Russian attack on Austria,' it might, 'to his great regret, render a European conflagration inevitable.' In this case, Bethmann 'hoped Great Britain would remain neutral.' Had he ended his remarks there, Goschen would have had little to object to. How, after all, could England have justified *not* remaining neutral (that is, declaring war on Germany) if the *casus foederis* was a Russian attack on Austria? This, indeed, would follow the logic of what Bethmann had just proposed to Falkenhayn and Moltke: that Germany refrain from countermobilising in order to put the onus of starting the war onto Russia.

Bethmann did not, however, stop there. Thinking that he needed to offer England something tangible in order to win

---

* Fortunately for the chancellor's fragile nerves, he had, at this point, not yet received the Warsaw consul's report that 'Russia is already fully in a state of preparation for war. . . . The troops ranged against Germany are assembling between Lomza and Kovno along the Niemen,' which was decoded only on Thursday. Had Bethmann read this on top of everything else Wednesday night, he might have broken down completely.

a genuine, across-the-board neutrality pledge – and unable to give her the German fleet, as he would have wished – the chancellor began doling out inside information. In exchange for British neutrality, he promised Goschen that, 'in the event of a victorious war, Germany aimed at no territorial acquisitions at the expense of France.' This pledge, in itself, was harmless, but its very formulation opened Bethmann up to a broad range of questions regarding German intentions. If not France, then what about her colonies? Goschen asked. The chancellor, foolishly, admitted that he was unable to guarantee that Germany would not take them. Holland? Bethmann 'said he was . . . ready to assure the British Government that Germany would respect neutrality and integrity of Holland as long as they were respected by Germany's adversaries.' Now Goschen got to the point: Would Germany respect Belgian neutrality, guaranteed by all the powers since the creation of the state (largely under British auspices) in 1839? 'As regards Belgium,' Bethmann blurted out without thinking, he 'could not tell to what operations Germany might be forced by the action of France, but he could state that, provided that Belgium did not take sides against Germany, *her integrity would be respected after the conclusion of the war.*'[40]

Here was a diplomatic blunder of the first order. Under the stress of the night, Bethmann had given away the store. Rather than reassure London about Germany's peaceful intentions, his artless bid for neutrality signalled a desire for war. Having himself opened up a dangerous line of questioning, Bethmann had then tacitly admitted that Germany had imperial designs on France's colonies (if not on France herself). Worst of all, in his answers to the questions on Holland and Belgium, he had unwittingly betrayed the most sensitive secret of Germany's war plan: a march through Belgium. Why else had he promised to respect Dutch but not Belgian neutrality? Indeed, as Sir Eyre

Crowe, senior clerk at the British Foreign Office, minuted on Goschen's report, 'Germany practically admits the intention to violate Belgian neutrality.' The only comment necessary on these 'astounding proposals,' Crowe drily remarked, 'is that they reflect discredit on the statesman who makes them.'[41] Prime Minister Asquith, when he learned of the proposal, felt almost sorry for Bethmann, noting that 'there is something very crude & almost childlike about German diplomacy.'[42]

In Bethmann's defence, he seems to have realised his error almost as soon as he made it. Just minutes after his audience with Goschen concluded, the chancellor was handed a third telegram from Lichnowsky, which showed him just how forlorn his hope of British neutrality had been. After days of confusing feints at mediation, Foreign Minister Grey had finally summoned the courage to issue a real warning to Germany. While still hoping that a four-power conference, including Germany, would mediate between Austria and Serbia, Grey for the first time gave a hint of what England's policy might look like if this did not happen. If an armed Austro-Russian clash over Serbia drew France and Germany into a European war, Grey told Lichnowsky around six Wednesday evening, 'the British Government would be forced into taking rapid decisions. In this case it would not do to stand aside and wait.'[43] So King George's vague reassurance had been hollow. Britain would not remain neutral after all.

Lichnowsky's latest telegram dealt Bethmann a crushing blow. But it was also salutary, in that it forced him to abandon the wishful assumption on which he had been basing his policies. Here it must be said that Grey had done almost nothing before 29 July to discourage this assumption. As early as Friday, 24 July, Sir George Buchanan had urged the foreign secretary to make a clear statement at Berlin and Vienna 'that if war became general, it would be difficult for England to remain neutral.'[44]

Had Grey done so over the weekend, or even as late as Monday, 27 July, Bethmann would have been under no illusions about British neutrality. He might then have warned off Austrian foreign minister Berchtold from declaring war on Serbia on Tuesday – or at least passed on, unedited, the kaiser's more genuine version of the 'Halt in Belgrade' proposal, under which Austria would negotiate on the basis of the Serbian reply. Had Grey issued his veiled threat even as late as Wednesday morning (in time for Bethmann to learn of it before his fateful ten thirty PM encounter with Goschen), the chancellor would have spared everyone the embarrassment of his sublimely stupid bid for neutrality. Instead, Grey had consistently maintained a phony posture of disinterestedness, even as Churchill (admittedly without Grey's knowledge) was priming Britain's navy for war against Germany and as Russia commenced far-reaching preparations for war without a peep of British disapproval. By leaving the Germans in the dark about British intentions for so long, Grey had fed Bethmann's illusions, which had encouraged him to urge on Austria's reckless behaviour.

Sir Edward Grey, of course, was facing his own painful dilemmas. Churchill's bold preparatory manoeuvres were possible only because he had not run them by the cabinet, on the spurious grounds that moving the fleet around was his prerogative as first lord of the Admiralty and did not necessarily signify a policy. As His Majesty's foreign secretary, Grey's every utterance was, in essence, a declaration of policy, which is why he was so careful with them. The cabinet was deeply divided, with a thin stratum of Francophile Liberal imperialists – Asquith, Grey, Churchill – running foreign policy even as the domestic officers were mostly 'Little Englanders' suspicious of all foreign entanglements – particularly those with France and Russia. At a cabinet meeting held earlier on Wednesday, Grey had not dared to speak strongly against Germany, knowing that he and Asquith 'faced a clear non-interventionist majority.'[45] Churchill himself believed – notwithstanding his own unauthorised manoeuvres – that had Grey issued a real ultimatum to Germany, the Liberal cabinet would have 'broken up.'[46] Conversely, a clear declaration of neutrality that left France in the lurch would have prompted the loud resignations of Liberal-imperial interventionists (starting with Churchill). For fear of a cabinet meltdown, it had therefore been Grey's policy not to have a policy – until he had finally summoned the courage to issue his belated warning to Lichnowsky (even then watering it down enough so as to not stir up cabinet opposition). Sir Edward Grey had, in effect, impaled Bethmann on the horns of the Briton's own policy dilemma.

Faced with diplomatic and now military encirclement by the burgeoning Triple Entente, Bethmann at last did what he should have done days (if not weeks) earlier: wire Berchtold in Vienna, demanding 'urgently and emphatically' that the Vienna cabinet accept four-power mediation with Serbia, without reservation or qualification. If Germany and Austria did not negotiate based on the 'honourable terms' Grey had originally offered, they would be 'faced with a conflagration in which England will go against us, Italy and Romania to all appearances will not go with us, and we should be two against four Great Powers.'* At 2:55 AM Thursday morning, Bethmann sent off this historic wire to Vienna.[47] Five minutes later, he sent Ambassador Tschirschky another, demanding that Austria resume direct talks with Russia, emphasising that the Germans were 'prepared to fulfil our duties as allies, but must decline

---

* It is not clear whether Bethmann meant Italy or Romania as the fourth 'Great Power' joining England, France, and Russia (and Serbia). But the basic point was clear enough: the Central Powers would be outnumbered and outgunned.

to let ourselves be dragged by Vienna, wantonly and without regard to our advice, into a world conflagration. In the Italian question, too, Vienna seems to disregard our advice. Pray speak to Count Berchtold at once with great emphasis and most seriously.'[48] In this way Bethmann, on the evening of 29–30 July 1914, at last rescinded the blank check he had foolishly offered Austria three weeks earlier.

It was too late. At midnight, Sazonov called in Ambassador Pourtalès for an urgent audience at Chorister's Bridge. It was an awkward moment for Russia's foreign minister. Just three hours earlier, he, Sukhomlinov, and Yanushkevitch had convinced the tsar to order general mobilisation – although the tsar had then, to their horror, changed his mind. Plainly, Sazonov could not inform Pourtalès about any of this. He would have to give the Germans something, though, to put them off their guard. Gamely, Sazonov offered all kinds of ideas about how the Germans might mediate in Vienna, while refusing to be drawn into a discussion of Russia's own military preparations. Pourtalès objected that it was 'difficult, if not impossible' for Germany to put pressure on her ally 'now that Russia has taken the fateful step towards mobilisation.' Sazonov changed the subject back to Serbia, only for Pourtalès to bring it back to the 'danger of a general European conflagration.' Realising that he was getting nowhere over Serbia, Sazonov confronted Pourtalès with the 'contradiction' between the telegrams received Wednesday from the chancellor and the kaiser, the former all but threatening war, the latter promising to mediate in Vienna. Pourtalès had his answer ready. Even if all the powers mobilised, he insisted, it was still the kaiser's prerogative to work for peace. All Bethmann's telegram had contained was a 'friendly warning' about Germany's alliance obligations: if Russia mobilised against Austria, Germany was treaty-bound to mobilise against Russia on behalf of her ally. Hearing this again, Sazonov lost his temper. Just before 1:30 AM Thursday morning, Russia's foreign minister told Pourtalès point-blank that '*reversing the [Russian] mobilisation order was no longer possible*,' and that 'Austrian mobilisation was to blame.'[49]

In a remarkable coincidence, over at Peterhof Palace, the tsar was confessing nearly the same thing at almost exactly the same time. The kaiser's 9:40 PM telegram, which Nicholas believed to have been dispatched in response to his urgent 8:30 PM plea for a clarification of German intentions, had so shaken him that he had called off general mobilisation. He was still shaken when he composed his reply at 1:20 AM. Hoping to reassure the kaiser about Russian intentions, Nicky now told Willy – having evidently forgotten his lines under the emotional strain of the night – that 'the military measures which have now come into force were decided five days ago.'[50] Even as Bethmann was deciding, in the wee hours of Wednesday night, to rein in the Austrians just as Russia had been demanding for days, even as the tsar's conscience had forced him to call off general mobilisation, Russia's foreign minister and her loose-lipped sovereign were fessing up to Russia's secret war preparations against Austria and Germany – and that these preparations had been underway since Saturday.

Bethmann could only hope that he would not be within earshot when the kaiser heard this.

20

Slaughter It Is

THURSDAY, 30 JULY

A S THE NEWS OF THE NIGHT trickled into Berlin and Potsdam, it began to dawn on the Germans that they had been had. Bethmann had exposed the secrets of German policy to the British ambassador in a kind of diplomatic burlesque act, shortly before learning from Lichnowsky that British neutrality was hollow after all. The Russian foreign minister's pretence of desiring direct negotiations with Vienna – or accepting Grey's four-power conference – was blown to pieces by Sazonov's own admission that Russia's mobilisation 'could no longer be reversed.' France had begun preparing for war only a few days behind Russia, while feigning interest in British mediation efforts. British naval preparations were accelerating, too. It is true that Bethmann himself had come around to favour genuine German mediation in Vienna only on Wednesday night, 29 July, after receiving the shattering news from London. But then he had gone out on a limb not only in his bid for English neutrality and his last-minute withdrawal of blanket support for Austria, but also by restraining the German army from ordering pre-mobilisation measures akin to those already underway in Russia and France, over the objections of Falkenhayn and Moltke – and this despite the fact that the German mobilisation

284

plan relied more heavily than any other on the speed of its execution. In diplomatic-strategic terms, the Germans had been caught with their pants down.

No one felt this more keenly than Kaiser Wilhelm II. Having just laid himself bare, as he saw it, by taking up the tsar's request that he mediate in Vienna, Willy awoke just past six Thursday morning, 30 July, to read Nicky's confession that 'the military measures which have now come into force were decided five days ago.' 'So that is almost a week ahead of us,' the kaiser scribbled furiously in the margin; 'the tsar has been secretly mobilising behind my back.'[1] Lending credence to this view, Wilhelm next read a telegram from Pourtalès, dispatched on Wednesday afternoon, reporting Russia's 'partial mobilisation' of the four military districts facing Austria on Tuesday, ostensibly undertaken in response to Austria's declaration of war on Serbia. The kaiser noted, on this second telegram, that Russia's mobilisation measures had,

> according to the Tsar's telegram of 29 July actually been ordered 5 days previously, that is, on the 24th, immediately after the delivery of the ultimatum to Serbia, therefore long before the Tsar telegraphed me asking for mediation. His first telegram expressly said he would probably be compelled to take measures which would lead to a European war . . . in reality the measures were already in full swing and he has simply been lying to me. . . . I regard my mediation as mistaken, since, without waiting for it to take effect, the Tsar has, without a hint to me, been mobilising behind my back.

What this meant to Willy was simple: 'That means I have got to mobilise as well!'[2]

Kaiser Wilhelm II has been judged harshly for his impulsive conduct at this and other key moments in July 1914. And yet on this occasion, his gut reaction was not far from the mark. Just as he wrote, the mobilisation measures against Austria *had* been ordered by Russia's Council of Ministers on 24 July, then signed into law by the tsar on Saturday, 25 July, with the corollary that they would only be made public after Austria attacked (or declared war on) Serbia. The tsar had then personally confirmed on the night of 29–30 July that all this had been 'decided five days earlier,' as, indeed, it had been. Also inaugurated 'five days earlier' (although the tsar had not mentioned this) was Russia's Period Preparatory to War, which, judging by the mushrooming reports from German consuls on the ground, was directed at both Germany and Austria. This may have been what the kaiser was hinting at when he scribbled – twice, once on both the 'Nicky' and the Pourtalès telegram – that the tsar was 'mobilising behind my back.' He may also have been working merely on a hunch.

Whatever the root of the kaiser's reasoning, it was sound. Just hours after he wrote this, Consul Brück's Wednesday telegram from Warsaw arrived, reporting that 'Russia is already fully in a state of preparation for war. . . . The troops ranged against Germany are assembling between Lomza and Kovno along the Niemen, while those ranged against Austria are assembling at Lublin and Kovel.' All this had transpired before Tsar Nicholas II had, under pressure from his own military chiefs, ordered general mobilisation on Wednesday night (before changing his mind based on an erroneous reading of a telegram from Potsdam). The kaiser's judgment of the nature of Russia's secret mobilisation accorded well with the facts – better than did the wishful thinking of his chancellor, who had trusted Sazonov's word.

As was so often the case in their difficult relationship, the chancellor and the kaiser were not on the same page on Thursday morning. After receiving Lichnowsky's telegram containing Grey's veiled threat from London, Bethmann had begun favouring a diplomatic solution overnight, even as his sovereign, receiving the tsar's inadvertently revelatory telegram, had resolved to jettison diplomacy and mobilise. As soon as the chancellor forwarded Lichnowsky's telegram to Wilhelm at midday, however – with the accompanying commentary about the need to force Austria to the negotiating table – the kaiser backed down. He and Bethmann composed a reply to the tsar's telegram that contained (at the chancellor's insistence) no suggestion that he was going to abandon his 'mediatory role,' much less mobilise against Russia. Instead, Willy sought to clear up the apparent contradiction that Nicky had asked him to clarify in his earlier telegram of Wednesday night. His chancellor, the kaiser explained, had simply told Pourtalès 'to draw the attention of your government to the danger and grave consequences involved by a mobilisation; I said the same in my telegram to you.' He then reminded the tsar that

Austria has only mobilised against Serbia and only a part of her army. If, as is now the case, according to the communication by you and your government, Russia mobilises against Austria, my role as mediator you kindly entrusted me with, and which I accepted at you[r] express prayer, will be endangered if not ruined. The whole weight of the decision lies solely on you[r] shoulders now, who have to bear the responsibility for Peace or War.[3]

The last loaded line, which stated flatly that Russia bore sole responsibility for 'Peace or War,' was likely Bethmann's idea. The chancellor, with a keen eye on British opinion, had been focused for days on putting the onus for starting the war on Russia. Even though Grey had dashed his hopes of British neutrality, Bethmann still needed to foster the appearance of Russian responsibility so that Germany's powerful Social Democrats would support the war if it came. He would not be doing his job as chancellor if he did not do this.

The line was not all politics, however. As the kaiser's latest telegram pointed out, Russia's own government had announced that she had mobilised against Austria. According to the terms of the Austro-German alliance, this in itself could be a *casus foederis* for war, as Moltke had pointed out in his memorandum to Bethmann: 'unless Germany means to break her word and allow her ally to succumb to Russia's superior strength, she must also mobilise.' On Wednesday night, the chancellor had overridden this argument with Moltke and Falkenhayn, clutching desperately to Sazonov's questionable assurance that Russian mobilisation 'did not mean war.' Both Sazonov and Tsar Nicholas II had then provided strong evidence that this claim was bogus when they inadvertently revealed that Russia had resolved to mobilise against Austria five days earlier and that this mobilisation, once underway, 'could not be reversed.' And yet even now that Russia's warlike intentions had been exposed by her own sovereign and foreign minister, even now that Grey had dashed Bethmann's hopes of British neutrality, the chancellor did not invoke the *casus foederis* for German mobilisation or even pre-mobilisation, as, by every possible right, he could have. Bethmann, facing the ruin of his policies, wanted to give Russia one last chance to back down. So, too, did the kaiser, who, entirely in character, following an outburst of belligerence had lost his nerve as soon as the dogs of war began seriously howling.

Moltke, losing time vis-à-vis Russia's mobilisation with every passing hour, was not so sanguine. True, he had yielded to Bethmann on Wednesday, whereas Falkenhayn had pressed strongly for the declaration of *Kriegsgefahrzustand*. As late as Thursday morning, Moltke even told Captain Fleischmann, the Austrian liaison officer at the German General Staff, that 'Russia's mobilisation is not yet a cause for mobilisation. Not until state of war exists between Austria and Russia. . . . Do not declare war on Russia, but await Russia's attack.'[4]

Around midday on Thursday, 30 July, however, Moltke made a dramatic shift towards belligerence – dramatic enough that, at one PM, he barged into a meeting with the chancellor at the Wilhelmstrasse uninvited.[5] While Moltke himself never explained exactly what it was that changed his mind, it was almost certainly his receipt of the same two telegrams – from Pourtalès and the tsar – that had set off Kaiser Wilhelm II. Even more than his sovereign, Moltke was floored to learn that Russia had begun preparing for war five (now six) days earlier. That fact helped to explain why German army intelligence that day had concluded that Russia's Period Preparatory to War was 'far advanced.' Compounding his sense of panic on Thursday, Moltke learned from Vienna that Conrad 'intended to adhere rigidly to Plan B' – that is, mobilise solely against Serbia and not against Russia. With Russia having just admitted to having long since begun her mobilisation against Austria – and, to all appearances, mobilising secretly against Germany as well – Moltke was confronted with the prospect that the Russians could concentrate all their forces against Germany and overwhelm the German 8th Army, which, according to the latest German war plan, would alone defend East Prussia.[6]

We do not know exactly what was said at the one PM meeting at the Wilhelmstrasse, but it is clear that Moltke, in his new state of mind, asked the chancellor to proclaim *Kriegsgefahrzustand* immediately. Bethmann, still clinging to his 'Halt in Belgrade' initiative, refused. The Austrian military attaché, Lieutenant-Colonel Bienerth, whom Moltke summoned immediately following his meeting with Bethmann, found the chief of staff 'extremely agitated, as I had never before seen him.' As Bienerth reported to Conrad, 'Moltke said that he regards the situation as critical if the Austro-Hungarian monarchy does not mobilise immediately against Russia [that is, abandon Plan B and activate Plan R]. *Russia's announced declaration concerning mobilisation she has ordered* makes necessary countermeasures by Austria-Hungary and must also be cited in the public explanation. . . . Standing firm in a European war is the last chance of saving Austria-Hungary. Germany will go with her unconditionally.'[7]

Moltke's clearly insubordinate message to Conrad has sometimes been seen as the moment when the 'politicians' lost control of events and the 'military men' took over. His intervention certainly undermined Bethmann's last-ditch efforts to get Berchtold to accept diplomatic mediation. As Berchtold himself asked, upon learning of Moltke's instructions from Conrad, 'Who rules in Berlin, Moltke or Bethmann?'[8]

The fact remains, however, that Moltke did not get his way on Thursday. He failed to achieve either of his two principal goals: (1) getting Germany's chancellor to proclaim *Kriegsgefahrzustand*, so as to belatedly catch up to everyone else's war preparations; or (2) convincing Conrad to abandon Plan B and concentrate Austria's forces against Russia. Moltke had gummed up the works of his chancellor's diplomacy, but then Bethmann had done the same to Moltke's efforts to influence the military odds in Germany's favour. The real failure on Wednesday was the kaiser's. As sovereign, he should have butted heads together and forged a common imperial policy between his army chief of staff and his chancellor. The deeply worrying overnight news from Russia had jolted him awake briefly, before he retreated into his usual nerve-wracked passivity.

IN THEIR OWN WAY, France's civilian leaders were just as flummoxed as Germany's by Russia's early mobilisation.

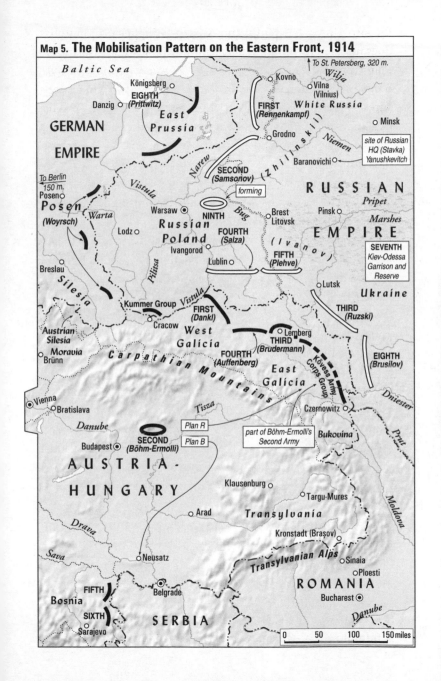

Map 5. The Mobilisation Pattern on the Eastern Front, 1914

Wednesday night, Ambassador Paléologue had been informed straightaway of the tsar's decision for general mobilisation. Nikolai Bazili, director of the Chancellery (or political department) of the Ministry of Foreign Affairs, had run back and forth between Chorister's Bridge and the French embassy to impart the critical information personally. The reason he returned to Chorister's Bridge from the embassy accompanied by Paléologue's secretary, Charles de Cambrun, was significant: in order to foil German surveillance, it had been agreed that telegrams to Paris announcing general mobilisation would be sent with Russian ciphers (which were tougher to crack than the French ones). As Bazili explained his task to Yuri Danilov, architect of Russia's mobilisation Plan 19 against the Central Powers: 'M. Paléologue had of necessity to communicate this news to Paris immediately, not being able to wait until the following morning, when the [general mobilisation] order was to be published; but at the same time we had to keep the news hidden from our enemies.'[9] The original message that Bazili encoded for Paris had contained the phrase 'and secretly to commence general mobilisation' (that is, to commence it on Thursday, 30 July, as originally resolved), only for the French embassy secretary to delete it after learning that the tsar had changed his mind. Instead, the Russian-encrypted telegram, wired to Paris at one AM, spoke only of the partial mobilisation of 'thirteen corps destined to operate against Austria.'[10]

Paléologue has come in for a good deal of criticism for his role in urging on Russia's secret war preparations without authorisation from Viviani and Poincaré, as in his vow given on Tuesday, when they were still at sea, of 'the complete readiness of France to fulfil her obligations as an ally.'[11] Likewise, he has been faulted for deliberately misleading them about the critical events of Wednesday, 29 July. Certainly, in order to fulfil his primary duty as intermediary for the Franco-Russian military alliance, the ambassador should have informed Paris that the tsar had decided on general mobilisation, even if he later changed his mind.

It would be going too far, however, to claim that Paléologue was acting as a free agent. He and General Laguiche had kept Army Chief of Staff Joffre and War Minister Messimy fully informed about Russia's Period Preparatory to War since the weekend, and there is no reason to doubt that they, in turn, had fully briefed Poincaré – who took a greater interest in military matters than Viviani – upon the president's arrival in Paris on Wednesday. As for his tacit endorsement of Russia's move from partial to general mobilisation, Paléologue was acting on the express instructions of France's General Staff (if not also its civilian government) to discourage any Russian tendency to mobilise against Austria alone, as he confessed in a post-war interview.[12] In his communications with the Quai d'Orsay about Russian mobilisation measures, the ambassador was indeed being cagey – but with good reason. Whenever it would come, the announcement of general mobilisation was so explosive that Paléologue had been ordered by the Russians not to use his own cipher, ostensibly in order to keep German cryptographers in the dark. But then Paléologue, like Sazonov, was keeping a watchful eye on British opinion as well – and on Viviani, whom he knew to be far less fervently committed to the Franco-Russian cause than Poincaré. The longer he could delay news of Russian mobilisation from reaching policymakers in London – and his own wavering premier – the more difficult it would be for them to stop it.

Sazonov was just as careful in informing Paris about Russia's mobilisation. In his own message to Ambassador Izvolsky (copied also to Ambassador Benckendorff in London, which required still more deftness of tone), Russia's foreign minister hinted only obliquely at the drama that had transpired on Wednesday evening in Petersburg. 'The German ambassador,' Sazonov wrote, 'informed me today of the decision of his government to mobilise its forces if Russia did not cease her military preparations. As we are unable to accede to Germany's desire, it only *remains for us to hasten our armaments and regard war as imminent.'*[13]

Izvolsky recognised the significance of this cryptic, but suggestive, message as soon as he received it at just past two AM on Thursday, 30 July. At once he sent his secretary to the Quai d'Orsay for urgent consultations, while ordering Count Ignatiev, Russia's military attaché, to deliver Sazonov's message to the French War Ministry on Rue Saint-Domingue, with urgent instructions that the war minister be awakened with the news. For good measure, Ignatiev went over to Messimy's house, in full dress uniform, to demand how France would respond to Russian partial mobilisation. Izvolsky then personally delivered Sazonov's telegram to Premier Viviani, waking him up in the process. Messimy, in turn, phoned Viviani, finding him awake but not in a good mood. 'Good God!' the premier exclaimed. 'These Russians are even worse insomniacs than they are drinkers.' Viviani then roused Poincaré. The president, recognising the gravity of the moment, dressed quickly and summoned Viviani and Messimy to the Elysée Palace at four AM.[14]

The meeting lasted clear through the night. We do not know what was said, but it is not hard to guess at the subject. Back on Sunday, Jules Cambon, France's ambassador in Berlin, had reported that 'any mobilisation orders issued in Russia will certainly be followed by mobilisation orders in Germany.'[15] Sazonov had just confirmed the veracity of Cambon's report by informing the French government that Ambassador Pourtalès had warned him that if Russia mobilised, Germany would have to as well. Sazonov had then hinted that this was exactly what Russia was about to do ('it only remains for us to hasten our armaments'). Whether or not Viviani and Poincaré had signed off on Russian mobilisation measures taken since the weekend, they needed to weigh in now. In a wire sent off to Paléologue in St Petersburg at seven Thursday morning, 30 July, Viviani recounted what he had learned from Sazonov's telegram – and from Izvolsky – about the 'inevitability of war' (*l'imminence de guerre*) and the need to 'hasten [Russia's] armaments,' commenting that Russia was evidently 'counting on the support of her ally, France, and she considered it desirable that England would join Russia and France without further delay.' Viviani instructed Paléologue to tell Sazonov that, while 'France was resolved to fulfil all obligations of her alliance, in the interest of general peace and in view of the conversation pending between the less interested powers, I believe that it would be opportune that, *as regards the precautionary and defence measures which Russia believes it necessary to adopt*, she should not immediately take any step which might offer to Germany a pretext for a total or partial mobilisation of her forces.'[16]

There are several contradictory notes in this ambiguous message. The phrase 'in the interest of general peace' was clearly Viviani's (he also inserted a reminder that he had written Paléologue in this vein back on Monday, 27 July, from aboard the *France*). There is no reason to doubt Viviani's sincerity in desiring to avert a European war, no matter how ineffectual his policies had been so far in furthering this aim. Just as clearly, we can detect the hands of Poincaré and Messimy in the telegram's tacit approval of the 'precautionary and defence measures' Russia was taking, conditioned only by a gentle hint that she should avoid giving the Germans a too obvious casus belli. In a diary entry that day, Poincaré explained his thinking: the idea in 'warning' the Russians was not to prevent war from breaking out but to avoid 'offering Germany a pretext,' 'because of the ambiguous attitude of England' (*à cause de l'attitude ambiguë de* l'*Angleterre*).[17] Poincaré's tacit approval of Russia's impending general mobilisation is further confirmed in a telegram Izvolsky sent to Sazonov Thursday morning, reporting that he had been assured privately that 'the French government had no desire to interfere in our military preparations.'[18] Just as Bethmann, in Berlin, was busy trying (and largely failing) to put the diplomatic onus on Russia, so Poincaré wanted the Russians not to blow their cover in England by tipping their hand too early.

Considering how far Russia's mobilisation had gone by Thursday, this was easier said than done. Still, though it had infuriated War Minister Sukhomlinov and Chief of Staff Yanushkevitch, the tsar's decision to reverse the general mobilisation order had opened a diplomatic lifeline of sorts. By intervening to cancel his own general mobilisation order of Wednesday night, Tsar Nicholas II had given not only the Germans but also his own French allies a brief stay of execution. So long as Russia refrained from raising the red placards of general mobilisation, there remained a faint glimmer of hope that everyone would back down from the brink.

R USSIA'S SOVEREIGN, however, still had to reckon with his own advisers. It was not only the military men who had been taken aback by his rescinding of the general mobilisation order. By Thursday morning, it was clear that most of his cabinet was against him as well. Krivoshein, the bellicose agriculture minister, was livid. So, too, was M. V. Rodzianko, the president of the Duma. In light of the common view of Nicholas II both in Russia and abroad as a lightweight,* it is interesting to note that,

---

* It is true that the tsar's diary entries on these momentous days were marked by triviality. Thus, on Wednesday, 29 July: 'played tennis; the weather was magnificent.' On Thursday, 30 July: 'The weather was hot. . . . Had a delightful bathe in the sea.' Still, these entries tell us little about the tsar's state of mind when he was making the key decisions.

on this critical day, he stood rather like the formidable Tisza had against the war party in Vienna – alone against all others.[19]

Sazonov was at the centre of the storm. It was he who had first pushed Russia into the Period Preparatory to War over the weekend and who had convinced Nicholas II to order general mobilisation on Wednesday night (before the tsar changed his mind). On both occasions, he had acted decisively, belying his reputation for hesitation and cowardice. And yet because Sazonov had long been viewed as a cautious moderate in the cabinet, Nicholas II trusted his counsel now, more than that of any other adviser. The tsar categorically refused to see Krivoshein. Next to try their luck were Sukhomlinov and Yanushkevitch, who phoned the palace around eleven AM and tried to persuade their sovereign that 'it was indispensable to proceed to a general mobilisation,' so as to 'prepare for a serious war without loss of time.' After hearing his chief of staff make the same case as the war minister – the same case, indeed, that both men had made the previous night – the tsar curtly declared that 'the conversation was at an end.' Yanushkevitch, thinking quickly, said that Sazonov was in the room, too: Would the tsar hear out his foreign minister, at least? After a 'lengthy silence,' he agreed. Realising that mobilisation talk was a non-starter, Sazonov asked for an audience so that he could 'present a report concerning the political situation which admitted of no delay.' After another pause, the tsar agreed to see him at three PM.[20]

Sazonov had just over three hours before his date with destiny. He did not waste his time. First, he huddled with Yanushkevitch to discuss his strategy for persuading the tsar to mobilise. The chief of staff had been thinking about this all night, but the tsar had cut him off on the phone before he could make his full argument. He urged that Sazonov impress on Russia's sovereign the 'extreme danger that would result for us if we were not ready for war with Germany.' General mobilisation, he explained, 'would be very seriously dislocated by the partial mobilisation already ordered; this dislocation could only be avoided by an immediate general mobilisation.' Every hour, every minute counted. If the tsar continued objecting to technical arguments, Yanushkevitch said, Sazonov should switch to a political tack and warn his sovereign that if he continued hesitating, Germany's cunning kaiser would then 'coax out of the French a promise of neutrality,' leaving Russia alone to face the German military machine. Assuming that this barrage of arguments would be enough, Yanushkevitch asked that Sazonov phone him from the palace once the tsar had decided. As soon as the order was received, Yanushkevitch vowed, 'I shall go away, smash my telephone, and generally adopt measures which will prevent anyone from finding me for the purpose of giving contrary orders.' To Yanushkevitch's relief, Sazonov 'agreed completely.' The chief of staff then phoned Dobrorolskii, the army's mobilisation chief, and ordered him to 'be ready to come to me with all the documents immediately upon my telephone call in the afternoon.'[21]

After dismissing Yanushkevitch, Sazonov called in German ambassador Pourtalès, who had been demanding an audience after their dramatic encounter of the night before. According to the foreign minister, the ambassador 'appealed to Sazonov to hold out a last straw and to make some suggestion which Pourtalès could telegraph to his Government.'[22] Sazonov then quickly composed the following 'formula,' in French: 'If Austria, recognising that the Austro-Serbian question has assumed the character of a question of European interest, declares herself ready to eliminate from her ultimatum points which violate the sovereign rights of Serbia, Russia engages to stop her military preparations.'

Although, as Pourtalès noted optimistically in his report to Berlin, Sazonov had not – as before – demanded that Austria suspend her own military preparations, on the central ultimatum issue he had not budged an inch.[23] Far more important than what Sazonov did or did not include in his hastily scribbled 'formula,' however, was the fact that it was Germany's ambassador, and not Russia's foreign minister, who was begging to keep diplomatic channels alive.

At noon, Sazonov called in Buchanan and Paléologue. Acquainting the British and French ambassadors with the gist of his exchange with Pourtalès, Sazonov claimed, erroneously, that this audience had taken place at two AM (the encounter that had ended with Sazonov vowing that Russia's mobilisation 'could not be reversed') rather than minutes earlier.* The reason Russia's foreign minister lied becomes clear when we read Buchanan's account of the proceedings: it was in the 'two AM audience,' Sazonov claimed, that Pourtalès, 'seeing war as inevitable, broke down completely' and asked the Russian to compose his peace formula as a 'last straw.' To buttress his claim that it was the Germans who were committed to war, Sazonov told Buchanan and Paléologue that Russia had 'absolute proof of military and naval preparations being made by Germany against Russia more especially in the direction of the Gulf of Finland' (whether or not he had any such proof – unlikely, as no such preparations had begun – he did not show evidence of them).** Because it was Germany's ambassador who supposedly saw war as inevitable, and the Germans were up to, well, something or other 'in the direction of the Gulf of Finland,' it was therefore clear, Sazonov told Buchanan and Paléologue, that 'Russia can hardly postpone converting partial into general

---

* Aside from the part about him 'breaking down completely,' and when it took place, Pourtalès's account of the meeting agrees with Sazonov's. That the meeting took place between eleven AM and noon is confirmed by the numbering of Pourtalès's telegrams to Berlin.

** Sazonov may have been referring to the return of Germany's Baltic fleet from Norway to Kiel, ordered by the kaiser on Monday. But this was hardly 'in the direction of the Gulf of Finland' – a body of water nearly a thousand miles distant from Kiel.

mobilisation now that she knows that Germany is preparing and excitement in [Russia] has reached such a pitch that she cannot hold back if Austria refuses to make concession.'[24]

In this way, Sazonov ingeniously covered his diplomatic flank, offering up a last-minute initiative with Germany (however cynically contrived and inaccurately reported) as evidence of Russia's peaceful intentions, along with evidence of the enemy's warlike intentions (however specious) to justify the general mobilisation order he was about to demand of Tsar Nicholas II. If Buchanan had any suspicions about what Sazonov was up to, he failed to express them – or report them to London. Nor did Paléologue object to Sazonov's suggestion that Russian general mobilisation was about to begin, but then, as he had been in the loop on Russia's war preparations all along, there was no reason to expect that he would have.

Buoyed by the implied endorsement from the French and British ambassadors, Sazonov lunched with Krivoshein and Schilling. If Russia's foreign minister was beset with any remaining doubts, the ever-war-ready Krivoshein did his best to scotch them. The atmosphere, Schilling wrote in his diary, 'was tense and the conversation was almost exclusively concerned with the necessity for insisting upon a general mobilisation at the earliest possible moment, in view of the inevitability of war with Germany, which every moment became clearer.'[25] After returning to Chorister's Bridge, Sazonov found Sukhomlinov waiting to fire him up, along with Duma president Rodzianko, who handed him a memorandum for the tsar. 'As head of the representatives of the Russian people,' the message stated simply, Rodzianko, speaking on their behalf, 'would never forgive a delay which might precipitate the country into fatal confusion.'[26]

Fortified by this unanimous Greek chorus of Russia's civilian and military leaders, Sazonov headed over to the Peterhof, arriving, as requested, at three PM. Nicholas II, endeavoring not to be cornered, had insisted that the meeting include General

Tatistchev, who, incongruously, was to be handed orders for an urgent posting as the tsar's personal liaison to Kaiser Wilhelm II (as Nicky had informed Willy in his ill-thought-through 1:20 AM telegram, the one in which he had confessed that Russia's mobilisation measures had been 'decided five days ago'). Russia's foreign minister would have to make his case for war in the presence of the man being posted to Potsdam to work for peace.

Fortunately for Sazonov, General Tatistchev was so overwhelmed by the gravity of the moment that he remained silent as the foreign minister spoke. Having evidently forgotten Yanushkevitch's instructions – or realising that they would not work on the tsar – Sazonov skipped all the technical bits about partial versus general mobilisation and focused instead on German intentions. 'It was clear to everybody,' he declared, according to Schilling's diary, 'that Germany had decided to bring about a collision, as otherwise she would not have rejected all the pacificatory proposals that had been made and could easily have brought her ally to reason.' It was better, Sazonov continued, 'to put away any fears that our warlike preparations would bring about a war, and to continue these preparations carefully rather than by reason of such fears to be taken unawares by war.' Assuming that war was now unavoidable, the foreign minister summed up his case in language similar to that of his telegram to Izvolsky the previous night: 'it only remained to do everything that was necessary to meet war fully armed and under the most favourable conditions for ourselves.'[27]

By the conclusion of Sazonov's remarks, the tsar was 'deadly pale.' As sovereign, he felt a heavy weight on his shoulders. Finally he replied, 'in a choking voice': 'Just think of the responsibility you are advising me to assume! Remember it is a question of sending thousands of men to their deaths.'[28] Another long silence followed. As the fate of Europe hung in the balance, suddenly and without warning, General Tatistchev spoke up. Despite the ostensible importance of his brief, he had been ignored, and he may have taken offence. Or he might simply have wanted to help alleviate the agony of his emperor. 'Yes,' Tatistchev intoned gravely, 'it is hard to decide.' Russia's sovereign replied 'in a rough and displeased tone, "I will decide,"' making clear that he would brook no further intervention. At last, shortly before four PM on Thursday, July 30, Tsar Nicholas II agreed to order general mobilisation. Sazonov, on cue, rushed down to the palace telephone, called Yanushkevitch, and uttered the magic words: 'Now you can smash your telephone!'[29]

After Yanushkevitch had the ministers sign the tsar's new mobilisation order, Dobrorolskii headed over to the General Telegraph Office. 'Every operator,' he recalled,

> was sitting by his instrument waiting for the copy of the telegram, in order to send to all the ends of the Russian Empire the momentous news of the calling up of the Russian people. A few minutes after six, while absolute stillness reigned in the room, all the instruments began at once to click. That was the beginning moment of the great epoch.[30]

This time, unlike the previous evening, no contrary instructions were delivered. The tsar had made up his mind. There was no going back.

THE COUNTDOWN FOR European war had now begun. According to joint agreements between the French and Russian general staffs, the Franco-Russian offensives against Germany would begin by M + 15 (August 14). Unless she wanted to leave her ally in the lurch, France would now have to mobilise as well. Germany, faced with hostile forces mobilising on both her eastern and western borders, would respond by mobilising, as she had indeed publicly pledged to do. To win time against the Germans, and with an eye on Britain, Sazonov insisted to Yanushkevitch that Russia should 'proceed to the general mobilisation as far as possible secretly and without making any public announcement concerning it.'[31] Officially, Russia's general mobilisation would begin at midnight, at which time, the tsar's directive stipulated, the army and navy would be 'placed on a war footing' – but there was no reason to let the Central Powers in on the secret before then (or even afterwards).[32] As for Russia's French ally, Sazonov wired to Izvolsky another cryptic telegram announcing merely that, 'as long as we do not receive a fully satisfactory reply from Austria via the German government as intermediary, we shall continue our military preparations.'[33] Sazonov did inform Paléologue what had been decided at the Peterhof, but with a careful twist. Owing to 'disquieting information concerning preparations of the German Army and Navy,' Paléologue wired misleadingly to Paris at nine fifteen pm on 30 July, 'in consequence the Russian government has decided to proceed secretly to the first measures of general mobilisation.'*[34]

To Ambassador Benckendorff, in London, Sazonov sent an even more cryptic wire, the meaning of which can only be deciphered if we understand that Russia had resolved to go to war:

> It is a matter of the highest degree of importance that Turkey not receive the two Dreadnoughts 'Rio de Janeiro' [aka the *Sultan Osman I*] and 'Reshadieh' [*Reshad V*] being built for her in England. The construction of these ships is so far advanced, that the first of them

---

* This critical passage in Paléologue was purged from the original *Yellow Book* published by the French government after the war, in order to rebut German accusations that Paris had prior knowledge of Russia's 'secret' decision for general mobilisation.

could be sent off to Turkey within weeks. . . . Please make the English government aware of the overriding importance of this question for us, and impress upon them energetically that these ships must be retained in England.[35]

Having decided on war, Sazonov needed to make certain that Russia would be able to seize Constantinople and the Straits – an impossibility if Turkey were to float these dreadnoughts.

Meanwhile Russia's still-secret general mobilisation cranked into motion. At seven PM, the first confirmation telegrams from Russia's military districts were wired back to Dobrorolskii. Commanders in the Warsaw District (Russian Poland), facing both Austria and Germany, received the general mobilisation orders at eight PM and acted on them at once.[36]

At almost the same hour, France's government took a decisive step towards war. A report from French military intelligence on Thursday morning had convinced Army Chief of Staff Joffre that the Germans were moving 'covering forces' to the frontier and that he must respond. The report was not true, but Joffre believed it. In the afternoon, a German newspaper, *Berliner Lokal-Anzeiger*, reported – erroneously – that Germany had already mobilised. Although Jules Cambon, France's ambassador in Berlin, quickly relayed to Paris Foreign Minister Jagow's denial of the report, the story heightened tensions in the French capital still further. After resisting Joffre's demands all day, just before five PM (seven thirty PM Russian time), Viviani and Poincaré agreed to allow France to inaugurate *couverture*, or the covering of the border – with one important condition: France's covering troops, Viviani insisted, were to be instructed to hold back ten kilometres (about six miles) from the frontier, so as to avoid border incidents.

France's vaunted 'ten-kilometre withdrawal' was largely phony. According to a telegram that Viviani dispatched on

Thursday night to his ambassador in London, Cambon was to tell Sir Edward Grey that the Germans had already sent covering troops 'within several hundred metres' of the border, whereas France would hold her own 'covering troops' back and 'thus leave a strip of our national territory undefended against sudden aggression.' Curiously, there was no mention of 'ten kilometres' in this misleading communication, nor in the orders transmitted to the French army at 4:55 PM, which stipulated only that 'no troops or patrols under any pretext are to approach the frontier or go beyond [a] line' designated by 50 frontier villages.[37] It was an entirely conventional pre-mobilisation manoeuvre, involving five army corps ordered to 'cover' the German border (not to withdraw from it). Viviani revealed the real purpose of the 'ten kilometres' in the last line of his telegram to Cambon: 'In so doing we have *no other reason* than to prove to British public opinion and the British Government that France, like Russia, will not fire the first shot.'[38]

The timing of all this was uncanny. Even as the French army was receiving orders to cover the German frontier, Russia was ordering general mobilisation against Germany and Austria-Hungary. And yet, if the British were to believe Viviani's protestations, it was the Germans who were mobilising first! Franco-Russian deceptions ensured that German diplomats faced an uphill struggle to enlighten London as to what was really happening on Germany's eastern and western frontiers.

Sazonov's dissembling, along with Viviani's ruse about the ten-kilometre withdrawal, won precious time for France and Russia in the mobilisation race against Germany. As long as the news of Russia's general mobilisation remained secret, Moltke's hands would remain tied in Berlin, as the army chief of staff would have no justification for ordering *Kriegsgefahrzustand*, much less German general mobilisation. A secret this big, however, could not remain secret for long.

21

Last Chance Saloon

FRIDAY, 31 JULY

MOLTKE ROSE AT DAWN Friday morning in an uneasy state of mind. At around eleven PM Thursday night, he had picked up alarming reports of Russian war preparations near the Prussian frontier, but he had no confirmation of general mobilisation. Bethmann, still waiting for a firm answer from Berchtold about accepting mediation on the basis of a 'Halt in Belgrade,' had been alarmed enough when Moltke shared this intelligence to suspend his latest urgent instructions to his ambassador in Vienna.[*1] The chancellor had also agreed to give Moltke an answer on the proclamation of *Kriegsgefahrzustand* by noon Friday. Before taking the final plunge, however, Bethmann wanted proof that Russia had taken the fateful step towards war.

---

* Confusingly, at 9 PM Thursday, Bethmann recommended 'most urgently that Austria should accept Grey's proposal,' and then wired again at 11:20 PM for Tschirschky to disregard this message on account of news of Russian military preparations; then, upon receiving a peace-minded telegram from King George V around midnight, Bethmann changed his instructions again. Coupled with Moltke's insubordinate message to Conrad on Thursday afternoon, the effect was to convince Berchtold that Bethmann was irresolute; thus there was no need for Austria to back down.

At seven AM, Moltke rang General Hell, commander of the German XX Army Corps at Allenstein, to get the latest intelligence on the border. 'Have you the impression that Russia is mobilising?' he asked. Hell replied swiftly: 'Yes, *I have thought so for several days.*' Moltke asked for evidence. 'The frontier is hermetically sealed,' Hell offered, and 'nobody crosses in either direction. Since yesterday they have been burning the frontier guard-houses, and red mobilisation notices are said to be posted up in Mlava.' This was the news Moltke was waiting for, except that he wanted not a *rumour* that the placards were up, but an actual placard for proof. 'Why have you not got hold of one of the notices?' he asked. The answer was simple: the frontier was sealed. Moltke therefore ordered General Hell: 'You must get me one of those red notices; I must make certain whether they are mobilising against us. *Till then I cannot obtain the promulgation of a mobilisation order.*'[2]

There are several observations to be made here. First, Moltke, reading the intelligence on Russia's mobilisation, had made up his mind that war was imminent. This was already evident in his wire to Conrad on Thursday afternoon, in which he demanded that Austria shift to mobilisation Plan R against Russia. His goal in demanding proof of Russian mobilisation was plainly to gain a pretext to mobilise – as soon as possible.

Second, despite his act of diplomatic insubordination in communicating directly with Conrad in Vienna, Moltke was still bowing to civilian authority in Berlin. He needed a red placard as indisputable proof so that Bethmann – and the kaiser – would allow him to proclaim *Kriegsgefahrzustand*, something he could not authorise on his own. Even at seven Friday morning – nearly sixteen hours after the tsar had finally bowed to the Russian war party in Petersburg, and twelve hours after the French had covered the German border – the German government had not inaugurated even pre-mobilisation of her armed forces. Mere rumours of what Russia had done, picked up on Thursday night, were not sufficient, nor was a firsthand report by phone from a ranking general in Allenstein. German standards of proof were higher than that.

Third, Sazonov's instinct – to keep Russia's general mobilisation secret – was diplomatically and strategically sound. The Germans were tying themselves in knots trying to figure out what was going on, wasting valuable time in the process. Meanwhile, any protests the Germans might mount in London would fall flat, as long as British diplomats did not themselves know about the momentous events of the past night.

The latter was made painfully clear in Bethmann's first audience on Friday morning, with Britain's Ambassador Sir Edward Goschen. Goschen arrived at the Wilhelmstrasse unprompted just before ten, although, as the chancellor told him, he had been about to summon him anyway. Goschen's own intention was to pass on Grey's emphatic refusal of Bethmann's embarrassing 'neutrality' bid from two nights ago, but Bethmann, with more pressing matters on his mind, paid this little mind. He told Goschen that he had just received 'news from the Russian frontier which, if confirmed, would create a very grave and dangerous situation and might oblige Germany to make a serious communication to the Russian Government.' The news was this: the Russians 'had destroyed their customs houses on the German frontier, and had carried off their money chests into the interior.' Goschen, unimpressed, retorted that 'these proceedings, if true, seemed to me to be not so much a menace to Germany, as measures of precaution . . . to meet all emergencies.' Bethmann countered, 'on the contrary that, taken with other reports which had reached him both from Russia and Sweden, the above news threatened general mobilisation.'[3] The chancellor then issued a pointed warning, which Goschen passed on to London: 'If the news he had received proved true, and [Russian] military measures were also being taken against Germany . . . he could not leave his country defenceless while other powers were gaining time. He was now going to see the Emperor and he wished me to tell you that it was quite possible that in a very short time, perhaps even today, they would have to take some very serious step.'[4]

Of course, as we know today, Bethmann was correct in his suspicion, and Britain's ambassador – owing to a week of misleading reports from the gullible Buchanan in Petersburg – was wrong. But, lacking the magic red placards as proof, Bethmann had no way of convincing Goschen or Grey.

After Goschen left, Bethmann huddled in conference with Moltke and Falkenhayn. Before Moltke's own sources could confirm the news from Russia, at 11:40 AM a telegram from Pourtalès was decoded, announcing: 'General mobilisation army and navy ordered. First day of mobilisation 31 July.'[5] Here, at last, was proof. Bethmann agreed that *Kriegsgefahrzustand* be proclaimed, provided that the sovereign approved. The chancellor got Wilhelm on the phone at once and read out Pourtalès's telegram. The kaiser then motored from Potsdam to Berlin and signed the order inaugurating *Kriegsgefahrzustand* or 'Imminent Danger of War,' operative at 3 PM. This put German railways under full military control; inaugurated martial law and military censorship; cancelled all leaves, returning troops to their garrisons; strengthened frontier defences; and suspended postal traffic across the border.[6] *Kriegsgefahrzustand* was equivalent in every way to Russia's Period Preparatory to War except in its Germanic efficiency. Although the Russians had a six-day head start in pre-mobilisation, the tighter timetable of *Kriegsgefahrzustand* meant that they would likely have only a two- or three-day advantage in general mobilisation. Barring a miracle, German general mobilisation – and war – would now follow in two days' time.

Bethmann, Falkenhayn, and Moltke understood this, although it is by no means clear that their sovereign did. Kaiser Wilhelm II, prone to mood swings in the best of times, was swerving wildly back and forth between abject war lust and plaintive desperation for peace. Just past seven PM Thursday evening, upon reading (after nearly 24 hours' delay) the Pourtalès telegram in which Sazonov had declared that Russia's mobilisation 'could no longer be reversed,' the kaiser had unleashed one of his most furious tirades ever. 'England, France, and Russia,' he wrote in the margins, 'are in league to wage a war of annihilation against us, taking the Austro-Serbian conflict as a pretext.' Concluding (again) that all hope for peace was lost, he wrote, 'Now this whole trickery must be ruthlessly exposed and the mask of Christian peaceableness roughly and publicly torn off the face [of England]! . . . And our consuls in Turkey and India, agents, etc., must fire the whole Mahometan world to fierce revolt against this hateful, lying, unprincipled nation of shopkeepers; for if we are to bleed to death, England shall at least lose India.'[7]

Extreme rhetoric (and visions of Islamic holy war) aside, the kaiser's basic intuition, once more, was correct. Just as his angry marginalia of Thursday morning had accurately divined the chronology of Russia's war preparations, so now, on Thursday evening, did he grasp the essence of the dire strategic situation better in his fevered state of mind than later, when he had calmed down. At the very time he was scribbling these bloodthirsty marginalia – seven PM on Thursday, 30 July – Russia's general mobilisation against Germany and Austria-Hungary was cranking secretly into motion, although neither the kaiser nor his advisers would learn this until the next morning. At the same hour, meanwhile, France had ordered her troops to cover the German border. Unhinged as the kaiser's anti-English outburst was, Britain's pose of neutrality ('trickery . . . mask of Christian peaceableness') was indeed hollow, as borne out by her biased negotiating posture, ignorance of Russian war preparations, and Grey's recent threat (as against Grey's frequent, and disingenuous, vows of neutrality). It was when his inner demons took over that Kaiser Wilhelm II saw things most clearly.

On Friday morning, by contrast, Germany's sovereign fell prey again to happy illusions. Shortly before learning of Russia's general mobilisation around noon, he penned one more telegram to the Peterhof, warning the tsar that he had received 'authentic news of serious preparations for war on my eastern frontier.' Again putting his faith in Nicky's goodwill, Willy concluded with a plea that 'the peace of Europe may still be maintained by you, if Russia will agree to stop the military measures which must threaten Germany and Austro-Hungary.'[8] Even after learning of Russian general mobilisation, the kaiser wrote to George V at Buckingham Palace (burying his white-hot anger against Albion of the night before), thanking the king for his 'kind telegram' of the night before and promising that he was still 'working at' mediation in Vienna. His efforts were made difficult, however, by the fact that 'this night Nicky has ordered the mobilisation of his whole army and fleet.' With remarkable – and misleading – understatement, the kaiser then informed England's sovereign that he was 'off to Berlin to take measures for ensuring safety of my eastern frontiers, where strong Russian troops are already posted.'[9]

Of course, these 'measures' went much further than 'ensuring the safety' of Germany's eastern frontier. Germany's pre-mobilisation, if not interrupted, would lead inexorably to general mobilisation, targeting also her *western* frontier – facing France and Belgium. The kaiser did not fully understand this, but his chancellor did. As Bethmann had told Tirpitz and Falkenhayn on Thursday, 'proclamation of imminent danger of war meant mobilisation and this in our circumstances – mobilisation on both fronts – meant war.'[10] It was precisely because he viewed *Kriegsgefahrzustand* as tantamount to war that the chancellor had delayed ordering it for so long.

Now that the decision had been made, Bethmann wasted no time relaying it to his ambassadors. Unlike Sazonov, who had continued dissembling with even Izvolsky, Russia's most senior diplomat, after the tsar had proclaimed general mobilisation, Bethmann simply told the truth. By three thirty PM on Friday, he had informed his ambassadors in Vienna, Petersburg, Paris, Rome, and London about the proclamation of *Kriegsgefahrzustand*, and that Germany had been forced to take this measure in response to Russian general mobilisation. Bethmann further informed his ambassadors that he was sending Russia a twelve-hour ultimatum to rescind her general mobilisation and demobilise (beginning at midnight and expiring at noon on Saturday, 1 August), failing which Germany would be forced to mobilise herself. All this, the chancellor instructed his diplomats, was to be made public. Schoen, in Paris, was asked to discern by noon Saturday what France's attitude was in the case of European war. In this way, Europe was first made aware that war was about to begin – not by the Russians, who were the first to mobilise, but by the Germans, who informed everyone about what Russia had done in secret and then, for good measure, about their own response to it.[11]

Still, rumours will out. Despite Russia's delay in announcing mobilisation, panic-selling began on Friday on all Europe's bourses; those in St Petersburg, Vienna, Berlin, Budapest, and Brussels all closed. The City of London saw the worst panic-selling, as financial firms exposed to Europe saw their share values plunge. At ten fifteen AM, at the London stock exchange, attendants in 'gold-braided silk hats' posted the closure notice on the doors. Soon newsboys were shouting the news through the streets: 'The stock exchange is closed!' It was London's first outright closure since 1773. There was a bank run too, although few banks remained open long enough for depositors to cash out. By early afternoon, there was an enormous line on Threadneedle Street, outside the Bank of England – the last institution in London still open to convert pound notes into gold coins.[12]

Sentiment in the City of London and in the House of Commons was almost unanimously against British intervention in the war. As Prime Minister Asquith noted that day, 'the general opinion at present . . . is to keep out at almost all costs.'[13] Thanks to Churchill, the navy was primed and ready at Scapa Flow. Aside from the bellicose first lord of the Admiralty, however, no one in the cabinet was sure what to do. In theory, Asquith and Grey shared Churchill's view on the need to defend France against possible German aggression. But they knew that there was no Liberal majority in the cabinet for this position, which is why Sir Edward Grey had tiptoed so carefully all week around anything resembling an actual policy statement. Luckily for the beleaguered foreign secretary, there had been no cabinet meeting on Thursday, which fact he had used as a convenient excuse to demur when the French and German ambassadors asked where he stood.

On Friday morning, even as the City of London went into war-scare meltdown, Grey continued talking calmly about peace-mediation plans with Germany's Anglophilic ambassador, both men blissfully unaware that Russian general mobilisation had already begun. With improbable timing, shortly after the London bourse shut down owing to war hysteria, Grey told Lichnowsky, 'I have today for the first time the impression that the improved relations with Germany of late years and perhaps also some friendly feeling for Germany in the cabinet makes it appear possible that, in case of war, England will probably adopt an attitude of watchful waiting.'[14] Grey was dissembling, but he was not wrong about the cabinet, which met Friday afternoon. The French had been demanding all day – all week – that he take a stand. Everyone in the cabinet knew this;

in fact, the main subject of debate Friday was what Grey should say to France's ambassador, Paul Cambon, after the session was over. We have no transcript of the Friday meeting, but there is no doubt that the Little Englanders again won the day. Lord Morley, a leading anti-interventionist in the cabinet, 'tapped [Churchill] on the shoulder' to say, 'Winston, we have beaten you after all.' As Grey reported to his ambassador in Paris, 'nobody here feels that in this dispute, so far as it has gone yet, British treaties or obligations are involved.' Grey could offer France no 'definite pledge to intervene in a war.'[15]

Grey said as much to the French ambassador on Friday evening, although he added several wrinkles. His encounters with Cambon were always difficult. Grey's spoken French was as poor as Cambon's spoken English, so they both conversed slowly in their own tongue rather than in one common language.[16] In the current case, this worked to Grey's advantage, as, lacking authorisation to give Cambon the pledge of support he wanted, the Briton's goal was to obfuscate. And so Grey assured the Frenchman vaguely that 'we had not left Germany under the impression that we would stand aside.' In fact, Grey claimed, he had told Lichnowsky on Friday morning that, in case of war, 'we should be drawn into it' (this was untrue, although Grey had spoken to Lichnowsky in this sense on Wednesday). When Cambon asked for a commitment, Grey said evasively that he 'could not give any pledge at the present time.' The French ambassador 'expressed great disappointment' at this reply and tried to pin Grey down as to 'whether we would help France if Germany made an attack on her.' Grey's answer was the same: 'as far as things had gone at present, we could not take any engagement.'

Grey then introduced a stunning bit of news into the conversation. As if to change the subject, Grey informed Cambon that he had just learned that 'Russia had ordered a complete mobilisation of her fleet and army.'* Russia's action, Grey informed Cambon in a rare moment of clarity, 'would precipi- tate a crisis, and *would make it appear that German mobilisation was being forced by Russia.*' Returning to his usual manner of obfus- cation, Grey dropped the subject and concluded by promising Cambon that 'the Cabinet would certainly be summoned as soon as there was some new development, but at the present moment the only answer I could give was that we could not undertake any definite engagement.'[17] Russian general mobili- sation against Austria and Germany, apparently, did not qual- ify as 'some new development.'

Cambon, infuriated by the foreign secretary's evasions, went and 'unburdened himself' to Sir Arthur Nicolson, the permanent undersecretary of state, with whom he was on much better terms. Nicolson, concerned that Britain was offering France nothing, then sought out the foreign secretary to see what he could do for Cambon. Grey reminded Nicolson that he had sent a telegram to Paris and Berlin, demanding a pledge from each power that she was 'prepared to engage to respect neutrality of Belgium so long as no other Power violates it.' If the Germans refused, perhaps Grey could use this in the cabinet to make a case for interven- tion.[18] The idea that Russia's unprovoked general mobilisation against Germany might be used by British policymakers to make a case *against* intervention did not occur to him.

Meanwhile Churchill continued preparing the British fleet for war, whatever the sentiments of the cabinet. On Friday he outdid even himself, ordering British naval crews to board and seize the two dreadnoughts, *Sultan Osman I* and *Reshad V*, being

---

* Grey did not mention his source, but we can confirm from Foreign Office sources that it was the secretary of the German embassy, who called at five PM with the news of Bethmann's telegram from Berlin, reporting on Russian general mobilisation. Certainly Grey did not learn this from Cam- bon or Benckendorff; neither the French nor Russians had fessed up yet.

built for the Ottoman navy. Based on the timing – Sazonov had asked Britain to detain these very warships on Thursday night – one is tempted to conclude that Churchill had an intuition about Russian general mobilisation before learning of it. And yet there is no evidence that Churchill, when he carried out this provocative action (for which planning had been underway since Wednesday), knew that Russia had mobilised or that Sazonov had asked him to hold the ships in port. At any rate, detaining them was far from Churchill's purpose, and the Russo-Ottoman naval rivalry in the Black Sea was far from his thoughts. He was commandeering these state-of-the-art dreadnoughts for the British navy, as added strategic insurance against the German High Seas Fleet.[19]

IN PARIS, THINGS WERE MOVING FASTER. France, expecting to bear the brunt of the German assault, could not afford the attitude of 'watchful waiting' Sir Edward Grey had adopted. Mobilisation Plan XVI had envisioned France completing the concentration of its active army corps by M + 10 or M + 11, which would leave little margin for error, as the Germans were expected to finish concentration by M + 12 and go on the offensive by M + 13. Plan XVII, adopted in May 1913, cut off a full day, which would theoretically allow the French armies to begin their principal offensive two days before the Germans were ready to begin theirs (and with five days to spare regarding France's obligations to Russia) – so long as Moltke did not beat his counterpart, Joffre, to the punch by mobilising first.*

---

* France's reserve corps would still lag nearly five days behind this (although a portion of them would be ready by M + 11). The Germans had decided to throw their reserve divisions right into the front lines, which would allow them to move faster and flank much further north than the French assumed they could. This was a serious flaw in Plan XVII. But Joffre, despite receiving credible intelligence reports about German plans for reserve deployment, did not believe them.

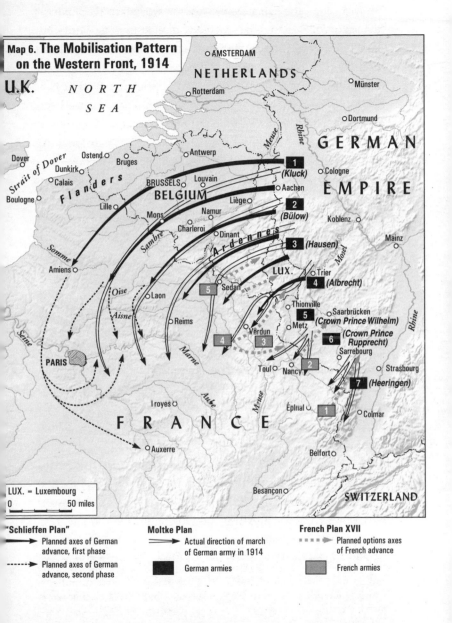

Map 6. The Mobilisation Pattern on the Western Front, 1914

U.K.

NORTH SEA

NETHERLANDS

GERMAN EMPIRE

FRANCE

SWITZERLAND

LUX. = Luxembourg

0   50 miles

"Schlieffen Plan"
→ Planned axes of German advance, first phase
--→ Planned axes of German advance, second phase

Moltke Plan
⇒ Actual direction of march of German army in 1914
■ German armies

French Plan XVII
▸▸▸ Planned options axes of French advance
▨ French armies

1 (Kluck)
2 (Bülow)
3 (Hausen)
4 (Albrecht)
5 (Crown Prince Wilhelm)
6 (Crown Prince Rupprecht)
7 (Heeringen)

In a sense, the French and German war plans were mirror images of each other. Plan XVII envisioned thrusts into 'occupied' Lorraine left and right of the German fortified area at Metz (there was flexibility as to which side would be emphasised, depending on what the Germans did). If the French, as hoped, broke through the weaker left wing of the German armies and wheeled north, they could cut off the German right wing. Moltke hoped to do the same thing by sending his right wing through Belgium, enveloping the French armies from behind in a gigantic flanking manoeuvre. While the French plan of march was not as detailed as the German one and had greater flexibility, the basic idea was the same. Under the dynamic, offence-minded doctrine prevailing in both general staffs – the French called it *offensive à outrance* – it was imperative to reach the enemy's flank first. Speed was everything. Every day counted.[20]

For this reason France, as we have seen, had begun quietly preparing for war on Tuesday, when troops were ordered back from Algeria and Morocco. With an eye on Britain, France did not want to show her hand too early. Even so, at each stage, Joffre remained a day or two ahead of Moltke, from the heightening of railway security to 'the return to garrison of troops on manoeuvre,' the cancellation of leaves, and the *couverture* ordered Thursday afternoon – conditioned by the mythical 'ten-kilometre withdrawal.'[21]

Now, on Friday, Joffre wanted to go further still. Notwithstanding the less than fully informative dispatches that Paléologue and Sazonov had sent to Paris, there is no reason to doubt that Poincaré, Messimy, and Joffre understood the gravity of these cryptic messages. Whether Russia had 'decided to proceed' to general mobilisation publicly or (as Paléologue had it) secretly, she had evidently *proceeded to general mobilisation*, as would be confirmed for the Quai d'Orsay at 3:30 PM Friday afternoon, by France's ambassador in Berlin, Jules Cambon, in a wire

Joseph Joffre, chief of staff of the French army, who re-oriented France's Mobilisation Plan XVII in a more offensive direction. While France's president was at sea, Joffre quietly endorsed Russia's secret early mobilisation and urged that it proceed still faster. *Source: Getty Images.*

dispatched at 2:17 PM. (Sazonov and Paléologue having fudged the truth, it was again left to the Germans to report what Russia had done.) Because, as Cambon himself had reported from Berlin the previous weekend, Germany had pledged herself to respond to this by mobilising against France and Russia, it did not take too great a leap of imagination to divine that European war was about to break out. As Cambon himself concluded, 'in these conditions we can expect the almost immediate publication of the German order for general mobilisation.'[22]

The gist of this report was soon confirmed by Germany's own ambassador to Paris, Baron Schoen, who called at the Quai d'Orsay at around six thirty PM, even as the cabinet was meeting at the Elysée Palace to discuss Jules Cambon's telegram. Viviani, after conferring with Poincaré about what line to take, dismissed the cabinet and hurried over to the Quai d'Orsay to receive the ambassador. Schoen did not mince his words: in response to Russia's '*total* mobilisation of its land and sea forces,' he informed the French premier, Germany had activated the 'Imminent Danger of War' at three PM Friday. The Russian government, he continued, was being asked to demobilise on both her German and her Austrian frontiers, within a twelve-hour time limit, from midnight until noon Saturday. Barring this, Germany would be forced to mobilise, which meant war.*[23]

Viviani claimed that he 'had no information at all about an alleged total mobilisation of the Russian army and navy.' This transparent lie did not impress Schoen. Plowing right ahead, he asked the premier what the 'attitude of France' would be 'in the case of a war between Germany and Russia.' Viviani was still evasive. Not unlike Grey in his dealings with the French ambassador, France's premier replied that he could not, as yet, give an answer. When, Schoen asked, might he be able to give one? Viviani said he would reply by Saturday at one PM Paris

---

* Curiously, both Viviani and Poincaré later maintained that Schoen had not specified that German mobilisation would be tantamount to war. Schoen insists that he *did* specify this, as a 'last urgent appeal to co-operate in saving the peace that was in dire peril.' Whether or not Schoen was telling the truth, it is hard to see what Viviani and Poincaré wanted to prove: the ambassador clearly issued a very serious warning, without sugarcoating. Viviani himself confirmed as much when, later that evening, he told the British ambassador that the 'the German Embassy is packing up.'

time (two PM German time, or two hours after Russia's deadline to demobilise would expire). In one final gambit to tease out French intentions, Schoen asked if he should get his passports ready. Viviani told him to wait.[24]

The sequence of events that followed is bewildering. Viviani, returning home for dinner after his meeting with Schoen, ran into Joffre and briefed him on Schoen's quasi-ultimatum to France. Joffre then urged Messimy, the war minister, 'to give orders for our general mobilisation without an instant's delay, for I considered it imperative. Messimy promised me to insist on this step when the Cabinet assembled in the evening.'[25] At eight thirty PM, while Viviani was dining at home, a telegram from Paléologue was received at the Quai d'Orsay, announcing that 'an order has been issued for the general mobilisation of the Russian army.'*[26] While this could not have come as news, this laconic, single-line message still had a sobering effect, as it threatened to undermine plausible deniability. When the cabinet reconvened at nine PM, the first item of business was composing a careful message to Paléologue, in which Viviani asked the ambassador 'to report to me, as a matter of urgency, as to the reality of the alleged general mobilisation of Russia.' Considering that Paléologue had reported Thursday night that Russia 'had decided to proceed secretly' to general mobilisation, and then wired again Friday morning confirming it was public, this wire, dispatched to Petersburg at nine thirty PM, must

---

* The telegram was wired from Petersburg at 10:43 AM Friday, meaning that it took twelve hours to reach Paris (after being dispatched eighteen hours after the tsar had ordered general mobilisation!). Paléologue later concocted an elaborate story explaining why he had taken 30 hours to report the world-historical news to Paris: he only saw the placards on the streets Friday morning; his messenger got lost on the way to the telegraph office; finally, the telegram went via Scandinavia instead of Berlin. Rarely has the imperative of 'plausible deniability' been put so nakedly on display.

have struck Paléologue as a rhetorical question.*[27] The only logical explanation is that it was diplomatic camouflage, as France sought to extend plausible deniability a little longer.

Scarcely had the cabinet put together this cover story denying French knowledge of Russian general mobilisation than a bombshell came in from the streets. Jean Jaurès, the great pacifist orator, had just returned to Paris after addressing an anti-war congress of the Socialist International in Brussels, at which he had locked arms with Hugo Haase, leader of the German Social Democratic Party, in a gesture of internationalist solidarity. Addressing journalists at the Chamber of Deputies, Jaurès was seen to 'explode' in anger over Russia's malign influence on French foreign policy: 'Are we going to unleash a world war because Izvolsky is still furious over Aehrenthal's deception in the Bosnian affair [of 1908–1909]?'[28] At 9 PM, Jaurès went to dine with friends at the Café Croissant in Montmartre. At 9:40 PM, a young nationalist fanatic out to avenge the murder of Gaston Calmette by Mme Caillaux** – the improbably named Raoul Villain – walked up to the open window and fired two shots into Jaurès's back. By 9:45 PM Jaurès was dead.[29]

Word of Villain's terrible deed rifled across Paris. The cabinet was informed at 9:50 PM. Whatever their views of the Socialist orator, everyone was stunned by the news, which seemed a terrible omen. Even Poincaré, Jaurès's bitter opponent over the Three-Year Service Law, took the time to compose a heartfelt message to Jaurès's widow, expressing 'great admiration' for

---

* Paléologue's wire contained only one line of thirteen words. It cannot have taken more than five minutes to decode. Considering its importance, it beggars belief that Viviani was not apprised of its contents immediately – which would help explain the urgency with which the cabinet approved his strange covering message to Paléologue.

** Villain apparently aimed to murder Caillaux next. He had inscribed two pistols, one marked 'J,' for Jaurès and one 'C,' for Caillaux.

his rival.[30] But it was not all hugs and kisses. Public commotion over the Mme Caillaux trial had finally died down; now it threatened to begin all over again. The prefect of police phoned to warn that 'there will be a revolution in Paris in three hours.' The Socialists, after all, had vowed, in a series of international congresses, to stage a general strike to sabotage any European war. Jaurès himself was the most famous partisan of the idea, although he had always been careful to avoid direct exhortations to sedition. Suddenly, it seemed imperative to invoke the notorious Carnet B, the long list of anti-war agitators, anarchists, pacifists, and spies the French government planned to arrest on the day of mobilisation. Viviani, a former Socialist who knew some of the men on the list, predictably opposed the idea as an outrage. In the end the cabinet, hoping to cool tensions in the wake of the Jaurès murder and to preserve national unity, agreed not to invoke Carnet B against French citizens (although foreigners suspected of spying were still to be arrested). As an added precaution, Joffre agreed to order two cavalry regiments, about to depart for the frontier, to remain in the capital.

There remained urgent business. Despite Joffre's impatience, Viviani refused to authorise general mobilisation yet, insisting that everyone sleep on the question one more night. In a sense, the point was moot: it was already too late to issue orders to take effect by midnight Friday. To make midnight Saturday, the French had until four PM the next day. Meanwhile, Joffre wired his corps commanders to prepare for war.[31]

At ten thirty PM, Britain's ambassador, Sir Francis Bertie, arrived at the Elysée Palace, demanding an answer to Grey's query about respecting Belgian neutrality. Viviani demurred, responding with a question of his own: What would Britain do? To give a hint as to where things stood, he then told Bertie that 'the German Embassy is packing up' (this was untrue, although it was true that Schoen had asked him whether he should begin packing).[32] After conferring with his colleagues in the cabinet, Viviani dispatched Bruno de Margerie, his political director, to give Bertie an answer. The message for Grey was emphatic: 'French Government are resolved to respect the neutrality of Belgium, and it would only be in the event of some other Power violating that neutrality that France might find herself under the necessity . . . to act otherwise.' Poincaré had promised to repeat this assurance personally to King Albert of Belgium.[33]

Equally important was what the French cabinet did *not* discuss Friday night. Aside from the curious rhetorical 'query' about Russian mobilisation sent to Paléologue, no message of any kind about avoiding provocative Russian military measures on the German frontier was addressed to Izvolsky or Sazonov – not even as mild a warning as the one Viviani had sent off on Thursday morning. Then, everyone had been awakened at three AM to respond to Sazonov's cryptic message that, as Russia was 'unable to accede to Germany's desire [to cease mobilising], it only *remains for us to hasten our armaments and regard war as imminent*.' Now that the Germans themselves had inaugurated *Kriegsgefahrzustand* in response to Russian general mobilisation, there was no more need for dramatic late-night consultations between Russia and France. France would order mobilisation when she (that is, Viviani, the last holdout) was ready – probably at four PM Saturday. In the meantime, Messimy was dispatched to give the Russian ambassador a private assurance, 'in solemn, heart-felt tones of the [French] Government's firm resolve to fight.' In exchange, France's war minister 'begged' Izvolsky 'to confirm the hope of the French General Staff that all [Russia's] efforts will be directed against Germany and that Austria will be regarded as a negligible quantity.'[34] It was not quite a guarantee of co-belligerence, but it was close.

Nor was there any cabinet discussion of mediation in Vienna. The Austrian ambassador to Paris, Count Szécsen, visited the Quai d'Orsay just after ten PM, about the same time the cabinet was reacting to the Jaurès assassination. His brief was to inform the French government that Austria had officially declared to Russia that she did not intend to annex Serbian territory or infringe Serbian sovereignty. Szécsen assured Philippe Berthelot, the director of the Ministry of Foreign Affairs, who met him in Viviani's stead, 'it ought to be possible still to settle the question, [Austrian] mobilisation not being war, and leaving a few days still for conversations.' Serbia, he proposed, could ask Austria for terms. Not surprisingly, Berthelot dismissed the proposal, on the grounds that it was 'extremely late' and had already been 'overtaken by events.' Szécsen did not put up much protest, conceding to Berchtold in his own report of the encounter that, owing to the German *Kriegsgefahrzustand* ordered in response to Russia's general mobilisation, 'the Serbian question fell entirely into the background.'[35] Certainly the French cabinet saw things this way, as there was no discussion of Serbia on Friday night. Despite Berchtold having catalysed the entire crisis a week earlier with the ultimatum to Belgrade, with the decisive events of Friday in Petersburg, Berlin, and Paris, Vienna had become almost an afterthought.

Austria, however, had one more surprise in store for everyone. On Friday morning, yet another war council had convened in Vienna, this time with Emperor Franz Josef presiding. Conrad, as usual, was ready to move and declare general mobilisation. Berchtold had been willing to wait in order to humour Bethmann, but the mixed signals coming from the German chancellor had elicited his contempt. In the end, it was the pressure from Moltke – who wired two more messages to Conrad during the day, begging that he mobilise against Russia – that wore down the resistance of Tisza, Berchtold, and the emperor, who agreed to order general mobilisation just after noon. Oddly, although entirely consistent with Austria's behaviour so far, the mobilisation would not actually begin until August 4, and it was still not made clear to Moltke's satisfaction whether Conrad would follow Plan B (or 'Balkans,' focusing on Serbia) or Plan R (for Russia).[36]

It was another Austrian blunder that worked to Germany's detriment. By announcing general mobilisation on Friday, 31 July, five days before it would actually begin, Vienna handed yet another talking point to France and Russia in their goal of bringing Britain into the war. In reality, the decision was such a non-event that almost no one in Petersburg, Berlin, London, or Paris took note of it at first – with the curious exception of Jules Cambon, France's ambassador in Berlin, who learned about Russia's general mobilisation at about the same time. Indeed, in the same telegram in which he officially informed Viviani about Russia's general mobilisation, Cambon had erroneously reported that 'Russia had just decided on total mobilisation in response to Austrian total mobilisation' – despite the fact that Russia's decision had preceded Austria's by twenty hours.[37] The fact that no one in Paris took heed of this message on Friday – Austrian general mobilisation was not mentioned in the nine thirty PM telegram to Paléologue in which Viviani demanded clarification on Russian mobilisation – shows how little thought anyone gave Austria that day. But she would shortly make a comeback. The weekend would see a battle royale over British belligerence or neutrality, in which every new revelation – whether truthful or not – threatened to tip the balance.

22

'Now You Can
Do What You Want'

SATURDAY, 1 AUGUST

A T EIGHT AM, Joffre handed Messimy a note outlining 'the
imperative necessity of ordering our mobilisation.' Citing
reports of German mobilisation (actually pre-mobilisation)
measures – the call-up of reservists, requisitions, and pur-
chases of horses – France's chief of staff insisted that, in order
not to give Moltke a head start, 'the last possible time limit
for publishing the order would expire at four PM.' To drive
the point home, Joffre threatened to resign if France did not
mobilise on Saturday. If the government delayed any further,
he told Messimy, 'I cannot possibly continue to bear the crushing responsibility of the high office which has been entrusted
to me.' Messimy, sympathetic but unable to promise anything,
suggested that Joffre come to the Elysée Palace himself to make
his case. Joffre agreed.

At nine AM, the French cabinet convened. Joffre made his
case for immediate mobilisation. According to Messimy's recollection, 'there was no protest, no comment.'[1] There was also no
great urgency, as the German ultimatum to Russia had several

hours left to run, and, as Joffre himself conceded, the government had until four PM to decide. Meanwhile, important news came in from Rome. Camille Barrère, France's ambassador, reported that Italy's foreign minister, Antonio San Giuliano, had told him, 'in the most complete secrecy,' that 'the Italian Government was inclined to regard the Austrian attack on Serbia as an act of aggression of a nature to absolve it from action in favour of Austria.' Moreover, the articles of the Triple Alliance 'were such as to enable Italy . . . to abstain from participation in any conflict' – that is, on behalf of Germany as well. The only condition San Giuliano attached to this pledge of neutrality was that France and Russia show 'restraint.'[2] Without delay, Joffre was authorised to send the army 'additional instructions . . . prescribing that in case of mobilisation the covering troops designated for the south-eastern frontier should remain in their mobilisation centres, ready to entrain for the northeast.' So confident was the cabinet of San Giuliano's neutrality pledge that France would leave her Italian border undefended.[3]

At the same time, the British cabinet was meeting in London. In a sense, the fact that it was convening on a Saturday morning was historic. For well-born Britons, weekends were when one went to the country. Prime Minister Asquith liked to golf, Grey to fish, Churchill to play with his children. Others, such as Conservative MPs Arthur Balfour and Andrew Bonar Law, preferred lawn tennis. What no one liked to do was stay in town. But this Saturday was different. The burgeoning rift in the cabinet, growing for days, was threatening to burst it apart.

Overnight, more disquieting news had come in from Paris and Berlin that made nonsense of Grey's stated position of 'watchful waiting.' The French communiqué had actually been composed at twelve thirty PM Friday, although it was only delivered to Downing Street at midnight. In it, Viviani reported that 'German patrols had twice penetrated our territory,' and asserted (again falsely) that 'our advance units have retreated 10 kilom. behind our frontier.' 'The populations thus left exposed to enemy attack protest,' he continued, 'but the [French] Government is determined to show English public opinion and the [British] Government that the aggressor will in no case be France.'[4] This message was alarming enough that Sir Arthur Nicolson was awakened to receive it. He, in turn, awakened Asquith – although oddly, not Sir Edward Grey.[5]

The news from Germany, which came in only minutes later, was still more disturbing. After recounting the events of the past few days, including the Willy-Nicky telegrams and the kaiser's efforts to mediate in Vienna, Bethmann reported that, in view of Russia's general mobilisation that began on Friday, 'we were compelled, unless we wanted to abandon the safety of the Fatherland, to answer this action, which could only be regarded as hostile, with serious counter-measures. We therefore told Russia that if she did not stop her warlike measures against Germany and Austria-Hungary within twelve hours we should mobilise, and *that would mean war*. We asked France whether in a Russo-German war she would remain neutral.'[6]

Regardless of whether Viviani's claim that Germany had already invaded France was true (it was not), the Germans' own message suggested that a Russo-German war would begin Saturday. It would be hard to avoid a cabinet meltdown over this.

Nevertheless, Nicolson and Asquith did their best. With Grey asleep, they called in his private secretary, Sir William Tyrrell, in his stead. They decided to deal with the German question first, as it seemed more urgent. Showing that they gave credence to Bethmann's message about Russian general mobilisation (even if it was a little late to be noticing now – a day and a half after it had been ordered), Tyrrell, Nicolson, and Asquith penned an appeal from King George V to Tsar Nicholas II, passing on Bethmann's note about Russian mobilisation and asking vaguely that the tsar 'remove the misapprehension which I feel must have occurred.'[7] At one AM, they took

329

a taxi to Buckingham Palace and awakened the king. Asquith, having never done anything like this before, was rather embarrassed to see his sovereign 'in a brown dressing gown over his night shirt & with copious signs of having been aroused from his first "beauty sleep."'[8] Still, the king did as he was told and signed the telegram. At two AM, after everyone had gone home, Asquith's secretary rang the German embassy to inform Lichnowsky that a direct appeal asking Russia to 'stop the mobilisation' had been sent to the tsar (although in fact the telegram was not dispatched until three thirty AM; it was sent not directly to Tsarskoe Selo but to Buchanan at the Petersburg embassy; and, more significantly, it said absolutely nothing about stopping Russian mobilisation).[9]

Saturday morning, at seven AM, Nicolson at last called on Grey, who was staying with Lord Haldane, the former secretary of state for war (now lord chancellor). He was accompanied by General Sir Henry Wilson, director of military operations, in charge of liaising with the French army (it was Wilson who had drawn up plans for the dispatch of the British Expeditionary Force to France in case of war). Nicolson's idea was that Wilson, a keen interventionist for obvious reasons, might put some steel into Grey. But Grey, sluggish as usual, was still in bed. Nicolson declined to wake him.[10] Instead, he returned to the Foreign Office and wrote out another sovereign appeal for the king to sign, this time to France. This one was no less evasive, promising President Poincaré only that 'you may rest assured that my Government will continue to discuss frankly and freely }with M. Cambon all points touching the interests of both peoples.'[11]

When Grey finally awoke, his first priority before the cabinet meeting, scheduled for 11 AM, was to sound out the German ambassador. Still not quite stirring himself to action, he sent his secretary, Sir Tyrrell, to the embassy. Grey's idea for limiting (if not staving off) the war, judging from 'a remark of Sir W. Tyrrell's,' Lichnowsky reported to Berlin at 11:14 AM, was 'that in the event of our not attacking France, England, too, would remain neutral and would guarantee France's passivity.' More details, Tyrrell told the ambassador, would come after the cabinet meeting. Even while Lichnowsky was thinking through this stunning proposal, Grey phoned and asked him, as Lichnowsky reported to Germany's State Secretary Jagow, 'whether I thought I could give an assurance that in the event of France remaining neutral in a war between Russia and Germany we should not attack the French.' Lichnowsky, guessing how euphorically Grey's amazing offer would be received in Berlin, assured Grey that he 'could take responsibility for such a guarantee,' and that that the foreign secretary could use this German guarantee in the cabinet. Tyrrell then 'urgently begged' Lichnowsky to use his 'influence to prevent [German] troops from violating the French frontier. Everything depended on that.'[12]

Having thus sent messages urging moderation to Petersburg, Paris, and Berlin, Grey and Asquith had covered their flank with the Little Englanders before the start of the cabinet meeting. But they still had to satisfy the interventionists, foremost among them Churchill. Over the past few days, the bellicose first lord had made overtures to Conservative and Unionist opposition leaders,* in case the Liberal cabinet split over the war. Churchill had once been a Conservative and still had good contacts in the party. Among them was F. E. Smith (the future

---

* The old Conservative (Tory) and Liberal Unionist Parties, which had first formed a coalition in opposition to Gladstone's Liberals over Home Rule in 1886, had merged in 1912 to form the 'Conservative and Unionist Party,' a single political party with two names. For purposes of economy I will refer to them as Conservatives and Unionists interchangeably.

Lord Birkenhead), who assured him on Friday night that he 'was unreservedly for standing by France and Belgium.' After consulting with Andrew Bonar Law, leader of the Conservative opposition, Smith had given Churchill a written assurance that, 'on the assumption (which we understand to be certain) that Germany contemplates a violation of Belgian neutrality – the Government can rely on the support of the Unionist Party in whatever manner that support can be most effectively given.'[13] Churchill had then showed this note to Asquith.

During the cabinet meeting, Churchill quietly passed notes to David Lloyd George, the chancellor of the Exchequer, who had served him as a mentor in the Liberal Party. Although leaning against intervention, Lloyd George had not yet made up his mind. Churchill 'implored' him to 'come and bring your mighty aid to the discharge of our duty.' The question of war or peace, he told Lloyd George, 'is our whole future – comrades – or opponents.' Having thus staked out his position and won over (so he hoped) the prime minister and the chancellor of the Exchequer, Churchill summoned all his 'daemonic energy' and demanded 'the immediate calling out of the Fleet Reserves and the completion of our naval preparations.' The cabinet said no. Churchill issued forth a 'torrent of rhetoric,' which Asquith judged to have lasted over an hour. The cabinet still said no.[14]

To give succor to Churchill and the interventionists, Grey warned everyone that he would resign if, as Lord Morley and the Little Englander faction he led desired, 'an out-and-out and uncompromising policy of non-intervention at all costs is adopted.' The implications were clear: because Asquith and Churchill would almost certainly follow, Grey's resignation would bring down the government. Not even Morley wanted to risk this yet. Still, the cabinet remained deadlocked. There was no support for Churchill's belligerent stance, but none to force a vote on unconditional neutrality either.[15]

The deciding issue, it seemed, would be Belgian neutrality. While a hard core of Liberal MPs in Parliament were pushing a motion that afternoon that England should stay out of war 'whatever happened in Belgium,' the non-interventionists in the cabinet were not so sure. Morley did not like the idea of intervening on behalf of Belgium, but he admitted that the matter was tricky. 'There was,' he recalled of this historic cabinet session, 'a general, but vague, assent to our liabilities under the Treaty of 1839, but there was no assent to the employment of a land force.' At some point in the discussion of the Belgian issue, Grey saw his opportunity. He asked permission to address a warning to Lichnowsky that if Germany was unable to give the same guarantee on Belgium that France had, 'it would be very hard to restrain public feeling in this country.'[16] It was an odd sort of warning: threatening Germany with the wrath of English public opinion. But it offered Grey a possible way out of the cabinet impasse. He seized it.

Back in Paris, the cabinet meeting had been interrupted at eleven AM, when Ambassador Schoen arrived at the Quai d'Orsay to demand an answer as to French neutrality in a Russo-German war. Viviani was dispatched to give the reply that was prearranged by the cabinet on Friday evening: 'France will act in accordance with her interests.' Schoen could not have been in much doubt as to what this meant, but still, he had to ask. 'I confess,' he said, 'that my question is rather naive. But, after all, do you not have a treaty of alliance [with Russia]?' Viviani replied, again ambiguously: 'So it would appear' (*Évidemment*). Seeking some kind of answer that could be interpreted unambiguously in Berlin, Schoen pressed again, but all that Viviani would tell him was that 'he regards situation as changed since yesterday.' As to *what* had changed, he informed Schoen that 'Sir Ed. Grey's proposal that all sides cease military preparations has been accepted by Russia in principle and that Austria-Hungary has announced that she will not infringe Serbian integrity and sovereignty.'[17] The latter statement was true; the former 'revelation' – that Russia had agreed to cease military preparations – was utterly false, although Schoen did not know this.

It was an impressive performance by Viviani, who seemed to be warming to his role as foreign minister for the first time. He had given away nothing, while throwing a good deal of diplomatic smoke in the air. As Viviani himself noted in his own report of the encounter that he sent to France's ambassadors, Baron Schoen had answered 'that he did not know the developments which had taken place in this matter in the last 24 hours, that there was in them perhaps a "glimmer of hope" for some arrangement . . . and that he was going to get information.'[18] In any case, the German ambassador was nonplussed enough by Viviani's ambiguous answers that he did not ask for his passports. Viviani's misleading remarks, relayed by Schoen to Berlin, left the Germans guessing a little longer as to French intentions.

Viviani may still have been harbouring doubts himself. It is not entirely clear from the record when the pacifist-minded premier finally shifted towards belligerence. Judging from his refusal to issue even halfhearted warnings about Russian mobilisation on Friday, 31 July, or to press harder for mediation with Austria, he may have given up hope for peace by then. This shift, however, may have been more in the line of passive resignation than active conversion to belligerence. Viviani had not, after all, agreed to order mobilisation on Friday night. Nor had he done so in the Saturday morning cabinet meeting, despite the welcome news from Italy.

Whether or not he had made up his mind beforehand, Viviani's last resistance crumbled following his encounter with Schoen. The hostile audience may have got his blood up, or it may have simply confirmed suspicions he already harboured about German intentions. According to Joffre, when Viviani 'returned to his seat' at the cabinet meeting, 'he was now fully convinced that I was right, and in face of the dangerous preparations already made by the Germans, he was ready to sign the order for general mobilisation.'[19] Viviani's only condition was that he and Poincaré draft a manifesto to the French people, explaining why the decision was made (i.e., for purely defensive reasons), insisting on national unity and the setting aside of party differences, and arguing – with an eye on the British public and government – that '*mobilisation is not war.*' France's general mobilisation order was signed into law by Poincaré, Viviani, Messimy, and the naval minister.[20]

At three thirty PM, Messimy's aide, General Ebener, along with two officers delegated to deliver the order to the telegraph office, arrived at Rue Saint-Domingue to perform their duty. Messimy handed them the mobilisation order 'in dry-throated silence.' Everyone, he recalled, 'conscious of the gigantic and infinite results to spread from that little piece of paper . . . felt our hearts lighten.'[21] At three forty-five PM, the order was delivered to the central telegraph office in Paris and swiftly dispatched to all military commanders.

At four PM, the first mobilisation placards went up in Paris. Orchestras across the city played 'The Marseillaise,' alongside the Russian and, as if in plaintive hope, British national anthems. Contributing to the air of gaiety, the boulevards were empty of cars – Messimy had already requisitioned them for the army. Crowds of patriotic Frenchmen glided through the streets. Reservists were seen marching to the Gare de l'Est, from where they would embark for the frontier, as French civilians waved and cheered. English and other foreign tourists mobbed the Gare du Nord, hoping to get out of France before the war began. The trains, one Briton recalled, were 'packed to suffocation point.' Raymond Recouly recalled the moment when a 'small blue paper' announcing mobilisation was posted: 'An innumerable crowd surged to and fro. "Mobilisation is not

Soldiers on leave re-joining their garrisons in Paris as France mobilises in 1914. *Source: Getty Images.*

war" said M. Poincaré in his message to the people. To tell the truth no one believed him. If it was not war, it was certainly something terribly near to it.'[22]

Viviani himself had a similar premonition. Just before four PM, he called on Messimy to ask whether mobilisation could be postponed a little longer. The only news he had received since midday was a message from Paléologue claiming that Germany would order mobilisation on Sunday. This confirmation that a terrible war was about to begin may have stirred Viviani's conscience.* To his regret, Messimy replied that 'the order had

---

* Viviani told Messimy that he had just had a second meeting with the German ambassador, which 'gave a gleam of hope of an arrangement.' But this cannot be true, as he did not meet Schoen again until five thirty PM. It is possible that Messimy misremembered the time of this meeting – that it took place on Saturday evening, not just before four PM. This seems unlikely, however, as Joffre and Messimy had told Viviani repeatedly that the mobilisation order would go out at four PM. By nightfall, he would have known that the order was irreversible.

already gone and that the first measures were being carried out. It was too late, the mechanism had been set in motion.'[23]

I N BERLIN, BETHMANN WAS CLINGING to hopes just as forlorn as Viviani's. Although Germany's ultimatum deadline to Russia would expire only at noon, when he awoke on Saturday morning Bethmann received a preliminary reply that was not encouraging. Ambassador Pourtalès, after receiving the ultimatum at 11:10 PM, had presented it to Sazonov at midnight. The Russian foreign minister repeated his exhortation of two nights previously, that 'it was impossible on technical grounds to stop [Russia's] war preparations.' Playing for time, Sazonov insisted that 'the meaning of Russian mobilisation could not be compared to [Germany's],' the implication being that it could stop short of war.[24]

Bethmann was not impressed by Sazonov's sophistry about general mobilisation not meaning war. Addressing the Bundesrat Saturday morning – a higher parliamentary body whose endorsement, unlike the Reichstag's, was constitutionally necessary before a declaration of war – the chancellor informed the deputies that 'Russia tries to make out that her mobilisation is not to be regarded as an act of hostility against us.' Meanwhile, he informed the Bundesrat, France was also undertaking serious war preparations. If Germany took Sazonov's assurance at face value, Bethmann warned, she would 'lose advantage of our greater speed of mobilisation, putting us then in danger of having, in the immediate future, fully mobilised, battle-ready armies on our eastern and western frontiers,' ready to take 'entire provinces of East Prussia, even while, in the West, the Rhineland was endangered.' For this reason, the chancellor informed the Bundesrat, he had dispatched a twelve-hour ultimatum to Russia and a note to Paris demanding clarification as to French intentions. 'If the Russian reply is unsatisfactory,' he declared, 'and there is no absolutely unambiguous declaration of neutrality from France,'

> then the Kaiser will have the Russian Government informed that he must regard himself as in a state of war with Russia brought on by Russia herself, and to France he will have the statement made that we are at war with Russia and that, as France does not guarantee her neutrality, we must assume that we are also in a state of war with France. . . . We have not willed the war, it has been forced upon us.

The Bundesrat voted unanimous support for the chancellor. 'If the iron dice now must roll,' Bethmann concluded his remarks, 'then may God help us.'[25]

The noon deadline passed without further reply from Russia. Germany's state secretary, Jagow, therefore drew up a (French-language) declaration of war on Russia, which he wired to Pourtalès at 12:52 PM. Aside from some preliminaries having to do with the failure of mediation efforts, the document was fairly straightforward, citing Russia's general mobilisation, and failure to stop it, as casus belli. The only twist was that, not knowing whether Sazonov would still give a formal answer (his midnight reply had been ambiguous) or simply remain silent, a sort of 'choose one' clause was included, where Pourtalès could circle either 'having refused' or 'having not felt it necessary to reply' as grounds for ending diplomatic relations. In either case, however, the ambassador was to inform Sazonov that 'H. M. the Emperor, my august Sovereign, in the name of the Empire, accepts the war which has been thrust upon him.' To give time for both transmission and decoding, and – just possibly – second thoughts from Sazonov or the tsar, Pourtalès was instructed to hand the note to the Russian government at 5 PM Central European Time (6:30 PM Russian time). So the deadline had some time to run still.[26]

The French deadline of one PM (two PM Berlin time), too, passed without reply, other than Viviani's vague declaration that 'France will act in accordance with her interests.' While Bethmann and Jagow could not have seen either this or Sazonov's declaration as grounds for hope, they agreed to hold back. France, Bethmann wired to Schoen, could have another two hours to answer: until three PM (four PM Berlin time).[27]

There was good reason for the Germans to wait. Whereas both France and Russia were able to mobilise against Germany while *claiming*, at least, that doing so did not 'mean war,' the timetable of Moltke's plan meant that German general mobilisation was more serious. If Germany mobilised on Saturday afternoon, troops from the Sixteenth Division at Trier were to move into neutral Luxembourg (although not yet Belgium) overnight, in order to seize control of her railways (already, by treaty, under German management) and deny them to the French. An ultimatum had already been dispatched to the German ambassador in Brussels, demanding that Belgium allow the free passage of German troops, although it would not be presented to the Belgian government until the following night, giving Brussels time to answer before the Germans would cross the Belgian border on M + 3. While no German troops would violate Belgian territory for three days – and French territory for two weeks later still – the move into Luxembourg would be an unambiguous act of war (even if not, in the first instance, against France or Russia). For Germany to mobilise was therefore a decision of tremendous gravity. Perhaps, Bethmann hoped, there was still time for someone in Paris or Petersburg to develop cold feet.

Of course, Bethmann was the author of his own dilemma. It was not simply that his fait-accompli policy vis-à-vis Vienna had brought things to this pass in the first place. It was also the chancellor's insistence that German mobilisation must be accompanied by declarations of war. The paradox of Moltke's mobilisation plan was that it required immediate action in the direction of France and only a defensive posture on the Russian border. But because Russia was the power providing the casus belli, it was necessary to declare war on her first, before France, even though German troops had no immediate plans to attack Russia. Then, Germany must declare war on France before beginning hostilities against her. Declaring war first was diplomatic suicide, as Bethmann himself realised after the war: 'by so doing we appeared as the aggressors,' especially to Britain.[28] In fact, it was worse than this, because, as the naval secretary, Tirpitz, recalled explaining to Bethmann, both Italy and Romania had treaties with Germany, dating back to Bismarck's time, that obliged them to come to her aid if she were attacked. 'By our declaration of war on Russia,' Tirpitz pointed out, the Germans would 'give the Romanians the right to leave us alone in the war.' In the same way, a declaration of war on France would allow Italy to go her own way. Moreover, even given the inevitability of war with Russia, by declaring war first Germany would 'inspire the [Russian] moujik with the conviction that the kaiser intended to attack the White Tsar.' Tirpitz asked 'why the declaration of war had to coincide with our mobilisation.' Bethmann's answer was that mobilisation required Germany to 'send troops over the frontier,' which was by definition an act of war. In a kind of reductio ad absurdum of Germanic propriety by which diplomacy was made the servant of military necessity, the chancellor thereby reduced the question of declaring war to a tautology. It must be done, because it must be done. Bethmann knew it spelled strategic doom for Germany. But the logic remained unassailable. He would not be budged.[29]

As the day wore on without word from Paris or Petersburg, tensions in Berlin grew acute. Crowds were milling about the city. The air, one journalist observed, 'was electric with rumour. People told each other Russia had asked for an extension of time. The Bourse writhed in panic. The afternoon passed in almost insufferable anxiety.'[30]

Compounding the anxiety in the General Staff was the latest intelligence from the eastern front. By Saturday, Russia's mobilisation was so far advanced that German reconnaissance could identify specific Russian units in the order of battle.[31] At four PM, Falkenhayn, the Prussian minister of war, unsure why mobilisation still had not been declared four hours after the expiration of Russia's deadline, sought out Bethmann. He demanded that the chancellor convince the kaiser to mobilise immediately. 'After considerable resistance,' Falkenhayn recalled, 'he consented and we rang up Moltke and Tirpitz.' The kaiser then summoned everyone to the palace in Charlottenburg. At five PM on Saturday, 1 August, Germany's sovereign signed the order for general mobilisation – the last of the four principal belligerents to do so. He gave Falkenhayn a long handshake. Both men, Falkenhayn remembered, 'had tears in their eyes.'[32]

Scarcely had this momentous decision been made than Jagow appeared, having raced over from the Wilhelmstrasse to tell everyone that 'a very important dispatch had come in from England which would soon be decoded and brought along.'[33] He was referring to Lichnowsky's 11:14 AM telegram, which had been received at 4:23 PM. Not wanting to give Bethmann and the kaiser another chance to back down, Moltke, his face now 'bathed in perspiration,' left with Falkenhayn to transmit the mobilisation order to the army, without waiting to hear Jagow's news from London.[34]

Ten minutes later, they were summoned back. To general astonishment, Jagow informed everyone that Sir Edward Grey had promised 'that in the event of our not attacking France, England, too, would remain neutral and would guarantee

German mobilisation is proclaimed in 1914. *Source: Getty Images.*

France's passivity.' The news, General Lyncker, chief of the military cabinet, recalled, 'hit everyone like a bomb.' It suddenly appeared that Germany would only have to fight, in Lyncker's words, 'one opponent instead of three.'[35] No wonder Moltke, on his return to the palace, found everyone 'in a joyful state of mind.' The kaiser, overcome with relief, exclaimed aloud, 'Now we can go to war against Russia only. We simply march the whole of our army to the East!'[36]

Moltke was speechless. His plan had no provision for reversing the direction of German mobilisation 180 degrees from west to east. His intricate timetable, which one historian elegantly described as 'precise down to the number of train axles that would pass over a given bridge within a given time,' would be wrecked.[37] 'Your Majesty,' Moltke protested after recovering himself, 'the deployment of an army of a million men cannot be improvised. . . . If Your Majesty insists on leading the whole army to the east it will not be an army ready for battle but a disorganised mob of men with no arrangements for supply.' Besides, France would remain fully mobilised on Germany's western frontier and she would hardly leave Germany alone if she struck Russia. 'Your uncle,' Kaiser Wilhelm II replied angrily, 'would have given me a different answer!' This remark 'wounded me deeply,' Moltke later remembered: as he told the kaiser sheepishly, he had never considered himself 'to be the equal of the field marshal.' Over Moltke's strenuous objections, the kaiser insisted that his chief of staff sign an order to the commander of the Sixteenth Division in Trier to halt his imminent march into neutral Luxembourg. Moltke refused to sign, but an unofficial order was given by aides over the phone at 6:40 PM.[38]

Meanwhile, the heated discussion over the British proposal continued. Falkenhayn pulled Moltke aside to assuage his hurt feelings. He agreed with the chief of staff that there was no way to reverse the mobilisation against France, but he insisted that they humour the kaiser so long as England's offer was on the table. Moltke, though chastened, agreed to consider it. Tirpitz pointed out to everyone that, whether Grey's proposal 'was a bluff or not a bluff,' if the Germans refused to parley, their refusal would be published in London, 'putting us flagrantly in the wrong.' The kaiser agreed. Whether or not Grey was sincere, it seemed imperative to reply, to show good faith.[39]

And so Bethmann and Jagow, with input from Moltke and Falkenhayn, began writing up urgent pleas to London on the basis of Grey's offer. The first was a sovereign-to-sovereign appeal in which Kaiser Wilhelm II informed King George V that he had 'just received the communication from your Government offering French neutrality under guarantee of Great Britain. Added to this offer,' the message continued, 'was the enquiry, whether under these conditions Germany would refrain from attacking France.' The kaiser confessed that Germany's mobilisation against France and Russia could no longer, 'on technical grounds,' be halted, but he promised that 'if France offers me neutrality which must be guaranteed by the British fleet and army I shall of course refrain from attacking France and employ my troops elsewhere.' As a pledge of German good faith, the kaiser assured King George that 'the troops on my frontier are in the act of being stopped by telegraph and telephon[e] from crossing into France.'[40]

This was untrue. German troops were not expected to cross the French frontier for nearly two weeks, and so there was no need to 'stop' them from doing so now. Bethmann tacitly admitted this in his own telegram to Grey, which, in order to give England time to negotiate with Paris, promised that German troops would refrain from crossing the French frontier until Monday, 3 August, at seven PM.[41] (This, too, was misleading – it was *Belgium*'s frontier they would cross on Tuesday morning, not France's.) Because this telegram was sent almost simultaneously with the kaiser's, the intention was obviously to connect the idea that German troops were 'being stopped by telegraph' with the pledge that they would not enter France. In fact these promises meant nothing, as they simply reflected the prerogatives of Moltke's mobilisation plan.

The kaiser had, of course, already taken steps to 'stop troops' from crossing frontiers – the Sixteenth Division, slated to move into Luxembourg – but he could hardly reveal this to the British, as it would betray Germany's intention to violate neutral territory. Nor could he get his chief of staff to sign the order (although instructions had already been given over the phone). Failing to receive satisfaction from Moltke, the kaiser dismissed him just before eight PM. The chief of staff was 'crushed' as he left the palace; he 'burst into tears of abject despair.' He went home, sat on his bed, and pouted.[42]

Moltke might have taken solace if he had stuck around for the next twist. A second telegram from Lichnowsky was delivered just minutes after the chief of staff left, this one even more astonishing than the first. Sir William Tyrrell had come by the embassy early on Saturday afternoon, ostensibly to report on the cabinet meeting, and informed the German ambassador that 'Sir E. Grey has made an offer this afternoon for the neutrality of England, *even in the case that we make war with Russia as well as with France.*' Hearing this, the kaiser ordered champagne for everyone. Britain would remain neutral no matter what Germany did![43]

Of course, there were still France and Russia to worry about. At eight forty-five PM, Jagow wired Schoen in Paris, passing on Grey's offer, 'whereby England would guarantee France's neutrality, if we do not attack France.' Jagow promised that 'from our side no hostile action against France was in view, aside from mobilisation,' and asked that Schoen give this assurance to Viviani in order to 'keep the French quiet for the time being.'[44]

The situation with Russia was stranger still. After the twelve-hour ultimatum deadline had expired, Germany's declaration of war had been sent to Pourtalès at 12:52 PM, although his instructions were not to deliver it until 5 PM Central European time (6:30 PM in Petersburg). So a state of war between Germany and Russia almost certainly existed when Grey's neutrality offers were being digested in Charlottenburg – although, failing any new report from Pourtalès, no one could be quite sure of this. The most recent news from Russia was the latest 'Nicky-Willy' telegram, which had been received in Berlin just after 2 PM. In it, the tsar had said that he understood the kaiser was 'obliged to mobilise,' but asked for 'the same guarantee from you as I gave you, that these measures do not mean war and that we shall continue nego[t]iating.'[45] Germany's sovereign had, in effect, already answered this question in the negative by having a declaration of war sent to Petersburg, although he was not sure it had been delivered. Seeking to cover all possible bases, Bethmann had a reply written up in the kaiser's name, which was wired to Pourtalès at 9:45 PM.

'Although I requested an answer by noon today,' Willy's note began, 'no telegram from my ambassador conveying an answer from your government has reached me as yet. I therefore have been obliged to mobilise my army.' Failing receipt of a satisfactory answer as to Russian demobilisation, he was 'unable to discuss the subject of your telegram' (i.e., whether German mobilisation meant war). 'Immediate affirmative clear and unmistakable answer from your government,' Willy concluded, 'is the only way to avoid endless misery.'[46]

It was an awkward and unnecessary communication. As Bethmann must have known, by the time it reached Petersburg just before midnight, the question of peace or war would already have been resolved by Germany's own ambassador. Although it took several hours for his orders from Berlin to be transmitted and deciphered, Pourtalès had the declaration of war in hand by 5:45 PM Russian time, and he headed over to Chorister's Bridge about an hour later, only fifteen minutes behind schedule. Sazonov received him at 7 PM (5:30 PM German time), about the same time that Moltke and Falkenhayn were being called back to the palace owing to the bombshell from London. Knowing nothing of this, Pourtalès calmly asked, one more time, whether 'the Imperial Government was agreeable to giving him a favourable reply to his note of yesterday' (i.e., the twelve-hour ultimatum asking Russia to demobilise). Sazonov said no, he was unable to comply with Germany's request. Pourtalès drew the declaration of war out of his pocket and repeated his question a second time, emphasising the 'serious consequences' that would attend a refusal. Sazonov confirmed his refusal. 'With increasing emotion,' Pourtalès repeated his question a third time. Sazonov, as if to relieve the German's agony, confessed, 'I have no other reply to give you.' The ambassador, 'deeply moved and drawing a deep breath,' presented the declaration of war, 'with trembling hands,' to Sazonov.

The two men, both overcome with emotion, then embraced (although their accounts differ as to who embraced whom).[47]

According to Pourtalès, a brief exchange followed in which the men tried to fix blame on the other country for starting the war. Sazonov fingered Tschirschky, Germany's ambassador in Vienna, for urging on Austrian aggression against Serbia. Pourtalès retorted that the men responsible were 'those who had encouraged the Tsar to mobilise against us.' To this accusation, Sazonov replied with a question: 'What could I as Minister of Foreign Affairs have done, when the War Minister [Sukhomlinov] explained to the Tsar, that the mobilisation was necessary?' Pourtalès replied that it was precisely Sazonov's job, as foreign minister, 'knowing from [our] previous negotiations what would necessarily be the consequences of this mobilisation . . . to restrain the Tsar from this fateful step.' Had Pourtalès known that it was Sazonov himself who – deputised by Sukhomlinov and Yanushkevitch – had convinced the tsar to mobilise, he would have been angrier still.

However the historic exchange at Chorister's Bridge really ended, Pourtalès asked for his passports as soon as it was finished. He was to leave Petersburg at eight AM.[48] Sazonov wired the news of the declaration of war immediately to his ambassadors and then went to dine with Buchanan and Paléologue. Once everyone knew that Germany had declared war, the kaiser's last telegram could only appear to be a deliberate provocation. Bethmann had handed France and Russia another diplomatic gift.

B ACK IN CHARLOTTENBURG, oblivious to what was happening in Petersburg, Kaiser Wilhelm was in a euphoric mood. After relaxing for a bit with his family in the garden, he retired to bed. Scarcely had the kaiser nodded off when he was awakened with an urgent telegram from King George V (although

Grey was its real author). 'In answer to your telegram just received,' it read,

> I THINK THERE MUST BE SOME MISUNDERSTANDING AS TO
> A SUGGESTION THAT PASSED IN FRIENDLY CONVERSATION
> BETWEEN PRINCE LICHNOWSKY AND SIR EDWARD GREY THIS
> AFTERNOON WHEN THEY WERE DISCUSSING HOW ACTUAL FIGHT-
> ING BETWEEN GERMAN AND FRENCH ARMIES MIGHT BE AVOIDED
> WHILE THERE IS STILL A CHANCE OF SOME AGREEMENT BETWEEN
> AUSTRIA AND RUSSIA. [49]

Misunderstanding there certainly had been – but not on Lichnowsky's part. Sir Edward Grey had indeed made both neutrality offers during the day. Remarkably, he had even told the French ambassador, Paul Cambon, of his first one, and forwarded it to Sir Francis Bertie in Paris, where the suggestion that (as Bertie interpreted Grey's proposal on reading it through carefully) Britain would 'remain neutral so long as German troops remain on defensive and do not cross French frontier, and French abstain from crossing German frontier' was received with even more astonishment than in Berlin (although it was not happy astonishment).[50] Grey himself was astonished when, summoned to Buckingham Palace at eight PM, he read the kaiser's cable from Berlin. He had not really thought through what it meant to 'guarantee the passivity of France' – namely, to pledge the British army and navy to uphold French neutrality, even while Germany went to war with France's closest ally. 'There must have been some misunderstanding' was Grey's way of disclaiming his own proposals once he realised how foolish they were.*

---

* Lichnowsky, who was close to Sir Edward Grey, later defended his friend's reputation by playing along with the idea that he had misunderstood him. But Grey's two dispatches to Sir Francis Bertie in Paris, both dated 1 August 1914, give the lie to both men. Grey may not have been in his right mind Saturday, but he did say what he said.

The kaiser's heart was broken by this terse telegram from his cousin. The longed-for British olive branch had been withdrawn. Although rousing himself to send the summons to Moltke, he had not dressed but simply thrown a coat over his pajamas. It was in this disheveled state that the all-highest warlord received his chief of staff shortly after eleven PM. Moltke, expecting to be given another impossible, halt-the-mobilisation order, was instead handed the telegram from Buckingham Palace. 'Now you can do what you want' was all the kaiser could say. Moltke, relieved, 'drove home at once and telegraphed to the Sixteenth Division that the invasion of Luxembourg was to proceed.'[51] Germany had declared war on Russia first, but it was her war against France that would now begin.

23

Britain Wakes Up
to the Danger

SUNDAY, 2 AUGUST

A FTER THE KAISER WENT TO BED, his advisers huddled to discuss what to do next. In the evening drama over Grey's neutrality offer, Russia had nearly been forgotten. Pourtalès had been instructed to deliver Germany's declaration of war at five PM. Nine hours later, no news had been received from Petersburg. Was Germany at war with Russia, or not? No one knew. And as Bethmann argued, the strange thing was that if she were not at war with Russia, she could hardly justify going to war with France. Falkenhayn dismissed this as twaddle, arguing that 'the war was there after all and the question of a declaration of war on France was of no account.' Moltke agreed: 'The war was there, and that was that.' Still, Bethmann would not budge. He would not allow Germany's war with France to proceed, declared or otherwise, until he had 'some confirmation under international law' that she was at war with Russia.

At this Moltke grew angry. The Russians had mobilised first, he reminded Bethmann; shots had been fired on the East Prussian border; there was obviously a war, whether or not

Germany had declared it. A 'violent scene' ensued, Tirpitz recalled, 'followed by mutual apologies for loss of temper.' The chancellor finally conceded that, if the Russians had indeed fired first, then the case was 'clear, that means the Russians have been the first to start and I shall have the declaration of war [on Russia] handed over the frontier by the nearest General.' One might think this was unnecessary, considering that a declaration of war had already been sent to St Petersburg. Yet Bethmann did not know whether Pourtalès had handed it to Sazonov. He needed legal proof.[1]

The argument, arcane on the surface, was fundamental. With impeccable German logic, Bethmann insisted that war could not begin until a declaration was made. After all, it said so in the Geneva Convention of 1907. France or Russia might sneakily start a war without declaring one, but Germany was too honest for that. Moltke and Falkenhayn, by contrast, worried only about getting the war underway as smoothly as possible. War was war; declarations were superfluous and possibly counterproductive. It did not occur to any of the three men that the diplomatic-strategic question of the hour – and of subsequent history – was: Which side appeared to be starting the war?

The only man thinking clearly was Tirpitz. This owed a great deal to the nature of his job. Moltke and Falkenhayn thought of England as a country capable of sending a small handful of divisions to France – barely enough to slow down the German armies. The chief of Naval Staff, by contrast, was obsessed with the question of British belligerence, because the British fleet was his principal strategic adversary. Even now that it was too late, Tirpitz objected that he did not understand 'why the declaration of war on Russia had been published before [German] mobilisation.' He could also 'see no use in launching the declaration of war on France before we actually marched into France.' Above all, he did not understand why the war plan required the German army to march through neutral Belgium. Moltke replied 'that there was no other way open, we must go through with it.' In that case, Tirpitz informed everyone, 'we must at once reckon on war with England.' At least, he pleaded, Germany must postpone the declaration of war on Belgium so as to delay British mobilisation.

By this point, Bethmann seemed to have lost the plot. Tirpitz, who was listening to the proceedings with mounting concern, recalled a scene bordering on farce. Herr Kriege, head of the legal department of the Foreign Office, was furiously raising objections to the invasion of Belgium, only to be 'sharply snubbed' by Moltke. Bethmann seemed barely to be listening anymore; it appeared to Tirpitz that the 'reins have slipped entirely out of the Imperial Chancellor's hands.' Bethmann, Tirpitz surmised from the look on the chancellor's face, must either have had 'no previous knowledge about the march through Belgium, or had tried [but failed] to prevent it.'* Someone then pointed out, as if in passing, that Austria had still not promised to 'take the field with us against Russia' – rather a large oversight. Nor had Italy, a military ally since 1882, been informed that Germany had declared war on Russia. Nor had Romania, another country with which Germany had a mutual defence alliance. When they learned this, Moltke and Falkenhayn were 'horrified.' Tirpitz's lasting impression from this historic night was that Germany's 'political leadership has completely lost its head.'[2]

In one area, at least, the Germans were thinking ahead. After learning from reports at four AM and six AM that Russian troops had crossed the border into East Prussia, Bethmann

---

* While Bethmann knew in a general sense about the planned march through Belgium, it is true that he learned of the M + 3 assault on Liège only on Friday, 31 July.

was able to confirm to the kaiser, the German public (via a press communiqué), Vienna, and Rome that 'an actual state of war' existed with Russia. Getting Austria to back Germany by declaring war should not have been difficult (although, owing to Conrad's unwillingness to abandon Plan B focused on Serbia, Austria did not do so for another four days). No one in Berlin knew it yet, but Italy was a lost cause even before Bethmann and Jagow had given her leeway to wiggle out by declaring war on Russia first. Romania, too, was not likely to join in.

With Ottoman Turkey, at least, there were grounds for hope. Back on 22 July, just before Austria's ultimatum had been delivered in Belgrade, Enver Pasha, the Ottoman war minister, had proposed an outright military alliance to the German ambassador, Hans von Wangenheim – only for Wangenheim to turn down the idea. Kaiser Wilhelm II, on learning this, had thoroughly rebuked Wangenheim and ordered alliance talks to be resumed. By Friday night, 31 July, negotiations had proceeded to the point where Bethmann asked Wangenheim whether Turkey was prepared to 'undertake some action worthy of the name against Russia.' On Saturday at two thirty PM, after Russia's ultimatum to demobilise had expired, Bethmann, desperate, had given up his last reservations about taking on Turkey, wiring Wangenheim that he was authorised to sign an alliance treaty so long as Germany's military attaché, Liman von Sanders, assured him that the Turkish army was battle-ready.[3] Wangenheim was also thinking along these lines, proposing at the same time – in a wire that crossed with the chancellor's – that Germany send her one Mediterranean dreadnought, the SMS *Goeben*, to Constantinople. Once through the Straits, he informed Bethmann, it might protect both Bulgaria and the Bosphorus from Russian amphibious operations, while securing the underwater cable line linking Germany and Austria to Constantinople (by way of Romania) against Russian sabotage. It might also help push Turkey into the war.[4]

Now that the war with Russia was on, Germany needed all the help she could get, and Turkey – sharing borders with both Russia and British Egypt – was ideally placed to give it. At four PM on Sunday, 2 August, Wangenheim and the Ottoman grand vizier, Said Halim Pasha, signed a secret alliance treaty valid until the end of 1918, under which Germany pledged to defend Ottoman territory in exchange for a Turkish engagement to declare war on Russia if she attacked Germany, according to the same *casus foederis* that applied to Austria-Hungary. It was not as great a coup as British neutrality would have been, but it was something.*

MEANWHILE THE GEARS of Germany's mobilisation were cranking methodically into motion. Shortly after midnight on Sunday, 2 August, German troops had entered Luxembourg over the bridges at Wasserbillig and Remich. They proceeded to secure the principal rail lines, which were, by treaty, under German management. No resistance was offered, although Prime Minister Paul Eyschen of Luxembourg wired a formal protest to Berlin at eight AM Sunday. A series of telegrams was now dispatched from the Wilhelmstrasse to Paris, London, and the Hague, explaining the action as a precautionary measure 'to secure the railways under our management from French attack.' To Eyschen, the Germans further claimed that they had reports of hostile French manoeuvres on Luxembourg's soil (he swiftly denied that this was true, as it was not). Berlin even requested that France's minister to

---

* So incompetent was German diplomacy that this treaty was invalid even before Wangenheim signed it. Because Germany had declared war on Russia (and not the other way around), the *casus foederis* did not, technically, apply to *any* of her allies, not even Austria-Hungary. The clever Ottoman grand vizier, it seems, knew this: Turkey did not declare war on Russia until months later, despite furious protests from Berlin.

Luxembourg be expelled. Eyschen complied, although clearly under duress.[5]

On the French-German frontier between Strasbourg and Metz, the situation remained murky. Both Joffre and Moltke, with an eye on London, had issued orders that troops were not to cross the frontier or fire first, but rumours were running rife about border incidents. The French embassy in London, for example, protested to Grey that '20,000 German troops have invaded France near Nancy.'[6] The Germans, for their part, reported that French aircraft were bombing 'the environs of Nuremberg,' that a French cavalry patrol had crossed the frontier, that two French saboteurs had been caught trying to blow up a tunnel, and that a French pilot had been shot down on German territory.[7] Almost none of these reports was true.

Even if they had been true, they likely would not have swayed British opinion decisively. In the cabinet, all eyes were fixed on the Belgian frontier, which German troops might, or might not, cross en route for France.* Belgium's own army had already begun mobilising three days earlier, as if in defiance of all the powers. By Friday, the Meuse bridges had been wired for destruction; by Saturday, the fortress city of Liège had been armed, and the eastern viaducts and tunnels, facing German Trier and Aachen, were wired for demolition. While Belgium's mobilisation was theoretically a 'call-up without deployment,' targeting neither France nor Germany, reports that the Germans had invaded Luxembourg, which reached the Belgian foreign ministry at six AM Sunday, were alarming. Germany's minister in

---

* In a sense, it was curious that no one in London seemed much exercised by the violation of Luxembourg's neutrality, guaranteed by a treaty also signed in London in 1867. But then Luxembourg was tiny and landlocked, whereas Belgium was Britain's main continental buffer along the English Channel. Sentiment and sympathy there might have been regarding the Grand Duchy of Luxembourg, but not national interest.

Brussels, Klaus von Below-Selaske, was asked for an explanation. His answer was not entirely reassuring: 'Your neighbour's roof may catch fire but your own house will be safe.'[8]

Non-interventionists in England keenly hoped that this would remain true. Despite the dramatic events of the past few days, many Britons remained complacent on Sunday morning, happy in their ignorance. Owing largely to Sir George Buchanan's lazy reporting from St Petersburg, the picture even cabinet insiders had of events in Europe was murky and incomplete. True, Buchanan had wasted no time reporting Germany's declaration of war on Saturday night, but he had neglected to mention that Russia had provoked this by ordering general mobilisation on Thursday (and the Period Preparatory to War five days before that). The French, too, were deliberately misinforming London about such matters as the ten-kilometre withdrawal. On Saturday, Poincaré had gone so far as to tell Sir Francis Bertie, in what was almost certainly a conscious lie, that 'the Emperor of Russia did not order a general mobilisation until after a decree of general mobilisation had been issued in Austria' (in fact, Russia's had preceded Austria's by twenty hours; her mobilisation against Austria herself had preceded Austria's general mobilisation by *three days*).[9] With such a distorted picture of events, it is understandable that no firm policy had been decided on in London.

Yet, in light of the successful French and Russian manipulation of British opinion, the cabinet, surprisingly, was still leaning against intervention. As Prime Minister Asquith wrote on Sunday morning, 'a good 3/4 of our party are for absolute non-interference at any price.' Grey confronted one Liberal MP and demanded what he would do if Germany invaded Belgium. 'She won't do it,' was the reply. Grey: 'I don't suppose she will, but supposing she does.' 'She won't do it,' came again the reply, like a metronome. Preoccupied with Ireland, ill-informed about events on the Continent, most Liberals did not want to hear about obligations to France, much less to Russia. Even Asquith, despite his Francophile sympathies, assured the German ambassador on Sunday morning that, although much would depend on what happened in Belgium, 'we had no desire to intervene.'[10]

At the same time, Paul Cambon was meeting with Sir Edward Grey. Presenting a report from Viviani of the German invasion of Luxembourg, the ambassador demanded that Grey use this in the cabinet to make a case for intervention. To his disappointment, not even this news could sway His Majesty's foreign secretary. The integrity of Luxembourg, Grey argued, was upheld 'collectively' by the powers in the Treaty of London of 1867, whereas England had guaranteed Belgium 'severally and individually' in the 1839 treaty. So the cases were different. After hearing Grey's latest elliptical sophistry, Cambon unburdened himself to Henry Wickham Steed, the foreign editor of the London *Times*: 'I do not know whether this evening the word "honour" will not have to be struck out of the English vocabulary.'[11]

As if channelling the French ambassador, the Conservative opposition goaded the Liberal cabinet in a similar manner Sunday morning. Bonar Law, Unionist leader in the Commons, and Lord Landsdowne, on behalf of the Lords, issued a declaration that 'It would be fatal to the honour and security of the United Kingdom to hesitate in supporting France and Russia at this juncture.' As if to offer help, but with an obvious hint of menace in the direction of wavering cabinet Liberals, they added that 'we offer our unconditional support to the Government in any measures they may consider necessary for this object.'[12]

The cabinet was bitterly divided when it met at eleven AM. The sense of occasion was tremendous. If meeting on Saturday was rare, convening on a Sunday was almost unheard of; no one could even remember the last time it was done. With Germany and Russia at war, and France and Germany poised on the knife's edge, it seemed imperative to declare a policy of some kind. And yet Asquith knew that there was 'a strong party . . . against any kind of intervention in any event,' led by Lord Morley's Little Englander faction and the Right Honourable John Burns, president of the Board of Trade. Lloyd George, the chancellor of the Exchequer, was still wavering, although he seemed to be leaning towards Morley's faction. On the other side, Churchill was poised to resign if the cabinet dithered any longer, with Bonar Law and the Conservatives cheering him on from the sidelines, ready to form a new government if this one fell. 'We are on the brink of a split,' Asquith would write after the midday session.[13] Churchill himself was convinced the government would fall, with a majority resigning over any nudge in the direction of intervention. 'The grief and horror of so many able colleagues,' he recalled, 'were painful to witness.'[14]

To postpone an open breach, Grey made his case as gingerly as possible. He denounced the hypocrisy of the Central Powers, which had foiled his mediation efforts (the lack of positive responses to them from France or Russia was not mentioned) and 'marched steadily to war.' Grey avoided, as he had all week, any discussion of Russia's secret early military preparations or of the fact that St Petersburg had been the first power to mobilise (if he had believed Bertie's Saturday report, Grey may have erroneously thought the Austrians had mobilised first). He reminded his colleagues that, owing to joint agreements with Paris, France's navy was concentrated in the Mediterranean, with the British fleet covering the Channel. The French had, in effect, left their northwestern coast undefended against the Germans. When these agreements had been negotiated by Grey and Cambon in 1912, Morley and the Little Englanders had insisted that this engagement was not 'based

on any agreement to cooperate in war.' Now they realised –
as, surely, they should have known all along – that this was
precisely what the agreements had intended to bring about. For
what was the purpose of dividing the oceans into spheres of
naval coverage if not to ensure cooperation in wartime? At last,
Grey had found the issue on which to make or break the cabinet. 'If the Channel is closed against Germany,' he argued, 'it
is in favour of France, & we cannot take half measures – either
we must declare ourselves neutral, or in it.' If it was neutrality,
then Grey would resign; if not, then he expected other resignations. He therefore 'asked for a sharp decision.'[15]

He did not quite get it. Around two PM, just as everyone
was getting hungry, the cabinet agreed on a compromise that
would allow it to adjourn for lunch. Even Morley was forced to
admit that 'we owed it to France' to defend the Channel. And
so Grey was authorised to tell Paul Cambon that 'if the German
fleet comes into the Channel or through the North Sea to undertake hostile action against French coasts or shipping, the British
fleet will give all the protection in its power.' The statement
was conditional enough not to break up the cabinet, although
it did prompt one resignation. With what Morley described
as 'remarkable energy, force, and grasp,' Burns of the Board
of Trade insisted that a guarantee to defend the French coast
was 'neither more nor less than a challenge to Germany, tantamount to a declaration of war against her.'[16] This, indeed, was
the French ambassador's own interpretation of Grey's statement. As Cambon wired to Paris: 'in truth a great country does
not wage war by halves. Once it decided to fight the war at sea
it would necessarily be led into fighting it on land as well.'[17]

The true implications began to sink in among the remaining non-interventionists over lunch. Lord Morley dined with
Lloyd George and Sir John Simon, the attorney general. The
overall sentiment, Morley recalled, was that 'Burns was right':

the cabinet 'was being rather artfully drawn on step by step to war for the benefit of France and Russia.' Together, the men agreed to make a stronger stand when the cabinet reconvened at six thirty PM. Burns, having agreed at Asquith's insistence to attend despite his resignation, would strengthen their hand.[18]

Despite growing opposition, Asquith and Grey did not back down. Having already won everyone but Burns over to a naval commitment to defend the French coastline, they now pressed for armed intervention if the Germans violated Belgian neutrality. To keep the waverers on board, Grey agreed to make the case for belligerence in the Commons on Monday only if the Germans committed a 'substantial violation' of Belgium, not merely a crossing of the small corner of Belgian territory that abutted Luxembourg. Implied, although not directly stated, was that Britain would intervene only if the Belgians themselves offered resistance to a German invasion. As Asquith put it, Britain could hardly be 'more Belgian than the Belgians,' going to war with Germany if Brussels did not.[19]

Opinion was far from unanimous. Morley threatened to follow Burns and resign. Sir John Simon complained that 'the Triple Entente was a terrible mistake. Why should we support a country like Russia?' To Grey's warning that France would be overwhelmed if Britain stayed out, Lloyd George retorted, 'How will you feel if you see Germany overrun and annihilated by Russia?'[20] As the cabinet broke up for the evening, the government seemed ready to fall. British belligerence hung by a thread.

E VEN AS THE BRITISH CABINET was debating what to do in case the Germans violated Belgium, Klaus von Below-Selaske was en route for the Belgian Foreign Ministry to propose that she do so. At 2:05 PM, Jagow had wired, ordering him to open the sealed envelope sent to him several days previously.

Dressed up with specious warnings that the French were preparing to attack Germany by way of the Meuse River valley,
the note demanded that Belgium answer within twelve hours
– by 8 AM Monday – whether she would resist the movement
of German troops through her territory. While 'intending no
acts of hostility towards Belgium,' and promising to evacuate
her territory 'as soon as peace is concluded,' the note stipulated
that, if opposition were encountered, it would be met by force.[21]
The ruse was transparent. It was an ultimatum.

The Belgian cabinet met at nine PM, presided over by King
Albert himself. It faced a dreadful dilemma. Submitting to the
German ultimatum would forfeit national honour. And yet
Belgium had but six infantry and one cavalry divisions to face
the might of Germany – possibly as much as several dozen
divisions. Of course, once the Germans invaded, Belgium might
count on French and possibly British aid, but this would likely
come too late to affect the outcome. King Albert was himself
convinced that 'our answer must be "no," whatever the consequences. Our duty is to defend our territorial integrity.' But he
realised that a hostile German invasion would bring devasta-
tion upon his people. It was hardly the kind of decision one
wanted to rush into. At ten PM, most cabinet members were
dismissed and the military chiefs called in for their input. While
there remained considerable debate over the plan of deployment, opinion on the ultimatum was unanimous: the answer
could only be no.[22]

At midnight, the ministers dispersed, and a drafting committee set to work on the reply. Below-Selaske, desperate for
news, showed up at the Foreign Ministry at one thirty AM,
reporting that the French army had crossed the German frontier
'in a breach of international law' (that is, before war had been
declared; the Germans were fanatics on this point).[23] As French
troops had reportedly crossed German, not Belgian, territory,

Below-Selaske's complaint was dismissed as irrelevant. It was obvious that the German simply wanted an answer on which way the Belgians would go. At two thirty AM, the final text of the reply was approved. The 'infringement of [Belgium's] independence with which the German Government threatens her,' the note declared, 'would constitute a flagrant violation of international law. No strategic interest justifies such a breach of law. Were it to accept the proposals laid before it, the Belgian Government would sacrifice the nation's honour while being false to its duties towards Europe.' While expressing a hope that the Germans might change their minds, the note concluded that, 'if this hope were disappointed, the Belgian Government is firmly resolved to repel every infringement of its rights by all the means in its power.'[24]

As everyone turned in on Sunday night, policymakers in Berlin, London, and Paris were awaiting news from Belgium with almost unbearable anxiety. By morning, they would have it.

24

Sir Edward Grey's Big Moment

MONDAY, 3 AUGUST

B Y MONDAY MORNING, news of the German ultimatum to Brussels had reached London, although it was not yet clear what Belgium's response had been. Bonar Law and Lord Landsdowne met with Asquith to reconfirm Conservative support for intervention. Public opinion seemed to be shifting in their direction. As Lloyd George recalled, 'the war had leapt in popularity between Saturday and Monday . . . the threatened invasion of Belgium had set the nation on fire from sea to sea.' The chancellor of the Exchequer, always adept at reading shifts in the popular mood, now came over to the war party.[1]

Not everyone felt the same way. Morley and Simon both sent Asquith resignation letters on Monday morning (although they did promise to attend that day's cabinet). Even Sir Edward Grey seemed to be having cold feet. Scheduled to address the Commons in the afternoon, he had stayed up late the night before, jotting down notes for his speech. When he arrived at the Foreign Office around ten AM, the German ambassador was waiting for him, desperate for news on which way Britain would go. Grey was almost apologetic, leaving Lichnowsky with the impression that, although Britain would 'not be able to regard the violation of Belgian neutrality calmly,' he, personally, 'would like, if at all possible, to remain neutral.' Lichnowsky, hoping to give Grey grounds for doing so, promised that Germany, 'even in the event of a conflict with Belgium . . . would maintain the integrity of Belgian territory,' and that, providing England stayed neutral, the German fleet would not attack France's northern coastline. Grey listened politely but promised nothing.[2]

When the cabinet met at eleven AM, the very gravity of the moment did much to dissolve the bitterness of the weekend. Everyone knew that Grey was going to address the Commons at three PM, and everyone knew, more or less, what he would say about Britain's obligations regarding Belgium. Burns had already gone; Morley and Simon were going, too. Now, the first commissioner of works, Lord William Beauchamp – 'Sweetheart,' as Asquith called him – announced that he, too, would resign.* Lloyd George, having switched sides, made a 'strong appeal' to the waverers 'not to go, or at least to delay it.' It was, Asquith wrote after the session, 'a rather moving scene in which everyone all round said something.'[3]

Ordinarily, a wave of resignations like this would be enough to sink a government, but with a European war on the immediate horizon, they had the opposite effect, convincing the remaining ministers to stand firm. With the deck cleared of the most vociferous non-interventionists, the cabinet at last approved Churchill's previous, unauthorised mobilisation of the British fleet. When news arrived confirming the German

---

* Lord Beauchamp's homosexuality was an open secret. He is believed to have been the model for Lord Marchmain in Evelyn Waugh's *Brideshead Revisited*.

ultimatum, and that 'Belgium has refused categorically,' Asquith (in his temporary role as secretary of state for war) ordered the army to mobilise, too. Most important, Grey was authorised to tell the Commons that afternoon that Britain would defend the French coast against German attack and that she would take action if Germany invaded Belgium. Simon and Beauchamp, overwhelmed with emotion, withdrew their resignations (although Morley did not). Even Morley agreed to 'say nothing today,' to attend the Commons debate, and not to walk out in protest when His Majesty's foreign secretary made his case. At two PM, the cabinet broke up to give everyone time to dine and to allow Grey to gather his energy for his speech.[4]

Anticipation for the big event had been building all day. Since 1871, the first Monday in August had been a bank holiday in England. Most years, this meant the city would be empty, with vacationers staying away for a third day. But with the cabinet in constant session owing to the war crisis, the tourist traffic had reversed course. Masses had descended on London, keen for news. The weather remained superb, so even in the city people were enjoying the outdoors. By afternoon, the crowd of pedestrians in Westminster, Lloyd George recalled, 'was so dense that no car could drive through it.' 'Had it not been for police assistance,' he wrote, 'we could not have walked a yard on our way.'[5]

By three PM, the House of Commons was 'crowded to the roof and tense with doubt and dreadful expectation,' the historian G. M. Trevelyan recalled. For the first time since 1893, every member was in attendance. The diplomatic gallery was packed (although Lichnowsky was not there). So many visitors wanted to witness history that extra chairs had to be brought into the gangway. All eyes were on Sir Edward Grey as he rose to speak – especially those of Ambassadors Benckendorff and Cambon, desperate to learn at last whether England would join Russia and France. The endless crisis meetings had taken a severe toll on Grey, who was normally accustomed to regaining his strength in the country each weekend. To those close enough to see his face, he looked 'pale, haggard, and worn.'[6] In Grey's own recollection of the moment in his memoirs, he strikes an oddly passive note, as if he were merely submitting to fate rather than shaping world-historical events: 'I do not recall feeling nervous. At such a moment there could neither be hope of personal success nor fear of personal failure. In a great crisis, a man who has to act or speak stands bare and stripped of choice. He has to do what it is in him to do; just this is what he will and must do, and can do no other.'[7] Grey's elliptical manner of speaking, his inability to simply come out and say what he meant, had long infuriated ambassadors trying to tease out an understanding of British policy. This speech would be no different.

'It has not been possible to secure the peace of Europe,' he began, characteristically using indirect language, but he did not 'want to dwell on that.' To allay suspicions that he had secretly committed Britain to fight, Grey stated that he had 'given no promise of anything more than diplomatic support' (to *whom* this promise of diplomatic support had been given, Grey did not say). Grey did share with the House a letter he had written to Ambassador Cambon in November 1912, relating to the disposition of the British and French fleets, but he insisted that, read literally, it did not constitute 'an engagement to co-operate in war.' As to the Franco-Russian alliance, Grey insisted that 'we are not parties' to it and that 'we do not even know the terms of that Alliance.' After a half hour of this aimless, uninformative meandering, members of the House could have been forgiven for wondering why Grey was addressing them at all.

At last Grey came to the point – or so it seemed. 'For many years,' he remarked as if stating an unremarkable fact, 'we have had a long-standing friendship with France.' ('And with

Germany!' one MP was heard to shout.) As if discouraged by this protest from the back benches, Grey started backing down again. 'But how far that friendship entails obligation,' he continued, 'let every man look into his own heart, and his own feelings. . . . I construe it myself as I feel it, but I do not wish to urge upon anyone else more than their feelings dictate as to what they should feel about this obligation.'

Grey then explained his own 'feelings' as to what Britain owed France. Because of the concentration of the French fleet in the Mediterranean – a concentration owing, Grey explained as elliptically as possible, to 'the feeling of confidence and friendship which has existed between [our] two countries' – 'the French coasts are absolutely undefended.' As if stating a hypothetical, Grey explained that his own 'feeling is that if a foreign fleet engaged in a war which France had not sought, and in which she had not been the aggressor, came down the English Channel and bombarded and battered the undefended coasts of France, we could not stand aside.' Expanding the hypothetical, Grey offered that if Britain *did* stand aside, France would be forced to withdraw her fleet from the Mediterranean, which would leave Britain's weak squadron there exposed to attack from Italy, in case she abandoned her current posture of neutrality and joined the Central Powers. This, he informed the House with something less than great conviction, would disturb 'our trade routes in the Mediterranean.' As if to undermine his own argument, Grey now revealed that Germany's ambassador had assured him that 'if we would pledge ourselves to neutrality, [Germany would] agree that its Fleet would not attack the Northern coast of France.' At this stage, Grey's case for intervention rested on a naval attack on France's channel coast that the Germans had expressly promised not to carry out if England remained neutral and a far-fetched hypothetical involving an Italian threat to Britain's Mediterranean shipping interests. Little wonder that Lord Derby, an interventionist Tory, was heard whispering angrily, 'By God, they are going to desert Belgium!'

Just when it seemed that Grey had lost his line of thought, he gathered himself for a final push. He had avoided mentioning Belgium for more than an hour. Now, as if revealing a trump, he did. After reading out France's positive reply to his question about respecting Belgian neutrality, along with Germany's evasive one, Grey finally dropped his bombshell: Germany had issued an ultimatum to Brussels the previous night. Even this news, he confessed, was unconfirmed ('I am not yet quite sure how far it has reached me in an accurate form'). 'We have great and vital interests,' Grey now stirred himself to declare, 'in the independence – and integrity is the least part – of Belgium.' At last finding his voice, Grey channeled Gladstone, the great moralist, who had asked regarding a violation of Belgium by a European power whether Britain 'would quietly stand by and witness the perpetration of the direst crime that ever stained the pages of history, and thus become participators in the sin.' True, Gladstone was discussing a hypothetical, but it now appeared that it was about to become real. And if Belgium fell and France were 'beaten to her knees,' Grey predicted, 'the independence of Holland will follow,' followed by Denmark: before long, Germany would dominate the entire Channel coastline and have England at her mercy. In an ill-judged prophecy, Grey argued that 'we are going to suffer, I am afraid, terribly in this war, whether we are in it or whether we stand aside.' If Britain did stand aside, forfeiting her 'Belgian Treaty obligations,' then she would 'sacrifice our respect and good name and reputation before the world.'

After listening to Grey in 'painful absorption' for nearly an hour and a half, the Commons, one eyewitness recalled, 'broke into overwhelming applause, signifying its answer.'[8] Grey had carried the day.

He had not, however, won over everyone. Trevelyan, disappointed, complained that Grey had given 'not a single argument why we should support France' – as, indeed, he had not. Nor had there been any mention of Russia's secret early war preparations, nor of her having been the first power to mobilise – these revelations, of course, had not reached Grey himself, owing to French and Russian deception and his own incuriosity. Strangest of all, considering the aim of his speech, Grey, despite alluding to the German ultimatum to Brussels delivered the previous night, had not noted that Belgium had already refused it and vowed to fight – although this had been confirmed by Britain's minister to Belgium in a wire received by the Foreign Office at 10:55 AM.* Considering how much was riding on his speech – and that his meandering remarks went on for 90 minutes – it is astonishing how much Grey did *not* mention. Small wonder that the Labour Party registered dissent with Grey's case for intervention. Grey's own party had similar reservations. No fewer than 28 dissident Liberals met in the lobby to adopt a resolution stating that he had failed to make the case for war.[9]

Nor did Grey succeed in convincing Germany that Britain meant war. Not wanting to provide a focal point for the interventionists, Lichnowsky had not attended the Commons. Having digested only the highlights from Grey's remarks, he reported to Jagow on Monday night that, 'although the speech is marked by a deep distrust of our political intentions, one can nevertheless gather from it that the British Government has in all probability no immediate intention of taking part

---

* In his memoirs, Grey claims that he received the report 'after the speech was over.' If so, this suggests appalling incompetence in the Foreign Office. If Grey was making a case for intervention, the latest report from Brussels should have been the keynote of his speech.

in the conflict or of abandoning the neutrality she has so far observed.' Lichnowsky noted that he had already defused Grey's concerns about a German attack on France's channel coastline, and that even regarding Belgium, all that Grey had made clear was that 'England would oppose any encroachment on Belgian territory or sovereignty.' Overall, he concluded, 'we can regard the speech as satisfactory. . . . I am convinced that the British Government will strive to remain neutral.'[10] If Lichnowsky's optimistic interpretation proved true, it would be welcome news in Berlin. But then one could never really tell with Grey. Until he actually spelled it out clearly, British policy would remain an enigma.

A FTER RECEIVING TWO DAYS of reports of border violations by French troops – most, though not all of which, were exaggerated or untrue – Bethmann had instructed Baron Schoen to hand Viviani a declaration of war at six PM. In the event, Schoen arrived at the Quai d'Orsay nearly an hour late, owing both to difficulties in deciphering his instructions from Berlin and to his car being attacked en route by two French patriots (whereupon he was provided an escort by the Paris police). At seven PM on Monday, 3 August, Schoen solemnly handed Viviani a note declaring that, in response to various violations of the German border by French troops, 'the German Empire considers itself in a state of war with France.'*[11] He then asked for his passports and left Paris by train. In Berlin, Jules Cambon was given his passports later Monday night and sent home by

---

* In Jagow's instructions, Schoen was to mention that a French pilot had been shot down over Germany, which was true. Owing to transmission difficulties (or to French jamming?), this part did not come through, and the incidents Schoen cited were mostly false.

way of Denmark (and made, insultingly, to pay the fare of the special train, although the Germans later refunded his money via the Spanish embassy). France and Germany were at war.

Disputed border incidents aside, the real reason for the timing of Germany's declaration of war was that German troops were scheduled to cross into Belgium first thing Tuesday morning, to secure the rail junction at Liège. It was the latest German blunder, brought about by the rigid structure of Moltke's mobilisation plan, which, as one military historian pointed out, required forcing 'more than 600,000 men through the narrow aperture of Liège.'*[12] Although France's own concentration on the frontier was far more advanced than the Germans – the first battles on the Alsatian front would all be fought on German, not French soil – Bethmann had again declared war first. This was hardly the way to impress the British.

Back in London, despite a general sense that the public was getting behind the war, the outlook was far from clear. Histories generally record that something dramatic was decided by Grey's Monday speech in the Commons, although it is hard to determine precisely what this was. When Churchill saw Grey after his speech, he asked 'what happens now?' Grey told him that an ultimatum would be dispatched to Berlin, warning the Germans not to violate Belgian neutrality (this was something he had conspicuously failed to mention to Parliament).[13] To France's ambassador, Grey gave the same assurance, along with a promise that the British fleet would defend the French coast from German attack. And yet when the cabinet met at six PM, no ultimatum to Berlin was drafted. Nor did Grey summon

---

* The lightning strike on Liège on M + 3 was Moltke's own idea. It was meant to clear a path for the right wing and obviate the need to cross Dutch territory, as in Schlieffen's conception. Considering the consequences, it was arguably Moltke's single greatest mistake.

Lichnowsky to brief him. The only 'warning' that the cabinet authorised was a telegram to Sir Edward Goschen, who was to inform Berlin that 'His Majesty's Government are bound to protest against this violation of a treaty to which Germany is a party in common with themselves, and must respect an assurance that the demand made upon Belgium *will not be proceeded with*, and that her neutrality will be respected by Germany.' Even this toothless protest, containing not even a hint of armed intervention, was sent off only on Tuesday morning.[14] If Grey had – supposedly – won over the Commons to belligerence on Monday, he had not yet won over himself.

Sir Edward Grey had always been more prone to reflection than to action. Having failed all week to exert the slightest influence on events in Europe, he was in no hurry to do so now. He remained lost in his thoughts after he returned to his office in Whitehall. Watching, with his failing eyes, the lamps being lit in St James Park, Grey was heard to remark that 'the lamps are going out all over Europe; we shall not see them again in our lifetime.'[15]

25

World War:
No Going Back

TUESDAY, 4 AUGUST

A T 8:02 AM, THE FIRST GERMAN UNITS, in field grey, rolled across the Belgian frontier at Gemmenich. In Berlin, Moltke was still half-hoping the Belgians would mount a token defence for honour and then agree to terms. Instead, as soon as he learned that German troops had crossed the border, King Albert rode his horse to Parliament and opened the historic session at eleven AM, wearing not his regalia but a simple field uniform. He asked the deputies whether they wished 'to maintain intact the sacred gift of our forefathers.' The reply was unanimous. Belgium would fight.[1] The German force, consisting of six infantry brigades and three cavalry divisions, was tasked with seizing Liège, some 50 kilometres (30 miles) away, in a lightning assault. Considering that German intelligence had learned as early as Saturday that Liège was mobilised and ready, and that a new estimate prepared on Monday reported that the Belgian army had sent reinforcements to the town, it is surprising that Moltke did not call off the attack. Not unlike Chancellor Bethmann pursuing his fait-accompli policy into diplomatic oblivion, the chief of Army Staff ignored warnings and plunged right in.

The assault on Liège was a fiasco. Although the Germans' mobile siege artillery scored hits on the main forts, none surrendered. The Belgians performed all planned demolitions, including those of the Meuse bridges, which the Germans had counted on capturing intact. The Germans, not expecting to meet such resistance, had not brought pontoons to bridge the river, and so they had to turn back. One infantry brigade made it into the town but was forced swiftly to retreat.[2] In a kind of strategic hari-kari, Moltke had insisted that – British opinion be damned – the first engagement of the war would be fought in neutral Belgium, two weeks before Germany's concentration against France would be complete, and the Germans had been routed by the Belgians anyway.

The wages of Moltke's folly were brought home almost immediately. Shortly after news of the German violation of Belgium arrived in London, the British cabinet met and had what Asquith called 'an interesting session.' We do not know exactly what was said in the Tuesday morning session – curiously, no summary was sent to the king, as was customary – but according to Asquith, the news from Belgium 'simplified matters.'[3] Everyone agreed to send an ultimatum to Berlin, although it was left up to Grey to formulate its exact terms. Citing the German ultimatum delivered to Brussels on Sunday, the fact that Germany had 'declined to give the same assurance respecting Belgium as France gave last week,' and not least the news that 'Belgian territory has been violated at Gemmenich,' Grey informed Sir Edward Goschen that he was to give the German government until midnight to reverse course and guarantee Belgian neutrality. Failing a satisfactory reply, Goschen was to ask for his passports. Grey's ultimatum was wired to Berlin at two PM, which meant that – given time for transmission, decoding, and delivery by Goschen to the Wilhelmstrasse – the Germans would have five or six hours to comply.[4]

Meanwhile, the war between France and Germany, although implied by the departures of ambassadors Schoen and Cambon, awaited ratification in both countries' parliaments. In Paris, Tuesday morning saw the public funeral of Jaurès. Although it was a fellow Frenchman who had felled the great Socialist orator, the memorial service served to rally opinion on the Left behind the government: it was as if Jaurès had been the first victim of the war. Léon Jouhaux, leader of the confederated French trade unions (CGT), spoke for 'all the working men' in declaring that 'we take the field with the determination to drive back the aggressor.'[5]

At three PM, the two houses of France's parliament met in joint session to debate the war – that is, whether to fund it by voting 'war credits.' President Poincaré addressed the deputies first, declaring that 'France has been the object of a brutal and premeditated aggression.' This was perhaps not literally true, as Germany's aggression consisted so far of mere *declarations* of war on France and Russia and a violation of Luxembourg and Belgium – not of France. Still, the fact that Germany had declared war on Paris first made 'self-defence' an easy sell. Viviani, following the president, claimed that the German army had crossed the French border at three points, and he denied German allegations that France had done the same. More helpfully, he informed the deputies that Italy had vowed neutrality, which would free up four French divisions from having to guard her southern borders. This revelation received the biggest ovation of the entire session. Neither Viviani nor Poincaré breathed a word about Russian mobilisation or its timing, insisting instead that Russia had continued negotiating up to the last minute. In the end Viviani, seeking to shore up support on the Left, staked out the case in moral terms, as a matter of 'right and liberty.' He implored the deputies, and the French people, 'to help us in bearing the burden of our heavy responsibility, the comfort of a clear conscience and the conviction that we have done our duty.'[6]

The applause was deafening. Both the Senate and the Chamber of Deputies voted unanimously for war credits – even the Socialists, who thereby abandoned pre-war pledges that they would prevent or sabotage a war by staging a general strike (an idea dear to the departed Jaurès). In this way France forged a *union sacrée*, or sacred union, in which all parties were united behind the war effort. As Poincaré recalled afterwards, 'Never has there been a spectacle as magnificent as that in which they have just participated. . . . In the memory of man, there has never been anything more beautiful in France.'[7]

The scene at the Reichstag in Berlin was just as dramatic when Bethmann Hollweg mounted the podium at three thirty to ask for war credits.* Waxing more lyrical than his counterparts in Paris, the chancellor declared that 'only in defence of a just cause shall our sword fly from its scabbard. . . . Russia has set fire to the building. We are at war with Russia and France – a war that has been forced upon us.' Stating the German case, he said that the aim all along had been localisation of the Austro-Serbian conflict, only for Russia to mobilise. Like Viviani and Poincaré, he omitted facts that complicated his case – Austria's unilateral declaration of war on Serbia, Germany's insincere forays at mediation until it was too late to force Austria to change course. Still, given the head start Russia had in mobilising against both Austria and Germany, it was not hard to convince the Reichstag that Russia had 'set

---

* Having not received Grey's ultimatum yet, Bethmann still harboured hope that he could make a case for a just, defensive war that might impress London.

fire to the building.' Nor, given France's own (although less dramatic) head start, were the deputies inclined to disagree when Bethmann asked them, 'Were we now to wait further in patience until the nations on either side of us chose the moment for their attack?' (At this there were 'loud cries of "No! No!" Acclamation.') To clinch the case for war with France, Bethmann invoked the 'ten kilometre' myth, noting that, despite the promise to hold back, French troops, cavalry patrols, and pilots had crossed the German border without declaring war, in a 'breach of international law.'

The most delicate part of Bethmann's presentation concerned Belgium. Here the case rested on the specious claim that 'France stood ready for an invasion' and that, owing to Germany being encircled, 'France could wait, we could not.' For this reason, Bethmann explained awkwardly, 'we were forced to ignore the rightful protests of the Governments of Luxembourg and Belgium.' In a stunning admission, Germany's chancellor admitted that the violation of Belgian territory was 'a breach of international law' – the same 'international law' he had just invoked to condemn French behaviour. Bethmann then went still further, promising that this 'wrong (*unrecht*) – I speak openly – the wrong we thereby commit we will try to make good as soon as our military aims have been attained.' To explain why Germany had been 'forced' to commit a wrong, Bethmann argued that 'he who is menaced as we are and is fighting for his highest values, can only consider how he is to hack his way through' (*sich durchhaut*). Although Tirpitz, for one, thought the brazen honesty of this confession of wrongdoing constituted 'the greatest blunder ever spoken by a German statesman,' the Reichstag deputies did not agree: they broke into 'great and repeated applause.'

Having made his way through the most difficult issue, the chancellor addressed the matter of British neutrality. Citing

Sir Edward Grey's speech before the Commons, Bethmann reiterated Lichnowsky's promise that the German fleet would not 'attack the northern coast of France, and that we will not violate the territorial integrity and independence of Belgium' – that is, in any post-war settlement. These assurances, the chancellor continued, 'I now repeat before the world.' He then concluded:

> now the great hour of trial has struck for our people. But with clear conviction we go forward to meet it. Our army is in the field, our navy is ready for battle – behind them stands the entire German nation – the entire German nation united down to the last man.

The applause was deafening. Amidst 'frantic applause and highest enthusiasm,' Reichstag party leaders rose as one to vote war credits – even Hugo Haase, on behalf of the Social Democrats.[8] Just as in France, Socialist internationalism had evaporated in a frenzy of patriotism.

On Bethmann's instructions, the passage in his speech addressed to Britain was wired immediately to Lichnowsky in London – en clair, so that the British could read it themselves.[9] Even now, the chancellor had not given up his dreams of reconciliation with England. True, Bethmann may not have been thinking clearly, as suggested by his desperate and self-indicting revelations before the Reichstag. Beaten down a week earlier when the folly of his fait-accompli policy first became apparent, the chancellor had given the appearance to Tirpitz of a 'drowning man.'[10]

The illusion was not all Bethmann's fault, however. His hopes for British neutrality had been encouraged all along by Grey, who had twice promised neutrality on Saturday and told Lichnowsky on Monday morning that Britain 'would like, if at all possible, to remain neutral.' Even after his supposedly decisive speech in the Commons on Monday afternoon, Grey's wire to Goschen Tuesday morning contained only a pro forma protest against Germany's violation of Belgian neutrality, giving no hint of armed intervention. One can hardly blame Bethmann for thinking that the British might, still, stay out.

After dithering for days, however, Sir Edward Grey had finally got his act together. As against his earlier vague or misleading communications with the Germans, the ultimatum he wired to Berlin at two PM on Tuesday contained no grounds for ambiguity. When Sir Edward Goschen arrived at the Wilhelmstrasse at seven PM, he informed Jagow calmly and clearly that, failing a German vow to disengage from Belgium by midnight, he would be forced to ask for his passports: Britain meant war. The state secretary replied that, unfortunately, he could not give such an assurance, even if Germany were given 24 (rather than five) hours to reply. Jagow then, Goschen reported to Grey, expressed 'poignant regret at the crumbling of his entire policy and that of the Chancellor, which had been to make friends with Great Britain.' He then 'begged' Goschen to call on Bethmann, the man who had waged – and lost – so much on the mirage of British neutrality.

Sir Edward Goschen was gentleman enough to comply with Jagow's wish, although he regretted his decision almost immediately. The ambassador found Bethmann 'very agitated.' Goschen knew that the chancellor had staked his policy – his very reputation – on rapprochement with England, a policy that had now 'tumbled down like a house of cards.' Goschen's ultimatum, Bethmann kept repeating, was 'terrible, terrible.' Simply for the word 'neutrality,' he complained – 'a word which in war-time has so often been disregarded – just for a scrap of paper, Great Britain was going to make war on a kindred nation who desired nothing better than to be friends with her.'

Britain's taking up arms against Germany in the current war, he fumed, 'was like striking a man from behind while he was fighting for his life against two assailants.' Goschen countered that Britain's 'solemn engagement' to defend Belgium's neutrality was just as much 'a matter of "life and death" for the honour of Great Britain' as it was supposedly 'a matter of life and death for Germany to advance through Belgium.' Bethmann, in turn, asked 'at what price will that compact have been kept. Has the British Government thought of that?' By this point Bethmann was 'so excited, so evidently overcome by the news of our action and so little disposed to hear reason' that Goschen decided to end the interview so as not to 'add fuel to the flame by further argument.' According to Bethmann, it was Goschen who was overcome and 'burst into tears.' They both may have done so.[11] In four hours, the two greatest military powers in the world, Germany and Great Britain, would be at war.

EVEN AS THESE EVENTS were taking place, a fascinating drama was underway in the Mediterranean over the fate of the SMS *Goeben*, the dreadnought that Germany's Ambassador Wangenheim had requested be ordered to proceed to Constantinople. Wangenheim's objective was to give ammunition to the war party in the Ottoman government, which, despite signing an alliance treaty with Berlin on Sunday, had still not declared war on Russia. At nine thirty AM Tuesday, while Grey was being authorised by the cabinet to send an ultimatum to Berlin, the *Goeben*, commanded by Admiral Wilhelm Souchon, and its support cruiser, the *Breslau*, had come into range of the superior British dreadnoughts *Indomitable* and *Indefatigable*. Because Britain was not at war, her ships could not fire. Throughout the day, as Grey waited for his answer from Berlin, Souchon raced across the Mediterranean for neutral Sicily, riding his coal-stokers so hard in the August heat that four men died from exhaustion. At five PM, just as Ambassador Goschen was receiving his instructions from London, Souchon slipped out of firing range of the British warships. At seven PM, as Goschen was arriving at the Wilhelmstrasse to deliver Grey's ultimatum, a fog descended off the Sicilian coast. At nine PM, as the ambassador's tearful audience with the German chancellor was concluding, only three hours before Britain would declare war, the *Goeben* and *Breslau* disappeared from British view in the thickening fog.[12] While no one knew it yet, Souchon's lucky escape would allow the dreadnought *Goeben* shortly to reach Constantinople, neatly cancelling out Churchill's commandeering of the *Sultan Osman I* for Britain and making all but certain the entry of the Ottoman Empire into the war as a co-belligerent of Germany – thereby spreading the war to the Middle East, with consequences still being felt today.

EPILOGUE: THE QUESTION
OF RESPONSIBILITY

IF THE OUTBREAK OF THE FIRST WORLD WAR WAS, as Winston Churchill wrote, 'a drama never surpassed,' its first month was only slightly less dramatic.[1] After the initial disaster at Liège, the Germans regrouped and crashed violently through Belgium into northern France, very nearly reaching Paris before being pitched back by the French armies (with an assist from the British) at the Battle of the Marne in early September. On the eastern front, Russia's earlier-than-expected offensives against both Austrian Galicia and East Prussia allowed Moltke finally to persuade Conrad to abandon Plan B and reroute Austria's 2nd Army northward to Galicia at a crucial stage in the Serbian campaign. Russia received her own comeuppance at Tannenberg, in East Prussia, in late August, when most of Samsonov's 2nd Army was encircled and destroyed by the Germans. Despite the possibilities opened up by a war of movement in the conflict's first month, neither of the two warring coalitions could achieve a decisive advantage. In the West, the outnumbered Germans took the high ground and dug in behind fortified positions; in the East the Russians proved they could beat the Austrians but not the Germans.

With both sides thinking they could win, periodic peace parleys came to nothing. So evenly matched were the belligerent coalitions that the recruitment of allies – Turkey and Bulgaria for the Central Powers; Italy, Romania, and Greece for the Entente – scarcely disturbed the stalemate. Only in 1917, when the United States came in and Russia dropped out, was there a prospect of victory for either side – and even then the two events nearly cancelled out, so the carnage continued for another year. By 1918, the war had rung up a butcher's bill of nearly nine million dead and as many wounded, and had brought about the grisly end of empires that had endured for centuries. Millions more died in the Russian Revolution and Civil War, in the bloodletting surrounding the collapse of the Ottoman and Habsburg empires, and of course in the Second World War, born of Hitler's ambition to refight the First.

Why did all this happen? As one learns from standard textbooks, a number of long-term structural factors made the catastrophe of 1914 possible. The deadliness of the conflict required the rise of mass conscription armies along with industrialisation and the improvement of weapons of death, resulting in that strange gap between 'weight and mobility' that made it difficult for armies to manoeuvre quickly enough to take advantage of modern firepower and that gave such a decisive advantage to entrenched defenders. In diplomacy, one can go back to the Austrian-Russian break in the Crimean War to unravel the skein of causation that led to the creation, by the early twentieth century, of two alliance blocs of nearly equal strength, with Britain leaning towards (but not quite joining) one side owing to Germany's foolish naval buildup.

None of this structural background, however, is sufficient to explain what happened in 1914. Mass conscription and the arms race were not less advanced during the First Bosnian Crisis of 1908–1909 and the Balkan Wars of 1912–1913. France and Russia were just as free to determine whether or not to go to war in 1914 as in all previous years of their military alliance dating back to 1894. Austria had just as much interest in cutting Serbia down to size in 1912 and 1913 as she did in 1914;

the Germans had no particular interest in the Balkans in any of these years. Russia could have found cause to go to war over Serbia – or the Straits – in 1908, 1909, 1912–1913, or the winter of 1913–1914, during the Liman von Sanders crisis. Britain, having decisively won her naval race with Germany by 1914, could easily have stayed out of this Balkan imbroglio, as she had in all previous ones.

Absent the Sarajevo incident, a great power war might still have broken out at some point in 1914 or shortly thereafter. But there are good reasons to think otherwise. Without the diplomatic crisis born of Sarajevo, France would have remained consumed by the Caillaux affair in July 1914 – until Caillaux's wife was acquitted, which would have paved the way for a triumphant Caillaux-Jaurès cabinet. Caillaux and Jaurès, to emasculate the president, might have exposed Russia's covert subsidies for Poincaré's election campaign. Whether or not they succeeded in jettisoning the Franco-Russian alliance in favour of détente with Germany, their tussle with the president would have lit up the political skies. The French political and strategic landscape of 1915 might have looked very different from the one in July–August 1914.

This was just as true in Great Britain. Before the July crisis sparked by Sarajevo, the drift in British diplomacy was towards rapprochement with Germany and growing tensions with Russia over Persia. Absent Sarajevo, this trend would have continued. More important, the Home Rule crisis over Ireland was building towards a climax in summer 1914. There is no telling how it would have ended. Catholic Ireland might have taken up arms against the Protestant Ulstermen, or vice versa. The threat of Irish civil war might have split the British army into hostile factions, as nearly happened anyway after Curragh. Or Churchill might have sent in the navy again, this time in anger (in March, he had vowed privately to 'pour enough shot and shell into Belfast to reduce it to ruins'), to enforce Home Rule. In any case, without Sarajevo and the war it sparked, Irish affairs would have preoccupied British statesmen for years.

Absent the murder of the heir to the throne in 1914, Austria-Hungary would still have seethed with ethnic tensions. She would not, however, have gone to war with Serbia, for one very simple reason: Franz Ferdinand, who had blocked Conrad every single time he had advocated doing so – all 25 of them in 1913 alone! – would have remained alive. The archduke, who cared little for the opinion of others, was nothing if not stubborn. One could imagine him getting angry after surviving an assassination attempt in Sarajevo – if, say, his car had not taken the wrong turn onto Franz-Josef Strasse. He would almost certainly have cursed Serbia, and Serbs, once he learned who was behind the plot. But then, he already hated Serbs, which had not prevented him from developing an almost religious aversion to the idea of war with Serbia. If anything, surviving a murder attempt would have strengthened his conviction that Hungary was to blame for the ills plaguing the dual monarchy, owing to her persecution of racial minorities. The archduke might have pulled off his longed-for Austrian reconciliation with Romania, quieting tensions in the Balkans. Or his quarrel with Tisza might have plunged the dual monarchy into a crisis between Hungary and Austria. Or some combination of the two. What Austria would not have done was fight a war with Serbia.[2]

As for the Germans, absent Sarajevo, there remains a lingering suspicion that Moltke would have continued advocating a preventive war with Russia before the latter's Great Programme came to fruition in 1917. But then he, and other hawks at the General Staff and Wilhelmstrasse, had pushed for such a war before 1914, too, without success. Moltke was not sovereign of Germany; he was not even her chancellor. There is no evidence – none – that either Bethmann or Kaiser Wilhelm II – the 'two old women,' as German hawks called them – advocated *Präventivkrieg* before the Sarajevo incident nor, indeed, after it.

The idea that Berlin's strategic position was uniquely favourable for war in 1914 is absurd. By 1912, Germany had decisively lost the naval race with Britain. As recently as 1911, her position vis-à-vis France and Russia had been reasonably strong, but France's Three-Year Law, and Russia's recent acceleration of her mobilisation schedule under French pressure, had already wiped out any advantage Germany might accrue from her speedier deployment even before the Great Programme would take effect. In 1914, the Austro-German strategic position was, in the words of military historian Terence Zuber, 'nearing a "worst possible case" scenario.' Indeed German planners, recognising that they were decisively outnumbered on both fronts, were hoping to add six corps to the peacetime army by 1915 (if the Reichstag would pay for this), which might have restored parity, as France was already scraping the bottom of the recruitment barrel, conscripting nearly 90 per cent of her available manpower. Expansion of the army could have given the Germans decisive superiority on the western front, with enough covering troops in the east to hold off any Russian attack.[3] This would have soured even Poincaré on the strategic point of a Russian alliance. Or real détente with a Caillaux-Jaurès ministry in Paris might have ended the Franco-German arms race altogether. If any, all, or none of these scenarios transpired, Moltke – or the belligerent Prussian minister of war, Falkenhayn – might still have bent the kaiser's ear with pleas for preventive war. They would not have been listened to. Talk of *Präventivkrieg* among German generals was qualitatively no different than French whispers of *revanche* in Alsace-Lorraine, Conrad's entreaties that Austria must crush Serbia, or Russian conferences plotting the conquest of Constantinople. Talk was talk. It was not war.

With St Petersburg, it is easier to imagine alternative scenarios leading her into war in 1914. With the *Sultan Osman I* scheduled to arrive in the Bosphorus in July, the clock was ticking – as soon as Turkey floated a single dreadnought, Russia's 'Straits window' would close for the foreseeable future. This fear, even more than the Liman von Sanders crisis, is what prompted the strategic planning conference of February 1914 focused on the Ottoman Empire, and Sazonov's demand, following the Sarajevo outrage, for up-to-date information on the timetable for an amphibious strike on Constantinople. Even absent the assassination of the Habsburg heir, some kind of crisis over Turkey's dreadnoughts would have come to a head for Russia in summer 1914.

This is not to say, however, that any crisis between Russia and Turkey would have led to general European conflagration. The Eastern Question had produced wars and crises before, but they had all followed their own logic, depending on circumstances. The Russo-Ottoman war of 1877–1878 might have – but did not – produce a larger war, owing to Russia's diplomatic isolation and the exhaustion of her troops when they neared Constantinople; this gave both sides cause to start negotiating. The First Bosnian crisis of 1908–1909 had very nearly produced an Austrian-Russian clash, only for this to be averted when Russia backed down owing to her weakness following her 1905 revolution.

The two Balkan Wars of 1912–1913 had threatened the European equilibrium still more seriously. If then–chairman of the Council of Ministers Kokovtsov had not blocked the war party, Russian mobilisation in November 1912 might have led Germany to counter. Still, without the provocation of an Austrian attack on Serbia, as happened following Sarajevo (but not during the Balkan Wars), Petersburg would have been hard-pressed to win French, much less British, support for a war with the Central Powers.

A crisis over the arrival of Turkey's first dreadnought in July 1914 might have spiraled into war. Still, prior to Sarajevo, most of the diplomatic chatter in Europe concerned the possibility of another war between Turkey and Greece, not Russia. The Greeks, pursuing their own naval buildup, might have launched a pre-emptive strike before the Ottoman Empire floated the *Sultan Osman I*. A Greco-Turkish clash might have led to a Third Balkan War, as Bulgaria would have taken advantage of the crisis to make good her losses in the Second. Still, it need not have spread to Europe. What made July 1914 different was the direct involvement of a Great Power – Austria-Hungary – in the initial clash, which brought in Russia.

Had Russia herself launched an amphibious strike on Constantinople in summer 1914, a Great Power war might have resulted. Still, advanced as operational planning for such a strike was, it is hard to see what pretext Sazonov would have used to justify it. A Greco-Turkish war might have provided the spark, but if it seemed as if Petersburg was piggybacking on Turkey's distress to seize the Straits, then Russia would not have been able to count on support from France, let alone Great Britain. As Sazonov wrote in his memoirs, the general understanding at the February 1914 planning conference was that Russia's leaders 'considered an offensive against Constantinople inevitable, should European war break out.' The European war, that is, had to come *first*. Such a war might provide Russia with the pretext to conquer Constantinople, but she could not be seen to start it, or she would find herself just as isolated as in 1878 – or, worse still, 1853, when Britain and France had gone against her in the Crimean War. Only the unique sequence of events following Sarajevo – which led Austria to move against Serbia, backed by Germany – produced a European war in which both France and Britain would back Russia. Although there were bilateral agreements between London and the other two capitals, this unlikely tripartite battlefield coalition had never existed before and will never be seen again.*

Still, contingent and clearly preventable as the Sarajevo outrage was, it happened; the July crisis ensued; world war broke out in August, with all of the fearful and long-lasting consequences mentioned above. All of these world-shaking events were man-made. They are therefore quite properly subject to human judgment.

WHEN WE EXAMINE the key moral question of 1914 – responsibility for the outbreak of European, then world war – it is important to keep *degrees* of responsibility in mind. Sins of omission are lesser ones than sins of commission; likewise, actions are not equivalent to the reactions they occasion. Above all, intentions are important, but the hardest to divine, because we cannot peer into men's hearts. To begin at the beginning: Gavrilo Princip and his fellow assassination plotters bear ultimate responsibility for provoking the July crisis by murdering Archduke Franz Ferdinand. True, there was no intention on Princip's part, or that of Black Hand organisers in Belgrade, to cause a world war;** nevertheless some of them clearly sought to provoke a confrontation with Austria. Historians continue to

---

* Not even in World War II. When France dropped out in 1940, the Soviet Union was allied to Nazi Germany. Not unless we count de Gaulle's 'Free French' as a sovereign co-belligerent could a British-French-Russian wartime coalition be said to have repeated itself.
** Asked on his deathbed by a prison psychiatrist whether he had any regrets about his deed, Princip replied, 'If I hadn't done it, the Germans would have found some other excuse.'

argue about the different motivations of Serbian leaders. Apis may have wanted to provoke a crisis with Vienna so as to furnish an opportunity for a coup d'état, or merely to embarrass Prime Minister Pašić enough for his party to be defeated in July elections. Pašić almost certainly did not approve of the plot when he learned of it, but he made only an ineffectual, halfhearted effort to foil the assassination, whether because he feared a coup or the reaction from Vienna if he revealed what the Black Hand was up to. The only things we know for certain are that high Serbian officials were complicit in the crime and that Pašić neither prevented it nor gave the Austrians any genuine help in investigating it.[4]

The Austrians must stand next in the dock of judgment. It was clearly the intention of Conrad, Berchtold, and every other imperial minister except Tisza to use the Sarajevo outrage as a pretext for a punitive war against Serbia. Emperor Franz Josef I, as ultimate arbiter and signator of all key decisions, also bears a grave responsibility, although he did not design the policies – he merely confirmed them. One could easily argue, of course, that the crime committed in Sarajevo was sufficient legal casus belli for war with Serbia: the war launched by the United States and her allies against Afghanistan in 2001 (if not also the Iraq war of 2003) was justified in very similar terms (the 'harbouring of terrorists'). There are significant differences between the two cases, however. The Serbian government, unlike Osama bin Laden, did not confess to (much less publicly boast about) committing the crime, and she did agree to arrest at least some of the conspirators, such as Major Tankositch, whereas the Taliban refused outright to hand over bin Laden (although Serbia did similarly shelter Apis).

More significantly, the United States received broad (if not quite universal) international support for her action in Afghanistan. No Great Power made clear her stout opposition to a United States punitive strike in 2001, as at least Russia clearly did to an Austrian one in 1914. True, Berchtold and Conrad did not know, at the beginning of July, what Russia's reaction would be. By the end of the month, they did, and they proceeded against Serbia anyway. The Austrian sin was therefore one of both intention and commission, although with the caveat that the goal in Vienna was a local war with Serbia, not a European war involving Russia, much less France, Britain, and all the other ultimate belligerents. This was made dramatically clear when Austria, despite having catalysed the July crisis in the first place, refused to declare war on Russia until August 6 – two days after even Britain went in. While this anticlimactic declaration of war has sometimes been seen as implicating Germany in 'war guilt' – as it was clearly the Germans who pressured the Austrians into it – what it really reveals is just how little desire there was in Vienna to fight Russia. Considering the Austrians' poor performance against Russian troops in Galicia at the start of the war, one can easily see why.

Tisza, for his part, bears significant responsibility for the final shape of the July crisis: its back-ended timing. Owing to the harvest leave issue, the two weeks Austria 'lost' after the Ministerial Council of 7 July may not have been as important as historians have claimed. Conrad probably would have had to wait before mobilising, anyway. It was, rather, at the very beginning that Tisza's opposition mattered. Had Austria-Hungary mobilised on 1 July (as Conrad wanted to), or after only a few more days of diplomatic spadework (as Berchtold and the emperor would have preferred), it is possible that the Austrians would have caught Europe by surprise with a fait accompli – an occupation of Belgrade, at least, conveniently located as the capital was right on the Austrian border.

True – in light of Austria's indecisiveness during the Balkan Wars and her notoriously incompetent military performance in 1914 – one should regard this counterfactual with scepticism. And yet part of the reason why Conrad fared so badly in Galicia is that his real goal – shared by everyone in Vienna – was to crush Serbia, not to fight Russia. Had Austria begun her mobilisation against Serbia in the first week, instead of the last week, of July, and implemented Plan B without interruption, there is no telling how the crisis would have played out. It might still have led to European war, or it might have led to some kind of face-saving compromise along the lines of a 'Halt in Belgrade.' It was largely Tisza's doing that Austria did not present her ultimatum until four weeks after Sarajevo. Of course, his motivation in blocking Conrad was honourable: he wanted, at least until 14 July, to *prevent* war, not to cause it. If there is any sin in Tisza's behaviour, it is a negative one of omission leading to unintended consequences.

The German sin, at the time of the Hoyos mission of 5–6 July, was more serious. By giving Austria-Hungary a blank check against Serbia, Kaiser Wilhelm II and Bethmann Hollweg made a broader escalation of the Balkan crisis possible. Given Tisza's opposition, there is reason to believe that Conrad would not have got his Serbian war at all without German intervention. It was not German support alone that changed Tisza's mind – his own revulsion against Serbia grew organically the first two weeks in July, as he learned more about Sarajevo – but without it Berchtold would have had a very hard time convincing the emperor to move forward, whatever Tisza's views. Austria's diplomatic isolation and military weakness meant that German backing was indispensable. The Germans gave it unambiguously. Still, although it is true that Arthur Zimmermann, the undersecretary of state, and many military chiefs in Berlin, were keen on the idea of 'preventive war,' it is equally clear that Kaiser Wilhelm II and Bethmann did not expect Russia to fight. While they recognised the risks and were willing to run them, they did not *intend* to provoke European war. Their real sin, at this stage of the crisis, lay in failing to mandate any particular Austrian course of action, or to establish firmer guidelines as to how Vienna would coordinate its strategy with Berlin. The blank check was foolish and self-defeating. It encouraged Berchtold to behave as recklessly as possible, under the mistaken impression that this was what the Germans wanted him to do.

Berchtold himself must shoulder the greatest blame for bringing the crisis to the danger point on 23 July. Having lost the chance for a military fait accompli, Austria's foreign minister settled for a diplomatic one, detonating his ultimatum bombshell without even clearing the text first with his German allies. True, this was partly Bethmann's fault for leaving Berchtold alone to do his worst and for failing to press Vienna for more information until it was too late. And yet Jagow did request to see the text; he also asked that Berchtold do his 'homework' and finalise a dossier of Serbian guilt before dispatching the ultimatum, and make sure of Italy's support. Berchtold did nothing of the kind. After sending the ultimatum under seal to Belgrade, he even lied to Germany's ambassador that it was not yet finished. Here was conscious intention to deceive not only a hostile power such as Russia, but even Austria's closest ally. Of all the what-ifs of the July crisis, this is one of the greatest. If Berchtold had done what the Germans asked and convinced Europe of Serbia's perfidy, he would have put the diplomatic onus back on Russia to advocate for her guilty client. With what we know today of Serbian complicity in the Sarajevo crime, it is astonishing that Austrian officials were unable to marshal a convincing case even a month after the crime in Sarajevo.

Still, serious as Berchtold's errors were, it was not he who began the countdown to European war. His blundering helped isolate Austria-Hungary and embarrass Germany for

supporting her, but his actions did not force Russia to mobilise, much less France or Germany. Here the timeline becomes
all-important. Because of Schilling's running diary at the
Russian Foreign Ministry, we know that Sazonov decided on
a military response before Serbia had replied to the ultimatum
on Saturday, 25 July – before, indeed, he had actually read
the ultimatum itself on Friday. True, his decision still had to
be ratified in the Council of Ministers Friday afternoon and
by Tsar Nicholas II the next day. In a sense, it had to be ratified by France, too. But even before running his decision by
anyone else, by eleven AM on Thursday, 24 July, Sazonov
had already instructed Russia's finance minister to repatriate
funds from Germany and her army chief of staff to prepare
for mobilisation. Sazonov had known about the impending
Austrian ultimatum (if not its exact form) since the preceding
Saturday. After he, the tsar, and France's president, and pre-
mier/foreign minister held four days of meetings from Sunday
to Wednesday, Sazonov had good reason to believe he had
their support for his course of action. The most recent research
strongly suggests (although it does not prove) that Poincaré
and Paléologue gave Sazonov verbal support for a strong line
against Vienna during the summit in Petersburg. The written
evidence proves that Paléologue gave this support afterwards,
with or without explicit authorisation from Poincaré. So, too,
did General Laguiche (France's liaison officer at Russian command) and Joffre and Messimy in Paris.

Tsar Nicholas II signed into law the Period Preparatory to
War at midday on Saturday, 25 July – before learning of Serbia's
reply to the ultimatum and before either Serbia or Austria
had mobilised. The Period Preparatory to War began at midnight, 25–26 July. Because it, unlike Germany's version (the
Kriegsgefahrzustand), was enacted and carried out in secret, historians have been able to deny warlike intent on Russia's part, the

idea being that, as Sazonov himself told Ambassador Pourtalès, preliminary mobilisation measures 'did not mean war.' Some have gone even further, saying that even Russia's general mobilisation, ordered at four PM on 30 July, did not 'mean war.'[5] In both cases, the claim is dubious, although it has slightly more surface plausibility with the Period Preparatory to War.

The measures inaugurated on Sunday, 26 July, viewed on their own terms, clearly fell well short of war. Just as clearly, they constituted preparations for war. This was, indeed, the entire reason why the secret Period Preparatory to War had been developed in 1912–1913: to allow Russia a head start in mobilising against the Austro-Germans. The statute of 2 March 1913 clearly states that the Period Preparatory to War 'means the period of diplomatic complications preceding the opening of hostilities.' Or, as laid down in the tsar's November 1912 directive, 'it will be advantageous to complete concentration without beginning hostilities, in order not to deprive the enemy irrevocably of the hope that war can still be avoided. Our measures for this *must be masked by clever diplomatic negotiations*, in order to *lull to sleep as much as possible the enemy's fears*.' Dobrorolskii, chief of the Russian army's Mobilisation Section, understood this to mean war. So did War Minister Sukhomlinov and Chief of Army Staff Yanushkevitch. Sazonov made a great show of believing otherwise, but then, that was his job: to handle the 'diplomatic complications.' In this sense, and this sense alone, was the Period Preparatory to War *not* war. However insincere, diplomacy could continue.

In a curious mirror imaging of Sazonov's approach, Austria's foreign minister, tiring of insincere 'diplomatic complications,' declared war on Serbia – by telegram – on Tuesday, 28 July. Considering that Conrad did not believe the army would be ready to fight until 12 August, Berchtold's manoeuvre was counterproductive, as it gave diplomatic ammunition to Russia and France in their goal of winning over Britain and other neutrals. Berchtold's motivation, however, is instructive: he wanted to cut off further outside mediation efforts. War cancelled diplomacy. Here was another sin of commission. Still, aside from its adverse strategic consequences, especially for Germany, Berchtold's move proves little more than that Austrian leaders wanted a war with Serbia, a fact we knew already.

Austria's declaration of war on Serbia has usually been seen as the point of no return in the outbreak of the First World War, the moment when the July crisis escalated into actual conflict. This, too, has a surface plausibility. And yet again, we need to be careful with chronology. While it is true that Berchtold's rash action gave Russia a pretext to escalate her war preparations, these had been underway for nearly three days when Austria declared war on Serbia. By keeping quiet about the Period Preparatory to War and then delaying the announcements of both partial and general mobilisation, Sazonov was able to convince Sir Edward Grey, along with generations of historians, that Russia had begun mobilising only after Austria's declaration of war on Serbia. This is untrue: Austrian, German, French, and most of all Russian sources confirm that Russia's mobilisation measures against *both* Austria and Germany were well advanced by 28 July, and even more so by 29 July. All Berchtold's telegram did was give Russia a public casus belli for war preparations she was undertaking anyway. The long-running argument about Russia's partial versus general mobilisation rests, ultimately, on a fiction. As Kokovtsov had pointed out in November 1912, and Dobrorolskii pointed out in July 1914, a partial mobilisation targeting Austria alone, without using the Warsaw railway hub and blanketing Poland, was technically impossible. Nor was it ever fully implemented. 'Partial mobilisation' was a diplomatic conjuring act designed to show France – and more so, Britain – that Russia was not giving Germany a pretext for war.

The decision for European war was made by Russia on the night of 29 July 1914, when Tsar Nicholas II, advised unanimously by his advisers, signed the order for general mobilisation. General mobilisation – as he knew, as Sazonov knew, as Schilling knew; as Krivoshein, Rodzianko, and Duma leaders knew; as Sukhomlinov, Yanushkevitch, and Dobrorolskii knew – meant war. So clearly did the tsar know this that, on being moved by a telegram from Kaiser Wilhelm II, he *changed his mind*. 'I will not be responsible for a monstrous slaughter' is the key line of the entire July crisis, for it shows that the tsar, for all his simplicity – or expressly because of his guileless, unaffected simplicity – knew exactly what he was doing when he did it. He knew exactly what he was doing when he did it again, sixteen hours later, after agonising all day about it. Sazonov knew it, which is why he told Yanushkevitch to 'smash his telephone' so that the tsar could not change his mind again.

The French knew it, too. Although the final decision and its timing needed to be massaged carefully for British ears, Poincaré, Joffre, and Messimy knew that Russia had resolved on war long before her general mobilisation was confirmed by Paléologue's 30-hours-late telegram Friday night. In a fascinating illustration of the importance of chronology, Barbara Tuchman, in her classic *The Guns of August*, narrates a middle-of-the-night drama that sees President Poincaré awakened in bed by Russian ambassador Izvolsky asking him, 'What is France going to do?' Messimy then wakes up Viviani, who exclaims, 'Good God! These Russians are even worse insomniacs than they are drinkers.' It is a wonderful set piece, but Tuchman gets the date wrong by two days.

This scene transpired not on *Friday* night, 31 July–1 August, after Germany had inaugurated *Kriegsgefahrzustand* and sent Russia and France her ultimatums, but on *Wednesday* night, 29–30 July. The catalyst for the late-night drama was not, as

Tuchman suggests, pressure from Berlin – on Wednesday and Thursday Germany still had not undertaken serious war preparations of any kind – but Izvolsky's receipt of Sazonov's cryptic telegram from St Petersburg announcing that, owing to Russia's inability 'to accede to Germany's desire' that she cease mobilising, 'it only remains for us to hasten our armaments and regard war as imminent.' Wednesday was the same night that Sazonov told the German ambassador that Russia's mobilisation measures 'could no longer be reversed.' Viviani, for his part, may still have entertained illusions that Russia could stop short of war, which is why he hesitated longer than the others before approving France's general mobilisation on Saturday. But Poincaré and Messimy knew perfectly well what Sazonov meant on Wednesday night, which is why they convened a crisis meeting from four to seven AM to craft a response.

France's response, as we have seen, was carefully calibrated to manipulate British opinion. In none of the messages Viviani sent to Paléologue in St Petersburg on either 30 or 31 July was there any endorsement of Russia's mobilisation, which was referred to only obliquely, but there was no request to halt it, either. Joffre, Messimy, Laguiche, and Paléologue had already endorsed and encouraged the acceleration of Russia's war preparations. Poincaré and Viviani, because they were at sea from 24–29 July, had plausible deniability of all this – plausible deniability they needed to maintain, even after returning to Paris, to convince London of their innocence. But the dramatic scene of Wednesday night (not Friday night) gives the game away. Whether or not they had known before that Russia was mobilising, they knew then. And they knew what it meant. It meant France had to mobilise, too. And mobilisation meant war.

France, even more than Russia, insisted publicly that mobilisation was not war. The 'ten-kilometre withdrawal' to allow the Germans the initiative was a brilliant public relations move then, and it continues to gull historians. Aside from Joffre's sensible orders to avoid border incidents until concentration of forces was complete (orders nearly identical to those Moltke gave), it was nonsense. Article 2 of the Franco-Russian military convention specified that, once the *casus foederis* was invoked, 'France and Russia . . . without a previous agreement being necessary, shall mobilise all their forces immediately and simultaneously, and shall transport them as near to the frontiers as possible.' As General N. N. Obruchev, Russia's signatory, explained, 'this mobilisation of France and Russia would be followed immediately by positive results, by acts of war, in a word would be inseparable from an "aggression."' Or as France's counterpart to Obruchev, General Raoul de Boisdeffre, put it after signing the accord, 'the mobilisation is the declaration of war.' Or as Dobrorolskii, architect of Russia's mobilisation in 1914, put it, 'once the moment has been chosen, everything is settled; there is no going back; it determines mechanically the beginning of the war.'[6] After this moment – midnight on 30–31 July, when Russia's general mobilisation took effect – France and Russia were expected to mount offensives against Germany by M + 15. Just as Dobrorolskii said, mobilisation moved like clockwork. The first Great Power battles of 1914 occurred on German territory, in France's case on *exactly* Russian M + 15, with her invasion of Alsace on 14 August. Russia, too, won her first engagement on German soil, at Stallupönen/Gumbinnen, on 17–20 August 1914.[7]

One can, of course, still argue that the Austrians fired first, at Serbia on 29 July. Austria also declared war first, on 28 July (although only against Belgrade). We must remember, however, that Austria-Hungary, for all her warlust against Serbia, had little desire to fight Russia, to the extent that Moltke had to beg Conrad repeatedly to do it. For all Berchtold's mischief with the ultimatum and declaration of war, it was clearly his intention, and Conrad's, to fight a war with Serbia alone. True, they realised that Russia might object, but to the extent they thought about this at all, they expected the Germans to handle Russia. The evidence shows that there was little real coordination between Berlin and Vienna, rather a great gap in understanding of what the other side was up to. The Germans were just as shocked when they learned of Berchtold's declaration of war on Serbia on 28 July – which they had just been assured would not come until August 12 – as the Austrians were when they learned that Germany planned to invade Belgium rather than concentrate her forces against Russia. None of this absolves anyone in Berlin and Vienna of responsibility for gross errors in policymaking. But it does make ridiculous the charge of cold, joint premeditation.

Only the Germans, of course, were responsible for the strategic stupidity of invading France by way of Belgium. Although recent research casts doubt on the notion that there was ever an immutable Schlieffen Plan, all this means is that Moltke himself is to blame for the decision – and even more so for the strike on Liège on M + 3.[8] Questionable as the German occupation of Luxembourg was, the fact that its railways were, by treaty, under German management mitigates some of its significance, along with the fact that Britain did not see the occupation as a plausible casus belli against Germany. Belgium was what mattered to outside powers, especially Britain; indeed the French understood this so well that Poincaré intervened with Joffre in 1912 to ensure that France's initial deployment would not violate her territory. Germany's decision to violate Belgian neutrality – on M + 3, two weeks before the concentration of her armies would be complete – was a political, diplomatic, strategic, and moral blunder of the first magnitude. For this, Moltke was directly to blame, although Bethmann, Jagow, or the kaiser should have called him to account over it.

Important as the German violation of Belgium was, it did not cause the First World War. It may not even have brought Britain into it. Until the Germans gave him the gift of Liège on 4 August, Grey's ammunition against non-interventionists in the cabinet came from the informal naval agreement with France he had personally arranged with Cambon in November 1912, about which the Commons (although not the cabinet) remained ignorant. It was over this issue – not Belgium – that Morley and Burns resigned. Morley and Burns, along with some historians, paint Grey in a Machiavellian light, as a master manipulator who brought his own party, against its will, into an agreement with France (by encouraging her to move her fleet to the Mediterranean and leave her Channel coast undefended) and then co-belligerence with her and Russia.[9] While there is an element of truth here insofar as the semisecret French naval agreement did encourage French hawks and tie Britain's hands in the case of war between France and Germany, Grey hardly had the intention of fomenting such a war.

Sir Edward Grey's sins during the July crisis were of omission, not commission. By failing to develop a clear policy (owing to the lack of a mandate from the cabinet or Commons, although he could have showed courage and overridden them), Grey missed his chance to put a scare into Berlin that Britain might intervene until it was too late for the Germans to pull Vienna back from the brink. Grey's misleadingly positive signals, up to and including his bizarre neutrality pledges of 1 August and his ambiguous speech in the Commons on 3 August, left the Germans guessing until he finally sent Berlin an ultimatum on 4 August. By feigning neutrality and yet clearly taking the Franco-Russian side, by failing to notice Russia's secret early mobilisation and yet denouncing Austria and Germany for 'marching towards war,' Grey encouraged Russian and then French recklessness, as his attitude convinced Sazonov and

Poincaré that they had him in their pocket. Still, while he can be faulted for misleading the cabinet and Commons, and even, arguably, for failing to prevent the war by not earlier deciding on a policy, bringing about a Great Power war was the furthest thing from Grey's intention, and further still from that of some other cabinet ministers (even Churchill, who wanted the navy to be ready and was generally gung-ho, did not really wish for a European war to break out). Britain's role in unleashing the First World War was one born of blindness and blundering, not malice.

We can say something similar about Germany's role, although with allowance for the much greater sin of invading Belgium. For this colossal error in judgment, German leaders richly deserve the opprobrium they have been showered with ever since 1914. Like the blank check, it was a sin of commission, not omission. And yet with Belgium, too, Germany's sin was not one of intending a world war – British belligerence was the last thing anyone in Berlin wanted – but of botching the diplomacy of the European war's outbreak. Russia had mobilised fully two days before Germany; she had begun her secret war preparations against Austria and Germany five days earlier still. France had mobilised before Germany, too (although only by minutes). Austria had not mobilised against Russia at all. And yet somehow the prevailing opinion in London on 3–4 August was that Austria and Germany had started the war with France and Russia. The assault on Liège was not the cause of this error in British perception, which owed more to Franco-Russian deception, Sir George Buchanan's inept reporting, and Grey's misleading summaries. But Liège did help to confirm British prejudice against Germany. It also gave Entente diplomats, and pro-Entente historians, a ready-made argument for German war guilt – the idea that Germany 'caused' or 'intended' or 'willed' the First World War.

This argument is not supported by the evidence. As indicated by their earlier mobilisations (especially Russia's), in 1914 France and Russia were far more eager to fight than was Germany – and far, far more than Austria-Hungary, if in her case we mean fighting Russia, not Serbia. Germany declared war first on France and Russia because of Bethmann's misguided sense of legal propriety, but she mobilised last, and even then hesitatingly, with her leaders (except for the timetable-obsessed Moltke and Falkenhayn) clutching desperately for exits, as indicated by how eagerly the kaiser, Bethmann, and Jagow jumped on Grey's last-minute neutrality offers.

The reason for Germany's reluctance becomes clear when we examine the order of battle of the armies. With German forces outnumbered and outgunned on both fronts, with Britain primed to intervene against them with an expeditionary force and a naval blockade, French and Russian generals expected that they would win, so long as Russia's mobilisation began early enough. This is abundantly clear from the chatter at the time of the war's outbreak, which shows a widespread (although not unanimous) mood of optimism in the French and Russian general staffs. As Sukhomlinov wrote in his diary on 9 August 1914, as the assembly of the armies was nearing completion, 'it seems that the German wolf will quickly be brought to bay: all are against him.'[10]

The Germans, by contrast, went into the war expecting that they would lose, which is why they were so keen to wiggle out of it at the last moment. Moltke's unrealistic and ultimately suicidal war plan, involving a march across Belgium, reflected German weakness, not German strength. It is not hard to see why Sir Edward Grey was able to convince the Commons (or most of it, anyway) that Germany was the aggressor in 1914: she was indeed the Power that first violated neutral territory in Luxembourg and then in Belgium. She did so, however, out of desperation, out of Moltke's belief that only a knockout blow against France would give her the slightest chance of winning. So far from 'willing the war,' the Germans went into it kicking and screaming as the Austrian noose snapped shut around their necks.

NOTES

Notes to Prologue   Sarajevo, Sunday, 28 June 1914

1. Nikitsch-Boulles, 214.

2. 'Alone and without escort': Fay, vol. 2, 31n39. 'Wifeless toast': Morton, *Thunder at Twilight*, 241.

3. Cited in Albertini, vol. 2, 8.

4. Nikitsch-Boulles, 212.

5. Pharos, 7 (Chabrinovitch testimony), and 23 (Princip).

6. Fay, vol. 2, 88–89.

7. Ibid., vol. 2, 117.

8. Pharos, 27–29 (Princip testimony) and 51–52 (Grabezh).

9. Fay, vol. 2, 121; Pharos, 21 (Chabrinovitch testimony), 63–64, 68 (Ilitch), and 105–106 (Jovanovitch).

10. Nikitsch-Boulles, 213.

11. Morton, *Thunder at Twilight*, 243.

12. Fay, vol. 2, 121–124, 138–140.

13. 'Red-gold Moorish loggias': Morton, *Thunder at Twilight*, 245. 'That's rich . . . ': Würthle, 13.

14. Potiorek Abschrift, 28 June 1914, in HHSA, P.A.I. Liasse Krieg, Karton 810.

15. Pharos, 53 (Grabezh testimony).

16. Ibid., 40 (Princip testimony).

17. Würthle, 15–16.

Notes to Chapter 1   Vienna: Anger, Not Sympathy

1. Zweig, *The World of Yesterday*, 215.

2. Conrad, vol. 4, 17–18.

3. 'Solve the Serbian question once and for all': cited in Albertini, vol. 1, 538. Conrad proposed going to war 25 times in 1913 alone: see Strachan, *First World War*, 69. On Conrad's mistress and her beer merchant husband (see footnote), see Beatty, 5, 199.

4. Berchtold, 'monstrous agitation': cited in Hantsch, 551. On the atmosphere in Vienna, see also Rauchensteiner, *Der Tod des Doppeladlers*, 66.

5. Ritter to Berchtold, 29 June 1914, HHSA Liasse Krieg, Karton 810.

6. Citation and commentary (on the most likely phrasing of the emperor's remarks) in Albertini, vol. 2, 116, 116n2.

7. 'Consternation and indignation': cited in Morton, *Thunder at Twilight*, 267. 'Threads of the conspiracy': Tschirschky to Bethmann from Vienna, 30 June 1914, PAAA R19865.

8. 'War on everyone's lips': cited in Hantsch, 551.

9. Tisza to Franz Josef I, 1 July 1914, cited in Erenyi, 245–246.

10. Conrad, vol. 4, 33–34. 'War. War. War': cited in Hantsch, 558.

11. On the Common Army, language, and nationality issues, see especially Rauchensteiner, *Der Tod des Doppeladlers*, 45, and Stone, *Europe Transformed*, 315. Conrad spoke seven languages: Strachan, *First World War*, 282.

12. Conrad, vol. 4, 30–31.

13. Citations in Hantsch, 559–560.

14. 'Mandate of Heaven . . . stiff, Burgundian rituals': Stone, *Europe Transformed*, 304–305. 'Engine under steam . . . keen desire to spite his nephew': cited in Beatty, 201.

15. Tschirschky to Bethmann, 2 July 1914, in PAAA R19865.

16. Conrad, vol. 4, 34.

17. Citations in Fay, vol. 2, 191.

18. Ballplatz insiders: see discussion in ibid., 205–206.

19. Tuchman, 15.

20. Details on Ferdinand at funeral: Morton, *Thunder at Twilight*, 269. On Sophie: Albertini, vol. 2, 117. 'Provincial hole': Zweig, *World of Yesterday*, 217.

21. Bethmann to Franz Josef I (via Tschirschky), 2 July 1914, in DD, vol. 1, no. 6b, 9–10.

Notes to Chapter 2   St Petersburg: No Quarter Given

1. No condolences offered: Austrian consular reports from Belgrade (29 June 1914) and Sinaia (5 July 1914). Russian embassy in Rome not flying its flag at half-mast: Ritter from Belgrade, 6 July 1914. Russian Legation in Belgrade refused to lower flag during funeral requiem: Giesl from Belgrade, 13 July 1914. All in HHSA, P.A.I. Liasse Krieg, Karton 810.

2. Ritter to Berchtold, 29 June 1914, and again 13 July 1914, in HHSA, P.A.I. Liasse Krieg, Karton 810.

3. On Pašić and Hartwig, see especially Turner, 81.

4. Albertini, vol. 2, 85.

5. On Pašić's knowledge of the plot, see Fay, vol. 2, 152; Albertini, vol. 2, 98 and passim.

6. Cited in Turner, 38.

7. On Russia's Black Sea exports, see British Foreign Office study of the 'Russian Financial Situation,' 25 July 1914, in PRO, FO 371/2094.

8. On missing Russian and French correspondence, see McMeekin, *Russian Origins*, chapter 2.

9. 'Has [France] no other glory than to serve the rancors of M. Izvolsky?': cited in Beatty, 238. For Izvolsky's correspondence, see LN.

10. Buchanan to Nicolson, 9 July 1914, in BD, vol. 11, no. 49, 39.

11. Czernin to Berchtold, 3 July 1914, no. 10017 in Oe-U, vol. 8.

12. Paléologue to Viviani, 6 July 1914, no. 477 in DDF, ser. 3, vol. 10.

13. Pourtalès to Bethmann from Petersburg, 13 July 1914, reproduced in Pourtalès, 81–83.

14. Russian General Staff memorandum to Sazonov, 3 July 1914, no. 74 in IBZI, vol. 4. For 'telegraphs, telephones and four wireless stations' and the feverish tone of the requests: documents and annotations in Gooch, *Recent Revelations*, 173, 176.

15. Conference protocol in Pokrovskii, *Drei Konferenzen*, 40–42.

16. Original transcript of 21 February 1914 conference, in AVPRI, fond 138, opis' 467, del' 462.

17. Sazonov to Grigorevich, 30 June 1914, no. 24 in IBZI, vol. 4. 'They considered an offensive against Constantinople inevitable': Sazonov, 126–127.

Notes to Chapter 3   **Paris and London: Unwelcome Interruption**

1. Messimy, *Souvenirs*, 125–126.

2. Ahamed, *Lords of Finance*, 63. 'A thousand kisses': cited in Beatty, 212.

3. Citations in Beatty, 234, 237–238.

4. Quoted in ibid., 235. On Russian bribes: Fay, vol. 1, 270 and 270n79.

5. Keiger, *Poincaré*, 102. 'Possibility of recovering our lost provinces': cited in Beatty, 232.

6. Izvolsky to Sazonov, 21 May 1914, in LN, 267.

7. Cited in Keiger, *Poincaré*, 164.

8. *Times* citations in Neiberg, 29, 31; Fromkin, 140.

9. Cited in Marcus, 93.

10. Cited in Marcus, 192–193.

11. Grey to Goschen, 24 June 1914, reproduced in Grey, vol. 1, 294. 'Question of life and death for Germany': Jarausch, 156.

12. Tuchman, 74.

13. Benckendorff to Sazonov, 30 May/12 June 1914, in AVPRI, fond 138, opis' 467, del' 462. Imperial Russia used the Julian calendar, which in 1914 was thirteen days behind the Gregorian one used today. For all Russian documents dated by the Julian calendar, I have given the Gregorian date after a slash, as here.

14. 'Probably irreversible': Jannen Jr., 51. 'Master of the complex art': Marcus, 70.

15. Churchill, *The World Crisis*, 65.

Notes to Chapter 4   Berlin: Sympathy and Impatience

1. Cited in Fay, vol. 2, 39.

2. Cited in Balfour, *Kaiser and His Times*, 125.

3. Stone, *World War One*, 11.

4. Bülow, *Memoirs*, vol. 3, 148–149.

5. Cited in McMeekin, *Berlin-Baghdad Express*, 102. 'Friend for all time': Wilhelm II, 'Tischrede in Damaskus (8 November 1898),' in Johann, ed., *Reden des Kaisers*, 81.

6. Cited in Hull, *Entourage*, 263.

7. Cited in Fay, vol. 2, 207.

8. Tschirschky to Bethmann, 30 June 1914, with Kaiser's marginalia, no. 7 in DD, vol. 1.

Notes to Chapter 5   The Count Hoyos Mission to Berlin

1. Hoyos's report of conversation with Naumann, no. 3 in Geiss, *July 1914*.

2. Cited in Smith, *One Morning in Sarajevo*, 206.

3. Citations in Hantsch, 566. See also Albertini vol. 2, 132.

4. Cited in Hantsch, 562.

5. Memorandum of the Austro-Hungarian Government, presented to the German government 5 July 1914, in DD, no. 14, 30.

6. Franz Josef I to Kaiser Wilhelm II, handwritten note presented on 5 July 1914, in DD, no. 13, 19–20.

7. Cited in Hantsch, 573.

8. Erenyi, 247.

9. Szögyény to Berchtold, 5 July 1914, no. 6 in Geiss, *July 1914*.

10. Ibid.

11. Plessen diary, cited in Albertini, vol. 2, 142.

12. Falkenhayn to Moltke, 5 July 1914, no. 7 in Geiss, *July 1914*.

13. Cited in Jannen Jr., 32. 'Surprise attack without preliminary preparation . . . partition of her territory': cited in Albertini, vol. 2, 143.

14. Cited in Beatty, 227.

15. Szögyény to Berchtold, 6 July 1914, no. 27 in Geiss, vol. 1.

16. Citations in Albertini, vol. 2, 142.

Notes to Chapter 6   War Council in Vienna (I)

1. Conrad, vol. 4, 36–37.

2. Potiorek to Biliński, 5 July 1914, HHSA, P.A.I. Liasse Krieg, Karton 811.

3. Citations in Hantsch, 572.

4. Conrad, vol. 4, 42.

5. Ibid.

6. Citation in Hantsch, 575.

7. Tisza's confession that he was 'mistaken' was actually made in private to Berchtold shortly before the ministerial meeting, although he repeated the gist of it to the larger group, too. Cited in Hantsch, 575.

8. Transcript of the 7 July 1914 war council in Vienna, reproduced as no. 39 in Geiss, vol. 1.

Notes to Chapter 7   Radio Silence

1. Szögyény to Berchtold, 9 July 1914, no. 58 in Geiss, vol. 1. 'Everyone here awaits with impatience . . . not easily repeat itself': Szögyény to Berchtold, 8 July 1914, no. 46 in Geiss, vol. 1. 'Emphasize enough . . . without striking a blow': Berchtold to Tisza, 8 July 1914, cited in Hantsch, 583.

2. Williamson Jr., *Austria-Hungary*, 199–200; Sondhaus, *Franz Conrad von Hötzendorf*, 142–143.

3. Conrad, vol. 4, 61.

4. Cited in Hantsch, 583.

5. Tisza memorandum, 8 July 1914, cited in Albertini, vol. 2, 169.

6. Cited in Hantsch, 588. 'Concrete demands on Serbia': Tschirschky to Jagow, 10 July 1914, in PAAA, R 19865.

7. Tschirschky to Jagow, 10 July 1914, in PAAA, R 19865.

8. Giesl to Berchtold, 11 July 1914, no. 10193 in Oe-U, vol. 8.

9. Cited in Albertini, vol. 2, 277.

10. Giesl to Berchtold, 13 July 1914, in HHSA, P.A.I. Liasse Krieg, Karton 810.

11. Cited in Albertini, vol. 2, 175.

12. Wiesner report, 13 July 1914, reproduced in Conrad, vol. 4, 81.

13. Tschirschky to Jagow, 13 July 1914, in PAAA, R 19865.

14. Tschirschky to Bethmann Hollweg, 14 July 1914, no. 91 in Geiss, vol. 1.

15. Tschirschky to Bethmann Hollweg, 14 July 1914, no. 92 in Geiss, vol. 1.

Notes to Chapter 8   Enter Sazonov

1. Shebeko to Sazonov, 16 July 1914, cited in Albertini, vol. 2, 185.

2. Tisza to Hungarian Diet, 15 July 1914, cited in Erenyi, 253.

3. Cited in Hantsch, 595.

4. de Bunsen to Sir Arthur Nicolson, 17 July 1914, no. 56 in BD, vol. 11.

5. de Bunsen to Sir Edward Grey, 16 July 1914, no. 50 in BD, vol. 11.

6. de Bunsen to Grey, 18 July 1914, no. 59 in BD, vol. 11, no. 59. 'Strong note . . . to be sent in the next week probably not acceptable to Serbia': Berta de Bunsen diary, 18 July 1914, cited in Schmidt, 72.

7. Shebeko memoirs, cited in Albertini, vol. 2, 185.

8. Shebeko to Sazonov, 3/16 July 1914, no. 247 in IBZI, vol. 4.

9. Albertini, vol. 2, 185.

10. Entry for 3/16 July 1914, in Schilling, 25–26.

11. Entry for 4/17 July 1914, in Schilling, 26.

12. Entry for 5/18 July 1914, in Schilling, 26–27.

13. Szapáry to Berchtold, 18 July 1914, no. 10365 in Oe-U, vol. 8. For 'docile as a lamb': Russian Foreign Ministry log for 5/18 July 1914, no. 272 in IBZI, vol. 4.

14. Buchanan to Grey, 18 July 1914, no. 60 in BD, vol. 11.

15. Tsar Nicholas II, marginal note on 16 July 1914 Shebeko telegram from Vienna, Peterhof 6/19 July 1914, no. 247 in IBZI, vol. 4.

Notes to Chapter 9   War Council in Vienna (II)

1. Fay, vol. 2, 249.

2. All quotations from the meeting of the council on 19 July are from the transcript of 19 July Ministerial Council, chaired by Berchtold, no. 10393 in Oe-U, vol. 8.

3. Conrad, vol. 4, 92.

4. Austro-Hungarian ultimatum to Serbia, submitted 23 July 1914, reproduced as no. 155 in Geiss, vol. 1.

5. Berchtold to Macchio, 21 July 1914, cited in Fay, vol. 2, 253.

6. Jagow to Tschirschky, 11 July 1914, and Jagow to Tschirschky, 15 July 1914, nos. 31 and 46 in DD, vol. 1.

7. Berchtold circular to diplomats, 20 July 1914, no. 10400 in Oe-U, vol. 8.

Notes to Chapter 10   Poincaré Meets the Tsar

1. Citations in Jannen Jr., 66–67; 'Murderous heat' and 'tropical Africa': Viviani, *As We See It*, 90–91.

2. Cited in Turner, 89.

3. Paléologue, vol. 1, 13.

4. Cited in Turner, 89.

5. Poincaré, vol. 2, 165–166. 'Brilliance of the uniforms . . . black coat was a drab touch': Paléologue, vol. 1, 14.

6. Toast of Nicholas II, Tsar of Russia, no. 293 in IBZI, vol. 4.

7. Toast of Poincaré, President of France, no. 294 in IBZI, vol. 4. On Viviani's visible discomfiture during this and other ceremonies in Petersburg, see Poincaré, vol. 2, 165 and passim.

Notes to Chapter 11   Sazonov's Threat

1. Poincaré, vol. 2, 168–169.

2. Paléologue, vol. 1, 16–17.

3. Poincaré, vol. 2, 170. 'Create some incident that would furnish . . . a pretext for attacking [Serbia]': Buchanan to Grey, 22 July 1914, no. 76 in BD, vol. 11.

4. Paléologue, vol. 1, 18–19.

5. Szapáry to Berchtold, 21 July 1914, no. 10461 in Oe-U, vol. 8.

6. Paléologue, vol. 1, 19.

7. Citations in Schmidt, 75, 78.

8. Pourtalès to Bethmann by courier, 21 July 1914, in PAAA, R 19867 (emphasis added).

Notes to Chapter 12   Champagne Summit

1. Poincaré, vol. 2, 174–176.

2. Paléologue, vol. 1, 21 22. 'Interminable lane of troops . . . traditional shout': Poincaré, vol. 2, 177.

3. Tuchman, 332.

4. Paléologue, vol. 1, 22–23.

5. Barrère (from Rome) to Bienvenu-Martin, 21 July 1914, passed on to Paléologue, 22 July 1914, cited in Schmidt, 77. 'Plied [him] unceasingly with questions . . . ': Poincaré, vol. 2, 178.

6. Poincaré diary, cited in Schmidt, 81.

7. Paléologue, vol. 1, 23.

8. Ibid., 24–26.

Notes to Chapter 13   Anti-Ultimatum and Ultimatum

1. Krupenski to Sazonov, 22 July 1914, no. 329 in IBZI, vol. 4.

2. Sazonov to Shebeko, 4 AM on 23 July 1914, no. 322 in IBZI, vol. 4.

3. Viviani to Dumaine, by way of Bienvenu-Martin, 24 July 1914, in QO Autriche-Hongrie, vol. 32. 'Only with reluctance': Poincaré diary entry dated 23 July 1914, cited in Schmidt, 80.

4. Albertini, vol. 2, 589.

5. Dispatch from the chargé d'affaires in Vienna, cited in diary entry for 13/26 July 1914, in Schilling, 38.

6. Jagow to Tschirschky, 22 July 1914, no. 201 in Geiss, vol. 1.

7. Berchtold to Giesl, 23 July 1914, no. 10518 in Oe-U, vol. 8.

8. Conrad, vol. 4, 108. San Giuliano's quid pro quo: cited in Sondhaus, *Franz Conrad von Hötzendorf*, 144.

9. Crackanthorpe to Grey, 17 July 1914, no. 53 in BD, vol. 11.

10. Berchtold to Giesl, 23 July 1914, no. 10519 in Oe-U, vol. 8. 'Receive him in my place': cited in Albertini, vol. 2, 285.

11. Giesl to Berchtold, 23 July 1914, no. 10526 in Oe-U, vol. 8.

12. Giesl, as told to Albertini, in Albertini, vol. 2, 285.

13. Tagesaufzeichnung des russischen Aussenministeriums, 23 July 1914, no. 245 in Geiss, vol. 1.

Notes to Chapter 14   Sazonov Strikes

1. Albertini, vol. 2, 290; and Sazonov, 152.

2. See diary entry for 11/24 July 1914, in Schilling, 28–29.

3. Szapáry from Petersburg, 24 July 1914, no. 10619 in Oe-U, vol. 8.

4. Dobrorolskii, 17–18.

5. PBM, box 1, chapter 7, 5–7 (emphasis added).

6. Kokovtsov, 346–347 (emphasis added).

7. Dobrorolskii, 17–19.

8. Buchanan to Grey, 24 July 1914, no. 101 in BD, vol. 11.

9. PBM, box 1, chapter 7, pp. 9–10 and passim.

10. Sonderjournal des russischen Ministerrats, 24 July 1914, no. 286 in Geiss, vol. 1.

11. Prince Regent Alexander to Tsar Nicholas II, 24 July 1914, cited in Albertini, vol. 2, 352.

12. Spalaiković to Belgrade, 24 July 1914, cited (with commentary) in Albertini, vol. 2, 353–354.

13. Ibid.

14. Szapáry from Petersburg, 24 July 1914, no. 10620 in Oe-U, vol. 8.

15. Pourtalès letter by courier to Bethmann from Petersburg, 25 July 1914, no. 19 (204) in Pourtalès, 104–105.

16. Pourtalès telegram to Jagow, 25 July 1914 (1:08 AM), no. 283 in Geiss, vol. 1.

17. Entry for 11/24 July 1914, in Schilling, 31.

18. Pourtalès, 19; see also Albertini, vol. 2, 301.

19. Entry for 11/24 July 1914, in Schilling, 32. Conversation as recorded by Paléologue, in vol. 1, 33.

Notes to Chapter 15   Russia, France, and Serbia Stand Firm

1. Dobrorolskii telegram, 25 July 1914, cited in Hoeniger, *Russlands Vorbereitung zum Weltkrieg*, 80.

2. Minutes of the Russian Council of Ministers held on 25 July 1914, cited in Fay, vol. 2, 314 and passim.

3. Cited in Fay, vol. 2, 308 (emphasis added).

4. Cited in Albertini, vol. 2, 305.

5. Chelius to Berlin from Krasnoe Selo, 13/26 July 1914, in PAAA, R 19871 (emphasis added).

6. Buchanan to Grey, 25 July 1914 (8 PM), no. 125 in BD, vol. 11.

7. Paléologue from Petersburg, 25 July 1914, 6:22 PM, in QO Autriche-Hongrie, vol. 32.

8. Dupont to Laguiche, 25 July 1914, cited in Schmidt, 330.

9. Poincaré diary entries, 25 July 1914, cited in Schmidt, 81.

10. Crackanthorpe to Grey, 25 July 1914 (12:30 PM), no. 114 in BD, vol. 11.

11. Boppe to Bienvenu-Martin, cited in Albertini vol. 2, 359.

12. Serbian reply to the Austrian 'note with a time limit,' 25 July 1914 (6 PM), reproduced (with accompanying Austrian commentary) in Albertini, vol. 2, 364–371 (emphasis added).

13. Griesinger to Jagow, 24 July 1914, nos. 158 and 159 in DD, vol. 1.

14. As told to Albertini, in vol. 2, 363.

15. Giesl from Belgrade, 25 July 1914 (1 PM), no. 10645 in Oe-U, vol. 8.

16. Giesl recollection, cited in Albertini, vol. 2, 373.

17. Fay, vol. 2, 349.

18. Conrad, vol. 4, 122.

19. Berchtold to Giesl, 23 July 1914 (11:20 PM), no. 10521 in Oe-U, vol. 8.

20. Berchtold to Giesl, 26 July 1914, cited in Albertini, vol. 2, 379.

21. Chelius to Berlin from Krasnoe Selo, 13/26 July 1914, in PAAA, R 19871.

22. Paléologue, vol. 1, 35 (emphasis added).

23. Grey circular to ambassadors, 24 July 1914 (1:30 PM), no. 91 in BD, vol. 11.

24. Grey to Bertie, 24 July 1914, no. 98 in BD, vol. 11.

25. Grey to Rumbold, 24 July 1914 (7:45 PM), and accompanying 'Communication by the German Ambassador,' nos. 99–100 in BD, vol. 11.

26. Rumbold to Grey, 24 July 1914 (3:16 PM), no. 122 in BD, vol. 11.

27. Grey to Buchanan, 25 July 1914, no. 132 in BD, vol. 11.

Notes to Chapter 16   Russia Prepares for War

1. Journal of the Committee of the Russian General Staff, night of 12/25 July 1914, no. 79 in IBZI, vol. 5, and note 1.

NOTES TO PAGES 208–221

2. Hoeniger, *Russlands Vorbereitung zum Weltkrieg*, 19; and Stone, *Eastern Front*, 41.

3. Fay, vol. 2, 317 and passim.

4. Pourtalès, 22–23.

5. Pourtalès to Jagow, 26 July 1914 (3:15 PM), no. 23 in Pourtalès, 107–108.

6. Szapáry to Berchtold, reporting on a conversation the afternoon of 26 July 1914 (sent off at 2:15 AM on 27 July 1914), no. 397 in Geiss, vol. 2; see also Fay, vol. 2, 398n85, for elucidation of the timing of the interview and dispatch (the original was incorrectly labeled 2:15 PM, 27 July; Geiss, no. 397, has 2:15 PM, 26 July; in fact the dispatch was sent off at 2:15 AM on 27 July).

7. Ibid.

8. Pourtalès to Jagow, 26 July 1914 (10:10 PM), no. 29 in Pourtalès, 113.

9. Sazonov to Shebeko, evening of 26 July 1914, cited in Albertini, vol. 2, 406n1.

10. Paléologue, vol. 1, 36.

11. Pourtalès to Jagow, passing on Eggeling, 26 July 1914 (3:25 PM), no. 22 in Pourtalès, 107.

12. Szapáry to Berchtold, reporting on a conversation the afternoon of 26 July 1914.

13. Nicolson to Grey ('Communication from the German Ambassador'), 26 July 1914, no. 146 in BD, vol. 11 (emphasis added).

14. Lichnowsky to Jagow, 26 July 1914 (8:25 PM), no. 236 in DD, vol. 1.

15. Lichnowsky to Grey (postscript to note), 26 July 1914, no. 145 in BD, vol. 11.

16. Szögyény to Berchtold, 25 July 1914 (2:15 PM), no. 10656 in Oe-U, vol. 8.

17. Conrad, vol. 4, 131–132; gist of conversation also in Tschirschky to Jagow, 26 July 1914 (4:50 PM), no. 213 in DD, vol. 1.

18. Ibid.

19. Tschirschky to Jagow, 26 July 1914 (4:50 PM), no. 213 in DD, vol. 1.

20. Sazonov to Shebeko, evening of 26 July 1914.

21. Shebeko to Sazonov, 26 July 1914, no. 451 in Geiss, vol. 2.

22. Paléologue from Petersburg, passing on Laguiche, 26 July 1914, 1:55 PM (received Paris 4 PM) in QO Autriche-Hongrie, vol. 32.

23. Pourtalès from Petersburg, 9:30 PM, 26 July 1914, in PAAA, R 19871.

24. Eggeling to Berlin, 26 July 1914, cited in Turner, 101.

Notes to Chapter 17   The Kaiser Returns

1. Bethmann to Kaiser Wilhelm II, 25 July 1914 (10:45 PM), no. 191 in DD, vol. 1.

2. Bethmann to Kaiser Wilhelm II, 26 July 1914 (1 PM), no. 197 in DD, vol. 1.

3. Bethmann to Kaiser Wilhelm II, 26 July 1914 (8 PM), no. 221 in DD, vol. 1.

4. Kaiser Wilhelm II's marginal notes on Bethmann to Kaiser Wilhelm II, no. 221 in DD.

5. Ibid.

6. Bethmann to Kaiser Wilhelm II, 27 July 1914 (11:20 AM), no. 245 in DD, vol. 1.

7. Bülow, *Memoirs*, vol. 3, 161 (emphasis added).

8. Kaiser's marginal note on Baron von Schoen to Jagow, 24 July 1914 (8:05 PM), no. 154 in DD, vol. 1.

9. Schoen to Jagow, 26 July 1914 (9:50 PM, deciphered Berlin 1:55 AM 27 July). For interpretation, see Jannen Jr., 115.

10. Bethmann to Kaiser Wilhelm II, 27 July 1914 (11:20 AM), no. 245 in DD, vol. 1.

11. Moltke to his wife, 27 July 1914, cited in Turner, 102.

12. Plessen diary, 27 July 1914, cited in Albertini, vol. 2, 438.

13. Müller diary, 27 July 1914, cited in Turner, 102.

14. Grey to Buchanan, 27 July 1914 (3:30 PM), no. 177 in BD, vol. 11.

15. Brück to Jagow from Warsaw, 27 July 1914 (3:45 PM), no. 276 in DD, vol. 1. For Dvina river mined/rolling stock commandeered: Pourtalès to Jagow, passing on Chelius, passing on the Swedish consul in Riga, 27 July 1914 (7:17 PM), no. 274 in DD, vol. 1. For Kiev: Pourtalès to Jagow, passing on Kiev consul, 27 July 1914 (7:43 PM), no. 275 in DD, vol. 1.

16. Tschirschky to Jagow, 27 July 1914 (3:20 PM, arrived Berlin 4:37 PM), no. 257 in DD, vol. 1.

17. Goschen to Grey, 27 July 1914 (6:17 PM), no. 185 in BD, vol. 11.

18. Jagow to Kaiser Wilhelm II, 27 July 1914 (9:30 PM), first marked on by the Kaiser 28 July 1914, nos. 270 and 271 in DD, vol. 1, n2 and n3.

19. See Lichnowsky to Jagow, 27 July 1914 (arriving in Berlin 4:37, 8:40, and 8:40 PM), nos. 258, 265 and 266 in DD, vol. 1. The two telegrams received from the German naval attaché in London on 28 July are reproduced in Churchill, vol. 1, 222–223.

20. Lichnowsky to Jagow, 27 July 1914 (1:31 PM, arrived Berlin 4:37 PM), no. 258 in DD, vol. 1.

21. Lichnowsky to Jagow, 27 July 1914 (6:17 PM, arrived Berlin 8:40 PM), no. 266 in DD, vol. 1.

22. Lichnowsky to Jagow, 27 July 1914 (5:08 PM, arrived Berlin 8:40 PM), no. 265 in DD, vol. 1, 255.

23. Riezler diary, cited in Jarausch, 159.

24. Riezler diary entries, 25–26 July 1914, cited in Jarausch, 165–166. (emphasis added).

25. Riezler diary entry for 27 July 1914, cited in Jarausch, 167.

26. Bethmann to Tschirschky, passing on Lichnowsky from London (with edits and commentary), 27 July 1914 (11:50 PM, arrived Vienna 5:30 AM July 28), no. 277 in DD, vol. 1.

27. Szögyény to Berchtold, 27 July 1914 (9:15 PM), no. 10793 in Oe-U, vol. 8.

28. Albertini, for example, devotes nearly twenty pages to unpacking what he calls Bethmann's 'double game,' in vol. 2, 443–460.

29. Bertie to Grey, 27 July 1914 (2:45 PM), no. 183 in BD, vol. 11.

30. Lichnowsky to Jagow, 27 July 1914 (6:17 PM, arrived Berlin 8:40 PM), no. 266 in DD, vol. 1.

31. Buchanan to Grey, 26 July 1914, 8 PM (received 11 PM), no. 155 in BD, vol. 11.

32. Buchanan to Grey, 27 July 1914 (8:40 PM), no. 198 in BD, vol. 11.

33. Cited in Churchill, vol. 1, 218.

34. Viviani to Paléologue, 27 July 1914, cited in Schmidt, 93.

Notes to Chapter 18   'You Have Got Me into a Fine Mess'

1. Plessen diary, 28 July 1914, cited in Albertini, vol. 2, 467.

2. Kaiser Wilhelm II, marginal notes on Serbia's reply to the Austrian ultimatum, scribbled at 10 AM on Tuesday, 28 July, no. 271 in DD, vol. 1.

3. Kaiser Wilhelm II to Jagow, 10 AM on Tuesday 28 July, marked received, afternoon 29 July, no. 293 in DD, vol. 1 (emphasis in original).

4. As noted by Jannen Jr., 148.

5. The Austrian declaration-of-war telegram is reproduced (in French original facsimile) in Fay, vol. 2, 419.

6. Albertini, vol. 2, 461.

7. Yanushkevitch to Yudenich at Tiflis command, 14/27 July 1914, in RGVIA, fond 2000, opis' 1, del' 3796, list' 13.

8. Odessa consul report, passed on by Pourtalès to Berlin, 28 July 1914 (1:21 PM, arrived Berlin 2:25 PM), no. 296 in DD, vol. 2.

9. Consul Brück from Warsaw, 28 July 1914 (received 29 July), no. 49 in Pourtalès, 132.

10. Cited in Zuber, 157.

11. Cited in Turner, 'The Russian Mobilisation in 1914,' 77.

12. Buchanan to Grey, 28 July 1914, 8:45 PM (received 10:45 PM), no. 234 in BD, vol. 11.

13. Buchanan to Grey, 28 July 1914 (8:45 PM), no. 247 in BD, vol. 11.

14. Buchanan, *My Mission to Russia*, 197.

15. Paléologue, vol. 1, 39 (emphasis added). Buchanan recalls the conversation almost identically, in *My Mission to Russia*, 199.

16. Sazonov to Bronevski, with instructions to circulate secretly, 15/28 July 1914, no. 168 in IBZI, vol. 5.

17. Sazonov to Benckendorff, 15/28 July 1914, no. 167 in IBZI, vol. 5.

18. Fromkin, 222. *London Times* citation: Neiberg, 75. 'Crowd of stone-throwing Dubliners': Beatty, 119.

19. Grey to Goschen, 28 July 1914 (4 PM), no. 218 in BD, vol. 11.

20. Fromkin, 227.

21. Citations in Jannen Jr., 165. 'Ferocious melee of shouts': Beatty, 242.

22. Citation in Jannen Jr., 149.

23. Lichnowsky to Jagow, 28 July 1914 (12:58 PM, received Berlin 3:45 PM), with Bethmann's marginal notes, no. 301 and footnotes in DD, vol. 2, 23.

24. Bethmann to Tschirschky, 28 July 1914 (10:15 PM, received Vienna 29 July 4:30 AM), no. 323 in DD, vol. 2 (emphasis added).

25. Bethmann to Tschirschky, 28 July 1914 (3:20 PM, received Vienna 6 PM), no. 299 in DD, vol. 2. For Berchtold's request that Bethmann warn Russia: Tschirschky to Jagow, 27 July 1914, cited in Albertini, vol. 2, 483.

26. Bethmann to Pourtalès, copied to Vienna, Paris, and London, 28 July 1914 (9 PM), no. 315 in DD, vol. 2.

27. Willy to Nicky telegram, 28 July 1914 (10:45 PM), sent off at 29 July 1914 (1:45 AM), with accompanying notes on which phrases the kaiser rewrote from the original draft, no. 335 in DD, vol. 2, and footnotes.

28. Nicky to Willy, 29 July 1914 (1 AM), received at Neues Palais Potsdam at 7:30 AM, 29 July 1914, no. 332 in DD, vol. 2, and footnotes.

29. Citations in Turner, 104. Doumergue: cited in Turner, 89.

30. Entry for 15/28 July 1914, in Schilling, 43.

31. Sazonov to Izvolsky, copied to London, Vienna, Rome, and Berlin, 29 July 1914, no. 221 in IBZI, vol. 5.

32. Albertini, vol. 2, 544.

33. Paléologue to Paris, 28 July 1914 (7:35 PM, received 11:10 PM), no. 216 in DDF, ser. 3, vol. 11.

34. Yanushkevitch to commanders of all of Russia's military districts, 28 July 1914, no. 210 in IBZI, vol. 5. Incidentally, the Russian sources from this night are not precisely dated by hour – even in Schilling's Foreign Ministry logbook (Schilling, 16, 43–45), which is more informative for other dates – but a reconstruction of the timeline is still possible by comparing the dispatches of the French and German ambassadors with the memoir accounts left by Sazonov, Sukhomlinov, Dobrorolskii, and Danilov. I have followed here Albertini's excellent reconstruction of the most likely sequence of events, in vol. 2, 539–545.

Notes to Chapter 19   'I Will Not Be Responsible for a Monstrous Slaughter!'

1. Churchill, vol. 1, 225.

2. Viviani, *As We See It*, 98.

3. Poincaré diary, cited in Jannen Jr., 177. 'Many people here seem to think war imminent': Poincaré, *Au service de la France*, vol. 4, 361–362.

4. For analysis see Albertini, vol. 2, 590–591n6.

5. Entry for 15/28 July 1914, in Schilling, 43. 'They cannot send me any instructions': Paléologue, vol. 1, 41.

6. Viviani to Bienvenu-Martin, no. 190 in DDF, ser. 3, vol. 11.

7. Bienvenu-Martin to Viviani, 26 July 1914 (4:30 PM), no. 90 in DDF, ser. 3, vol. 11.

8. Viviani to Paléologue, 27 July 1914 (noon), no. 138 in DDF, ser. 3, vol. 11, and note; for analysis, Albertini, vol. 2, 593.

9. Citations in Jannen Jr., 177, and in Albertini, vol. 2, 597; for 'enormous pile of telegrams,' Poincaré, vol. 2, 215.

10. Poincaré, *Au service de la France*, vol. 4, 368–369.

11. Log entry, 11:15 AM on 29 July 1914, in QO Autriche-Hongrie ('Conflit austro-serbe'), vol. 31; and Sazonov to Benckendorff (passed on to Viviani by Izvolsky), 28 July 1914, no. 167 in IBZI, vol. 5.

12. See Article II of the Franco-Russian Military Agreement, updated in 1913, reproduced (with commentary) in Albertini, vol. 2, 585.

13. Consul Brück from Warsaw to Bethmann, 29 July 1914 (arrived afternoon 30 July), in PAAA, R 19873.

14. Viviani to Paul Cambon, 29 July 1914, no. 260 in DDF, ser. 3, vol. 11.

15. Moltke memorandum to Bethmann, 'Zur Beurteilung der politischen Lage,' 29 July 1914 (marked received same day), no. 349 in DD, vol. 2.

16. Cited in Albertini, vol. 2, 491.

17. Moltke memorandum to Bethmann, 'Zur Beurteilung der politischen Lage.'

18. Bethmann to Schoen, 29 July 1914 (12:50 PM), no. 341 in DD, vol. 2.

19. Bethmann to Pourtalès, 29 July 1914 (12:50 PM), no. 342 in DD, vol. 2.

20. Szapáry to Berchtold, 29 July 1914 (11 PM), reporting a conversation with Sazonov, in which Sazonov learned (by telephone) about the bombardment, no. 11003 in OeE-U, vol. 8. For the sequence of events detailed here, see Foreign Ministry log entry for 16/29 July 1914, in Schilling, 47–48.

21. Pourtalès to Jagow, 29 July 1914 (8 PM), no. 378 in DD, vol. 2.

22. Schilling, 48–49 (I have translated the internal quotes, which Schilling gives in the original French).

23. Entry for 16/29 July, in Schilling, 49; and, for the timing (which Schilling gets wrong), see Nicky-Willy telegram of 8:20 PM, cited immediately following.

24. Nicky to Willy from Peterhof, 29 July 1914 (8:20 PM), arrived Potsdam 8:42 PM, no. 366 in DD, vol. 2.

25. 'Permission to S. D. Sazonov . . . ': Entry for 16/29 July, in Schilling, 49–50. 'A war with a coalition': Yanushkevitch to Yudenich, 16/29 July 1914, in RGVIA, fond 2000, opis' 1, del' 3796, list' 19. On the mobilisation orders being carried around in his pocket: citation in Albertini, vol. 2, 547.

26. Entry for 16/29 July, in Schilling, 49–50.

27. Dobrorolskii, 25 and passim.

28. Willy to Nicky, 29 July 1914 (6:30 PM): deciphered at 9:20 PM and delivered to Peterhof Palace at 9:40 PM, according to Schilling, 55.

29. Citations in Albertini, vol. 2, 558–559.

30. Dobrorolskii, 25 and passim. Dobrorolskii claims this all happened at 9:30 PM, but as the tsar did not read Willy's telegram until 9:40 PM, this is too early; 10 PM is a likelier estimate.

31. Tirpitz, 287–288.

32. Cited in Albertini, vol. 2, 500.

33. Chelius to Jagow, 29 July 1914 (2:30 PM, received Berlin 3:15 PM), no. 344 in DD, vol. 2.

34. Cited in Zuber, 157.

35. German General Staff to Wilhelmstrasse, 29 July 1914 (4 PM), no. 372 in DD, vol. 2, 91–94.

36. Lichnowsky to Jagow, 29 July 1914 (2:10 PM, arrived Berlin 4:34 PM), no. 355 in DD, vol. 2.

37. Lichnowsky to Jagow, 29 July 1914 (2:08 PM, arrived Berlin 5:07 PM), no. 357 in DD, vol. 2.

38. Falkenhayn notes of 29 July 1914 meeting, cited in Albertini, 502.

39. Prince Heinrich of Prussia to Kaiser Wilhelm II, 28 July 1914, no. 374 in DD, vol. 2, 96–97. On the timing of the prince's arrival in Potsdam, see Fay, vol. 2, 500.

40. Goschen to Grey, 30 July 1914 (1:20 AM), reporting 10:30 PM conversation with Bethmann, no. 293 in BD, vol. 11.

41. Sir Eyre Crowe, minuting on Goschen to Grey, 30 July 1914 (1:20 AM).

42. Asquith, 30 July 1914, 136.

43. Lichnowsky to Jagow, 29 July 1914 (6:39 PM, arrived Berlin 9:12 PM), no. 368 in DD, vol. 2.

44. Buchanan to Grey, 24 July 1914 (5:40 PM), no. 101 in BD, vol. 11.

45. Cited in Jannen Jr., 198.

46. Churchill, vol. 1, 216.

47. Bethmann to Tschirschky, passing on Lichnowsky's 6:39 PM telegram with commentary, 30 July 1914 (2:55 AM), no. 395 in DD, vol. 2.

48. Bethmann to Tschirschky, 30 July 1914 (3:00 AM), no. 396 in DD, vol. 2.

49. Pourtalès to Bethmann Hollweg, 30 July 1914, 4:39 AM (arrived Berlin 7:10 AM), in PAAA, R 19873.

50. Nicky to Willy from Peterhof Palace, 30 July 1914 (1:20 AM, received Potsdam 1:45 AM), no. 390 in DD, vol. 2.

Notes to Chapter 20   Slaughter It Is

1. Kaiser's marginal notes on Nicky to Willy from Peterhof Palace, 30 July 1914 (1:20 AM, received Potsdam 1:45 AM), no. 390 in DD, vol. 2.

2. Kaiser's marginal notes on Bethmann to Kaiser Wilhelm II, written 29 July 1914 and sent to Neues Palais 6 AM on 30 July 1914, passing on Pourtalès of previous day, marked read by Kaiser 7 AM, 30 July, no. 399 in DD, vol. 2.

3. Willy to Nicky, 30 July 1914 (3:30 PM), no. 420 in DD, vol. 2; and, for immediate backdrop, Bethmann to Kaiser Wilhelm II, passing on Grey/Lichnowsky of previous night, 30 July 1914 (dispatched to Potsdam 11:15 AM by automobile), no. 407 in DD, vol. 2.

4. Cited in Conrad, vol. 4, 151–152; see also Fay, vol. 2, 506–507 and 507n62.

5. Albertini, vol. 3, 6.

6. Turner, 108–109. 'Far advanced': Zuber, 157.

7. Conrad, vol. 4, 152 (emphasis added).

8. Cited in Turner, 109.

9. Danilov, *La Russie dans la guerre mondiale*, 39.

10. Cited in Albertini, vol. 2, 586–587.

11. Entry for 15/28 July 1914, in Schilling, 43.

12. See Schmidt, 334.

13. Sazonov to Izvolsky, 17/30 July 1914, in LN, 289 (emphasis added).

14. The best documentation of the evening's timeline is in Schmidt, 231–232. For 'Good God! . . . ,' see citations in Jannen Jr., 182–183, and Tuchman, 109 (her translation from the French is somewhat more colourful). Tuchman, however, gets the date of these encounters dramatically wrong: by two days. See also epilogue.

15. Jules Cambon to Bienvenu-Martin, 25 July 1914, 1:15 AM, received Paris 2:50 AM, in QO Autriche-Hongrie, vol. 32.

16. Viviani to Paléologue, 30 July 1914 (7 AM), no. 305 in DDF, ser. 3, vol. 11; also no. 294 in BD, vol. 11 (emphasis added). For further analysis of this critical dispatch, see Albertini, vol. 2, 604n1; Schmidt, 319.

17. Poincaré diary entry, 30 July 1914, cited in Schmidt, 322.

18. Izvolsky to Sazonov, 30 July 1914, in LN, 290.

19. Tsar Nicholas II, diary entries for 16 (29) and 17 (30) July 1914, in GARF, fond 601, opis' 1, del' 261, list' 158–160.

20. Entry for 17/30 July 1914, in Schilling, 62–63.

21. Ibid., 63–64. For 'coax out of the French a promise of neutrality . . . upon my telephone call in the afternoon': cited in Fay, vol. 2, 469–470.

22. As reported by Buchanan to Grey, 30 July 1914 (1:15 PM), no. 302 in BD, vol. 11.

23. Pourtalès to Jagow, 30 July 1914 (1:01 PM), no. 421 in DD, vol. 2.

24. Buchanan to Grey, 30 July 1914 (1:15 PM), no. 302 in BD, vol. 11. That the Sazonov-Pourtalès meeting Sazonov discussed in Buchanan's presence took place between 11 AM and noon on 30 July 1914 is confirmed by the numbering of Pourtalès' telegrams to Berlin (when compared against Sazonov's noontime meeting with Paléologue/Buchanan, and his 12:30 PM lunch with Krivoshein): Pourtalès's 30 July 1914 (1:01 PM) telegram was no. 192, directly following no. 191, sent off at 11 AM; the one reporting the previous night's confrontation with Sazonov, by contrast, was no. 189, sent off at 4:30 AM. For more on the timing of these meetings, see Pourtalès, 46–47.

25. Entry for 17/30 July 1914, in Schilling, 64.

26. Cited in Albertini, vol. 2, 570.

27. Entry for 17/30 July 1914, in Schilling, 64–65.

28. Paléologue, vol. 1, 45.

29. Entry for 17/30 July 1914, in Schilling, 65–66.

30. Dobrorolskii, 28.

31. Entry for 18/31 July 1914, in Schilling, 69.

32. Tsar's mobilisation directive, 30 July 1914, to be made active at midnight, cited in Schmitt, vol. 2, 245.

33. Sazonov to Izvolsky, 17/30 July 1914, in LN, 292.

34. Paléologue to Viviani, 30 July 1914 (9:15 PM), no. 359 in DDF, ser. 3, vol. 111. On the purging of the key sentence from this telegram from the *Yellow Book*, see Albertini, vol. 2, 620.

35. Sazonov to Benckendorff, 17/30 July 1914, no. 281 in IBZI, vol. 5.

36. Dobrorolskii, 28 and passim.

37. Cited in Fay, vol. 2, 491.

38. Viviani (via Abel Ferry) to Cambon, 30 July 1914: reproduced as no. 319 in BD, vol. 11. For analysis of *couverture* and its real nature, see Schmidt, 344–345.

Notes to Chapter 21   Last Chance Saloon

1. Bethmann's first urgent instructions to Vienna: Bethmann to Tschirschky, 30 July 1914 (9 PM), received Vienna 3 AM on 31 July, no. 441 in DD, vol. 2. Wired again to disregard: Bethmann to Tschirschky, 30 July 1914 (11:20 PM), no. 450 in DD, vol. 2. Changed instructions again: Bethmann to Tschirschky, 31 July 1914 (2:45 AM), arrived Vienna 9 AM, no. 464 in DD, vol. 2.

2. Cited in Albertini, vol. 3, 33 (emphasis added).

3. Goschen to Grey (by private letter), undated but presumably 31 July 1914, no. 677 in BD, vol. 11.

4. Goschen to Grey, 31 July 1914 (11:55 AM), no. 337 in BD, vol. 11. This precisely dated dispatch confirms the gist of the conversation described in the longer letter, although with less detail.

5. Pourtalès to Jagow, 31 July 1914 (10:20 AM), received Berlin 11:40 AM, no. 473 in DD, vol. 2.

6. Details regarding *Kriegsgefahrzustand* in Albertini, vol. 3, 38; on the timing, see Fay, vol. 2, 523.

7. Kaiser Wilhelm II, marginalia on Pourtalès to Jagow, 30 July 1914 (4:30 AM), received Berlin 7:10 AM, read by Kaiser at 7 PM on 30 July 1914, no. 401 in DD, vol. 2.

8. Willy to Nicky, 31 July 1914 (2:04 PM), no. 480 in DD, vol. 3.

9. Willy to King George V, 31 July 1914 (12:55 PM), no. 477 in DD, vol. 2.

10. Protocol of the meeting of the Prussian State Ministry on 30 July 1914, no. 456 in DD, vol. 2.

11. Bethmann's 31 July 1914 telegrams to his ambassadors comprise nos. 479, 488, 490–492 in DD, vol. 2 and vol. 3. The one to Schoen is no. 491, dispatched at 3:30 PM. The ones to Petersburg, Rome, and London were sent between 3:10 PM and 3:30 PM. No. 479, to Tschirschky in Vienna, was sent a bit earlier (1:40 PM), such that it mentioned everything but the twelve-hour deadline to Russia for compliance.

12. Details in Marcus, 244, and Liaquat Ahamed, *Lords of Finance*, 29–30.

13. Asquith, 31 July 1914, 138.

14. Cited in Jannen Jr., 252.

15. Grey to Bertie, 31 July 1914 (7:30 PM), no. 352 in BD, vol. 11. 'Tapped on the shoulder . . . beaten you after all': cited in Marcus, 235–236.

16. As noted by Jannen Jr., 253.

17. Grey to Bertie, 31 July 1914, no. 367 in BD, vol. 11, 226–227. On Grey's source as to Russian mobilisation, see Albertini, vol. 3, 373.

18. Grey to Bertie, 31 July 1914 (5:30 PM), no. 348 in BD, vol. 11. 'Unburdened himself': cited in Jannen Jr., 254.

19. McMeekin, *Berlin-Baghdad Express*, 107 and passim.

20. On the French mobilisation plan and how it intersected with the German one, see Schmidt, 343–344.

21. Albertini, vol. 3, 67.

22. Jules Cambon to Viviani, 31 July 1914 (2:17 PM, received 3:30 PM), no. 402 in DDF, ser. 3, vol. 11.

23. On the dispute over whether Schoen specified that German mobilisation was tantamount to war, see Albertini, vol. 3, 76–80.

24. Viviani to Paléologue, 31 July 1914 (9/9:30 PM), no. 438 in DDF, ser. 3, vol. 11; and, for Viviani's promise to reply by 1 PM on Saturday, Schoen to Jagow, 31 July 1914 (8:17 PM, received 1 August 12:30 AM), no. 528 in DD, vol. 3.

25. Cited in Albertini, vol. 3, 91.

26. Paléologue to Viviani, 31 July 1914 (10:43 AM, received 8:30 PM), in QO Autriche-Hongrie, vol. 32.

27. Viviani to Paléologue, 31 July 1914 (9/9:30 PM), no. 438 in DDF, ser. 3, vol. 11. For the point about decoding taking only a few minutes: Albertini, vol. 3, 89.

28. Cited in Beatty, 244.

29. Tuchman, *Proud Tower*, 461; for the details on the pistols, Berenson, *Trial of Madame Caillaux*, 242.

30. Cited in Albertini, vol. 3, 87–88.

31. Jannen Jr., 274. On the *Carnet B*: Tuchman, 108.

32. Bertie to Grey, 1 August 1914 (1:10 AM), no. 380 in BD, vol. 11.

33. Bertie to Grey, 1 August 1914 (1:12 AM), no. 382 in BD, vol. 11.

34. Izvolsky to Sazonov, 1 August 1914 (1 AM), cited in Albertini, vol. 2, 85.

35. Cited in Albertini, vol. 3, 94–95.

36. Fay, vol. 2, 518–519.

37. Jules Cambon to Viviani, 31 July 1914 (2:17 PM, received 3:30 PM).

Notes to Chapter 22   'Now You Can Do What You Want'

1. Cited in Albertini, vol. 3, 99–100.

2. Barrère to Viviani, 31 August 1914, no. 411 in DDF, ser. 3, vol. 11.

3. Cited in Albertini, vol. 3, 100.

4. Viviani to Cambon, 31 July 1914, no. 338 in BD, vol. 11.

5. Albertini, vol. 3, 379.

6. Bethmann 'communication,' as translated and passed on to the British Foreign Office, 31 July 1914, no. 372 in BD, vol. 11 (emphasis added).

7. King George V to Tsar Nicholas II, passed on, Grey to Buchanan, 1 August 1914 (3:30 AM), no. 384 in BD, vol. 11.

8. Asquith, 1 August 1914, 140.

9. Lichnowsky, *Heading for the Abyss*, 13, as compared to King George V to Tsar Nicholas II, 1 August 1914 (3:30 AM).

10. Albertini, vol. 3, 379.

11. King George V to President Poincaré, no. 550 in DDF, ser. 3, vol. 11.

12. Lichnowsky to Jagow, 1 August 1914 (11:14 AM, received 4:23 PM), no. 562 in DD, vol. 3, 66.

13. Churchill, vol. 1, 229–230.

14. Cited in Fromkin, 237–238. 'Daemonic energy': Morley on Churchill, cited in Tuchman, 113.

15. Asquith, 1 August 1914, 140.

16. Cited in Albertini, vol. 3, 388. For 'whatever happened in Belgium': cited in Tuchman, 113.

17. Schoen to Jagow, 1 August 1914 (1:05 PM, received 6:10 PM), no. 571 in DD, vol. 3. For *Évidemment*: cited in Tuchman, 110.

18. Viviani to ambassadors, 1 August 1914, no. 505 in DDF, ser. 3, vol. 11.

19. Cited in Albertini, vol. 3, 103.

20. Citations in ibid., vol. 3, 105.

21. Cited in Tuchman, 110–111.

22. Recouly, cited in Albertini, vol. 3, 107. 'Packed to suffocation point': cited in Marcus, 253. Other details: Tuchman, 110–111.

23. Recouly/Messimy, cited in Albertini, vol. 3, 103.

24. Pourtalès to Jagow, 1 August 1914, no. 536 in DD, vol. 3.

25. Protocol of the Bundesrat, 1 August 1914 (morning), no. 553 in DD, vol. 3.

26. Jagow to Pourtalès, 1 August 1914 (12:52 PM), no. 542 in DD, vol. 3.

27. Bethmann to Schoen, 1 August 1914 (1:05 PM), no. 543 in DD, vol. 3.

28. Bethmann, vol. 1, 165.

29. Tirpitz, 290–291.

30. Cited in Tuchman, 94.

31. Zuber, 157.

32. 'Aufzeichnung Falkenhayns,' no. 1000a in Geiss, vol. 2.

33. 'Aufzeichnung Tirpitz,' no. 1000d in Geiss, vol. 2.

34. Jannen Jr., 297.

35. 'Tagebucheintragung Lynckers,' no. 1000b in Geiss, vol. 2.

36. 'Aufzeichnung Moltkes,' no. 1000c in Geiss, vol. 2.

37. Tuchman, 95.

38. 'Aufzeichnung Moltkes'; for the phone order, 'Aufzeichnung Falkenhayns,' no. 1000a in Geiss, vol. 2, 556n4.

39. 'Aufzeichnung Tirpitz,' in Geiss, vol. 2.

40. Kaiser Wilhelm II to King George V, no. 575 in DD, vol. 2.

41. Bethmann to Lichnowsky, 1 August 1914 (7:15 PM), no. 578 in DD, vol. 3.

42. 'Aufzeichnung Moltkes.'

43. Lichnowsky to Jagow, 1 August 1914 (2:10 PM, received Berlin 6:04 PM, marked read by Kaiser Wilhelm II 8:30 PM), no. 570 in DD, vol. 3. Champagne for everyone: Jannen Jr., 299.

44. Jagow to Schoen, 1 August 1914 (8:45 PM), no. 587 in DD, vol. 3.

45. Nicky to Willy, 1 August 1914 (2:06 PM, received Berlin 2:05 PM), no. 546 in DD, vol. 3.

46. Willy to Nicky, 1 August 1914 (9:45 PM), no. 600 in DD, vol. 3.

47. Schilling, 76–77; compare Sazonov, 212–213, and Pourtalès, 73–74.

48. Pourtalès, 73–74.

49. King George V to Kaiser Wilhelm II, 1 August 1914, no. 612 in DD, vol. 3.

50. Bertie to Grey, 2 August 1914 (2:15 AM), no. 453 in BD, vol. 11, responding to Grey to Bertie, 1 August 1914 (5:25 PM), no. 419 in BD, vol. 11. For Grey mentioning the offer to an incredulous Paul Cambon: Grey to Bertie, 1 August 1914 (8:20 PM), no. 426 in BD, vol. 11.

51. 'Aufzeichnung Moltkes.'

Notes to Chapter 23   Britain Wakes Up to the Danger

1. Tirpitz minute, cited in Albertini, vol. 2, 195.

2. Ibid. On Bethmann's learning of the assault on Liège only on 31 July: Turner, 'Schlieffen Plan,' 213.

3. Bethmann to Wangenheim, 1 August 1914 (2:30 PM), no. 547 in DD, vol. 3.

4. Wangenheim to Bethmann, 1 August 1914 (12:20 PM), no. 652 in DD, vol. 3.

5. Bethmann to German consul in Luxembourg, 11:30 AM, no. 640 in DD, vol. 3, and Eyschen's reply to Bethmann and Jagow, 3 August 1914 (10:14 AM), no. 730 in DD, vol. 3.

6. Communication from French embassy, 2 August 1914 (4:40 PM), no. 486 in BD, vol. 11.

7. Jagow to Flotow, 2 August 1914 (4:35 PM), no. 664 in DD, vol. 3, and, for French pilot being shot down, Lichnowsky to Tyrrell, 3 August 1914 (12:25 AM), no. 539 (and enclosures) in BD, vol. 11.

8. Cited in Tuchman, 121.

9. Bertie to Grey, 1 August 1914 (12:30 PM), no. 403 in BD, vol. 11. For analysis of what Poincaré must have known when he lied to Bertie, see Albertini, vol. 3, 112–117.

10. Asquith, 2 August 1914, 146. For 'she won't do it..': Grey, vol. 1, 327–328.

11. Citations in Albertini, vol. 3, 401–402.

12. Cited in Albertini, vol. 3, 399.

13. Asquith, 2 August 1914, 146.

14. Churchill, vol. 1, 232.

15. Citations in Jannen Jr., 327–328.

16. Morley, *Memorandum on Resignation*, 12–15.

17. Cambon, cited in Albertini, vol. 3, 406–407.

18. Morley, *Memorandum on Resignation*.

19. Cited in Albertini, vol. 3, 410.

20. Cited in Jannen Jr., 332.

21. Jagow to Below-Selaske, 29 July 1914 (to be opened later), no. 376 in DD, vol. 2.

22. Citations in Tuchman, 130.

23. Jagow to Below-Selaske, 2 August 1914 (6:55 PM), and Below-Selaske back to Jagow, 3 August 1914 (3:05 AM), no. 677 and 709 in DD, vol. 3.

24. Belgian reply note in: Below-Selaske to Jagow, 3 August 1914 (12:55 PM), no. 779 in DD, vol. 4.

Notes to Chapter 24   Sir Edward Grey's Big Moment
1. Lloyd George, vol. 1, 61.
2. Lichnowsky to Jagow, 3 August 1914 (1:02 PM), no. 764 in DD, vol. 4.
3. Asquith, 3 August 1914, 148.
4. Ibid. For the news confirming the German ultimatum, and Belgium's refusal: Sir F. Villers to Sir Edward Grey (from Brussels), 3 August 1914 (9:31 AM, received 10:55 AM), no. 521 in BD, vol. 11.
5. Lloyd George, vol. 1, 60.
6. Tuchman, 137–139. Trevelyan: cited in Jannen Jr., 344.
7. Grey, vol. 2, 14.
8. This recollection (and the Derby quote) is cited in Tuchman, 140–141. For the full text of Grey's speech (including interjections from the benches): Grey, *Speeches on Foreign Affairs*, 297–315.
9. Trevelyan and Liberal/Labour dissent: cited in Jannen Jr., 348.
10. Lichnowsky to Jagow, 3 August 1914 (10 PM), no. 801 in DD, vol. 4.
11. Schoen, 'In Paris überreichter Text der Kriegserklärung,' 3 August 1914, no. 734b in DD, vol. 3; compare to Bethmann's originals, no. 734 and 734a.
12. Turner, 'Schlieffen Plan,' 213.
13. Churchill, vol. 1, 235.
14. Grey to Goschen, 4 August 1914 (9:30 AM), no. 573 in BD, vol. 11 (emphasis added).
15. Widely cited, as in Jannen Jr., 348.

Notes to Chapter 25   World War: No Going Back
1. Cited in Tuchman, 148. On the timing of the session: Schmitt, vol. 2, 391.
2. Zuber, 158.
3. Asquith, 4 August 1914, 150.
4. Grey to Goschen, 4 August 1914 (2 PM), no. 594 in BD, vol. 11.
5. Jouhaux, cited in Albertini, vol. 3, 225.
6. Poincaré and Viviani to French parliament, 4 August 1914, cited in Albertini, vol. 3, 225–228.
7. Cited in Jannen Jr., 355.
8. Bethmann Hollweg to Reichstag, 4 August 1914 (3:30 PM), no. 1146 in Geiss, vol. 2. Tirpitz on 'greatest blunder': cited in Tuchman, 152. 'Frantic applause and highest enthusiasm': cited in Albertini, vol. 3, 224.
9. German Foreign Office to German ambassador, London, 4 August 1914 (4:38 PM), no. 612 in BD, vol. 11.
10. Cited in Albertini, vol. 3, 225.

11. Goschen to Grey, 6 August 1914, no. 671 in BD, vol. 11. For Bethmann's recollection of Goschen bursting into tears: Bethmann, vol. 1, 180.

12. Tuchman, 176.

Notes to Epilogue   The Question of Responsibility

1. Churchill, foreword to Edward Spears, *Liaison 1914*.

2. This Austrian counterfactual, along with those on France and Britain, builds on those spun out in Beatty, chapters 3, 5, and 6.

3. Zuber, 177.

4. For a summary of the state of the art in research on Serbian complicity and policy, see Williamson and May, 'Identity of Opinion,' 351–353. Princip quote footnoted: in Stone, *World War One*, 19.

5. On this question, see the discussion in McMeekin, *Russian Origins*, chapter 2 (and notes).

6. Cited in Schmitt, vol. 2, 250–251.

7. Zuber, 159.

8. See Zuber generally, along with the discussion of his work in, among many other places, Strachan, *First World War*, and Williamson and May, 'Identity of Opinion.'

9. Again, the best summary of arguments regarding Grey is in Williamson and May, 'Identity of Opinion.'

10. Cited in Fuller, *Strategy and Power*, 450. Sukhomlinov's optimism was not unfounded. Initial Russian reconnaissance, completed by 10 August, revealed that the Germans had only four infantry corps in East Prussia, plus a few reserve divisions. Against this, the Russians deployed nine army corps. Because each Russian division contained 16 battalions, to 12 for German ones, the Russian battalion advantage was 480 to 130. In artillery, the breakdown was particularly lopsided: 5,800 Russian guns against 774 German. For a fuller discussion, see McMeekin, *Russian Origins*, chapter 3.

BIBLIOGRAPHY

THE PLACE TO BEGIN any study of the July crisis remains Luigi Albertini's superb three-volume history of *The Origins of the War of 1914*, available in English translation by Isabella M. Massey (Oxford University Press, 1952). Albertini's curiosity and energy were boundless; he not only tracked down thousands of documents but also conducted interviews with many of the principals. His history, owing in part to the collaborative effort of Professor Luciano Magrini (who finished assembling the volumes after Albertini's death), is thorough and meticulous, covering, annotating, and excerpting virtually all relevant diplomatic correspondence from the Austro-Hungarian Ausgleich of 1867 to August 1914. Today's historians are also indebted to Professor Samuel R. Williamson Jr., who brought out a new edition from Enigma Books in 2005 (this is the one I have used). As Williamson writes in the foreword, 'whenever I need to check a date, verify a name, or simply to be reminded of the qualities and attributes of a great historical work, I reach for Albertini.' I do the same.

The only thing one needs to be a bit wary about with Albertini is the translations. This is no fault of Albertini, Magrini, or Massey; rather it reflects the inevitable difficulty of rendering documents from a multitude of languages (English, French, German, Russian, Serbo-Croatian) into Albertini's Italian and then English. For the most part, Massey did a superb job. When I cite Albertini in the notes, I am using Massey's translation.

The volumes of Sidney Fay and Bernadotte Schmitt, which came out before Albertini's and thus missed some of the material that became available in the 1930s, nevertheless remain essential reading. Fay, in *The Origins of the World War*, 2 vols. (Macmillan, 1935), is particularly good on the Black Hand and the milieu in Sarajevo, and also on the Russian mobilisation. Schmitt's *The Coming of the War, 1914*, 2 vols. (Charles Scribner's Sons, 1930) is strong on the last days of July and the first days of August, and particularly on Belgium, where Fay's own volume tends to tail off.

Of course, many fine studies have appeared since those of Fay, Schmitt, and Albertini. Following Albertini's lead, Imanuel Geiss produced a kind of annotated documentary history in two volumes (*Julikrise und Kriegsausbruch 1914*, 1963–1964), which adds a number of documents, including those published by the Bolsheviks, to the ones originally reproduced in the 'Kautsky' volumes of German documents published after the war. An abridged English-language translation was also published as *July 1914*. Still, in his interpretation and selection of documents to include (or ignore), Geiss, along with Fritz Fischer (*Griff nach der Weltmacht*, 1961; *Krieg der Illusionen*, 1969) and Holger Herwig (recently, with Richard Hamilton, *The Origins of World War I*, 2003) has come to stand for a kind of Germanocentric orthodoxy that I find ultimately unsatisfying. The fashion in recent years, among many First World War historians, has been to say that the 'revelations' of Fischer-Geiss-Herwig relating to Germany's long-term ambitions and her short-term premeditation during July 1914 (the 'preventive war') have superseded the more balanced interpretations of Fay, Albertini, and Schmitt. In this vein, see especially David Fromkin, *Europe's Last Summer: Who Started the Great War in 1914?* (Knopf, 2004).

As I have already made clear in my own *The Russian Origins of the First World War* (Harvard, 2011), I do not agree with the German 'preventive war' thesis. Even in what we might call the 'high Fritz Fischer era' (i.e., the 1960s–1970s), thoughtful historians, refusing to buckle to the emerging orthodoxy, continued producing more nuanced interpretations of the July crisis. Among them I think L. C. F. Turner's work has best stood the test of time. Turner produced excellent studies on both Germany's role in the outbreak of the war (as in his critical study of the Schlieffen Plan in the 1979 Paul Kennedy volume on the *War Plans of the Great Powers*) and the importance of Russia's early mobilisation ('The Russian Mobilisation in 1914,' published in 1968). Turner's elegant, concise study, *Origins of the First World War* (1970), is one of the most balanced and useful narrative accounts since Albertini's.

As Samuel R. Williamson Jr. and Ernest R. May point out in their recent, illogically titled review essay, 'An Identity of Opinion: Historians and July 1914' (2007), there remains a multitude of interpretations of the origins of the war, even if consensus now exists on certain subjects – e.g., Apis and the Black Hand; that Austria took many actions independently of (or directly contrary to) German advice; the importance of the Franco-British naval agreement in buttressing and possibly outweighing Belgium in Britain's path to belligerence. Far from confirming an 'identity of opinion,' Williamson and May assert that, contrary to the Fischer-Geiss-Herwig school, 'no convincing evidence has surfaced to support a contention that the German generals actually launched a preventive war in 1914.' It seems that not even the Fischer debate – which so thoroughly dominated the field for decades that many historians nearly forgot about the other powers in their zeal to unearth evidence of plotting in Berlin – has resolved the issues of responsibility debated by Fay, Schmitt, and Albertini. While we know a fantastic amount today about the thinking of policymakers in Vienna and Berlin, it is not altogether clear to me that we know much more than Albertini did.

We do know far more about the social, economic, and military-technological sides of the war and its outbreak today than Albertini did. In these areas, the recent general histories by Hew Strachan (*The First World War, Volume 1: To Arms*, 2001) and David Stevenson (*Cataclysm: The First World War as Political Tragedy*, 2004) are essential. Stevenson is particularly good on economics. Strachan has mastered the literature on war planning, gaming, and execution of all the main belligerents, up to 2001 at least. If one wants to know about the latest research on British naval and expeditionary planning, French and Russian mobilisation scenarios, the debates surrounding Terence Zuber's critique of received wisdom on the Germans' Schlieffen Plan, or the best available information on the initial battles of the war (including extra-European theatres), Strachan is the place to start.

The areas where our knowledge of the war's outbreak is incomplete remain the same now as ever: the role of French officials in sanctioning or encouraging Russia's early mobilisation; the exact nature of that mobilisation and whether it 'constituted war'; whether Paléologue was acting as a free agent in St Petersburg, taking orders from the French General Staff, or working on prior authorisation from the president; and, finally, the enigmatic role of Poincaré at the summit and at sea – what he knew and when he knew it.

For this reason, one of the most important revisionist works published in recent years is Stefan Schmidt's *Frankreichs Aussenpolitik in der Julikrise 1914* (Oldenbourg, 2009). Because it has not been translated into English, the impact of Schmidt's book has not yet been fully felt among First World War historians. But it will be. Schmidt's close reading of Poincaré's thinking and intentions – especially through his diaries and diplomatic correspondence, including published Russian sources – has greatly undermined the less critical interpretation of John Keiger (most recently *Raymond Poincaré*, 1997). Complementing my own *Russian Origins*, which draws on Russian archival sources to explore the assumptions, interests, and intentions behind policymaking in Petersburg from 1914 to 1917, Schmidt's book rounds out the long-neglected Franco-Russian side of the July crisis.

Among recent histories, I have also found stimulating William Jannen Jr.'s *The Lions of July* (Presidio, 1996), Michael Neiberg's *Dance of the Furies* (Harvard, 2011), and Jack Beatty's *The Lost History of 1914* (Bloomsbury, 2012). Of these, Jannen Jr. is best on high politics; Neiberg and Beatty are better on the social backdrop of the war's outbreak. Although Beatty's work, unlike Jannen Jr.'s and Neiberg's, is based almost entirely on secondary sources, Beatty has devoured these with gusto. Beatty and Neiberg both display deep sympathy with the ordinary men and women swept up into a cataclysmic war they had nothing to do with and did not want. Beatty has written a fascinating alternative history, spinning out plausible scenarios in which Europe would *not* have plunged into war in 1914. He is particularly good on the Irish Home Rule crisis, the Caillaux affair and its possible echoes, and the contingencies relating to the assassination of Franz Ferdinand. While I did not find Beatty's take on the German and Russian sides of 1914 as convincing, I admire the spirit of his and Neiberg's studies, reimagining history as it might have been. Like Niall Ferguson, who has written at length on the issue, I see counterfactual reasoning as central to the historical enterprise – and far more constructive than 'consensus' interpretations designed to close off further argument. Albertini's classic volumes are replete with lively 'what if' scenarios, which are essential to his judgments on statesmen and their responsibility for the catastrophe; rather than close off further argument, they invite them.

In the end, historians must make up their own minds about controversial matters such as responsibility for the outbreak of the First World War. An issue as explosive as this, as central to our understanding of modern history, can never be fully resolved by consensus. I invite readers wishing to know more to consult the sources themselves and to draw their own conclusions.

Frequently Cited Sources

Below is a list of frequently cited sources, listed alphabetically by the abbreviation used in the endnotes.

Albertini	Albertini, Luigi. *The Origins of the War of 1914*. 3 vols. Translated by Isabella M. Massey. New and updated edition, with introduction by Samuel R. Williamson Jr. New York: Enigma Books, 2005. First published by Oxford University Press, 1952–1957. Page references are to the 2005 edition.
Asquith	Asquith, H. H. *Letters to Venetia Stanley*. Edited by Michael and Eleanor Brock. Oxford: Oxford University Press, 1982.
AVPRI	Arkhiv Vneshnei Politiki Rossiiskoi Imperii. Moscow, Russia.
BD	*British Documents on the Origins of the War, 1898-1914*. Edited by G. P. Gooch and Harold Temperley. 13 vols. London: H. M. S. O., 1926–1938.
Beatty	Beatty, Jack. *The Lost History of 1914: How the Great War Was Not Inevitable*. London: Bloomsbury, 2012.
Bethmann	Bethmann Hollweg, Theobald von. *Betrachtungen zum Weltkriege*. Edited by Jost Dülffer. 2 vols. Essen: Reimar Hobbing, 1989.
Churchill	Churchill, Winston. *The World Crisis*. 6 vols. New York: Charles Scribner's Sons, 1951–1959.
Conrad	Conrad von Hötzendorf, Franz. *Aus meiner Dienstzeit*. 4 vols. Vienna: Rikola Verlag, 1921–1925.
DD	*Die deutschen Dokumente zum Kriegsausbruch*. Edited by Karl Kautsky, Max Montgelas, and Prof. Walter Schücking. 4 vols. Charlottenburg, Berlin: Deutsche Verlagsgesellschaft für Politik und Geschichte, 1919.
DDF	*Documents diplomatiques français (1871–1914)*. 41 vols. Paris: Imprimerie Nationale, 1929–1959.
Dobrorolskii	Dobrorolskii, Sergei. *Die Mobilmachung der rusischen Armee 1914*. Berlin: Deutsche Verlagsgesellschaft für Politik und Geschichte, 1922.

Erenyi	Erenyi, Gustav. *Graf Stefan Tisza, ein staatsmann und märtyrer*. Vienna: E. P. Tal, 1935.
Fay	Fay, Sidney Bradshaw. *The Origins of the World War*. 2 vols. New York: Macmillan, 1935. All translations Fay's, unless otherwise noted.
Fromkin	Fromkin, David. *Europe's Last Summer: Who Started the Great War in 1914?* New York: Alfred A. Knopf, 2004.
GARF	Gosudarstvennyi Arkhiv Rossiiskoi Federatsii. Moscow, Russia.
Geiss	*Julikrise und Kriegsausbruch 1914*. 2 vols. 2nd ed. Bonn-Bad Godesberg: Verlag Neue Gesellschaft GmbH, 1976.
Grey	Grey, Edward, Viscount ('of Fallodon'). *Twenty-Five Years, 1892–1916*. 2 vols. New York: Frederick A. Stokes, 1925.
Hantsch	Hantsch, Hugo. *Leopold Graf Berchtold, Grandseigneur und Staatsmann*. Graz: Verlag Styria, 1963.
HHSA	Haus-, Hof- und Staatsarchiv. Vienna.
IBZI	*Internationale Beziehungen im Zeitalter des Imperialismus*. Edited by M. N. Pokrovskii. 8+ vols. Berlin: R. Hobbing, 1931–.
Jannen Jr.	Jannen Jr., William. *The Lions of July: Prelude to War, 1914*. Novato, CA: Presidio, 1996.
Jarausch	Jarausch, Konrad. *The Enigmatic Chancellor: Bethmann Hollweg and the Hubris of Imperial Germany*. New Haven, CT: Yale University Press, 1973.
Kokovtsov	*Out of My Past: The Memoirs of Count Kokovtsov, Russian Minister of Finance, 1904–1914, Chairman of the Council of Ministers*. Edited by H. H. Fisher. Translated by Laura Matveev. Stanford, CA: Stanford University Press, 1935.
Lloyd George	Lloyd George, David. *War Memoirs of David Lloyd George*. 6 vols. Boston: Little, Brown, 1933–1937.
LN	*Un livre noir: Diplomatie d'avant-guerre d'après les documents des archives russes, Novembre 1910-Juillet 1914*. Preface by René Marchard. Paris: Librairie du travail, 1922.
Marcus	Marcus, Geoffrey Jules. *Before the Lamps Went Out*. London: Allen & Unwin, 1965.

Neiberg   Neiberg, Michael. *Dance of the Furies: Europe and the Outbreak of World War I*. Cambridge, MA: Harvard University Press / Belknap, 2011.

Nikitsch-Boulles   Nikitsch-Boulles, Paul. *Vor dem Sturm: Erinnerungen an Erzherzog Thronfolger Franz Ferdinand*. Berlin: Verlag für Kulturpolitik, 1925.

Oe-U   *Österreich-Ungarns Aussenpolitik von der bosnischen Krise 1908 bis zum Kriegsausbruch 1914*. Edited by Ludwig Bitter et al. 9 vols. Vienna: Österreichischer Bundesverlag für Unterricht, Wissenschaft und Kunst, 1930.

PAAA   Politisches Archiv des Auswärtigen Amtes. Berlin.

Paléologue   Paléologue, Maurice. *An Ambassador's Memoirs*. Translated by F. A. Holt. 3 vols. London: Hutchinson, 1923–1925.

PBM   Peter Bark Memoirs. Rare Book and Manuscript Library, Columbia University, New York.

Pharos   *Der Prozeß gegen die Attentäter von Sarajewo*. Edited by Professor Pharos. Berlin: R. v. Decker's Verlag, 1918.

Poincaré   Poincaré, Raymond. *Memoirs of Raymond Poincaré*. Translated by Sir George Arthur. 3 vols. London: William Heinemann, 1930.

Pourtalès   Pourtalès, Friedrich. *Meine Letzten Verhandlungen in St Petersburg, Ende Juli 1914: Tagesaufzeichnung und dokumente*. Berlin: Deutsche Verlagsgesellschaft für Politik und Geschichte, 1927.

PRO   National Archives of the United Kingdom. Kew Gardens, London.

QO   Quai d'Orsay Archives. Paris. Correspondence politique et commerciale dite 'nouvelle série,' 1896–1918.

RGVIA   Rossiiskii Gosudarstvennyi Voenno-Istoricheskii Arkhiv. Moscow.

Sazonov   Sazonov, S. D. *Fateful Years, 1909–1916: The Reminiscences of Serge Sazonov, Russia's Minister for Foreign Affairs*. London: J. Cape, 1928.

Schilling   Schilling, M. F., Baron, ed. *How the War Began in 1914: Being the Diary of the Russian Foreign Office from the 3rd to the 20th (Old Style) of July,*

1914. Translated by Major W. Cyprian Bridge. London: G. Allen & Unwin, 1925.

Schmidt   Schmidt, Stefan. *Frankreichs Aussenpolitik in der Julikrise 1914: Ein Beitrag zur Geschichte des Ausbruchs des Ersten Weltkrieges.* Munich: Oldenbourg, 2009.

Schmitt   Schmitt, Bernadotte E. *The Coming of the War, 1914.* 2 vols. New York: Charles Scribner's Sons, 1930.

Tirpitz   Tirpitz, Alfred Peter Friedrich von. *Mémoires du Grand-Amiral von Tirpitz.* Paris: Payot, 1930.

Tuchman   Tuchman, Barbara Wertheim. *The Guns of August.* New York: Macmillan, 1962.

Turner   Turner, L. C. F. *Origins of the First World War.* London: Edward Arnold, 1970.

Würthle   Würthle, Fritz. *Die Spur führt nach Belgrad: Die Hintergründe des Dramas v. Sarajevos 1914.* Vienna: Molden, 1975.

Zuber   Zuber, Terence. *The Real German War Plan 1904–1914.* Gloucestershire: History Press, 2011.

Other Works Cited or Profitably Consulted for This Work

Ahamed, Liaquat. *Lords of Finance: 1929, The Great Depression, and the Bankers Who Broke the World.* London: Windmill/Random House, 2009.

Aksakal, Mustafa. *The Ottoman Road to War in 1914: The Ottoman Empire and the First World War.* Cambridge: Cambridge University Press, 2008.

Balfour, Michael. *The Kaiser and His Times.* London: Cresset, 1964.

Berenson, Edward. *The Trial of Madame Caillaux.* Berkeley: University of California Press, 1992.

Buchanan, Sir George William. *My Mission to Russia and Other Diplomatic Memories.* 2 vols. London: Cassell, 1923.

Bülow, Bernhard von. *Memoirs.* 4 vols. London: Putnam, 1932.

Churchill, Winston. *The World Crisis: The Eastern Front.* London: Thornton Butterworth, 1931.

Danilov, Yuri. *La Russie dans la guerre mondiale, 1914–1917.* Translated by Alexandre Kaznakov. Paris: Payot, 1927.

Erdmann, Karl Dietrich, ed. *Kurt Riezler: Tagebücher, Aufsätze, Dokumente.* Göttingen: Vandenhoeck & Ruprecht, 1972.

Ferguson, Niall. *The Pity of War.* New York: Basic Books, 1999.

Fischer, Fritz. *Griff nach der Weltmacht. Die Kriegszielpolitik des Kaiserlichen Deutschland, 1914–1918*. Düsseldorf: Droste Verlag, 1961.

————. *Krieg der Illusionen: Die deutsche Politik von 1911 bis 1914*. Düsseldorf: Droste Verlag, 1969.

Fromkin, David. *Europe's Last Summer: Who Started the Great War in 1914?* New York: Alfred A. Knopf, 2004.

————. *A Peace to End All Peace: Creating the Modern Middle East, 1914–1922*. New York: H. Holt, 1989.

Fuller, William C., Jr. *Civil-Military Conflict in Imperial Russia 1880–1914*. Princeton, NJ: Princeton University Press, 1985.

————. *Strategy and Power in Russia, 1600–1914*. New York: Free Press, 1992.

Geiss, Imanuel. *Der lange Weg in die Katastrophe: die Vorgeschichte des Ersten Weltkrieges, 1815–1914*. Munich: Piper, 1990.

————. *July 1914: The Outbreak of the First World War; Selected Documents*. New York: Scribner, 1967.

Geyer, Dietrich. *Russian Imperialism: The Interaction of Domestic and Foreign Policy, 1860–1914*. New Haven, CT: Yale University Press, 1987.

Gilliard, Pierre. *Thirteen Years at the Russian Court*. Translated by F. Appleby Holt, O.B.E. London: Hutchinson, 1921.

Gooch, G. P. *Recent Revelations of European Diplomacy*. London: Longmans, Green, 1940.

Grey, Edward, Viscount ('of Fallodon'). *Speeches on Foreign Affairs, 1904–1914*. London: G. Allen & Unwin ltd., 1931.

Hamilton, Richard, and Holger Herwig, eds. *Decisions for War, 1914–1917*. New York: Cambridge University Press, 2004.

————. *The Origins of World War I*. New York: Cambridge University Press, 2003.

Hayne, M. B. *The French Foreign Office and the Origins of the First World War 1898–1914*. Oxford: Clarendon, 1993.

Hoeniger, Robert. *Russlands Vorbereitung zum Weltkrieg auf Grund unveröffentlicher Russischer Urkunden*. Berlin: E. S. Mittler, 1919.

Hull, Isabel. *The Entourage of Kaiser Wilhelm II*. New York: Cambridge University Press, 1982.

Jarausch, Konrad. 'The Illusion of Limited War: Chancellor Bethmann Hollweg's Calculated Risk, July 1914.' *Central European History* 2, no. 1 (March 1969): 48–76.

Keiger, John F. V. 'France.' In *Decisions for War, 1914*, edited by Keith Wilson. New York: St Martin's, 1995.

————. *France and the Origins of the First World War*. New York: St Martin's, 1983.

————. *Raymond Poincaré*. Cambridge: Cambridge University Press, 1997.

Kennan, George. *Fateful Alliance: France, Russia, and the Coming of the First World War.* New York: Pantheon Books, 1984.

Kennedy, Paul, ed. *The War Plans of the Great Powers, 1880–1914.* London: Allen & Unwin, 1979.

Krasnyi Arkhiv: Istoricheskii zhurnal. 106 vols. Moscow: Gospolitizdat, 1922–1941.

Krivoshein, K. A. *A. V. Krivoshein (1857–1921 g.) Ego znachenie v istorii Rossii nachala XX veka.* Paris: s.n., 1973.

Lichnowsky, Karl Max. *Heading for the Abyss: Reminiscences.* London: Constable, 1928.

Lieven, D. C. B. *Nicholas II: Emperor of All the Russias.* London: J. Murray, 1993.

————. *Russia and the Origins of the First World War.* New York: St Martin's, 1983.

Linke, Horst Günther. *Das Zaristische Russland und der erste Weltkrieg: Diplomatie Und Kriegsziele 1914–1917.* Munich: Wilhelm Fink Verlag, 1982.

Massie, Robert K. *Nicholas and Alexandra.* New York: Atheneum, 1967.

McDonald, David MacLaren. *United Government and Foreign Policy in Russia, 1900–1914.* Cambridge, MA: Harvard University Press, 1992.

McMeekin, Sean. *The Berlin-Baghdad Express: The Ottoman Empire and Germany's Bid for World Power, 1898–1918.* London: Penguin/Allen Lane, 2010.

————. *The Russian Origins of the First World War.* Cambridge, MA: Harvard University Press / Belknap, 2011.

Menning, Bruce. *Bayonets Before Bullets: The Imperial Russian Army, 1861–1914.* Bloomington: Indiana University Press, 1992.

————. 'The Offensive Revisited: Russian Preparation for Future War, 1906–1914.' In *Reforming the Tsar's Army: Military Innovation in Imperial Russia from Peter the Great to the Revolution*, edited by Bruce Menning and David Schimmelpenninck van der Oye. New York: Cambridge University Press, 2004.

Messimy, Adolphe. *Mes Souvenirs.* Paris: Plon, 1937.

Moltke, Helmuth Johann Ludwig von. *Erinnerungen, Briefe, Dokumente 1877–1916: Ein Bild vom Kriegsausbruch, erster Kriegsführung und Persönlichkeit des ersten militärischen Führern des Krieges.* Stuttgart: Der kommende Tag, 1922.

Mombauer, Annika. *The Origins of the First World War: Controversies and Consensus.* New York: Longman, 2002.

Morley, John, Viscount. *Memorandum on Resignation, 1914.* New York: Macmillan, 1928.

Morton, Frederick. *Thunder at Twilight: Vienna 1913/1914*. London: Peter Owen, 1989.

Neilson, Keith, with Roy Arnold Prete. 'Russia.' In *Decisions for War, 1914*, edited by Keith Wilson. New York: St Martin's, 1995.

Poincaré, Raymond. *Au service de la France: Neuf années de souvenirs*. 10 vols. Paris: Plon, 1926–.

Pokrovskii, M. N., ed. *Drei Konferenzen (zur Vorgeschichte des Krieges)*. Berlin: Arbeiterbuchhandlung, 1920.

─────. *Tsarskaia Rossiia v mirovoi voine*. Vol. 1. Leningrad: 1926.

Rauchensteiner, Manfried. *Der Tod des Doppeladlers: Österreich-Ungarn und der Erste Weltkrieg*. Vienna: Verlag Styria, 1993.

Reynolds, Michael A. *Shattering Empires: The Clash and Collapse of the Ottoman and Russian Empires*. New York: Cambridge University Press, 2011.

Siegel, Jennifer. *Endgame: Britain, Russia, and the Final Struggle for Central Asia*. London: I. B. Tauris, 2002.

Smith, C. Jay, Jr. *The Russian Struggle for Power, 1914–1917: A Study of Russian Foreign Policy During the First World War*. New York: Philosophical Library, 1956.

Smith, David James. *One Morning in Sarajevo: 28 June 1914*. London: Phoenix, 2009.

Sondhaus, Lawrence. *Franz Conrad von Hötzendorf: Architect of the Apocalypse*. Boston: Humanities, 2000.

─────. *Naval Warfare, 1815–1914*. New York: Routledge, 2001.

Spears, Sir Edward. *Liaison 1914: A Narrative of the Great Retreat*. London: W. Heinemann, 1930.

Spring, Derek. 'Russia and the Coming of War.' In *The Coming of the First World War*, edited by R. J. W. Evans and Hartmut Pogge von Strandmann. Oxford: Clarendon / Oxford University Press, 1983.

Steinberg, John W. *All the Tsar's Men: Russia's General Staff and the Fate of Empire, 1898–1914*. Baltimore, MD: Johns Hopkins University Press, 2010.

Steiner, Zara. *Britain and the Origins of the First World War*. New York: St Martin's, 1977.

Stevenson, David. *Cataclysm: The First World War as Political Tragedy*. New York: Basic Books, 2004.

─────. *The First World War and International Politics*. New York: Oxford University Press, 1988.

Stone, Norman. *The Eastern Front 1914–1917*. New York: Charles Scribner's Sons, 1975.

─────. *Europe Transformed, 1878–1919*. Glasgow: Fontana, 1983.

─────. *World War One: A Short History*. London: Allan Lane, 2007.

Strachan, Hew. *The First World War*. New York: Viking, 2004.

Sukhomlinov, Vladimir Aleksandrovich. *Erinnerungen*. Berlin: R. Hobbing, 1924.

Tuchman, Barbara W. *The Proud Tower: A Portrait of the World Before the War, 1890–1914*. New York: Macmillan, 1966.

Turner, L. C. F. 'The Russian Mobilisation in 1914.' *Journal of Contemporary History* 3, no. 1 (January 1968): 65–88.

————. 'The Significance of the Schlieffen Plan.' In *The War Plans of the Great Powers, 1880–1914*, edited by Paul Kennedy. London: Allen & Unwin, 1979.

Viviani, René. *As We See It*. Translated by Thomas R. Ybarra. New York: Harper & Brothers, 1923.

Wilhelm II (Emperor of Germany). *Reden des Kaisers: Ansprachen, Predigten, und Trinksprüche*. Edited by Ernst Johann. Munich: Deutscher Taschenbuch-Verlag, 1966.

Williamson, Samuel R., Jr. *Austria-Hungary and the Origins of the First World War*. London: Macmillan, 1991.

————, with Ernest R. May. 'An Identity of Opinion: Historians and July 1914.' *Journal of Modern History* 79 (June 2007): 335–387.

Yasamee, F. A. K. 'Ottoman Empire.' In *Decisions for War, 1914*, edited by Keith Wilson. New York: St Martin's, 1995.

Zweig, Stefan. *The World of Yesterday: An Autobiography by Stefan Zweig*. Lincoln: University of Nebraska Press, 1943.

INDEX

responsibility for First World
War, 391
support for action against Serbia,
106
Tisza and, 32
urging caution in responding to
Serbia, 94–95
visit to Bosnia-Herzegovina, 4
war council and, 325–326
Fredericks, Count, 160
French, John, 70
Friedrich, Archduke, Duke of
Teschen, 108

Geneva Convention of 1907, 351
George V
appeal to Nicholas II regarding
Russian mobilisation, 329–330
British neutrality and, 276, 279,
343–344
peace-minded telegram, 306n
telegram on misunderstanding of
neutrality offer, 347–349
Wilhelm II and, 311
German dreadnoughts, 380–381
Germany
access to Ottoman Straits and, 54
alerting Europe to mobilisation in
response to Russians, 312
alliance with Austria, 40
alliance with Turkey, 353–354
anxiety over war rumours, 340–341
assassination of Franz Ferdinand
as factor in lead-up to First
World War, 386–388
assigning responsibility for war to
Russia, 287–288
Austria's need for support of, 42,
45–46
belief that Russia would not join
in war, 100, 106
British ultimatum to, 374–375, 379
claims of French invasion, 354
contents of Austrian ultimatum
and, 142–144
declaration of war on France,
350–352, 370–371
declaration of war on Russia,
345–347, 350
desire for British neutrality, 90,
120, 274–275, 276–281, 330–331

doubts about Austria's intentions,
100–102, 104
early battles in war, 383
events leading to declaration of
war on Russia, 337–347
failure of diplomatic-strategic
manoeuvres, 284–285
French response to mobilisation
of, 316–325
'halt in Belgrade' proposal,
252–255, 256–257
invasion of Belgium, 278–279, 371,
373–374, 377, 383
invasion of Luxembourg, 339, 343,
344, 349, 354, 355
localisation and, 205
military weakness of, 404–405
mobilisation, 340, 341–343,
354–355, 404
mobilisation, delay in, 274–276
mobilisation, in face of Russian
mobilisation, 302–303, 312
mobilisation, start of, 309–311
mobilisation plans, 267–269, 317
placing blame for war on Russia,
376–377
Potsdam council of 27 July, 227–229
response to assassination, 78–80,
85–86
response to Austrian and Russian
partial mobilisations, 266–269
response to British-Russian naval
talks, 72
responsibility for First World
War, 393–394, 401–402, 403–405
responsibility for movement
towards war, 234–235, 238
Russian mobilisation, knowledge
of, 209, 220–222, 275
Russian mobilisation, protest of,
214–217
Russian mobilisation, response on
learning of, 286–290
Russian mobilisation, seeking
confirmation of, 306–309
Sazonov claim of mobilisation by,
299–300, 301
strategic position in 1914, 387–388
support for Austrian action
against Serbia, 90–91, 99–100,
104–105, 114, 119–120